art·SITES—FRANCE
First Edition

PUBLISHED BY
art·SITES, 894 Waller Street, San Francisco, CA 94117

EDITOR
Fronia Simpson
DESIGNER
Lisa Schulz/Elysium
CARTOGRAPHER
Tracey Croom
PRINTED BY
Bertelsmann

ISBN: 0-9667717-3-7
Printed in USA.

art·SITES™

france

contemporary
art + architecture
handbook

sidra stich

san francisco

for
Phyllis Wattis
guardian angel of the avant–garde

table of contents

Introduction

This is the inaugural book in the **art·SITES** series. We hope to publish many others, eventually covering all the major countries and regions where contemporary art and architecture are flourishing. The aim is to identify and briefly describe the most significant sites where there is innovative, intriguing, top-notch work from the present and recent past. By providing background, analytic and practical information, we orient you to a place or project, both in advance and during a visit. The book is organized geographically so you can conveniently and efficiently arrange walking tours of a neighborhood or excursions to a region. Sites are keyed by number to detail maps and by icon to subject categories—museums, art centers (exhibition spaces), film centers, art galleries, architecture, public art, parks and bookstores. Recent exhibitions and artists associated with galleries are also named to broaden your knowledge of sites where such information is relevant.

The **art·SITES** handbooks gather all sorts of pertinent material on what's happening here and now in the arts within a given city, region or country. Whether you have only a few hours or several weeks to spend traveling around a particular place, **art·SITES** is an invaluable resource. Especially if you want to get to know a place beyond the scope of the main museums or typical tourist monuments, these handbooks will open up a new world for you. France is a perfect example. Most people think of the country in terms of Paris, and within Paris, the Centre Pompidou signifies contemporary art and architecture. Not only is there a wealth of other extraordinary sites in Paris itself, but a day trip to the outskirts of the city or a long weekend to most any province (readily accessible in a few hours by train) will expose you to amazing art sites, where you can see the best of emerging and celebrated works by a range of international and French artists and architects.

BACKGROUND AND DECENTRALIZATION As anyone who has traveled in France is aware, the country takes "culture" very seriously. Indeed, culture is a dominant element in France's identity and economy. But whereas many countries stop short of considering contemporary culture—especially its most avant-garde manifestations—under the same umbrella as historic treasures from the past, France has been proactive in embracing it. Moves in this direction began in the early 1960s. More than a decade had passed since the end of World War II and it was increasingly evident that Paris was no longer the preeminent art center. Nor were French artists at the helm of the international art world. The decision in 1962 to create a cabinet-level department, the Ministry of Cultural Affairs, and to appoint André Malraux as the first minister was pivotal. In terms of contemporary art, it mainly resulted in an overhaul and renewal of public art commissions. Nevertheless, this gave contemporary art a toehold within the State.

The real turning point unquestionably came in 1969 when the newly elected President Georges Pompidou announced plans for a national cultural center devoted to creativity in the arts from the recent past and the present. The project also sought to construct a monumental, innovative building in the center of Paris, designed by the winner of a worldwide architectural competition. Almost single-handedly, the Pompidou Center, completed in 1977, elevated contemporary art and architecture to preeminence, ensuring its stature as a major player in French cultural politics. In fact, the State formed the National Collection of Contemporary Art (FNAC) in 1976. Its charge was to manage the existing collection, promote contemporary art and enrich the country's holdings of creative work by living artists (both French and foreign). Contemporary art was expressly viewed as patrimony, a valued resource and an important sign of national grandeur. Since objects from the collection are loaned to museums, exhibitions and embassies, they have a public presence. Needless to say, having the State as a perennial collector and commissioner of contemporary art was a big boon to the art market in France and to the image of Paris within the art world.

All the activity in the art realm led to the establishment in 1982 of the Visual Arts Delegation (DAP), a central administrative body, still within the Ministry of Culture but more independent. Not only did the agency greatly expand its purview to include support for studios, exhibitions, research, art schools, fellowships, art production, public education, publications and the like, but it also broadened the definition of culture to encompass comic books, photography, new technologies, fashion, culinary arts, film, video, and so on. By 1983 decentralization played an equally strong role in dramatically changing the structure and nature of the contemporary art scene in France. Regional collections and exhibition centers throughout the country emerged or expanded. With assistance (financial and otherwise) from the State, many became viable, quite autonomous entities, offering a notable counterpoint to Paris. To a greater or lesser extent, most have become participants within the international arena. In terms of creative, provocative programs and support for exciting young artists and fresh ideas, art centers outside the capital are where it's happening in France.

FRAC—FONDS REGIONAL D'ART CONTEMPORAIN (REGIONAL COLLECTION OF CONTEMPORARY ART) These collections were conceived as a way to stimulate and upgrade contemporary art production and interest. Initially, the FRACs concentrated solely on purchasing art, strongly emphasizing work by French artists. Though a national focus is still apparent, collections have expanded into the international realm, and a few have particularized their attention to certain realms, like drawing or architecture. In addition, activities have mushroomed as each FRAC has developed ways to make its collection accessible to the public and to enhance public response to contemporary art. Most have instituted extensive and diverse programs of exhibitions, lectures, artist talks, performances, publications, school projects, and so forth.

As of 1998 there were 24 FRACs. Many now have their own facilities and have become art centers with year-round programs on-site. Like alternative spaces, they tend to favor new, experimental work, often by emerging artists. Exhibitions usually have a connection to an artist or object in the collection, but the collections as such are not on permanent display. Only small selections are visible occasionally within a temporary exhibition, either at the FRAC's location or elsewhere within the region.

In their 16 year history (from 1982 to June 1998), the FRACs have amassed a collection of 11,500 works by 2,500 artists. Like any collection of contemporary art oriented toward both recognized and emerging figures, it is extremely uneven, weighted with lots of mediocre art by second-string followers. However, it also includes a wealth of incredible work by some of the most innovative, talented artists of the contemporary period. Thus, when you see an announcement for an exhibition of a FRAC collection, check it out. You're likely to find a rich cross section of art and a good introduction to work by Europeans you probably haven't heard of yet. Don't be surprised if the exhibit is in a church, historic monument, market hall, library, park or other public place in some small town.

CENTERS OF CONTEMPORARY ART   The distinction between "art centers," FRAC and other institutions concerned with contemporary art has become quite blurred. Officially, an art center places priority on research, discovery and the production of art. Its mission also involves experimentation related to art theory and history, especially as this affects education and outreach programs. Many art centers in France have esteemed histories for producing extraordinary exhibitions, initiating engaging art projects and being very supportive of artists and eccentric ideas. As a group, they offer a gamut of possibilities: some are specialized, some have collections, some have artist residencies and some are affiliated with an art school or university.

PUBLIC ART   When public art commissions (*commandes publiques*) were revived in the aftermath of World War II, they were largely under the aegis of the 1% provision: the government allocated 1% of the construction cost of a new or expanded public building to the creation of an artwork specifically conceived for the site. It was not until 1983, when the State created a fund for public art, that this realm made its presence felt throughout the landscape. Contemporary art was commissioned for old and new buildings, courtyards and plazas, public gardens, métro stations, commemorative monuments, schools, railroad stations, traffic circles and highways.

Public art offers the most difficult challenge for an artist and the commissioning agency. It's not just a matter of selecting a talented artist or exciting object, for these determinants must merge with a creative mind plus an acute sensitivity to location, context, social habits, environmental conditions, safety, architectural restrictions, materials, public relations, among other considerations. Unfortunately, despite the best intentions of sponsors and all others involved, few public art commissions (in France or elsewhere) are success stories. Fewer still qualify within the stream of vanguard creativity. To its credit, not only has France sponsored a phenomenal number of public art projects, but it has also commissioned some of the most engaging, innovative work in this area. Keep your eyes open for public art when you travel in France and do go out of your way to see some of the choice projects described in this book. Consider it an adventure on many levels!

ART MOVEMENTS, 1960–80s   Within the realm of French contemporary art, several significant groupings occurred and still influence the direction or presentation of art. Nouveau Réalisme is a label with little stylistic relevance, applied by a critic to an eclectic circle of artists who were against traditional oil painting, personal or polemic expression, and for "pure sensibility." Often viewed as parallel to Pop art, the nouveaux réalistes who exhibited together during 1960–63 included Arman, César, François Dufrêne, Raymond Hains, Yves Klein, Martial Raysse, Niki de Saint-Phalle, Daniel Spoerri, Jean Tinguely, Jacques de la Villeglé.

During the 1970s, Supports-Surfaces dominated the French art scene. Somewhat comparable to the minimal and process orientation in America and Arte Povera in Italy, artists in this movement rejected formalism and severely structured art in favor of the free use of materials (especially raw or popular-culture materials), natural processes, dissociations between frames (supports) and fabrics (surfaces), serial formats, vivid colors and immense size. Emphasis on the power of the work itself, not symbolism, subject matter or a priori references, and statements like—"Here painting can appear in its materiality as signifying surfaces"—show the influence of semiotic theory. Artists associated with Supports-Surfaces include André-Pierre Arnal, Vincent Bioulès, Pierre Buraglio, Louis Cane, Marc Devade, Daniel Dezeuze, Noël Dolla, Toni Grand, Bernard Pagès, Jean-Pierre Pincemin, Patrick Saytour, André Valensi, Claude Viallat.

B.M.P.T. is the acronym for Daniel Buren, Olivier Mosset, Michel Parmentier, Niele Toroni—artists who banded together in the late 1960s and shared a conceptual approach to painting. Though against personal expression and traditional definitions of painting, they denounced declarations of the death of painting and readymade artworks. Instead, these artists focused on paint, color, the character of the brush, the method of production, paintings that are cut, reassembled, structured into three-dimensional objects, placed outdoors, and otherwise reconfigured.

A term used to describe a 1980s development in French art is Figuration Narrative or Figuration Libre. It refers to a mode of spontaneous creation, swarming with forms and signs from mass culture and media. References to comic strips, rock music, punk, Jules Verne science fiction and porno literature are meant to express a revulsion against contemporary society. Artists associated with this term include Jean-Michel Alberola, Jean-Charles Blais, Rémy Blanchard, François Boisrond, Robert Combas, Hervé di Rosa, Catherine Viollet.

GRANDS PROJETS Following the creation of Centre Pompidou, there was a hiatus during the presidency of Giscard d'Estaing, a conservative who did not approve of the radical new architecture. In contrast, the next president, François Mitterand, who held office from 1981 to 1995, used presidential patronage to create monumental, new structures and to revamp or develop from scratch neighborhoods and districts. In March 1982 he presented an architectural program, naming a series of important public projects—*the grands projets*—that would establish a new basis for socio-cultural interaction and secure a place for visionary, technologically innovative architecture in France. Mitterand's projects ultimately included 12 major undertakings in Paris and 36 in the provinces. Topping the list are the Grande Arche, Grand Louvre, Musée d'Orsay, Institut du Monde Arabe, Opéra Bastille, Parc de la Villette, Cité des Sciences et de l'Industrie, Cité de la Musique and Bibliothèque Nationale de France.

Because international competitions were held to select architects, the country became a locus of worldwide attention. Without question, the *grands projets* had a great impact on the communities of design and urban planning, not the least of which was a shift away from the stronghold of modernism and the dreary (often inhuman) aesthetics of postwar construction. A new generation of leaders also emerged, among them the French architects Philippe Chaix and Jean-Paul Morel, Adrien Fainsilber, Jean Nouvel, Dominique Perrault, Christian de Portzamparc and the collaborative team called Architecture Studio. As the momentum of the *grands projets* reverberated round the country, urban architectural activity flourished. In less than two decades, not only did the face of Paris and several other French cities change dramatically, but France became the site of numerous impressive buildings by some of the most esteemed figures in the field.

VILLES NOUVELLES The "new towns," launched in the late 1960s, have had ambitious goals and mixed results. Conceived as a means of controlling urban sprawl and alleviating the problem of overcrowding in city centers, they were planned as agglomerations or satellites around existing cities. At first the unified, garden-city idea prevailed, but by the 1980s suburban-type communities were rejected in favor of towns with architectural variety and a marked integration of private and public housing, small businesses and corporate headquarters, industry, cultural institutions, university and research centers, leisure facilities, transportation networks and other services. Planners aimed to make the new towns autonomous, each one structured with a particular, distinctive character suited to the growth of the region. But they also located them on major car, train and bus routes so both businesses and inhabitants would have easy access to the nearby hub city. On the one hand, pragmatic, economic realities guided the development of the *villes nouvelles*. On the other, utopian ideals held sway as a powerful counterforce.

Among the new towns, several around Paris and those associated with the expansion of Montpellier stand out. Among their virtues are town centers and residential areas where pedestrians are separated from car circulation; a comfortable balance between new construction, unrefined and landscaped nature; mass housing in other than block buildings; neighborhoods with ambience and diversity; and infrastructure systems in advance of other construction. Like the *grands projets*, in various cases, commissions were awarded to innovative architects. The new towns are therefore enriched with some extraordinary buildings—visually compelling and conceptually intriguing. In addition, there are public artworks— some even commissioned at the critical planning stage of a town or building.

To be sure, there are many mundane, typically suburban designs in the new towns. There is even evidence of deterioration and disrepair as well as social problems and a lack of necessary services. Nevertheless, they present fascinating examples of planned communities. Especially since most of the *villes nouvelles* are still in the process of being developed and built, it's a great time to visit them. You can also see some of the same modes of planning in the new neighborhoods under construction and renewal in Paris—Bercy, Tolbiac, La Villette.

MILLENNIUM IN FRANCE Should you be in Paris on December 31, 1999, you can count down the minutes until the new year and new century on the Eiffel Tower's digital clock, or you can be among the first to enter the renovated Centre Pompidou, which opens at the stroke of midnight with a grand exhibition, *Time, Quickly*. Upstairs in the Musée National d'Art Moderne, a series of special exhibitions on 20th-century art, titled *Outsider Voices*, will run throughout the year. Also in Paris, the year 2000 will be marked by a series of exhibitions at the Grand Palais, among them *Visions of the Future* and *Melancholia* (Dürer to the present).

Arts festivals celebrating the millennium are scheduled for Bordeaux, Cahors, Lyon, Marseille, Nice, Perpignan, Strasbourg, Toulouse and various other cities. Of particular note, three museums in Nantes will present *Invented Worlds* honoring the legacy of the city's native son Jules Verne. Europe as a whole will denote 2000 by thematic presentations in nine "cities of culture." Avignon will represent France with *beauty*, Bergen—*art, work and leisure*, Bologna—*information and communication*, Brussels—*the city*, Kracow—*thought, spirituality and creativity*, Helsinki—*knowledge, technology and the future*, Prague—*cultural patrimony*,

Reykjavik—*nature and culture*, Santiago de Compostella—*Europe and the world*. A grand marketing campaign will soon be flooding the media with announcements of these events.

Practicalities

Information provided is as of 1998 but changes are inevitable. Despite our best efforts, you are likely to find different admission prices, hours, new addresses or even that sites no longer exist. We apologize for the inconvenience and hope you will inform us of changes so we can make corrections and update the next edition.

H O U R S   The thing to keep in mind is that there is no consistency. Also beware that many galleries and some museums close at midday for two to three hours. Most galleries are closed on Sunday and Monday, and museums are typically closed on Monday or Tuesday. Virtually all galleries and many art centers are closed during August and some shut down for the entire summer.

H O L I D A Y   C L O S I N G S   Most galleries and many museums are closed on the following national holidays: January 1, May 1 (Labor Day), May 8 (V.E. Day), July 14 (Bastille Day) and November 11 (Armistice Day). Closures also occur on the following religious holidays: Easter, Easter Monday, Ascension Thursday, Pentecost Sunday and Monday, Assumption Day (August 15), All Saints' Day (November 1) and Christmas (December 25). In addition, some galleries close early the day before a public holiday, and when a holiday falls on a Tuesday or Thursday, they often take a four-day weekend.

A D M I S S I O N   C O S T S   Admission prices to museums are usually denoted in two categories: general and reduced. The reduced price normally applies to children, students, seniors and the unemployed. Free admissions may also exist for certain group classifications at some museums. Most FRAC and art centers are free to everyone.

T E L E P H O N E   N U M B E R S   Telephone and fax numbers are indicated throughout this guide with the two-digit area code (usually referred to as the city code). There are five area codes in France: 01 (Paris), 02 (northwest), 03 (northeast), 04 (southeast), 05 (southwest). The country code for France is 33. When calling France from other countries, omit the zero in the area code.

T G V   This is the acronym referring to the high-speed (*très grande vitesse*) trains that can cut travel time around France by hours.

SITE ICONS   The following icons are used to distinguish the sites in this handbook:

🏛 museum

🖼 art center and exhibition space

🎥 film and video center

🖼 art gallery

🏢 architecture

⚐ public art

⚘ park or garden

📖 arts bookstore

paris

Paris

CURRENT ART INFORMATION *Pariscope* (3F) and *L'Officiel des Spectacles* (2F) are two inexpensive weeklies listing current exhibitions and special activities for most cultural sites. In the galleries, you can get a free sheet with exhibition information organized by geographic area. The magazine *artpress* (40F), published monthly, has the most complete coverage of contemporary art and exhibitions in France. It includes English translations of the major articles.

FIAC (Foire Internationale d'Art Contemporain) is a big, international fair for contemporary art held annually, in Sept or Oct. For the past several years, it has been at Espace Eiffel Branly, 29–55 quai Branly, 75007. (Mon–Fri, 12–8; Sat–Sun, 10–8. admission: 70F. métro: Alma-Marceau.) As is typical of such fairs—which have flourished in the past decade—participating galleries rent spaces in a giant hall and show either a full selection of the artists they handle or an exhibition of a single artist. Depending on the scope and character of the galleries represented, the fair can be a terrific way to see a cross section of what's happening in the art world. In any event, there's always too much to see, and it's easy to get lost in the maze of look-alike spaces. If you go, try to keep track of your meanderings on the floor-plan handout—usually available for free at the entrance desk.

MOIS DE LA PHOTO Every other year (even-numbered years), a citywide celebration of photography is held during the month of Nov. This has become France's most popular festival with over 500,000 visitors partaking of exhibitions and events located in numerous places throughout Paris.

OPEN STUDIOS During weekends in Oct and Nov, different neighborhoods in and around Paris organize open-studio events. These give the public a chance to see a wide range of very current art and speak informally to artists. Not all artists participate and the quality is variable, but it's a good opportunity to see emerging artists and those not affiliated with Paris galleries.

OUTDOOR MURALS Here and there in the city, you will see murals painted on the blind walls of buildings. Since 1976, the city has financed five to seven each year. The state also supports a few, and many are created independently. Trompe-l'oeil depictions, especially those featuring architectural illusions and perspective distortions, are favored. Imagery referring to another time period, typically the romanticized past or the fantasized future, is also popular. Some of the best murals are filled with oddities that defy logic and explanation or use clever humor.

METRO Not only is the subway system the best way to get around in Paris, but the station names provide a helpful geographic reference.

RER (*réseau express régional*) refers to the faster métro system with routes extending into the outskirts and suburbs.

METEOR is the name of a new métro line, a section of which was inaugurated in October 1998. It has a mega-underground station at the national library stop (Bibliothèque), and its trains have as a special feature high-tech video monitors with a menu of video art. You might want to check this out even if you just ride back and forth between stations. Leave it to the French to add culture to public transportation!

Jan Dibbets

Hommage à Arago, 1994

This artwork is composed of 135 bronze medallions embedded in the ground along an imaginary line—the 10-km-long (over 6 mi) meridian axis of Paris from Porte Montmartre to Cité Universitaire. They create a path between the north and south borders of the city cutting through famous sites and centuries of history. Each medallion is identically stamped with the directional markers N and S and the name *Arago*—a 19th-century political reformer, distinguished physicist and astronomer who formulated meridian measurements. (Arago was also the persuasive force behind the French government's sponsorship of the daguerreotype. He envisioned the possible contributions photography could make to science.) The medallions, which are only about eight inches in diameter, can easily be missed and stepped on. You may come upon them by accident or you can search near such locations as the Observatoire de Paris, Jardin du Luxembourg, boulevard Saint-Germain, place de l'Institut, quays of the Seine, Louvre, Palais-Royal, boulevard Hausmann, place Pigalle, Moulin de la Galette or Sacré-Coeur.

By laying the medallions into the ground, the Dutch artist Jan Dibbets sought to challenge the conventional definition of a monument as a statue on a pedestal. His memorial was purposefully nonmonumental. Although the medallion format may seem to express an irreverent attitude toward commemorative sculpture and a lack of respect for Arago as a heroized individual, it in fact takes into account the nature of Arago's achievements and an actual circumstance relevant to the history of public statues. From 1893 to 1942 a bronze statue of François-Dominique Arago dominated a small plaza (Ile de Sein) located where the meridian of Paris crosses boulevard Arago. However, the statue, like many bronze sculptures, was melted down for use in armaments during World War II. Because it was never replaced, only an empty pedestal remains at the site. Using the missing statue as a point of departure, Dibbets chose to pay homage to Arago by spreading his name across the entire city of Paris. As with the meridian, a perception of the totality of artwork is only imaginary or virtual.

The project is a good example of Dibbets's art. His recurring concerns are with the concept of displacement, the relationship between distant and close-up vision, the sequential organization of space and the manner in which the mind compensates for the limits of visual perception. *Hommage à Arago* is also a strong example of an alternative type of public art.

Dibbets, *Hommage à Arago*

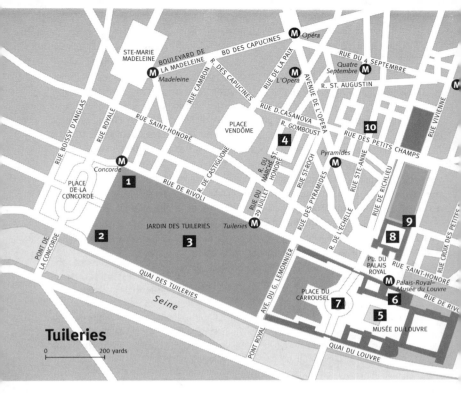

Tuileries–Louvre

Galerie Nationale du
1 Jeu de Paume

🖼 renovation: Antoine STINCO,
1987–91
🏛 1 place de la Concorde, 75008
📖 01-47-03-12-50 f: 01-47-03-12-51
Tues, 12–9:30; Wed–Fri, 12–7;
Sat–Sun, 10–7; closed Mon
admission: 38/28F
métro: Concorde

This exhibition space is located in the
northwest corner of the Tuileries
Gardens. It is relatively easy to find if
you arrive from within the Tuileries, but
if you come via the métro or neighboring streets the surrounding wall is a bit
baffling. Look for an unassuming, small
opening on the rue de Rivoli side of the
wall, just off the corner of place de la
Concorde. Enter and go up the short

stairway, turn into the gardens (it's
sand, not greenery) and head for the
nearest building—the one with a monumental portal composed of a glass cube
set within a tall, Italianate stone arch.

The building, originally constructed in
the mid-19th century to house an
indoor "jeu de paume" court (a tennis-
type game), was turned into an exhibition space for impressionist paintings in
1922. When the art was moved in the
mid-1980s to the Gare d'Orsay museum, the structure was totally and creatively renovated by Antoine Stinco to
accommodate contemporary art exhibitions. Though retaining most of the old
exterior, the redesign opens the interior
to natural light while also forming galleries that are well defined, proportioned for human comfort yet spacious
and adaptable to the diverse needs of
contemporary art. Considering the
inadequate, intrusive architecture of

many new museums, this is quite an accomplishment! But don't think the design is boring or merely functional. You'll immediately perceive the visual eccentricity of the renovation in the main staircase. Placed off-center in a narrow hall, it rises dramatically even as it invites visitors to go down to the video-film rooms on the lower level. Stinco has also added a mezzanine, which interrupts the spatial order and provides more intimate space for some galleries and a café.

With the renovation, the Jeu de Paume became a showcase for contemporary art. The idea was to develop a Kunsthalle—an art center similar to those developed in Germany, which have no permanent collection but are exclusively dedicated to the presentation of contemporary art—especially very current, innovative, if not brash art. For the first several years after the new Jeu de Paume opened, the exhibitions were exciting and well conceived. Curators were attuned to international activity and brought some of the most compelling art and artists to Paris. The art was fresh and experimental, and group shows called attention to hot topics or prevalent themes. In recent years, however, the pulse has changed to a more conservative selection and historic orientation. The program is largely composed of retrospectives of mid-career artists. Recent exhibitions: *Pierre Alechinsky*, *Arman*, *Jean-Marc Bustamante*, *César*, *Sam Francis*, *Kcho*, *Bernard Moninot*, *Jaume Plensa*, *Jean-Pierre Raynaud*, *Sean Scully*, *Jésus Rafael Soto*, *The Supports-Surfaces Years*, *A Century of English Sculpture*.

If it's not too crowded, enjoy the relaxed atmosphere in the café and don't miss a stop at the small but superb bookstore just to the left of the reception desk in the main lobby. It has an extensive collection of art, museum and theory publications.

2 | Alain Kirili

Le grand commandement blanc, 1985–86
Jardin des Tuileries
métro: Concorde

Located alongside the Orangerie—the building opposite the Jeu de Paume in the southwest corner of the Tuileries overlooking the Seine.

Originally created in 1985–86, *The Great White Commandment* was restored and relocated to this site in 1996. The work is composed of 17 small elements of various blocklike, abstract shapes forged in iron and painted white. The parts all sit on little pedestals scattered about a plot of grass which is off-limits to people. Both as a totality and in terms of its individual forms, the sculpture seems absurdly placed and out of scale with its surroundings. Although it features such traits as repetition (sameness) and difference—concerns that have preoccupied many artists during the past several decades—it is a very weak example of the minimalist mode (and of Kirili's work). Since this is the inaugural and currently the only work of contemporary sculpture on permanent display within the Tuileries, it's a shame that it is not exceptional.

3 | Café Véry

 architect: Antoine STINCO
Jardin des Tuileries
métro: Tuileries

Located near the Jeu de Paume along the main pedestrian path that cuts through the middle of the gardens.

As you walk through the fashionable Tuileries, take a look at this café, which gives good evidence of the way Paris thinks in aesthetic and functional terms when it comes to modernizing its landmark treasures. The café is a simple one-story kiosk-style building with a central service core, notably furnished with finely crafted wood cabinets. The dining area, enclosed by a wall of glass doors, is flooded with natural light and open to wraparound views of the surrounding garden and its visitors. In nice weather, the doors are pulled back, creating a seamless continuity between interior and exterior tables. Conversely, in inclement weather or at night, a wall of wooden-shutter doors covers the glass-door walls to provide intimacy and warmth. A glass pyramid-shaped cupola, which also brings light into the interior, adds a snappy, vertical element to the structure.

A second café of duplicate design has been situated just opposite the Café Véry. Farther down the Tuileries toward the Louvre, two fast-food cafés of similar kiosk design develop the archetype.

4 | Marché Saint-Honoré

 architect: Ricardo BOFILL, 1997
place du Marché Saint-Honoré, 75001
métro: Pyramides, Tuileries

This building has finally brought new life to a site that has been an eyesore since an ugly parking garage replaced a traditional city market in the 1960s. The site is a large square in the middle of an upscale district linking the Tuileries and the Opéra Garnier. Bofill's design gives priority to this path by constructing his contemporary *marché* (market) of shops and offices around a central "street" continuous with external alignments. The structure is reminiscent of 19th-century covered shopping arcades. Like them, its glass canopy roof high above a central passageway extending the full length of the building produces an open, airy feeling. But whereas they were elaborated by fine decorative details, here everything is reduced—or refined—to minimalist expression.

White concrete columns devoid of bases and capitals, exposed I-beams and expanses of glass stand out as elements in their own right. Yet they simultaneously emphasize design features, such as the curved walls of the passageway, the pitched roof, the continuity of the same elements inside and outside and spatial plays with the surrounding neighborhood. The building is actually encased by a glass wall that both endows the exterior with the appearance of openness and protects the interior from urban noise, pollution, light and other invasive forces. Bofill, an architect identified with housing projects full of appropriations from historic styles, here indicates his talent for creating a high-tech emporium without a brutal, dehumanizing industrial appearance.

Bofill, Marché Saint–Honoré

5 | Grand Louvre

renovation: I. M. PEI, 1983–89
34–36 quai du Louvre, 75001
01-40-20-50-50
Mon, Wed, 9–9:45; Thurs–Sun,
9–6; temporary exhibitions,
10–9:45; closed Tues
admission: 45F; 26F after 3 and
Sun; free 1st Sun each month;
30F major exhibitions
métro: Palais-Royal

The enlargement and renovation of the Louvre—the extravagant royal palace expropriated during the French Revolution (1793) and then developed as a national museum with an unequaled collection of art—was a top priority among President Mitterand's *grands projets*. Not only did the deteriorated building require fixing and updating, but Paris needed a new look and something dramatic to reclaim its stature as a leading cultural center. With visible panache, I. M. Pei's great glass pyramid, which provides a new main entrance and a spectacular cap over the new reception areas, did indeed revitalize the Louvre, the city and Paris's reputation as a cultural capital. This contemporary architectural project or, more precisely, this architectural image served to rekindle the spirit of modernity. Although the radical transformation initially provoked rage and criticism from the populace, Parisians soon adopted the pyramid as a favorite monument and symbol of the city.

The pyramid covers escalators and staircases that lead down into an expansive hall (cour Napoléon)—the hub of the museum's circulation network—where the east-west and north-south axes of the Louvre intersect. Besides allowing sunshine and light to penetrate the interior, its glass design and extended height obscure the sense of an underground environment. As modern as it appears with its minimalist form and geodesic structure of stainless-steel tubes and cables, Pei's pyramid harks back to an ancient icon. And though he has converted the closed, solid shape into a transparent, almost immaterial one, his image retains the awesome, visual presence of its historic predecessor. Indeed, its prominence is strengthened because its ultrageometric simplicity is in such stark contrast to the decorative grandeur of the surrounding architecture. By placing two smaller pyramids, seven triangular reflecting pools and a series of fountain jets alongside the giant pyramid, Pei both reiterates the contrast and further marks the site as the entrance.

In addition to the new grand entrance and huge reception area, the Louvre renovation (1981–99) has doubled the museum's size to the equivalent of 13 football fields, making it the largest museum in the world. The spatial expansion and reorganization of the gallery layout have greatly helped accommodate the crowds (now more than 3 million visitors a year). Moreover, they enhance the art. The renowned masterpieces are still on display, but galleries are more focused and viewing conditions are improved. The Grand Louvre is also very up-to-date as a public-service institution with rest and relaxation areas, elevators, restaurants, cafés and bookshops.

6 | Café Richelieu

architect: Jean-Michel WILMOTTE
Richelieu wing, first floor,
Musée du Louvre
01-40-20-53-63
Access only from within the Louvre.

Jean-Michel Wilmotte, in collaboration with several contemporary artists, has given this chic café a distinctive decor. Prior to the renovation, the Ministry of Finance was located in this section of the Louvre, and the minister himself used these rooms as his private office. Immediately visible as you enter are the signature stripes of Daniel BUREN. These mark the walls, tables, ceiling and floor in the entry room as well as some furniture in the adjacent dining room. Also in this dining room, Jean-Pierre RAYNAUD has metamorphosed existing recessed arches into celestial vaults in homage to the Louvre's painting *The Annunciation* by Fra Angelico. Taking a very different approach to the setting, Francis GIACOBETTI has translated the stone sculptures of great men located on the facade of the Louvre (visible from the café windows) into a frieze of photographs. The café also includes a crushed-metal sculpture by CESAR.

7 | Carrousel du Louvre

architects: I. M. PEI with Michel
MACARY, 1993–97
99 rue de Rivoli, 75001
Mon, Wed–Sun, 10–8; closed Tues
métro: Palais-Royal

At the same time as the Louvre museum was being renovated, an adjacent construction project created the Carrousel—a culture bazaar and upscale shopping mall. You can either enter through the allée du Grand Louvre, which extends directly from the museum's grand reception hall, harmonizing perfectly with a string of genteel shops selling coins, postcards, posters, casts and prints related to art objects. Or you can enter from the street or métro, where access is also a continuous route opening onto a panoply of businesses and public spaces. You'll find passageways lined with elegantly designed, chic boutiques specializing in high fashion, leisure and sportswear, jewelry, shoes, scarves, perfume, porcelain, kitchenware, souvenirs, etc. There's even a Virgin Megastore, a post office and an agency for châteaux rentals! And should you get hungry, you can go

to a gourmet restaurant or the Restagora—a self-service, international food emporium. The Carrousel also houses the new Studio Theater of the Comédie Française, an auditorium for the Ecole du Louvre (Louvre School) and two huge halls used for commercial shows but best known as the site of the seasonal presentations by Paris couturier houses. Occasionally you'll find something with a contemporary art focus here. Such was the case when *Paris Photo*, Europe's International Photography Fair, took over the space in Nov 1997.

As much as the Carrousel is basically a mall, it is so elegant and so permeated with sophisticated product displays that it raises mall standards to a new level. Architecturally, it sustains the flavor of the new Louvre with its marble floors and walls, its high ceilings and soft lighting. It even has a historic component: a 14th-century moat built by Charles V, which was discovered during construction of the Carrousel and then incorporated into its design. However, the dramatic focal point is another glass-and-steel pyramid. Unlike its counterpart, this one is suspended in space and positioned upside down. Despite its 150-ton weight, here too it has the aura of an immaterial presence suffusing the underground plaza with sunlight and rainbow reflections.

8 | Daniel Buren

Les deux plateaux, 1985–86
cour d'Honneur, Palais-Royal
winter, 7 am–8:30 pm; summer,
7 am–11 pm
métro: Palais-Royal

An easy way to enter this inner courtyard of the Palais-Royal is to walk straight back from place Colette or rue Saint-Honoré through one of the porticos or outdoor passageways in the building.

The Ministry of Culture often hails this installation sculpture as emblematic of its *commande publique* (public art) program. Without question, it is a superb, innovative creation embodying many aspects of late-20th-century art. Yet, as with many unorthodox projects, this one met with public furor. The outcries lasted for months, became a political scandal and even involved a court injunction to block construction under the claim that it defaced the Palais-Royal, a historic monument. A 1957 law guaranteeing an artist's right to finish a commissioned work already begun saved the project.

The controversy brought out in the open many concerns about art in public places. (These are still being argued.) At the same time, *Two Plateaus* effectively inaugurated a new form of public sculpture—a "living monument." For Buren —an incomparably sensitive, ingenious artist (known superficially for his signature stripes)—the question was, How to make a monumental sculpture that doesn't impose itself physically, that isn't a monument but has the stature of a monument. . . . How to make a very big object but one the spectator always dominates? At stake is the production of not an object, but a place. Public sculpture is not viewed as a statue on a pedestal or even a multipartite installation. Instead it is conceived as a means of reintegrating art with the human, social realms. In this case, Buren has placed 460 freestanding, black-and-white, vertically striped pillars (cement-composite shafts sheathed with marble and granite) across the ground plane of a courtyard in such a way that they become a compelling presence, precisely ordered and scaled with reference to the surrounding architecture. You can't help but walk among and over the columns and usually end up sitting on them. Thus your experience is both visual and physical. Moreover, the oddity of the arrangement and discovery of the subterranean dimension of the work provoke the intellect and imagination,

Buren, *Les deux plateaux*

not to mention on-the-spot interpersonal dynamics. The work also accommodates pedestrians who use the courtyard as an access route, children who treat it as a playground and romantic Parisians (or tourists) who come at night when the courtyard is a wonderland of stripes punctuated by red and green runway lights, which define the corners of the surface squares, and a blue glow illuminates the underground elements.

The design of *Two Plateaus* followed two main principles: "to reveal the underground of the courtyard, and to inscribe the project into the architectural composition of the Palais-Royal, which is essentially linear, repetitive and intertwined." The work creates a mesh or pattern of squares on the ground dictated by the alignment of the columns in the Galerie d'Orléans (the colonnade at the periphery of the courtyard). In addition, the whole is organized on two distinct plateaus. "The oblique one—where the line with the greatest slope is on the diagonal of the courtyard—reveals the underground. The horizontal one—created by the visual alignment of all the heights of the trunks of columns whose reference height is that of the pedestal of the columns in the colonnades of the Palais-Royal—reveals the ground level. These two plateaus are virtual." As Buren indicates, there are several different systems operating and interconnecting at once. Most immediately notable is the harmony of the checkerboard layout with the colonnades and the descending alignment. And indeed, the discovery of these surface-oriented systems leads to awareness of the underground plateau, where the placement of additional pillars and an H-shaped artificial stream echo the points and paths of the plateau on the ground surface. The stream is made visible and audible through steel grates (alongside the alignments of the tallest and slanting columns), and you can see one of the sunken pillars, set in a small pool of water and contained as a kind of relic inside a glass cube, at the end of the descending alignment. To those who are mystically minded, it's an interesting leap from Buren's creation to the prehistoric alignments at Carnac.

9 | Pol Bury

Untitled, 1985
cour d'Honneur, Palais-Royal
winter, 7 am–8:30 pm
summer, 7 am–11 pm
métro: Palais-Royal

Located just behind the Buren installation in an adjacent section of the Palais-Royal courtyard.

In contrast to the linearity and rigorous order of the Buren project, Bury's two fountains feature irregular groupings of huge, shiny stainless-steel balls set on a steel plate. As with many Bury compositions, you have to look carefully and not turn away too quickly because the elements move unexpectedly. They shift, sometimes imperceptibly, causing relational changes to occur continuously. Here, water serves as the catalyst. It slides across the surface, enters the balls through slits in their shells, and when it reaches a certain level it topples the balance, triggering a new arrangement of the parts.

10 | Galerie Françoise Paviot

57 rue Sainte-Anne, 75002
01-42-60-1001 f: 01-42-60-44-77
Tues–Sat, 2:30–6:30; closed Mon
métro: Pyramides, 4 Septembre

Though located a bit off the beaten track from other galleries, be sure to visit here if you like contemporary photography. Exhibitions present classic work as well as current themes and approaches. Group shows, like *Feminine Now*, diversify the program.

Artists: Anna and Bernhard Blume, Angela Grauerholz, McDermott & McGough, Ann Mandelbaum, Ray Metzker, Jean Painlevé, Mark Ruwedel, Arthur Siegel, Nancy Wilson-Pajic.

Les Halles–Centre Pompidou

The name *Les Halles* is used to refer variously to the giant area of Paris that was previously France's central fruit and vegetable market—a popular site of late-night tourism; the large, labyrinthine transportation hub for the métro system (Châtelet–Les Halles); an equally grandiose shopping-sports-culture complex (Forum des Halles and Nouveau Forum des Halles); and an extensive garden (Jardin des Halles). This was one of the early redevelopment projects in Paris, and plans for the radical transformation of the whole area suffered enormous public, professional and political criticism. Even after the demolition stage had been completed, there were years of indecision and opposition to the multitude of ideas proposed. Meanwhile, the site became known as *le grand trou* (the big hole). Indeed, it was the largest, most conspicuous urban eyesore in the world, made all the worse because it no longer contained the widely lamented, classic, 19th-century iron-and-glass food halls by Victor Baltard. A compromise, passed in 1975, called for a large park and shopping center, yet still battles continued. More proposals emerged from an international conference in 1979, but these too were rejected. If nothing else, the public outrage curtailed the high-density, high-rise developments that had begun to intrude on historic environments throughout France. Finally, a hybrid and incoherent (but commercially successful) complex was built at one end, and

the rest became open, landscaped space with an underground maze of rail lines, road tunnels, parking facilities, shops and activity centers. The fringes also acquired some new housing and commercial buildings that adhere to height limitations and display traditional mansard roofs and dormer windows.

1 | Forum des Halles

architects: Claude VASCONI and Georges PENCREAC'H, 1979
1–7 rue Pierre Lescot (between rue Berger and rue Rambuteau), 75001
métro: Les Halles

This four-level shopping mall centers on a sunken courtyard dominated by escalators carrying a crowded stream of people to and from the shops, fast-food restaurants and métro lines below. The above-ground architecture is a glitzy mix of glass-and-mirror chrome-ribbed walls and mushroom structures embellished by curious pink marble statuary by the Argentine sculptor Julio SILVA. In contrast, the subterranean zone is a bland, low-ceilinged, glass-and-concrete environment—not a place to spend time if you're susceptible to claustrophobia or agoraphobia. To the north and east of the Forum are terraces and pavilions housing offices, more stores and entertainment or exhibition spaces.

2 | Patrick Raynaud

Voyelles, 1988
passage Mondétour (off rue Rambuteau), Les Halles

The sculpture *Vowels* is one of the public artworks commissioned by the city as part of the renovation of Les Halles. It is located on a walkway marked by a transverse beam that connects shops on either side. Using the beam to his advantage, Raynaud has placed monumental, brightly colored steel letters—

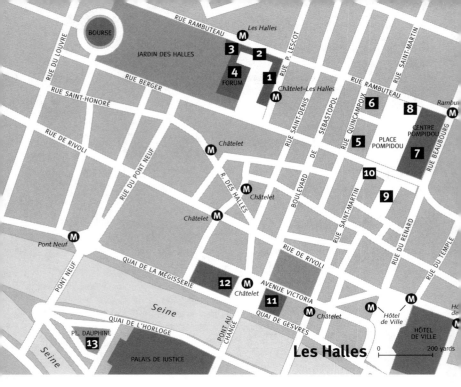

A, E, I, O, U—on and around it in play-ful, skewed positions. The letters are an homage to the sonnet "Les Voyelles" by Arthur Rimbaud. "In this environment, saturated with diverse advertising mes-sages and commercial signs," the artist saw his sculpture as offering "a mes-sage of the same type in colored letters but with a fundamentally different and strongly poetic content."

3 | Pavillon des Arts

🚇 101 rue Rambuteau, Forum des Halles, 75001
01-42-33-82-50 f: 01-40-28-93-22
Tues–Sun, 11:30–6:30; closed Mon
admission: 33/15F
métro: Les Halles

Located at porte Rambuteau, terrasse Lautréamont—the second level, in the last above-ground building on the north side (rue Rambuteau) of the Les Halles complex. Don't expect to see an exterior sign or a fancy entrance. The space lies

behind a mundane door in a generic office corridor.

This exhibition space, run by the city of Paris, is a well-kept secret and some-what difficult to find. It organizes excel-lent exhibitions, generally with historical themes. Although they rarely deal with the contemporary period, some—like the superb *Surrealism and Love*, 1997—focus on modern art. One exception is the pavilion's participation in the city-wide Month of Photography. If past exhibitions are an indication, it's well worth seeing the show they organize for this event.

4 | Nouveau Forum des Halles

🏛 architect: Paul CHEMETOV, 1985
🚇 métro: Les Halles

Located beneath the garden of Les Halles, continuous with the underground structure of Forum des Halles. The most direct entry is from porte Saint-Eustache off rue Rambuteau near the Saint-Eustache church.

Contrary to Forum des Halles, this complex has a spacious and architecturally interesting subterranean plaza (place Carrée). It's as high as a five-story building, lined with massive concrete-block walls and supported by huge buttresses and double-column piers. It makes no excuse for being a brutal, cold, oversized environment, but its exaggerated show of strength and openness is just what you want underground. In addition to the shops and eateries, this forum contains an incredible botanical garden, a spectacular glass-roofed swimming pool, billiard parlor, 15-screen movie theater and various culture enclaves. It's quite a potpourri. When meandering around, be sure to check out the exuberant portraits of J. S. Bach, Mick Jagger and everyone in between in the mural by ERRO, situated in the lobby of the music and dance concert auditorium.

Espace Photographique
4 de Paris

4 Grande Galerie, place Carrée,
Nouveau Forum des Halles, 75001
01-48-72-94-94
Tues–Fri, 1–6; Sat–Sun, 1–5;
closed Mon
métro: Les Halles

If you enter Les Halles complex from porte Saint-Eustache and take the escalator down, you'll arrive in place Carrée.

Before it moved into its new home in 1997, the Maison Européenne de la Photographie organized exhibitions in this space. The site still presents photography shows, most with intriguing themes. The emphasis is slanted toward cultural content and usually includes unfamiliar work. It's similar to an alter-

native space where each exhibition explores something different and you never know what to expect in terms of the subject matter and character of the work. Recent exhibitions: *Rock 'n Roll Attitudes*, *To the Discovery of Vietnamese Photography*, *Jazz Off Stage*.

4 Vidéothèque de Paris

2 Grande Galerie, Nouveau Forum
des Halles, 75001
01-44-76-62-00 f: 01-40-26-40-96
Mon–Sat, 1–9; closed Sun
admission: 30/25F
métro: Les Halles

Located just to the right when you get off the escalator from the porte Saint-Eustache entrance to Les Halles complex.

This is an amazing institution that gives the public easy access to 5,600 commercial films, documentaries, short footage and newsreels. The collection has a particular focus on Paris. There's a consultation room with 40 screens for individual viewings; three halls with film programs about Paris and other cities, shown four times each day; two rooms for group showings; and desks where you can search computer databanks and CD-ROMs for information. In addition to owning and showing videos made by others, the center produces videos that bear witness to the transformation of Paris—its architectural, cultural, sociological and human evolution. The Vidéothèque also organizes meetings, lectures, international conferences and multimedia festivals.

Galerie Chantal
5 Crousel

40 rue Quincampoix, 75004
01-42-77-38-87 f: 01-42-77-59-00
Tues–Sat, 11–1 and 2–7;
closed Mon
métro: Hôtel de Ville, Les Halles

Rue Quincampoix is a narrow pedestrian street with a calm that belies its location just one block away from the hullabaloo of the Centre Pompidou plaza. Although many galleries on this street are not visible as you walk along, it is worth the effort to go behind the street facades to find them. To get to the Galerie Chantal Crousel, pass through the large coach doors fronting the street and walk straight back across the courtyard to the old one-story building with a set of stairs up to its door.

This gallery consistently shows some of the most exciting, truly creative work by noteworthy European artists and a few Americans. Work shown here usually has a conceptually based orientation, though this is never at the expense of visual sensitivity. Exhibitions typically include a choice selection that is plentiful and varied. The gallery has a great record of supporting emerging artists, often giving them their first major show. Don't miss the downstairs exhibition spaces, which often include additional objects, installations or videos. Artists: Bas Jan Ader, Absalon, Nobuyoshi Araki, Sophie Calle, Tony Cragg, Avital Geva, Robert Gober, Dominique Gonzalez-Foerster, Marie-Ange Guilleminot, Mona Hatoum, Thomas Hirschhorn, Carsten Höller, Wolfgang Laib, Moshe Ninio, Gabriel Orozco, Tobias Rehberger, Wolfgang Tillmans, Rirkrit Tiravanija, Rosemarie Trockel.

Gabriel Orozco, *La D.S.* 1993 (Galerie Chantal Crousel)

5 | Galerie Nelson

⌂ 40 rue Quincampoix, 75004
01-42-71-74-56 f: 01-42-71-74-58
Tues–Sat, 2–7; closed Mon
métro: Hôtel de Ville, Les Halles

This gallery shares the same courtyard as Galerie Chantal Crousel. It is located on the second level, via a staircase to the left of the street entrance.

The gallery director, Philip Nelson (an American), is a friendly soul, well versed in what's going on in Europe. You may not be familiar with the artists he shows, but most have achieved considerable recognition within international art circuits. Don't be embarrassed to ask for assistance since the artists here tend to create "tough" work that's not always easy to grasp initially. Usually there is a short text (available at the reception desk), which describes the program or conceptual base for the objects on display. Artists: Sylvie Bächli, Joseph Bartscherer, Basserode, Dorothéa Breick, Frédéric Diart, Helmut Dorner, Lili Dujourie, Ludger Gerdes, Rodney Graham, Dianne Hagen, Axel Kasseböhmer, Harald Klingelhöller, Ken Lum, Jürgen Meyer, Reinhard Mucha, Hervé Paraponaris, Thomas Ruff, Anne-Marie Schneider, Thomas Schütte, Pia Stadbaümer, Mitja Tusek, Gert Verhoeven, James Welling, Stephen Wilks, Bruno Yvonnet.

Galerie du Jour,
6 | Agnès B

⌂ 44 rue Quincampoix, 75004
01-44-54-55-90 f: 01-44-54-55-99
Tues–Sat, 10–7; closed Mon
métro: Hôtel de Ville, Les Halles

Located at the back of a courtyard entered from a walkway between #44 and #46.

The same woman who successfully created the Agnès B clothing stores shaped the direction of this gallery. It has a fresh spirit, often showing art that tends to be provocative and satiric, if not bawdy. Some exhibitions seem to substitute gratuitous shock or flash humor for incisiveness and creative risk, but others use shock and humor to open the door to perplexing issues. In addition to the art on display, the gallery sells unusual art publications and posters. Artists: Kenneth Anger, Aurèle, Banger, Jean-Batiste Bruant, Roman Cieslewicz, Thomas Florschuetz, Futura, Rafael Gray, Katsuhiko Hibino, Joël Hubaut, Louis Jammes, Mike Lash, Thierry Lefébure, Claude Lévèque, Made in Eric, Jonas Mekas, Martin Paar, Paul Seawright, Vyakul, Neil Winokur.

Centre National d'Art et de Culture Georges Pompidou

7

architects: Renzo PIANO and Richard ROGERS, 1972–77
19 rue Beaubourg, 75191
01-44-78-49-19 f: 01-44-78-13-02
métro: Hôtel de Ville, Les Halles, Rambuteau

The main entrance is on the plaza side of the building off rue Saint-Martin. (The plaza and the center itself are variously referred to as place Pompidou/ Centre Pompidou and place Beaubourg/ Centre Beaubourg.)

Centre Pompidou is closed for renovation until the year 2000. During this period, performances (theater, dance, music, art) will still take place in a tipi set up in the Pompidou plaza. (01-44-94-98-00. admission: 50/40F) Special exhibitions organized by the National Museum of Modern Art and visits to the Brancusi Studio will continue during the renovation. (See below.) The activities of IRCAM (Contemporary Institute of Acoustic Music and Research), which is another part of the Pompidou Center,

located in an adjacent building, will not be affected. The grand reopening at midnight, December 31, 1999, will mark the millennium.

When plans for a cultural center (art museum, public library, live-event facilities) were being developed in 1971, the idea that it be a dynamic and accessible place and not a staid repository held sway. Reclaiming Paris as the center of the international avant-garde, heeding the lessons of the spring of 1968 about abolishing outmoded conventions and embracing the populace, affirming new technology, and revitalizing a neighborhood (the Marais) in serious decline were all factors determining the shape and character of both the building and its programs. It's unlikely anyone had an inkling of how successful the project would be in responding to these concerns. The Pompidou has indeed become a popular mecca. It has an average attendance of about 7 million per year—a figure that reflects the crowds who flock to blockbuster museum shows as well as the throngs of nonprofessional scholars who, for the first time in France, have had access to a free public library. The building is world famous, a 20th-century landmark—still presenting an image of ultra-radical, technically venturous design. The Marais is booming as a lively, commercially prosperous, upscale, chic area. And the center's exhibitions, presentations and collections are renowned, often challenging narrow, conventional definitions of "art" and "culture."

The design of Piano (Italian) and Rogers (English)—winners of the international competition for the project—is as bold in its rejection of the pure, sleek forms of modernism as it is in its emphatic industrial style dominated by a conspicuous display of technological and service elements on the exterior. Because the architects wanted to provide the utmost spatial flexibility on each of the seven levels, they conceived of the core as a stack of open platforms with a minimum of permanent subdivisions. The outside then became an exoskeleton articulated by structural beams, tension cables, giant colored tubes, service pipes, staircases, elevators, escalators, walkways. As in a diagram, the elements are color-coded: blue for air-conditioning, green for water circulation, yellow for electrical circuits, red for people-mover mechanisms. Moreover, Piano and Rogers situated the building with its rear facade on the streetside and its front opening onto an enormous, sloped plaza (occupying as much land as the building) bordered by streets closed to traffic. They gave preeminence to the outdoor plaza as a means of enhancing the public aspect of the building, and indeed it has become a space where people gather and engage in all kinds of activities. (Unfortunately, an incessant cacophony of loud noise and the presence of too many raunchy hang-abouts and peddlers often make the plaza uninviting and unpleasant.) The architects also increased the accessible, public face of the design by making a hanging escalator the dominant feature on the front facade. It's an amazing form, enclosed in a transparent tube, extending across the entire length of the building, stopping at every floor and giving some 3,000 people an hour a bird's-eye view of the plaza as well as a panoramic view of Paris.

Most people either love or hate the Pompidou building, and it continually elicits argumentative, vociferous comments. It will be curious to see how and if the renovation affects opinions. Although changes will expand and consolidate various aspects of the previous layout, the constituent parts of the center will largely remain the same. The lower levels and mezzanine will probably contain the children's center, post office, bookstore (a superb place to find art, film, theory, music, architecture books and contemporary exhibition catalogues), Internet café, exhibition spaces, five halls for film, lecture, audiovisual and live events, and underground parking garage. Levels 1 and 2 will house the redesigned public library. The newly organized National Museum of Modern Art will occupy all of levels 3 and 4, and restaurants and special exhibition spaces will still be on the top level.

Musée National d'Art Moderne—Centre de Création Industrielle
7 (MNAM-CCI)

Centre Georges Pompidou, 19 rue Beaubourg, 75191
01-44-78-12-33 f: 01-44-78-12-07
métro: Hôtel de Ville, Les Halles, Rambuteau

The museum is closed for renovation until the year 2000. During the interim, special exhibitions will be presented in Galerie Sud (South Gallery) on the mezzanine. Mon, Wed–Sun, 10–10; closed Tues. admission: 30/20F

The stated goal of MNAM is "to show every art form that has existed since the beginning of the twentieth century in France and in the world." Sounds a bit megalomaniac and yet it is precisely this encyclopedic urge that has produced one of world's richest collections of modern art. At least for the first half of the century, when Paris was the capital of the art world, the museum's collection is dominated by many incomparable treasures. Strengths in Bonnard, Braque, Delaunay, Duchamp, Ernst, Giacometti, Kandinsky, Klee, Léger, Magritte, Malevich, Matisse, Miró, Mondrian, Pevsner, Picasso, Rouault and other key figures make Fauvism,

Cubism, de Stijl, Suprematism, Constructivism, Dada and Surrealism come alive.

The layout (designed by Gae AULENTI in a 1986 renovation of the galleries) alternates box-like rooms of differing sizes and shapes with narrow passages covered by pitched glass. Paintings and sculptures are installed in the rooms whereas related drawings and documentary materials are set in protective, controlled-light vitrines in the adjacent passages. A main corridor, which extends the length of the building, provides entry into each section of the galleries as well as views of and access into outdoor sculpture courtyards. (In fact, the courtyards are not always open to the public.) In general, the museum is organized chronologically and stylistically—a mode now considered conservative and restrictive. Of course changes may well occur in both the gallery layout and installation arrangement when the museum reopens in 2000. With luck there will be a humanization of the antiseptic spaces and too sparse, too pedantic texts.

Although the MNAM collection gives a broad perspective on the pre–World War II period, galleries devoted to the second half of the century barely scratch the surface. During this period, Paris lost its place as a major center of vanguard activity. Though New York usurped the lead during the 1950s and 1960s, the last decades of the century are rife with international cross-currents and complexities. There is no progression of "isms," and individual efforts become more significant than group or chronological determinations. What emerges is a great diversity of art forms, themes, images, attitudes, concepts and materials—not to mention some overt references to socio-political-cultural issues and mainstream, information-age life.

The MNAM display (prior to the renovation) unfortunately didn't communicate the character of the age, and its groupings were a disservice to the art. Given its collection of exemplary works by such innovative figures as Joseph Beuys, Marcel Broodthaers, Anselm Kiefer, Yves Klein, Jannis Kounellis, Sol LeWitt, Mario Merz, Claes Oldenburg, Sigmar Polke, Jackson Pollock, Jean-Pierre Raynaud, Gerhard Richter, Jean Tinguely and many less familiar names, the museum could create a compelling display. The same holds true for coverage of the more recent years. Rumors suggest that the collection comprises prime objects—including new media and installation works—by many distinctive artists. The building's renovation offers a great opportunity to explore new modes of organization and presentation for the art from these years.

MNAM became a national museum in 1947, though it had been operating as a museum of modern art since 1937 when it moved into the Palais de Tokyo (the site now occupied by the City Museum of Modern Art). Just before its relocation to the Pompidou Center, the museum integrated the Center of Industrial Creation into its fold. (The two units fused totally in 1992.) CCI is concerned with the history and evolution of the 20th century in terms of architecture, interior architecture, urbanism, design, visual communication and related fields. Prior to the renovation, two galleries were devoted to architecture and design. These will be greatly enlarged in the new distribution of space. More of the museum's design objects and remarkable architectural models and drawings—including fascinating proposals for buildings that were never actualized—will be on exhibit.

A major part of the MNAM program is its special exhibitions. These generally were—and will still be—located in the North and South Galleries on the mezzanine and in the Grand Gallery on the top floor. In many ways, MNAM has been one of the most ambitious and creative forces producing major exhibitions. Aside from the fact they are usually far too big for normal human stamina, they are distinctive in dealing with ideas, historical and cultural context, multimedia and mass-media documentation, interdisciplinary connections and an expansion of the canon of relevant artists and art objects. Recent examples include: *The Impression*, *Feminine-Masculine—The Sex of Art*, *Art and Life—1952–94*, *The City—Art and Architecture in Europe (1870–93)*, *Manifest, Manifest—a Parallel History (1960–90)*, *Art and Publicity (1890–90)*, *Magicians of the Earth*. Complementing these projects are the museum's retrospective and one-person exhibitions, which are also impressive. Recent examples: *Francis Bacon*, *Joseph Beuys*, *Constantin Brancusi*, *Tony Cragg*, *Max Ernst*, *Luciano Fabro*, *Filonov*, *Gisèle Freund*, *Louis Kahn*, *Wassily Kandinsky*, *Henri Matisse*, *Bruce Nauman*, *Christian de Portzamparc*, *Georges Rouault*, *Kurt Schwitters*, *Andy Warhol*.

8 | Atelier Brancusi

architect: Renzo PIANO, 1995–97
place Pompidou, 95191
01-44-78-12-33
Mon, Wed–Fri, 12–10; Sat–Sun, 10–10; closed Tues
admission: 30F
métro: Rambuteau, Les Halles, Hôtel de Ville

Located at the north end of Pompidou plaza bordering rue Rambuteau.

In 1956 Brancusi bequeathed the whole of his studio and its contents to France on the condition that it be totally and exactly reconstituted. It was the studio he occupied from 1916 until his death in 1957 at impasse Ronsin in the Montparnasse area of Paris. MNAM (in its previous location in the Palais de Tokyo) provided the first re-creation of the studio within its exhibition space (1962). When it moved to Beaubourg (1977), it again constructed a faithful representation of Brancusi's live-work space, this time as a separate building (situated at the Saint-Martin/Rambuteau corner of Pompidou plaza). After floods caused the studio to be emptied and closed in 1990, a decision was eventually made to construct an enhanced studio building.

The new studio, designed by Renzo Piano, one of the original architects of the Pompidou, opened in 1997. Again located in the plaza, though closer to the Center, it is a far more elegant and spacious version than its predecessor. Now there is a large reception area, auxiliary galleries and a peripheral corridor for viewing and visitor circulation. Piano has strictly respected the size and original disposition of the four rooms, furnishings, tools and art objects. But by situating the studio in the middle of the building and then shielding the rooms behind glass walls, he has created a very controversial installation. Moreover, the cold austerity of the building's interior —which is in marked contrast to the sensuosity of Brancusi's sculptures and the lived environment of his studio— project a counterproductive ambience. Brancusi wanted visitors to experience his art as it existed in his studio, but the glass walls and setting have a distancing and imprisoning effect. Rather than functioning to protect the art (their ostensible purpose), they create a debilitating barrier. What a shame, since Brancusi's studio provides a unique opportunity to enter the habitat and mind-set of a great artist.

Brancusi placed great importance on the presentation of his art. He paid close attention to comparisons and contrasts among sculptures, juxtapositions, the space around works and changes in light and shadow. The positioning of each individual object as well as interactions within the ensemble were critical. For these reasons, he liked to show his art in his studio—the place where he had the greatest control over viewing conditions. This is also the reason he willed his studio replete with his art for public display.

Rooms 1 and 2 of the studio show numerous Brancusi sculptures in various stages of creation and in a range of materials—wood, stone, plaster, bronze. You can also see sculptures sharing pedestals; sculptures set on the floor without the intermediary of a pedestal; partially carved blocks of stone; the same work in different sizes (changes in height being particularly important); photographs by Brancusi; and monochrome backdrop paintings (red, white, gray) on the walls.

Beside providing exposure to his art as he wanted it to be seen, the studio reveals how Brancusi lived and worked. This is particularly evident in Rooms 3 and 4. Room 3 re-creates the additional room he rented in 1930 for use as a private domain. It includes a sanding machine, drills, a hoist and pulling device for moving sculptures, an entertainment area with his violin, guitar, books and large collection of jazz and folk music, and a sleeping loft. The adjacent room, added in 1941, is largely a storage area for casts, although it also contains more tools and an additional pulley device used to hold and move large blocks of stone during the carving process. You can see a piece of gray marble for a *Oiseau* (*Bird*) sculpture on the worktable. This room was the place where Brancusi set up his camera and photographic equipment. The photographs he took of his art and studio, some of which are on exhibit in the back gallery, are important documents. They provide further indication of Brancusi's interest in and ability to affect and change the character and appearance of his sculptures.

Jean Tinguely and
9 | Niki de Saint-Phalle

La fontaine Stravinsky, 1983
place Igor Stravinsky
métro: Hôtel de Ville, Les Halles

This fountain sculpture (located on the south side of the Centre Pompidou) is a spectacle of squirting water jets, colorful figures and gyrating, swirling sculptures. It brings together 16 objects: assemblages created by Jean Tinguely from wheels, ancient and new motors, corroded iron works and other metamechanical parts; and fanciful painted figures by Niki de Saint-Phalle. Inspired by the compositions of Igor Stravinsky, the artists gave the different elements of the fountain names like *key to the earth*, *nightingale*, *snake*, *firebird*, *spiral*, *life*, *elephant*, *death*, *ragtime* and *love*. The scene in the plaza is a perfect side show with its conglomerate of café-table people-watchers and profusion of camera-happy tourists, frolicking children and stray or pampered dogs.

Tinguely & Saint–Phalle, *La fontaine Stravinsky*

10 | Café Beaubourg

architect: Christian de PORTZAMPARC, 1985–86
100 rue Saint-Martin, 75004
métro: Hôtel de Ville, Les Halles

Though opening directly onto the clamor of the Pompidou plaza, this café offers a setting for solitary dreaming. Its design is by Portzamparc, the celebrated architect of Cité de la Musique. Looking somewhat like an old eating club from the 1930s, it has a wide curving staircase, an inconspicuous bar off to the side, rearrangeable tables and chairs (designed for the space), bookshelves, an airy central space punctuated by eight oval-shaped columns and a balcony with a bridge crossing from one side to the other. The faux-fresco walls and overall appearance is subdued and minimalist. Yet on closer inspection you become aware of intriguing details, like the cutout little squares or circles Portzamparc has added throughout. Not surprisingly, the café is a meeting spot favored by the art crowd and a chic place to sit, read, write or do nothing. Be sure to go down to the bathrooms. They are an unexpected design treat. Of note is the emphasis on curves (unlike upstairs), a seductive S-shaped mirror-wall, a tall chrome bar-table with two little seats, a little telephone room with centuries-old exposed stones and bricks, black cone-shaped sinks and a zigzag floor-mirror.

11 | François Morellet

Or et désordre, 1991
foyer, Théâtre de la Ville,
place du Châtelet, 75004
métro: Châtelet

Alhough the full installation can only be seen from the inside (accessible to ticket-holders during performances), it is possible to get a partial view from the street. Look through the arcade of windows on the upper level.

On the concrete framework of the foyer's ceiling—which is also the underpart of the auditorium's tiers—Morellet has laid out a linear composition using blocks of gold leaf. Within the align-

ments, the letters V-I-L-L-E-D-E-P-A-R-I-S appear. They are ordered in accordance with an improvisational system formulated by the artist in his exploration of "architectural disintegrations." The installation also relates to Morellet's desire to disturb habitual connections between a viewer and space. Within the title, *Or* means *Gold* but also doubles as *Order* when set in a punning combination with *Disorder*.

12 | Valerio Adami

Untitled, 1989
loggia, Théâtre du Châtelet,
place du Châtelet, 75001
métro: Châtelet

Visible from the street through the arcade of large windows on the upper level.

Adami, an artist inspired by classical culture, is well known in France for the narrative figure style he developed in the 1970s. To commemorate the bicentennial of the French Revolution, he was commissioned to create a work for the loggia of the Châtelet Theater. He chose to evoke theater, dance and music in terms of figures in six allegorical panels. The compositions, with their eccentric images, vivid colors, flat planes and bold black outlines, are prime examples of Adami's work.

13 | David Rabinowitch

Suite of Constructions in Conic Section in Four Arrangements. To Dominique Bozo in memoriam, 1984–87
place Dauphine, Ile de la Cité
métro: Cité

Located on the raised terrace of place Dauphine, a quiet little park behind the Palais de Justice at the opposite end of Ile de la Cité from Notre-Dame.

This sculpture of Cor-ten steel plates lying flat on the ground is easy to miss.

Unlike most sculpture, which has volumetric form and occupies space, here form and space are delineated rather than modeled. Each of the four units has a different shape and segmentation but all have components generated by the curves and planes of a cone—the circumference, ellipse, parabola and hyperbola. The holes that pierce the plates variously produce additional irregularities and play with ideas about depth, solid and void. Such cerebral considerations and the work's austere, brute appearance are typical of the minimalist mode of art that emerged in the mid-1960s. Rabinowitch dedicated this sculpture to Dominique Bozo, former director of Centre Pompidou, who introduced his art in France. The work was installed here in 1993, after Bozo's untimely death.

Marais

1 | Galerie Nathalie Obadia

⌂ 5 rue du Grenier Saint-Lazare, 75003
01-42-74-67-68 f: 01-42-74-68-66
Tues–Sat, 11–7; closed Mon
métro: Rambuteau

With its international scope and focus on new-generation artists, many of whom have gained attention in their own countries, this gallery offers a different perspective. The work covers the gamut of contemporary approaches and sensibilities. Artists: Georges Adeagbo, Angie Anakis, Carole Benzaken, Ricardo Brey, Nathalie Elemento, Stephen Ellis, Valérie Favre, Anthony Freestone, Clara Halter, Serge Kliaving, Charles Long, Pierre Moignard, Manuel Ocampo, Pascal Pinaud, Fiona Rae, Jeanne Silverthorne, Jessica Stockholder, Christophe Vigouroux, Paul Winstanley.

2 | Galerie des Archives

⌂ 4 impasse Beaubourg, 75003
01-42-78-05-77 f: 01-42-78-19-40
Tues–Fri, 11–1 and 2–7; Sat, 2–7; closed Mon
métro: Rambuteau, Hôtel de Ville

This gallery features the work of artists who have truly carved out a distinctive niche by developing a very personal brand of creativity. Although theoretically based, the art has a strong visual presence and evocative aura. The annual schedule of exhibitions includes emerging artists, as yet unknown in France. Artists: Pep Agut, Art Oriente objet, Elisabeth Ballet, Andrea Blum, David Boeno, Lynne Cohen, Patrick Corillon, Mark Dion, Lydia Dona, Gary Hill, Florence Paradeis, Erik Samakh, Thomas Shannon, Craig Wood.

3 | Galerie Daniel Templon

⌂ 30 rue Beaubourg, 75003
01-42-72-14-10 f: 01-42-77-45-36
Tues–Sat, 10–7 ; closed Mon
métro: Rambuteau, Hôtel de Ville
Located all the way in the back on the left side of the courtyard.

Templon's roster reads like a textbook of major artists from the past four decades. The gallery represents many Americans and a few young artists. It often accompanies exhibitions with catalogues. Artists: Jean-Michel Alberola, Martin Barré, Jean-Michel Basquiat, Ben, Ross Bleckner, Daniel Buren, Saint Clair Cemin, Jake & Dinos Chapman, Francesco Clemente, George Condo, Vincent Corpet, Enzo Cucchi, Olivier Debré, Eric Fischl, Raymond Hains, Keith Haring, Brian Hunt, Jörg Immendorf, Alain Jacquet, Ellsworth Kelly, Bertrand Lavier, Jean Le Gac, Sol LeWitt, Roy Lichtenstein, Malcolm Morley, Marc Mulders, Jules Olitski, Mimmo Paladino,

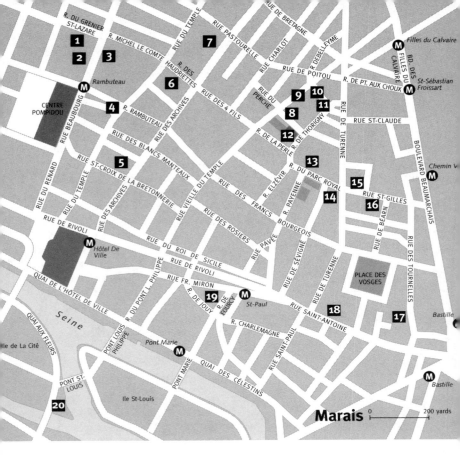

Jaume Plensa, Jean-Pierre Raynaud, Paul Rebeyrolle, François Rouan, David Salle, Tony Scherman, Julian Schnabel, Joel Shapiro, Ray Smith, Frank Stella, Donald Sultan, Gérard Traquandi, Juan Uslé, Claude Viallat, Andy Warhol.

Galerie
4 | Laage-Salomon

57 rue du Temple, 75004
01-42-78-11-71 f: 01-42-71-34-49
Tues–Sat, 12–7; closed Mon
métro: Hôtel de Ville
Enter through the courtyard.

This windowless, stark gallery always feels dreary, forbidding and compressed, even with its high ceilings. Because its installations are usually very spare, each work has room to breathe, but the gallery aura accentuates a sense of objecthood and austerity that often runs counter to the character of the art. Most of the artists are noteworthy, mid-career names, and the art on display does credit to their reputations. Artists: Roger Ackling, John Baldessari, Martin Barré, Georg Baselitz, Philippe Cognée, Hannah Collins, Mohamed El baz, Monique Frydman, Hamish Fulton, Fariba Hajamadi, Claudia Hart, Axel Hütte, Peter Joseph, Laurent Joubert, Per Kirkeby, Eugène Leroy, Mark Luyten, Georgia Marsh, Pierre Mercier, Gerhard Merz, Carmen Perrin, Yuki Onodera.

5 Galerie Gabrielle Maubrie

24 rue Sainte-Croix de la
Bretonnerie, 75004
01-42-78-03-97
Tues–Sat, 2–7; closed Mon
métro: Hôtel de Ville

Enter the courtyard and take the stairs on the left to the 2nd level.

The gallery favors art with a conceptual or socio-political edge or art that foregrounds humanistic issues. It's never just visual or chic. The work presented here is challenging and often ironic on all levels, so be prepared to spend enough time to give it serious attention. It's the kind of art that will probably never be mainstream though it has a real depth of conviction and personalized aesthetic. Artists: Dennis Adams, Etienne Bossut, Joseph Havel, Antonio Muntadas, Bill Owens, Allen Ruppersberg, Ernest T, Amikam Toren, Stephen Willatts, Krzysztof Wodiczko.

6 Galerie Ghislaine Hussenot

5 bis rue des Haudriettes, 75003
01-48-87-60-81 f: 01-48-87-05-01
Tues–Sat, 11–1 and 2–7; closed
Mon
métro: Hôtel de Ville, Rambuteau

From the street you will see only the gallery's name on a small plaque beside the carriage door. After you enter the courtyard you must go all the way to the back on the left side.

The gallery has earned a solid reputation for its choice of artists—a roster that includes both midcareer and emerging artists and many Americans. Exhibitions are usually very compelling, with installations taking advantage of the big open space, balcony and flood of natural light coming through a high glass roof. The rawness of the space tends to give the art a "studio" appear-

ance. This only serves to enhance the fact that the works are typically very recent creations being shown for the first time. The exhibitions are always worth a visit. Artists: Richard Artschwager, Vanessa Beecroft, Glenn Brown, Jean-Marc Bustamante, Wim Delvoye, Carroll Dunham, Fischli & Weiss, Bernard Frize, Andreas Gursky, Jim Hodges, Roni Horn, Cristina Iglesias, Mike Kelley, Karen Kilimnik, Juan Muñoz, Jean-Michel Othoniel, Tony Oursler, Miguel Rio Branco, Julie Roberts, Michal Rovner, Adrian Schiess, Alain Sechas, Cindy Sherman, Adriana Varejao, Franz West, Sue Williams, Christopher Wool, Chen Zhen.

7 Galerie Cadot

77 rue des Archives (between rue
des Haudriettes and rue
Pastourelle), 75003
01-42-78-08-36
Tues–Sat, 2:30–7; closed Mon
métro: Rambuteau

Often when you enter this gallery, it appears empty or in the process of reinstallation. Don't be misled. The art may be intentionally reductive and the installations are often quite sparse. The gallery's concentration on abstraction from the 1980s in both painting and sculpture belies a considerable diversity of work. Artists: Akin/Ludwig, Connie Beckley, Miguel Branco, Gerardo Delgado, Joel Fisher, David Hodges, Jorge Molder, Meret Oppenheim, Markus Raetz, Daniel Tremblay, Juan Usle.

8 Galerie Claudine Papillon

16 rue des Coutures Saint-Gervais,
75003
01-40-29-98-80 f: 01-40-29-07-19
Tues–Sat, 2:30–7; closed Mon
métro: Saint-Paul, Filles du Calvaire

Among the gallery's artists are various well-established and emerging Europeans who have had little exposure outside their homelands. Exhibitions feature new talent and marginal avant-garde artists as well. An energetic direction prevails and the work is always fresh, if not intriguing. Artists: Jean-Michel Alberola, Tony Carter, Patrick Caulfield, Marc Couturier, Michael Craig Martin, Erik Dietman, Hreinn Fridfinsson, Jürgen Klauke, Barbara & Michael Leisgen, Thierry Mouillé, Sigmar Polke, Dieter Roth, André Thomkins, Vassiliki Tsekoura, Françoise Vergier.

Galeries Côté Rue
9 and Yvon Lambert

108 rue Vieille du Temple, 75003
01-42-71-09-33 f: 01-42-71-87-47
street gallery: Tues–Sat, 2:30–7; closed Mon
main gallery: Tues–Fri, 10–1 and 2:30–7; Sat, 10–1 and 2:30–6
métro: Filles du Calvaire, Saint-Paul

The street-side space is a recent addition to the well-established, spectacular space behind the inner courtyard—a vast, light-filled, glass-roofed room that was formerly a commercial workshop. The arrangement enables the gallery to show photographs and work of modest size in a more intimate setting as well as large-scale objects and installations. They can also present two different one-person shows simultaneously. Exhibitions feature classic as well as recent work by well-known international artists, many of whom are leaders of the minimalist and conceptual approach and most of whom emerged during the 1960s and 1970s. Artists of the next generation and emerging artistis who are creatively using the medium of photography are also shown. Artists: Carl Andre, Miguel Barcelo, Robert Barry, Jean-Michel Basquiat, Jean-Charles Blais, Christian Boltanski, Robert Combas, Daniel Dezeuze, Bernard Faucon, Philippe Favier, Nan Goldin, On Kawara, Anselm Kiefer, Joseph Kosuth, Louise Lawler, Giulio Paolini, Edda Renouf, Julian Schnabel, Richard Serra, Andres Serrano, Daniel Spoerri, Haim Steinbach, Niele Toroni, Richard Tuttle, Cy Twombly.

9 Galerie Renos Xippas

108 rue Vieille du Temple, 75003
01-40-27-05-55 f: 01-40-27-07-16
Tues–Fri, 10–1 and 2–7; Sat, 10–7; closed Mon
métro: Filles du Calvaire, Saint-Paul

Located in the balcony and lower-level spaces above and below the Yvon Lambert Gallery.

Although the gallery spaces are oddities on the fringe, the art is center-stage caliber. The roster includes both young and established artists who work in various directions. Artists: Per Barclay, Torie Begg, José-Manuel Broto, Stephen Dean, Anne Deleporte, Thomas Demand, Nancy Dwyer, Gérard Fromanger, Franz Graf, Herbert Hamak, Joan Hernandez Pijuan, Ulrich Horndash, Robert Irwin, Joseph Marioni, Gerhard Merz, John Nixon, Richard Nonas, David Rabinowitch, David Reed, Lucas Samaras, Andreas Schön, Takis, Koen Theys, Kara Walker.

Galerie
10 Thaddaeus Ropac

7 rue Debelleyme, 75003
01-42-72-99-00 f: 01-42-72-61-66
Tues–Sat, 10–7; closed Mon
métro: Filles du Calvaire, Saint-Paul

The gallery is spread among various rooms on the main floor and lower level. It shows internationally known artists in exhibitions featuring their most recent work, an on-site project (like the installation by Gilbert & George, 1997) or a historic body of work (like the *Heads after Picasso* by Warhol, 1997). Sometimes the work of young newcomers is on display in small or group exhibitions. Once each year there is superbly curated theme show, like *Modern Ensemble: Still Lifes* (1998), *Transforming the Image of Woman in Contemporary Art* (1996) and *Beneath the Cloak* (1997). Artists: Martine Aballea, Shuji Ariyoshi, Donald Baechler, Georg Baselitz, Jean-Michel Basquiat, Joseph Beuys, Sandro Chia, Francesco Clemente, Christian Eckart, Julio Galan, Gilbert & George, Antony Gormley, Peter Halley, Jasper Johns, Per Kirkeby, Marie-Jo LaFontaine, Wolfgang Laib, Jonathan Lasker, Robert Longo, Markus Lupertz, Fabian Marcaccio, Hermann Nitsch, Walter Obholzer, Mimmo Paladino, Blinky Palermo, Anne and Patrick Poirier, Rona Pondick, Arnulf Rainer, Robert Rauschenberg, James Rosenquist, Edward Ruscha, David Salle, Hubert Scheibl, Sturtevant, Philip Taaffe, Andy Warhol, Robert Wilson.

10 | Galerie Marian Goodman

7 rue Debelleyme, 75003
01-48-04-70-52 f: 01-48-04-70-52
Tues–Sat, 11–7; closed Mon
métro: Filles du Calvaire,
Saint-Paul

Located in the same building as Thaddeus Ropac on the 6th floor.

Having attained a global reputation for its exhibitions in New York, the gallery opened a small space in Paris in 1995. It shows the same artists—international stars, mainly European, who gained prominence during the 1970s–80s. Unlike its exhibitions in New York, where space permits huge works and major installations, here the objects are more modest. Artists: Giovanni Anselmo, Lothar Baumgarten, Christian Boltanski, Marcel Broodthaers, James Coleman, Tony Cragg, Richard Deacon, Dan Graham, Rebecca Horn, Anselm Kiefer, Jannis Kounellis, Juan Muñoz, Maria Nordman, Gabriel Orozco, Giulio Paolini, Giuseppe Penone, Gerhard Richter, Edward Rusha, Thomas Schütte, Thomas Struth, Niele Toroni, Jeff Wall, Lawrence Weiner.

11 | Galerie Karsten Greve

5 rue Debelleyme, 75003
01-42-77-19-37 f: 01-42-77-05-58
Tues–Sat, 10–7; closed Mon
métro: Filles du Calvaire,
Saint-Paul

With its nicely renovated interior, which includes exposed excavations of old stone walls, the gallery itself is on display. In addition to the two-storied space with small rooms, entered directly from the street corner, there is a second space accessible through the courtyard. The pervasive focus is on classic objects from the 1960s–70s or art associated with American Minimalism. You may only see a few objects by a given artist, but they typically are superlative examples. Exhibitions tend to run for two to three months. Artists: Josef Albers, Carl Andre, Joseph Beuys, Louise Bourgeois, John Chamberlain, Joseph Cornell, Jean Dubuffet, Dominique Evrard, Dan Flavin, Lucio Fontana, Gotthard Graubner, Leiko Ikemura, Paco Knöller, Willem de Kooning, Jannis Kounellis, Catherine Lee, Loïc Le Groumellec, Sol LeWitt, Piero Manzoni, Nicola de Maria, Henri Michaux, Detlef Orlopp, Blinky Palermo, Pablo Picasso, Norbert Prangenberg, Karl Prante, Peter Schmersal, Carole Seborovski, Joel Shapiro, Bill Traylor, Richard Tuttle, Cy Twombly, Bernar Venet, Wols.

12 | Musée Picasso

renovation: Roland SIMOUNET,
1976–85
Hôtel Salé, 5 rue de Thorigny,
75003
01-42-71-25-21 f: 01-48-04-75-46
Mon, Wed–Sun, closed Tues
Apr–Sept, 9:30–6;
Oct–Mar, 9:30–5:30
admission: 30/20F—applicable to
everyone on Sun; additional fee
for special exhibitions
métro: Saint-Paul, Chemin Vert

The building, a spectacular private mansion from the 17th century, was painstakingly restored and tastefully renovated. The architect judiciously and superbly retained the character of the old building, including the grand baroque staircase and back garden. And yet he also provided appropriate, varied, even majestic exhibition spaces and a circulation pattern that is easy to follow. Such idiosyncratic touches as the bronze light fixtures, benches and chairs by Diego GIACOMETTI (brother of Alberto) add pizzazz to the ambience without detracting from Picasso's art.

The museum's collection was started by works donated to the government in lieu of payment of estate taxes after the artist's death in 1973. Additional works received after the death of Picasso's widow in 1990 further enhance the museum's holdings, which represent a complete panorama of Picasso's art: paintings, sculptures, collages, relief paintings, ceramics, drawings, notebooks, prints and illustrated books. Also included are works owned by Picasso (Donation Picasso): art by Balthus, Braque, Cézanne, Chardin, Corot, Courbet, Derain, Matisse, Miró, Rousseau and objects from Africa, Oceania and Iberia.

A visit to the Picasso Museum gives a general overview of an artist who is undeniably one of the 20th century's

great masters. Although the collection has many holes and weak spots, especially for the early years, it contains some of the most outstanding collage and wood sculptures from the cubist period, and many extraordinary paintings and mixed-media compositions from the 1920s–30s. For the most part, the collection is arranged chronologically beginning on the first level. Selections from the Donation Picasso are on the second level; the third level contains special exhibitions and a display of Picasso's prints and drawings; and works from the post–World War II years, including a multitude of ceramics made in Vallauris, are located in vaulted rooms in the basement and on the ground floor. Interspersed throughout are non-chronological alcoves devoted to special themes, as well as display cases and wall niches presenting archival items and contextual documents. The renovated chapel—exhibiting the large-scale collage *Femmes à leur toilette* (*Women at Their Toilet*) 1938—and the rear garden —embellished with several sculptures— are wonderful places to relax.

13 | Giulio Paolini

Fragments de culture, lecture, mémoire, 1990
Hôtel de Croisille,
12 rue du Parc Royale, 75003
Mon–Fri, 10–6
métro: Saint-Paul, Chemin Vert

To find the installation, go through the coach door fronting the street at #12; cross the courtyard to the door in the left rear corner for Siège du Service des Bibliothèques et des Archives du Patrimoine; enter the library's *salle de lecture* (reading room); and proceed into the garden just beyond the windows. You will probably have to ask a librarian to unlock the garden door for you. This is truly a hidden treasure. Because it is not located in a very acces-

Paolini, *Fragments de culture, lecture, mémoire* (detail)

of the goddess's body and frames that repeat the geometry in the grid are scattered across the trellis wall. Paolini thus plays with ideas about present and past, original and copy, same and different, part and whole, solid and void, order and disorder. He further confounds interpretation by conjoining the majestic beauty of ancient Greek figuration with the reductive structure and enigmatic content of late-20th-century art.

14 | Comptoir de l'Image

44 rue de Sévigné, 75003
01-42-72-03-92 f: 01-42-72-15-19
Mon–Sat, 11–1 and 2–7; Sun, 2–7
métro: Saint-Paul

If you have some time to browse, check out this wonderful little bookstore. It sells photography books, international exhibition catalogues and fashion magazines (current and past).

| IPM

46 rue de Sévigné, 75003
01-42-77-58-94 f: 01-42-77-74-27
métro: Saint-Paul

This is not a public gallery or sales-oriented shop but a business that arranges art fairs, most particularly the annual International ArtistBook fair. If you are interested in artists' books, you might want to make an appointment with Rik Gadella, a well-informed connoisseur who is a fountain of information about the latest productions.

Galerie Brownstone, 15 | Corréard

17–26 rue Saint-Gilles, 75003
01-42-78-43-21 f: 01-42-74-04-00
Tues–Sat, 11–1 and 2–7;
closed Mon
métro: Saint-Paul, Chemin Vert

The expertise of Gilbert Brownstone, an American with curatorial experience, is evident here in the quality and character

sible or visible place, even people who work near it are unaware of its presence. *Fragments of Culture, Reading, Memory* should, however, be considered one of the most ingenious works of contemporary public art.

Paolini, an acclaimed Italian artist who often appropriates figures from the classical past, here presents two mirror-image goddesses. They stand atop cubic-frame pedestals placed in front of and behind a transparent wall constructed from a trellis and an open grid of steel bars. Each statue, a replica of the same idealized maiden, gazes at a shard she holds in an upraised hand. The goddesses face one another through a square frame hanging on the wall between them. It appears like a mirror, albeit set in a skewed position. Marble fragments that duplicate parts of the exhibitions. The gallery specializes in art with a monochrome sensibility and work sometimes categorized as geometric abstraction, constructivist, minimalist, conceptual and materialist. These rubrics are, however, loosely applied to encompass innovative, very current work in various media, conceptual bases and even pictorial imagery. The creativity of young artists, like Seton Smith, is particularly noteworthy in terms of an adaptation of an abstract, monochromatic sensibility to photography. Artists: Ghada Amer, John Armleder, Yoo Bong Sang, Noël Dolla, Patrick Everaert, Dominique Figarella, Sylvie Fleury, Roland Flexner, Gottfried Honegger, Callum Innes, Imi Knoebel, Patrick Lebret, Philippe Mayaux, Elisabeth Mercier, Olivier Mosset, Jean Luc Mylayne, Maurizio Nannucci, Jean Nouvel, Edouard Prulhière, Philippe Ramette, Jean-Pierre Raynaud, Bettina Rheims, Matthew Ritchie, Claude Rutault, Seton Smith, Jésus-Rafael Soto, Günter Umberg, Franz-Erhard Walther, Carmelo Zagari.

16 | Galerie Philippe Rizzo

9 rue Saint-Gilles, 75003
01-48-87-12-00 f: 01-48-87-06-22
Tues–Fri, 11–1 and 2–7; Sat, 11–7;
closed Mon
métro: Chemin Vert, Saint-Paul

The focus here is on photography and conceptual work by emerging or midcareer artists. Distinctive subjects and eccentric, innovative formats make the exhibitions especially notable. If you go away from this gallery feeling neutral about the art, perhaps you should go back and look again at how the artist has manipulated the content or undercut familiar images, often with irony. Artists: Sarah Charlesworth, Nina Childress, Cheryl Donegan, Tracey Emin, Reza Farkhondeh, Olivier Goulet, Hallgrimur Helgason, Karen Knorr, Peter

Land, Florence Manlik, John Miller, Sarah Morris, Toby Mott, Grayson Perry, Jack Pierson, Christoph Rütimann, Gary Simmons, Laurie Simmons, Georgina Starr.

17 | Galerie Anne de Villepoix

11 rue des Tournelles, 75004
01-42-78-32-24 f: 01-42-78-32-16
Tues–Sat, 11–7; closed Mon
métro: Bastille

Despite its unassuming storefront appearance and modest size, this gallery consistently has some of the most provocative, spicy shows in Paris. Photography, video and mixed-media installations are favored. Often a single project fills the entire space. Don't be surprised if it's a multitude of found elements orchestrated to produce a cacophony of sounds, sequential movements and confrontational ideas, or an inventively crafted object of mammoth scale and provocative meaning. Art shown here tends to use familiar imagery derived directly from the mundane environment. But it is presented so as to raise consciousness about a particular issue or to upset conventional modes of thinking. The gallery has a roster of international artists with established reputations as well as unknown and young artists who are breaking new ground.

Artists: Vito Acconci, Chris Burden, John Coplans, Frédérique Decombe, Malachi Farrell, Mark Francis, Michael Joo, Valérie Jouve, Koo Jeong, Thomas Locher, Andrew Mansfield, Jean-Luc Moulène, Walter Niedermayr, Joyce Pensato, Sam Samore, Franck Scurti, Beat Streuli, Fred Tomaselli, Rosemarie Trockel.

18 Mission du Patrimoine Photographique

🚇 Hôtel de Sully, 62 rue Saint-
Antoine, 75004
01-42-74-47-75
Tues–Sun, 10–6:30; closed Mon
admission: 25/15F
métro: Saint-Paul, Bastille

A gallery in this grand old mansion is used to show temporary exhibitions of photographs from the National Heritage Collection. The focus is usually on artists from the early 20th century—*Cecil Beaton*, *Dorothea Lange*, *Roger Parry*, *Women Photographers with New Vision in France (1920–40)*, *Czech Photographers (1918–48)*.

19 Maison Européenne de la Photographie (MEP)

🏛 5–7 rue de Fourcy, 75004
01-44-78-75-00 f: 01-44-78-75-15
Wed–Sun, 11–8; closed Mon–Tues
admission: 30/15F; free Wed, 5–8
métro: Saint-Paul

The institution's name is somewhat confusing since it is a French operation dealing with international, not just European, photography. Created by the city of Paris in 1988, MEP moved into its current location in the renovated mansion Hôtel Hénault de Cantorbe in 1996. Even before it had official stature and a building, the organization was an active part of the Paris art community. Most notably, it initiated the biennial Month of Photography, which has become an extremely popular event in Paris. Encouraging attention to current activity in the sphere of photography is central to the MEP since its focus is specifically on the period from the late 1950s to the present. In its temporary exhibitions and installations from the permanent collection (which includes over 12,000 prints), there appears to be a tendency to give prominence to a traditional mode of straight, framed photography, rather than some of the more radical, vanguard presentations being explored. Experimental work and installations are relegated to a small, basement space called Ateliers (studios). However, MEP embraces new approaches to subject matter, conceptual art and photography associated with film, books, magazines and newspapers.

In addition to the exhibition areas, there are a book and video library, restoration workshop, auditorium for conferences and lectures, modest bookshop and small café—where you can read current photography magazines. Recent exhibitions: *Karl Blossfeldt*, *Erwin Blumenfeld*, *Alexy Brodovitch*, *Martine Franck*, *Esther and Jochen Gerz*, *Françoise Huguier*, *Shirin Neshat*, *Bernard Plossu*, *Jeanloup Sieff*, *Seton Smith*, *Joel Sternfeld*, *Paul Strand*, *Germany—the 1980s*, *Africa by Itself*, *What Is a Highway*?

20 Crypte de la Déportation

 architect: Georges-Henri PINGUS-
SON, 1962
square de l'Ile-de-France,
Ile de la Cité, 75004
métro: Cité

Located off quai de l'Archevêché at the east end of Ile de la Cité behind Notre-Dame.

This memorial is for the 200,000 Frenchmen, mostly Jews, deported to German concentration camps during World War II. The design is like a sunken garden, accessible by two narrow stairways that lead down to a bleak courtyard. In one corner facing downriver is a small window hole covered with iron bars. The sense of imprisonment and isolation is haunting. From the court-

yard, another narrow staircase goes farther down to the crypt itself. You
descend into a low-ceilinged, stark,
somber, hexagonal space from which
you can enter various chambers. One
section is a long gallery lit by 200,000
shimmering pieces of quartz. Another is
a tunnel with 200,000 pebbles, a reference to the Jewish tradition of placing a
stone on a grave to express commemoration. There is also a section containing
small tombs with earth from each of the
concentration camps and a tomb of the
unknown deportee. When you ascend
the stairs climbing back into the sunlight, the feeling of release is overwhelming. Thus, the memorial is both a
historic marker and a powerful, experiential design.

Bastille

1 | Opéra Bastille

 architect: Carlos OTT, 1984–89
120 rue de Lyon, 75012
01-40-01-19-70
métro: Bastille

Opéra Bastille was one of the *grands
projets* realized under President François
Mitterand. The international competition for this building, launched in 1982,
called for the most advanced stage and
acoustic technology available and a
structure widely accessible to the public
in the spirit of place de la Bastille, historically the populist heart of Paris.
Carlos Ott, a young Uruguayan-
Canadian architect, was selected, largely because of the way his design filled
the difficult, narrow and irregular site. If
you walk along rue de Lyon (the right
side of the building), you can see the
incredible extension of the structure
and its division into simple volumes.
Indeed, each space has a distinctive
character and houses a different func-

tion. Of course the most dominant volume is the cylinder in front, which
encloses the main 2,700-seat theater.
Reputed for its good acoustics, it also
privileges a frontal view for the entire
hall except for a few small balconies. On
the exterior, Ott exaggerated the cylinder by giving it a double curve even as
he reduced its vast expanse by structur-
ing the outer wall with a stepped
design. A cubic arch covers a grand
staircase and marks the main entrance.
Its square shape and black tone dramatically contrast with the surrounding
curves and white surface of the rest of
the building. And yet it is the core
image, replicated in the stepped pattern
of the adjacent walls and square modules in the grid pattern used across the
whole facade—regardless of whether
the sheathing is glass, stone or metal.

In addition to the main auditorium,
the building contains a "modulable
hall" for 600–1,000, a studio seating
280, two restaurants, rehearsal and
dressing rooms, numerous practice studios, workshops, storerooms and a
huge space for scenery construction
and costume workshops. If you attend a
performance, you may see sets, costumes or a stage curtain created by contemporary artists (Karel Appel, Jean-
Paul Chambas, Paul Jenkins, Cy
Twombly, Robert Wilson). Sculptures by
Torof Engstrom, Yves Klein and Niki de

Ott, Opéra Bastille

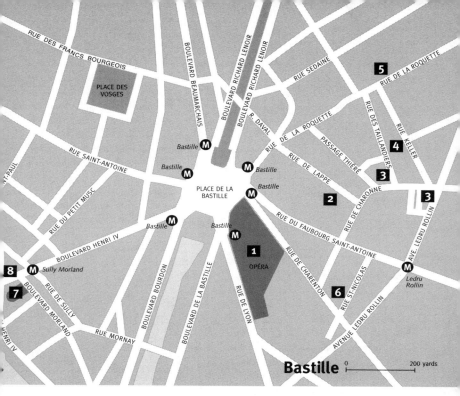

Bastille

0   200 yards

Saint-Phalle and paintings by Jean Miotte and Jean-Paul Riopelle decorate the lobbies (which also offer a panoramic view of the neighboring areas and the Paris skyline).

The design of the Bastille Opera has generally been considered functional but uninspiring, though its high cost (2.8 billion francs) has been loudly criticized. Despite the expense, the Opéra—like several major and expensive state-funded new buildings in Paris—seems to have been poorly constructed and is already in a sad state of disrepair. Most notable are problems with the exterior sheathing, which apparently wasn't properly affixed. The ugly fishnet, in place since 1997, was deemed a necessary stop-gap measure to protect pedestrians from falling panels. Conceptual errors in the stage design also plague performances in the main auditorium.

Galerie Liliane & Michel Durand-Dessert

2

🗔   28 rue de Lappe, 75011

📖   01-48-06-92-23   f: 01-48-06-92-24
Tues–Fri, 11–1 and 2–7;
closed Mon
métro: Bastille, Ledru-Rollin

Located in what was formerly a factory, the gallery profits from a naturally lit, two-story central space with a balcony and side rooms. When you enter from the street, walk straight back along the dark passageway to get to the main exhibition space. Additional displays are upstairs. The gallery focus is on conceptual, minimalist art by well-established Europeans and Americans. Often a single large work or installation piece takes over the entire lower space. Artists seem to derive great inspiration from the space since creations and selections typically explore new territory and take

45

advantage of scale dynamics. From time to time there are provocative thematic shows, like *The Body in Perspective* (1998). Artists: Giovanni Anselmo, Joseph Beuys, Troy Brauntuch, Marcel Broodthaers, Stanley Brouwn, Victor Burgin, Balthasar Burkhard, André Cadere, Alan Charlton, Gérard Collin-Thiebaut, Ger van Elk, Luciano Fabro, Helmut Federle, Hans-Peter Feldmann, Barry Flanagan, Gérard Garouste, Dan Graham, Hans Haacke, John Hilliard, Bertrand Lavier, Mario Merz, François Morellet, Yves Oppenheim, Claudio Parmiggiani, Pino Pascali, Yan Pei-Ming, Giuseppe Penone, Michelangelo Pistoletto, Gerhard Richter, Georges Rousse, Ulrich Rückreim, Fred Sandback, Patrick Tosani, David Tremlett, Jan Vercruysse, Michel Verjux, Carel Visser, William Wegman.

The gallery also operates a superb bookstore, located in the street-front room to the left of the entrance. It should not be missed. It's a great place to see the latest art publications, especially exhibition catalogues, small press editions and periodicals.

3 | Galerie Jousse Sequin

34 rue de Charonne and 5 rue de Taillandiers, 75011
01-47-00-32-35 f: 01-40-21-82-95
Mon–Fri, 10–1:30 and 2:30–7;
Sat, 11–7
métro: Bastille, Ledru-Rollin

Abiding by an intention to show young, avant-garde artists (mainly German, American and French), the gallery has presented work not otherwise seen or known in Paris. Its artists tend to deal with unusual, if not surreal, themes and imagery. The work is always fascinating but may also be confounding and disturbing. Artists: Michael Ashkin, Bernard Aubertin, Serge Comte, Thomas Grünfeld, Stephen Hepworth, Peter Hopkins, Richard Kern, Karin Kneffel, Philippe Meste, Chuck Nanney, Karin Sander, John Tremblay, Royce Weatherly.

At a second location (Grand Dia), just around the corner, the gallery has an impressive collection of furniture by architects and designers. Even if it's closed to the public, ask someone at the rue de Charonne office to let you in if you're interested. Sometimes there are actually public exhibitions in this space —like the offbeat show of architectural remnants saved by the architect Jean Prouvé from destroyed buildings. Artists: Pierre Jeanneret, Le Corbusier, Charles Perriand, Jean Prouvé and many others.

4 | Espace d'Art, Yvonamor Palix

13 rue Keller, 75011
01-48-06-36-70 f: 01-47-00-01-21
Tues–Sat, 2–7:30
métro: Bastille, Ledru-Rollin

Founded in Madrid in 1991, this gallery moved to Paris in 1993. With an energetic commitment to the work of young artists, it tends to focus on dynamic representations or manipulations of the image in photography, video, multimedia, performance and architectural projects. Although the modest storefront doesn't permit large, complex projects, you can get a good sense of the direction and sensibility of the artists from the objects and projects on display. Artists: Aziz & Cucher, BP, Daniel Canogar, Keith Cottingham, Diller & Scofidio, Yolanda Gutierrez, Robert F. Hammerstiel, Steve Miller, Orlan, Jorge Orta, Lucy Orta, Alicia Paz, Olivier Richon, Sandy Skogland, Alberto Sorbelli.

5 | Galerie J & J Donguy

57 rue de la Roquette, 75011
01-47-00-10-94 f: 01-40-21-83-84
Tues–Sat, 1–7; closed Mon
métro: Bastille

When you reach #57, walk all the way to the back, left side of the courtyard.

The gallery—one of the first in the Bastille neighborhood—has functioned in many ways as a meeting place for artists and poets. The exhibition space is very rough and raw, and the art also tends to have an unrefined, impulsive or expressionistic character. The dominant point of departure is Fluxus or a related mode of creativity in the realm of assemblage, installation, performance and experimental art. Videos and poetry often mix with the art objects, and many works are infused with a socio-political perspective. Soirées are held in the courtyard from time to time. The small bookstore surrounding the reception desk has some rare books and catalogues. Recent exhibitions: *Eric Andersen, Armand Behar, Jean-François Bory, Jacques-Elie Chabert, Heinz Cibulka, Pascal Doury, Jean Dupuy, Frédéric Grandpié, Daniel Hogue, Michel Journia, Alison Knowles, Xavier Moehr, Michel Mousseau, Orlan, Charlemagne Palestine, Serge Pey, Costa Picadas, Joan Rabascall, Denis Roche, Pierre Tilman, Everything Is Cold Except Ice.*

6 | Galerie Météo

4 rue Saint-Nicolas, 75012
01-43-42-20-20 f: 01-43-42-30-20
Tues–Sat, 2:30–7:30; closed Mon
métro: Ledru-Rollin

Adventurous, ambitious and energetic are adjectives that define this gallery. It supports young, mainly French artists and pays heed to notable emerging tendencies. Artists: Ghada Amer, Maurice Blaussyld, Noël Dolla, Patrick Everaert, Dominique Figarella, Roland Flexner, Patrick Lebret, Philippe Mayaux, Elisabeth Mercier, Jean-Luc Mylayne, Edouard Prulhière, Philippe Ramette, Matthew Ritchie, Carmélo Zagari.

7 | Pavillon de l'Arsenal

21 boulevard Morland, 75004
01-42-76-33-97 f: 01-42-76-26-32
Tues–Sat, 10:30–6:30; Sun, 11–7; closed Mon
admission: free
métro: Sully-Morland

If you have an interest in architecture, city planning or design, you should plan a visit to this site, officially called the Centre d'Information, de Documentation et d'Urbanisme et d'Architecture de la Ville de Paris. It's not listed in most guidebooks but is a treasure trove for anyone curious about the built environment of Paris or the French flair for style in the urban landscape. The Arsenal itself is a renovated 19th-century warehouse located a block from the Seine. The ground floor and mezzanine levels have temporary exhibitions on themes that offer interesting slices into the visual character of the city. Recent exhibitions: *Paris Boutiques, Architectural Store-Windows, From Roof to Roof,* and *Paris under Glass—The City and Its Reflections.* Two current-event galleries present outstanding designs from competitions. There is also a permanent exhibition (updated each year) that documents the city's growth and transformations. Along with a large model of Paris and an interactive computer, the presentation includes original drawings of present and future plans by contemporary architects. Don't forget to peruse the display of Arsenal publications at the reception desk or, if you want information on a specific building or project, visit the archives and photo files in the Centre de Documentation upstairs.

Institut du Monde
8 Arabe (IMA)

architects: Jean NOUVEL, ARCHI-
TECTURE STUDIO, Gilbert LEZENES,
Pierre SORIO, 1987
11 quai Saint-Bernard, 75005
01-40-51-38-38
Tues–Sun, 10–6; closed Mon
métro: Jussieu, Sully-Morland

This building is just across Pont de Sully, facing the Seine from the Left Bank.

Renowned as one of the most outstanding buildings of the 1980s, the Arab World Institute magically brings together high-tech architecture and motifs borrowed from traditional Arab culture. This conjunction is but one of the dialogues shaping the building's design and reiterating the primary function of IMA as a center promoting the diffusion of Arab culture in France and Franco-Arab cultural exchanges. The building was one of Mitterand's *grands projets*, created jointly with 60% of the costs paid by France and 40% by Arab States.

To get a good impression of the unique, brilliant character of the synthesis, start by walking around the exterior. Note that the structure, entirely sheathed in glass, is divided into two parallel parts. The side facing the Seine is a curving wedge shape with a horizontally oriented grid articulating its outer surface. The side facing the Jussieu campus of the University of Paris is a taller, emphatically rectangular unit with a square grid defining its glazed walls. Not only do differences emphasize the image of bilateral harmony within the IMA, but they also create scale and character correspondences between the IMA and the two dissimilar environments around its north and south facades. An exemplary aspect of the design is its masterful accommodation of a constraining, odd plot of land located in the midst of historic and modern-day Paris.

A dramatically tall, narrow passage lies between the two sectors, and an equally eccentric interior ramp in the form of a white marble spiral tower visibly occupies the front extremity of the building. By its anterior position and circular form, the tower recalls minarets on ancient mosques. But an even more discernible reference to Islamic culture lies just beyond in the image of the metal window screens. As geometrically patterned surfaces punctured with openings for light, these bear witness to the decoratively carved wood *mashrabiyya*—window coverings used in Islamic cultures to control sun exposure within interior spaces. To be sure, the dazzle of a wall patterned with 240 glistening metallic screens is a Western variant, though very unexpected in a modern glass building typically devoid of decoration. The screens appear like finely crafted, delicate handwork with

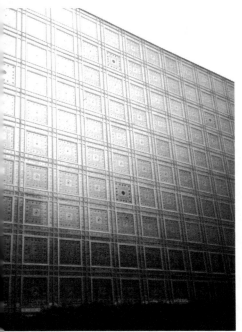

Nouvel et al., Institute du Monde Arabe

differently sized sequences of squares, twisting disks and light openings. In fact, they are machine-made, and the disk images are ocular devices belonging to a sophisticated technological system. Functioning somewhat like a camera lens, the devices open and close in response to the amount of sunlight received. This occurs automatically since they are activated by photoelectric cells and programmed by computer.

Going down the long, dark passage to the entrance is a surreal experience because the space is so odd, stark and almost imprisoning. And yet there's a fantasy, processional aura about it. Here again, architectural difference is manifest side to side with a glass wall on the right and stone on the left. A small patio with a small fountain, situated at the end of the passage, links the two sides. The door on the left takes you into the IMA museum and the opposite door leads into a spectacular atrium. It's a 10-story square space enclosing glass elevators and steel-cable staircases. Though the setting is industrial and high-tech, it's spellbinding—especially since you now get the full, dramatic thrust of the window screens and can experience their mystical lighting effects. Another place to see the screens is in the library (enter on the 3rd level), where you can also see and walk within the spiral tower.

Be sure to go up to the roof terrace (or roof-café) so you can enjoy the site of Notre-Dame and other nearby monuments from on high. The lobby outside the auditorium on the lower level is also interesting. The space is long, dimly lit, devoid of embellishment but oddly segmented by five rows of closely positioned columns. With its secluded pockets and staid serenity, the hall has the semblance of a public environment in the Arab world. Indeed, the low ceilings and subdued lighting throughout the building create an ambience common to traditional Islamic architecture.

IMA organizes five or six exhibitions of contemporary art by Arab artists each year. They are of uneven quality but sometimes include work of great interest by artists who have gained significant attention in recent years. Since there is no fixed space for these shows, which are not part of the special exhibition program presented in the gallery on the ground floor, they unfortunately tend to end up in basement rooms or hallways. A collection of contemporary art is also being developed by IMA, but it too has no gallery space at present.

Saint-Germain

1 | Musée du Luxembourg

19 rue de Vaugirard, 75006
01-42-34-25-94
Tues–Wed, Fri–Sun, 11–6; Thurs, 11–8; closed Mon
métro: Mabillon, Odéon

Adjacent to the Luxembourg Palace on its west side.

Exhibition spaces in this former Orangerie (greenhouse for growing oranges) are now used for a wide range of shows organized by the Ministry of Culture, including some on contemporary art. If you are in Paris during one such presentation, make time to go see it. You won't be disappointed since you will see a distinctively different, well-curated exhibition and high-caliber art. For example, *Cross-breeding* (1998) featured an amazingly unconventional collection of lace, embroideries, carpets and tapestries by Ghada Amer, John Armleder, François Bouillon, Erik Dietman, Bertrand Dorny, Sylvain Dubuisson, Philippe Favier, Paul-Armand Gette, Marie-Ange Guilleminot, Fabrice Hybert, Annette Messager, Jean-Michel Othoniel, David Rabinowitch and others.

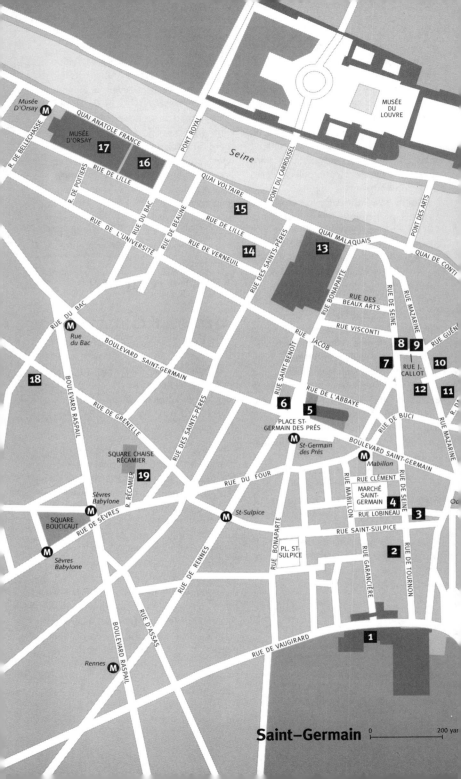

2 | Institut Français d'Architecture (IFA)

6 bis rue de Tournon, 75006
01-46-33-90-36 f: 01-46-33-02-11
Tues–Sat, 12:30–7; closed Mon
admission: free
métro: Mabillon, Odéon

The French Institute of Architecture is a cultural entity, created as a place for reflection, exhibition and recollection of 20th-century architecture and urbanism. If you want information about notable old and new buildings, this is a good place to go, though it is geared for professionals rather than tourist enthusiasts. The institute's lectures and conferences offer penetrating discussions about construction and design projects and issues. The gallery presents interesting shows on current design questions, thematic surveys and retrospectives of work by both leading and unheralded architects. Since here, too, it's directed toward a professional audience, others might find the displays difficult to grasp. Recent exhibitions: *The Emerging City*, *From Henri Sauvage to Claude Parent*, *The Other City*, *TransArchitectures*, *Jean Dubuisson*, *Sverre Fehn*, *Jacques Hondelatte*, *Jan Kaplicky*, *Lucien Kroll*.

3 | La Chambre Claire

14 rue Saint-Sulpice, 75006
01-46-34-04-31 f: 01-43-29-89-22
Mon–Sat, 10–7
métro: Mabillon, Odéon

This bookstore specializes in photography and has an extensive selection of current and past publications on individual artists, groups, themes and various topics related to photography. If you're searching for some out-of-print or hard-to-find book, or just want to browse, this is a great place to indulge yourself.

4 | Gérard Mulot

76 rue de Seine, 75006
01-43-26-5-77
Tues–Sun, 7 am–8 pm; closed Wed
métro: Mabillon, Odéon

Located on the corner of rue Lobineau, across from the Saint-Germain market.

In the opinion of many, this is the best pastry shop in Paris. In addition to its delectable taste, the pastry here is made with an incredible level of artistry. It has superb color, inventive imagery, a creative manipulation of form and a mind-boggling use of ingredients and flavors. Each production is an extraordinary work of art. It is unquestionably worth a visit to see these masterpieces, if not to eat them! (The breads and croissants are also delicious.)

5 | Pierre Buraglio

Interior renovation and liturgical furnishings, 1992
Chapelle Saint-Symphorien, Eglise Saint-Germain-des-Prés, 3 place Saint-Germain-des-Prés, 75006
01-43-25-41-71
Tues and Thurs, 1:30–5:30
métro: Saint-Germain-des-Prés

Just after you pass through the main doors of the church and before you enter the central nave, you will find the entrance to this small chapel to the right.

For the renovation of this medieval chapel, the French artist Pierre Buraglio created various discrete and subdued "interventions" and designed new functional objects. (The liturgical furniture, especially the altar, was actually made in collaboration with the sculptor Serge Landois.) Buraglio also showed extreme respect for the spare, massively proportioned architecture and historic fragments of the original chapel. Indeed, some small vestiges of 13th-century frescoes and stone sculptures have heightened visibility now thanks to their stark isolation.

Beginning with the steel-grill entrance gate and the nearby holy water basin—an extending drawer of thick frosted glass, set within a narrow, hollow box recessed into the wall—the artist gives evidence of the minimalist approach for which he is known. More particularly, he has used conspicuously simple, geometric forms and erratically positioned his artistic accouterments on the walls and within the chapel's space. Further indication of Buraglio's reductive, architectonic sensibility is visible in the small white ceramic tiles with blue markings hung on the wall to represent the 14 Stations of the Cross; the tall steel tube that serves as a candleholder; the wooden altar table with steel demarcating corner angles; the asymmetrical stainless-steel podium; the elongated cross of encrusted brass set within the masonry of the front wall; the cantilevered tabernacle box of white ceramic placed beside a tiny cubic space, recessed into the wall, painted red and containing an eternal flame; the window of frosted blue-gray glass; the wall drawing of a red rectangle, which marks the former location of the presumed original tomb of Saint-Germain and also signifies the blood of saints and martyrs whose remains were exhumed on this spot; and the white limestone floor tiles that pay homage to Saint-Symphorien. Although the environment is austere and cool, it is also mystical and serene.

6 | La Hune

170 boulevard Saint-Germain (corner of rue Saint-Benoît), 75006
01-45-48-35-85
daily, 10 am–11:45 pm
métro: Saint-Germain-des-Prés

If you enter this superb bookstore, be prepared to get lost among the labyrinth of tables and shelves chock-

full of great pickings. Upstairs in the art section there are lots of titles and the coverage extends to all the arts. You'll even find some exhibition catalogues not often found outside of museum shops.

7 | Galerie Georges-Philippe and Nathalie Vallois

38 rue de Seine, 75006
01-46-34-61-07 f: 01-43-25-18-80
métro: Odéon, Mabillon

The art here gets great exposure by being visible behind big storefront windows on a busy pedestrian street. The gallery's artists are diverse, some favoring a conceptual orientation and others having an abstract, assemblage, social commentary or figurative bent. The directors have a special penchant for Americans. Artists: Matthew Antezzo, Gilles Barbier, Alain Bublex, Jean-François Fourtou, Barry Le Va, Erik Levine, Saverio Lucariello, Paul McCarthy, Joachim Mogarra, Peter Nagy, Nedlo Solakov, Keith Tyson, Julia Wachtel.

8 | Galerie Darthea Speyer

6 rue Jacques Callot, 75006
01-43-54-78-41 f: 01-43-29-62-36
Tues–Fri, 11–12:45 and 2–7; Sat, 11–7; closed Mon
métro: Odéon, Mabillon

This gallery has a propensity for the type of brash figurative or funky art that emerged in America during the 1950s–60s. It also shows abstract art by both Europeans and Americans. Artists: Beauford Delaney, Leonardo Delfino, Christiane Durand, Lynn Foulkes, Sidio Fromboluti, Sam Gilliam, David Gista, Leon Golub, Roselyn Granet, Lionel Guibout, Caroline Lee, Ed Paschke,

Antoine Poncet, Peter Saul, Irmgard Sigg, Thierry Sigg, Nora Speyer, François Stahly, Viswanadhan, Zuka.

9 | Galerie Pièce Unique

4 rue Jacques Callot, 75006
01-43-26-54-58 f: 01-46-34-03-98
Tues–Sat, 11–1 and 3–7;
closed Mon
métro: Odéon, Mabillon

The name of the gallery refers to the focus on a single work of art in each exhibition. Thus, a "unique piece" is the exclusive, sole subject of the gallery's presentation. As if made to order, the space—a small, barren, all-white storefront room—is ideally suited for displaying one work in absolute isolation. A nice touch is having spotlights shine on the object after closing until 2 am. It is thus visible at night from the street. Needless to say, the works look extraordinary when seen under these conditions, especially to passersby who have just enjoyed a good French meal or wine at one of the nearby brasseries or restaurants.

Each exhibition features a different artist covering the gamut of stylistic orientations and subject matter. Most of the artists are well-established, internationally renowned figures though many have received relatively little exposure in France. The gallery has a knack for choosing artists who produce exceptional works that benefit from the peculiarities of the space. Past exhibitions: *Georg Baselitz, Domenico Bianchi, Christian Boltanski, Alighiero e Boetti, Louise Bourgeois, David Bowes, Enzo Cucchi, Marco Gastini, Ben Jakober and Yannick Vu, Bertrand Lavier, Sol LeWitt, Mario Merz, Annette Messager, Marta Pan, Giulio Paolini, Philippe Perrin, Fabrizio Plessi, Anne and Patrick Poirier, Jean-Pierre Raynaud, Philip Taaffe, Rosemarie Trockel, Cy Twombly.*

10 | Galerie Lucien Durand

19 rue Mazarine, 75006
01-43-26-25-35 f: 01-43-26-05-56
Tues–Sat, 11–7; Sun, 2–7;
closed Mon
métro: Odéon, Mabillon

This gallery recently altered its direction and now focuses on contemporary art by young and well-established international artists. The most risky and vanguard work, however, is to be found in the thematic group exhibitions featuring nongallery artists. Artists: Renaud Auguste-Dormeuil, Jean-Michel Basquiat, Lore Bert, Jean-Luc Bichaud, Jacques Bosser, Philippe Bouveret, Stéphan Braconnier, Hugues De Cointet, Jacques Farine, Christian Genty, Keith Haring, Eric Le Maire, Andreï Molodkin, Dennis Oppenheim, Marta Pan, Michel Ray-Charles, Sam Szafran, Leon Tutundjian, Xiao Fan. Recent group exhibitions: *The Body Photographed, Women Photographers—Pipilotti Rist, Annick Volle, Cindy Sherman, Nan Goldin.*

Anne and Patrick Poirier, *War Game—Snooker*, 1998 (Galerie Pièce Unique)

Galerie Montenay-Giroux

11

🔲 31 rue Mazarine, 75006
01-43-54-85-30 f: 01-43-29-42-21
Tues–Sat, 11–1 and 2:30–7;
closed Mon
métro: Odéon, Mabillon

As a means of promoting contemporary art, Montenay-Giroux presents exhibitions of French artists who are part of the gallery's ongoing program and alternates these with exhibitions of esteemed art from other countries and shows of young French artists. The art is very diverse and uneven but the strong work stands out. It's a real plus that the gallery calls attention to work not otherwise getting exposure in Paris. Gallery artists: Georges Autard, Philippe Berry, Yves Chaudouët, Eric Dalbis, Hubert de Chalvron, Claude de Soria, Errò, Gloria Friedmann, Catherine Ikam, Piotr Klemensiewicz, Denis Laget, Ange Leccia, Bernard Moninot, Michel Paysant, Anne Marie Pécheur, Jean Pierre Pincemin, Valérie Rauchbach, Emmanuel Saulnier, Vladimir Skoda. Other artists: Edward Allington, Donald Baechler, Georg Baselitz, General Idea, Mark Innerst, Ben Jakober and Yannick Vu, Komar & Melamid, Annette Lemieux, Nino Longobardi, Markus Lupertz, Brice Marden, Leonel Moura, Juliào Sarmento, Nancy Spero, Not Vital.

Architecture et Art du XX Siècle

12

📖 52 rue Mazarine, 75006
Tues–Sat, 4–7
métro: Odéon, Mabillon

This tiny bookstore, squeezed into a narrow alley, has hard-to-find books on art and architecture. It's a great place to browse—if you can squeeze your body through the narrow aisles and if you can

accommodate the limited, off-beat hours.

Ecole Nationale Supérieure des Beaux-Arts (ENSBA)

13

📷 13 quai Malaquai, 75006
01-47-03-50-50 f: 01-47-03-50-80
Tues–Sun, 1–7; closed Mon
admission: 20/10F
métro: Saint-Germain-des-Prés

Exhibitions organized by the National School of Fine Arts and held in this grand space are not always of contemporary art. When they are, they are usually very contemporary, if not aggressively avant-garde, very venturesome and distinctly international. Of note are such recent projects as *Transit*—work by artists born after 1960; *Implicit Connections*—bonds, exchanges and shared roots that weave artists together; *Biennial of the Image*—an international exhibition of young artists who use photographic, film, video or synthesized images; *Contemporary Creation in Japan*.

Renn Espace d'Art Contemporain

14

📷 7 rue de Lille (near rue des Saints-Pères), 75007
01-42-60-22-99 f: 01-43-20-38-50
admission: free
métro: Bac, Saint-Germain-des-Prés

This privately owned, classy exhibition space houses contemporary art exhibitions. However, its schedule is extremely erratic and not widely publicized. There are long stretches of time when the place lies dormant, the only clue about its program being the advisory sign on the door: "Closed until the next exhibition." Nevertheless, Espace Renn is an extraordinary site for displaying contemporary art. It has been renovated in a style related to a minimalist sensibility, which might best be called "refined warehouse chic." That is to say, the interior retains the aura of its past and yet all unnecessary embellishments (even doors) have been removed to create an utterly spare and spacious interior characterized only by its totally white walls, high ceilings and superb lighting. Exhibitions are equally austere with each artwork isolated and treated as an autonomous object. Past exhibitions: *Simon Hantaï, Yves Klein, Robert Ryman.*

15 | Caisse des Dépôts et Consignations

13 quai Voltaire, 75007
01-40-49-90-85
Tues–Sat, 12–6:30; closed Mon
métro: Bac, Saint-Germain-des-Prés

Selections from the Fonds National d'Art Contemporain—FNAC (National Collection of Contemporary Art) are regularly presented in this exhibition space. The room is quite limited by its long, narrow shape though exhibitions of photography and modestly sized work do fine. Since FNAC is a treasure trove of contemporary art, you'll see impressive work—including some by French artists who are not big names in international circles.

16 | Roy Lichtenstein

*Coups de pinceau,*1988
Caisse des Dépôts et
Consignations, 3 quai Voltaire,
75007
métro: Bac or RER: Musée d'Orsay

The building where this work is located is adjacent to the Musée d'Orsay. You can enter from either the river side (quai Voltaire) or in the back at 56 rue de Lille.

Installed in the interior courtyard of this regal and forbidding national bank building is a very tall sculpture by Roy Lichtenstein. With its bright colors and exaggerated stylizations, *Brushstrokes* is

the whimsical, incongruous focal point of its surroundings. In his inimitable way, Lichtenstein transformed gestures into an object, depicting them as an isolated entity so oversized and magnified that they paradoxically lose their identity at the same time as they are meticulously defined.

16 | Jean Dubuffet

Le réséda, 1972/88
Caisse des Dépôts et
Consignations, 3 quai Voltaire,
75007
métro: Bac or RER: Musée d'Orsay

Located beside the entrance door in a courtyard-parking area in front of the building.

Like the Lichtenstein work inside the bank, *Mignonette* (cute little girl), a buoyant sculpture by Jean Dubuffet, is delightful to encounter. It holds its own next to the staid grandeur of the bank's

Dubuffet, *La réséda*

exterior. In fact, it offers a marvelous counterpoint. Set atop a boulder, the image of a frolicking (or nerve-racked), screaming child with a giant bow in her hair is alive with expressive energy. The characteristic red, white and blue colors, stripes and black outlines of Dubuffet's late work animate the figure even as they further fragment its already contorted form.

17 | Musée d'Orsay

renovation: Renaud BARDON, Pierre COLBAC, Jean-Paul PHILLIP-PON, Gae AULENTI, 1980–86
1 rue de la Bellechasse, 75007
01-40-49-49-19
Tues–Wed, Fri–Sat, 10–6; Thurs, 10–9:45; Sun, 9–6; closed Mon
June 20–Sept 20, Tues–Sun, 9–6
admission: 40/30F; additional fee for special exhibitions
métro: Solférino or RER: Musée d'Orsay

The museum's collections cover the period from 1848 (2nd Republic) to World War I. They are unequaled in showing the beginnings, development and permutations of modernism with particular emphasis on France—the dominant center of avant-garde activity during the 19th century. There is no contemporary art here, but the dramatic transformation of a derelict railroad station and its hotel (built by Victor Laloux in 1900) into a postmodern museum is a hallmark of late-20th-century architecture, albeit a very controversial one. Most of the criticism and acclaim have centered on the interior design by Gae Aulenti.

It was President Giscard d'Estaing who saved the building from demolition in 1963 by declaring it a historic landmark and proposing that it be converted into a museum. Given the deteriorated state of the old Gare d'Orsay, its imposing size and elegant turn-of-the-

century industrial architecture (iron structure, massive stone walls, glass roof), the task of renovation and redesign was formidable. The approach taken by Aulenti was to consider "the building as a contemporary object without history. . . . The compositional principle we adopted was to be in conflict, in systematic opposition and not in symbiosis." Viewing the building through a process of decomposition and fragmentation, she chose to treat it as a conglomerate of edifices within one larger structure. Each constituent element, moreover, had its own language. But parts could be combined, decomposed and recomposed—especially if this produced the desired effect of jarring contrasts.

The museum interior is thus a panoply of different forms and colors, diverse materials, sharp angles, odd juxtapositions, multiple lighting systems, sudden shifts from restored decoration to heavy postmodern ornamentation and autonomous, deliberately clashing structures each independently styled. Some people say there is no serenity here and that the interior imposes itself on the art. Others call it spectacular and see the interior as an energizing foil for the art. Without question, it captures the spirit of the 1900 railroad station with all its dynamism and excessive, eclectic, monumental splendor.

The museum itself is an exciting, uniquely organized cultural facility. More than simply an art museum, it is dedicated to all forms of artistic expression of a specific era. This encompasses painting, sculpture, architecture, urban design, photography, graphic arts, the birth of cinema and everything concerned with the reproduction of images from this era—posters, the press, illustrated books, etc. Within the galleries there are theme-spaces, and even the permanent exhibitions denote the historical, social and cultural context for the art. If you can include at least a few of the auxiliary presentations or the little exhibitions in the tower during your visit, you'll find some fascinating bits of information relevant to the main displays.

It will be blatantly apparent the minute you pass through the front door that this is a huge, complex museum impossible to see in one visit. Roughly, there are three principal levels with galleries arranged as a series of rooms; the grand atrium space and its side terraces display sculpture; a somewhat detached pavilion at the far end of the atrium is devoted to architecture; the upper level contains the ever-crowded impressionist and post-impressionist galleries; the bookstore, souvenir shop and main restaurant are on the ground level; and small cafés are on the middle and upper floors.

Fondation Dina Vierny —Musée Maillol

18

 59–61 rue de Grenelle, 75007
01-42-22-59-58 f: 01-42-84-14-44
Mon, Wed–Sun, 11–6; closed Tues
admission: 40/26F
métro: Bac
Located off the corner of rue du Bac.

Dina Vierny, who was a model for Aristide Maillol (1861–1944) during the last decade of his life, created this museum in homage to the sculptor. In addition to its collection of his drawings and sculpture, the museum exhibits work by various 20th-century artists, including some from the contemporary era. Of particular note is a complete room dedicated to Marcel Duchamp. On display is the original plaster cast for the breast in *Prière de toucher* (*Please Touch*) and a full selection of Duchamp editions. There is also a multi-level installation by Ilya Kabakov, *The Communal Kitchen* (1992–95), that gives a gripping experiential perspec-

tive, replete with sounds, of an over-crowded, psychologically tense Soviet apartment.

Special exhibitions at the museum sometimes feature contemporary artists—like *Jean-Michel Basquiat*—or historically significant shows—like *Frida Kahlo Introduces Diego Rivera*.

19 | Espace Electra

🖼 6 rue Récamier, 75007
01-42-84-23-60
Tues–Sun, 11:30–6:30; closed Mon
admission: 20/10F
métro: Sèvres-Babylone, Saint-Sulpice

Located at the end of a very short street off rue de Sèvres, where it branches into rue des Saints-Pères. (The charming garden in the adjacent square Recamier is a nice place to relax.)

As you enter, be sure to take note of the blue neon sculpture, *Electravers* (1990) by François MORELLET. It simultaneously serves as the entrance wall, provides a welcome sign for Espace Electra and makes implicit reference to the gallery's sponsor—the Fondation Electricité de France. Though French corporations are only beginning to support art, this space, open since 1990, has an admirable record of organizing interesting shows. The projects vary greatly (not all deal with contemporary art), but more often than not they are curatorial feats of originality with compelling art. The inaugural show set the stage by presenting major installation sculptures by Dan Flavin, Bruce Nauman and James Turrell. Following this lead were such exhibitions as: *Gilles Clément*—visions of a celebrated landscape architect; *Deceptive Art*—three centuries of cinema from the magic lantern to cinematography; *Dialogues with Shadow*—symbolic conversations between contemporary artists and silhouettes of the night, elusive worlds, the ethereal, ephemeral and unknown; *Genre Games* —present-day art viewed according to the past classification system of still life, landscape, flowers, portrait and nude; *Photographic Fictions*.

Montparnasse

Fondation Cartier pour l'Art Contemporain

🏛 architect: Jean NOUVEL, 1991–94

🏢 261 boulevard Raspail, 75014

01-42-18-56-51 f: 01-42-18-56-52

🛉 Tues–Wed, Fri–Sun, 12–8; Thurs,

🍽 12–10; closed Mon

admission: 30/20F

Soirées Nomades (evening perfor-mances): Thurs, 8:30; reservations, 01-42-18-56-72

métro: Denfert-Rochereau, Raspail

When the Fondation Cartier, founded in 1984, moved to its radically contempo-rary building in the center of Paris from a previous location in the quiet country-side outside the city limits, it greatly expanded its audience, becoming a major player in Paris's contemporary art community. As with the Pompidou Center, the building itself signifies an avant-garde spirit at the highest level.

The site previously housed the American Center and has historic importance as the place where Chateaubriand lived. Though Jean Nouvel, world-renowned architect, retained a cedar tree planted by the famous writer-nobleman, he made few other concessions to the past in his industrial design of glass, exposed steel and cables. The building consists of a succession of sheer gridded-glass sur-faces beginning with a wall hugging the sidewalk and extending to the edges of the property. You instantly become

aware of Nouvel's architectural conceit when you pass behind the front wall into an intervening space (prominently displaying Chateaubriand's tree), which then brings you to the actual building— a structure far smaller than the mock facade suggests. Here, too, glass panels cover the exterior, allowing the architec-ture to conceal itself. Transparency, lightness and illusion effectively dimin-ish volume and scale, and the layering of planes confuse spatial distances and blur boundaries. (Glass panels in the floor on the ground level even aim to make parts of the horizontal structure disappear.) Thus, the design, ingenious-ly shaped by Nouvel's interest in dema-terialization, defies the concern with closed, discrete forms that was the essence of classic modernism.

Reflections on the glass walls also make the building permeable to its sur-roundings. Actual accessibility to the natural environment exists as well since sliding glass doors along the length of the building on the ground floor open onto the garden beyond. On the interi-or, the glass window-doors form the back wall of the prime exhibition gallery. The space is seemingly bound-less albeit harshly naked and cold. A second gallery on the lower level is also a grand expanse though cavernous and bleakly devoid of natural light. Both spaces present a big challenge for the hanging of art. Luckily, installation designers have done wonders by creat-ing inventive display rooms, cases and devices for each specific work.

Cartier's big thematic exhibitions, usually scheduled for the summer sea-son, are extraordinary. They include work from many centuries, various cul-tures and wide-ranging styles and media. For example, *L'amour* (1997) revealed an astonishing span of repre-sentations of love including the medieval *Tomb of the Good Marriage*, a

Nouvel, Fondation Cartier

Titian drawing, surrealist photographs by Man Ray, the 1936 newsreel announcing the abdication of Edward VIII and a video installation by Gary Hill. Complementing the astute choices of art are the displays developing provocative sequences and juxtapositions. In one-person and group exhibitions, Cartier also offers diversity. Aiming to break away from a European-U.S. centrism, it shows art from all regions of the world. Recent exhibitions: *As a Bird*, *By Night*, *To Be Nature*, Jean-Michel Alberola, Ron Arad, Nobuyoshi Araki, Matthew Barney, Chuck Close, Raymond Depardon, Gérard Deschamps, Alain Diot, Raymond Hains, Huang Yong Ping, Seydou Keita, Issey Miyake, Panamarenko, Alain Séchas, Francesca Woodman. Catalogues and a limited selection of related publications are on sale in a small bookshop on the mezzanine level.

For most exhibitions, Cartier commissions works that are often purchased for the permanent collection. Selections from the collection are on exhibit in the galleries once a year. It is truly unfortunate that the building does not have permanent collection galleries since the Fondation Cartier owns many exemplary and incomparable objects. Although the building has eight floors, only the ground and lower level are devoted to exhibitions. All other floors are occupied by foundation offices.

Thursday nights, when the Cartier has extended hours, its Soirées Nomades (Nomadic Evenings) take place in the garden. These are music, dance or theatrical performances deriving inspiration from current exhibitions or specific works on display in the galleries. Even if you don't manage to get to an evening event (it's a great way to catch a whiff of the Paris art scene), be sure to walk around the garden, designed by the conceptual artist, Lothar BAUMGARTEN (1992–95). The title he has given to his nature-based installation, *Theatrum Botanicum*, relates to monastic books from the Middle Ages that inventoried medicinal and aromatic, cuisine-oriented plants. In his turn, Baumgarten has created a garden with plants and flowers native to the region as it was in the distant past, before there were national boundaries. Despite the garden's appearance as a wild prairie, the artist rigorously planned all aspects of its creation, leaving nothing to chance. Numerous different species were chosen and each was placed in a setting related to its natural habitat. Precision in the preparatory stage did not, however, affect the appearance of the environment. Although it is an urban garden, it has an organic, omnipresent character in radical contrast to geometric, perspectively ordered French gardens. Baumgarten thus presents a very contemporary garden with historic roots and ecological-political underpinings.

Saint–Phalle, tomb sculpture

Niki de Saint-Phalle

Tomb sculpture
Cimetière Montparnasse (avenue du Nord, 6th division) 2 rue Emile Richard, 74014
Mar 16–Nov 5: daily, 8–6. Nov 6–Mar 15: daily, 8–5:30
métro: Raspail

Enter the cemetery at 2 rue Emile Richard, just off the intersection of boulevards Raspail and Quinet. Once inside go straight ahead on avenue du Nord, which begins in the 13th division and continues in the 6th division after you cross allée Principale. It's a short walk.

Before you come to the Saint-Phalle sculpture, you will pass the unusual tomb of Henri Langlois (1914–77) on the left side of avenue du Nord. He was the revered founder of the Cinémathèque Française. You can't miss the tomb since its uniquely designed in the curved shape of the Palais de Chaillot, the building that housed the Cinémathèque until 1998. In addition, all the surfaces of the tomb are covered with photographic stills from films or portraits of film stars.

Continue down the road a bit farther and you will come to Saint-Phalle's tomb sculpture. It's also on the left side, slightly set back and somewhat hidden behind a tall monument. Unexpectedly, it—a large, human-sized, brightly colored cat—comes into view. As if its smile and raised tail weren't enough to convey its charm, there are swirling flowers and hearts painted in red, yellow and blue across its rotund white body. The figure has all the marks of a Niki de Saint-Phalle sculpture, but as a tomb image it's truly unconventional—the utter antithesis in spirit, shape, color and character to all other tombs. The artist created the figure in commemoration of her assistant Ricardo (1952–1989) who loved cats.

Les Echelles du Baroque

architect: Ricardo BOFILL, 1979-84
78 rue du Château, 75014
métro: Gaîté

Located in the area behind Montparnasse station on a stretch of land bordered by place Catalogne, rue Vercingétorix and rue du Commandant Mouchotte.

Coming upon this housing development from the surrounding neighborhood, where you see its exterior facades—the ones that front the streets and urban life, you have no idea what lies within. These facades relate to others, at least enough so they don't stand out. But once you pass through one of the gigantic, Alice-in-Wonderland doorways and enter the interior realm of the complex, it's quite another story. (If possible, enter through the passageway off place de Catalogne.)

As its title suggests, *Baroque Ladders* was inspired by Italian baroque architec-ture, especially the circular piazzas and overwhelming sense of grandeur. Bofill borrowed freely from these sources to produce a witty, modernized pastiche. The complex has 270 units divided between two clearly differentiated interior plazas. On the right is *The Amphitheater*. To get the full effect of the design, walk to the end of the central passage, turn right at the end and then enter on axis. As if coming into a palace, you proceed through gates and bush-laden balustrades into a semi-circular grass courtyard. Walking across the stone stage to the slightly tiered, grass- and plant-covered section, you wallow in pseudo-baroque elegance and pomposity. The surrounding architecture—a seven-story building (plus underground garage) with a classic vocabulary of doors, windows, columns and pilasters—has all the stateliness of an imposing monument except that here the facades are prefabricated concrete panels, not hand-cut stone. What you see is literally a facade. None of the pillars and columns—including the

Bofill, *The Columns, Les Echelles du Baroque*

humongous ribbed ones around the edges—hold up anything. They're all surface-deep imitations.

Irreverent indulgence in baroque-modern construction is even more flamboyant in the second, elliptical plaza, *The Columns*. In this design, Bofill has transformed a colonnaded facade into mirrored glass. And here the columns are neither surface designs or structural supports: they are habitable spaces. Again there is a communal grass plaza in the center, although the "keep off the grass" signs suggest a reversal of Bofill's socialist orientation. Nevertheless, this public housing gives its residents privacy and a quiet, ennobling form of living space that accommodates its urban setting without succumbing to its mass, dehumanizing mundaneness.

Shamaï Haber

Le creuset du temps, 1987–88
place de Catalogne
métro: Gaîté

Located in the center of a traffic circle adjacent to Bofill's housing complex.

Haber's serene fountain, *The Crucible of Time*, seems a bit incongruous in its location in the midst of a busy traffic circle. Though it contrasts well with the baroque excesses of Bofill's housing and similarly styled buildings surrounding place de Catalogne, it literally gets lost amid speeding cars and big, noisy commercial vehicles. Rather than create an object, Haber has designed a simple waterscape structure that spreads across the entire traffic-circle island. Its form is a large, slightly sloped disk, and water flows continuously across it and down its sides. A wall of white cobblestones, arranged in a circular pattern, surrounds the pool and serves as the border of the island. Although the fountain's surface looks like smooth granite, it is actually composed of 300,000

stone blocks. Haber wanted the water to have a mirrorlike quality to give the illusion that the disk was floating on water. Unfortunately, the pool barely rises above the eyelevel of drivers, and pedestrians can't get near to appreciate its artistry. The fountain also suffers from neglect, often having no water but lots of garbage in and around it.

Assemblée Nationale– UNESCO–Parc Citroën

Walter de Maria

Sculpture for the Bicentennial of the National Assembly, 1990
cour d'honneur, Palais Bourbon/Assemblée Nationale,
place du Palais Bourbon, 75007
métro: Assemblée Nationale

Walk to the west side of this Napoleonic mansion—the side fronting the plaza between rue de Bourgogne and rue de l'Université. You do not want to be at the grand portico facing the river (the door for tours of the interior), but at the private entrance reserved for deputies and ministers.

Although you can't get past the guards at the gate, you can catch a glimpse of de Maria's sculpture installed just ahead at the far end of the courtyard. Unfortunately, this "public" art work is off limits to the public. The visible part is a large (6 1/2 feet in diameter) sphere of gray granite set on a pedestal. The distant perspective makes it impossible to see the dates of the French Revolution and Bicentennial inscribed on the pedestal or to read the complete text of the Declaration of the Rights of Man and Citizen engraved on the eleven bronze plaques set on a 25-meter, curved limestone table surrounding the sphere.

Erik Satie Conservatoire Municipal and Foyer de Personnes Agées

🏛 architect: Christian de PORTZAM-PARC, 1984
135 rue de l'Université and 17 rue Jean Nicot, 75007
métro: Latour-Maubourg

Portzamparc has created an amazing design here for contiguous buildings belonging to two very different institutions. One is a neighborhood school for music, dance, art and theater that largely serves children. The other is housing for the elderly. The school's main facade on rue de l'Université is a disjunctive composite of bold forms. There's a floating pitched roof, recessed entrance marked by an open-frame stilt structure, boxlike midsection raised on huge concrete columns, eccentrically arched window, asymmetrical tower housing a spiral stairway and much more. The building is clearly eccentric and autonomous. Its design fits well with the spirit of unfettered creativity one might assume goes on inside. In contrast, the housing units have a more conservative appearance. Yet they too have unique and dynamic features, many of which create playful correspondences with the design of the school. And they harmonize with nearby buildings, instead of asserting individuality as the school does. The residence and public center are thus each given an appropriate, different architectural image even as they share cross-currents.

UNESCO

🧍 7 place de Fontenoy, 75007
☎ 01-45-68-03-71
🕐 Mon–Fri, 9–6
🏛 admission: free
métro: Ségur, Ecole Militaire
Located across from Ecole Militaire, off avenues de Lowendal and de Saxe.

Although its architecture caused a stir in Paris when it opened (1958), the UNESCO headquarters—an ensemble of three buildings created by the international design team of Marcel BREUER (US), Bernard ZEHRFUS (France) and Pier Luigi NERVI (Italy)—now looks like a moderate version of 1960s modernism. Notably, the structures occupy only a small area within the UNESCO city block, and even when office expansion occurred in 1965 it was limited to underground offices with sunken patios so as not to disturb two side courtyards.

From its inception, UNESCO placed art in its environment.Works installed in the buildings and their surroundings have either been commissioned or donated as gifts by member countries. Selections of permanent objects evidently undergo rigorous evaluation since the choices are outstanding. For example, the most recent additions by Tadao Ando and Dani Karavan are first-rate exemplars of contemporary art. They alone are worth a special visit.

From the entrance door, cross the center hall and exit outdoors to the right onto a paved patio. Here you will find such classic examples of mod-

Portzamparc, conservatory and housing

ernism as *Reclining Figure* by Henry MOORE, *Walking Man* by Alberto GIA-COMETTI and *Spiral* by Alexander CALDER. These three works were part of the original construction plans for the building. Beyond the patio in the midst of the outlying area is *The Symbolic Globe* (1995) by the Danish engineer Erik REITZEL. It is an enormous, transparent sphere composed of 10,000 aluminum rods and joints with a small golden sphere suspended in the center. Before going back inside, look through the window to the right of the door and you will see *The Wall of the Sun* (1958) —an outstanding work by Joan MIRO and the ceramicist Josep Llorens ARTI-GAS. This work and its companion, *The Wall of the Moon*, were originally on the patio but had to be moved indoors to protect them from acid-rain damage. If the room where they are now located (Miró Hall) is not in use, you can go inside and see the walls up close.

As you re-enter the main building, turn to the right and take the passage-way into the adjoining building. On dis-play in the front of the lobby is a large abstract tapestry by LE CORBUSIER (1956) and a wood-panel painting, *The Fall of Icarus*, by PICASSO. The other end of the lobby is decorated with a mural, *Prometheus Bringing Fire to Mankind*, by the Mexican artist Rufino TAMAYO and a work by the Spaniard Antoni TAPIES. The latter is a strong example of the artist's mixed-media paintings on raw canvas. Here he com-bines common objects—a broom and paint-can cover—with words, loosely sketched images, intuitive markings and a big, bold, diagonal cross in a provoca-tive composition.

Retrace your steps to the main build-ing and exit to the right into the east courtyard. On your left is *Aeolian Signals* (1993), a sculpture in five parts representing the signs of the wind by the Greek artist TAKIS. If you now walk

ahead to the street gate facing avenue de Saxe, you will come upon *Square of Tolerance in Homage to Yitzhak Rabin*, a memorial project by the Israeli artist Dani KARAVAN. This work, inaugurated in 1996, consists of stone paths encir-cling a grass mound with an olive tree at its apex; a single stream of water falling from a stone block; and a wall inscribed with the first lines of the pre-amble to UNESCO'S constitution written in eleven languages. It states for all to read: "Since wars begin in the minds of men, it is in the minds of men that the defenses of peace must be construct-ed." This stirring monument is skillfully designed to be visible from the street and is well integrated into the courtyard landscape of which it is a part.

Encompassing the entire courtyard area between the main building and a small corner office building is *Garden of*

Ando, *Meditation Space*

Peace (1956–58) by the Japanese-American artist Isamu NOGUCHI. This is one of the most serene places in all of Paris. Noguchi's landscape, inspired by traditional Japanese garden design, includes a small pond, meandering stream, footbridge, flowers and a stone terrace with carved granite seating and a fountain, reflecting pool, mounded planting areas, stone walkways and dwarf cherry, plum, magnolia and bamboo trees. Not only is the garden authentically Japanese since all the plants and stones come directly from Japan, but it also expresses an age-old Japanese sensibility: the harmony between man and nature. Indeed, Noguchi was masterful in creating a garden in which natural and sculptural forms coexist. Reference to Japanese culture also occurs in the garden's patio, where round, square and triangular stone configurations are positioned to represent the tea ceremony. Nearby is the *Peace Fountain*—a rectangular pool with a tall "source stone" inscribed with mirror-image calligraphy denoting *heiwa* (peace). Finally, *The Nagasaki Angel*, located at the south end of the garden, provides a wondrous and disturbing reminder of modern Japanese history. The statue, originally on the facade of the Urakami Church in Nagasaki, was the only element spared from destruction by the atomic bomb dropped on the city on August 9, 1945.

Beyond the patio, at the most remote part of the courtyard, is a cylindrical structure commissioned to symbolize peace and to commemorate the 50th anniversary of the adoption of UNESCO'S constitution. Designed by the architect Tadao ANDO, *Meditation Space* (1996), is an extraordinary work that exemplifies the majesty and emotive power of a simple contemporary monument. To enter, you walk down a ramp and angle back across a shallow pond that encircles the structure with a continuous film of flowing water. The doorway is a cutout opening at the base of a two-story concrete form marked only by the regularity of the casting holes and grid lines. This doorway and a duplicate one on the opposite side also serve as windows, bringing light into the interior, which is otherwise a darkened sanctuary permeated by a deep aura of tranquility. Except for four high-backed armchairs that have a regal bearing despite their industrial, black-steel reductive shape, the space is empty. (The chairs are set back against the wall as pairs facing each other.) The design of the stone floor—concentric circles, radiating lines and a cross axis—only strengthens the circular, centering shape of the cylinder space without becoming an additive element or decoration. The interior floor and base of the pond bear symbolic meaning, however, since the granite comes from Hiroshima and was exposed to the atomic bomb fallout. It is just this subtle, unpretentious sense of symbolism and the expressiveness of basic elements that makes Ando's edifice an impressive monument to peace.

Canal+

 architect: Richard MEIER, 1988–91
quai André Citroën and 2 rue des
Cévennes, 75015
métro: Javel-A. Citroën

Located just beyond Pont Mirabeau and before Parc André Citroën.

Richard Meier, the famed architect who designed the Getty Museum, has here created the headquarters for the French television station, Canal+. Using an L-shaped plan, Meier divided the whole into two very different parts, each geared to the dominant function of the occupants. A tall, narrow wing stretched along the quay houses administrative offices, and a short block wing set perpendicular to it comprises studios and production management services. At the juncture where the two wings meet, is an entrance atrium. You probably won't be able to walk around the interior of the building, but try to enter, or at least look into the atrium. The space is high and narrow with glass sheathing on one side, an alignment of open corridors on the other and a bridge connecting the two wings at the back end. It has an eerie, otherworldly character, especially since sounds reverberate and Meier's trademark white enamel tiles, which cover both interior and exterior walls, produce super-shiny, antiseptic surfaces. If you walk around the building, this impression changes. On the river side, Meier balances a curved, transparent facade articulated by a rhythmic pattern with a straight, opaque facade delineated by horizontal and vertical elements. And in the rear, void and planar shapes accent the rooftop zone while meeting rooms and a restaurant open onto a public garden on the ground level.

Mark Di Suvero

Etoile du jour, 1985
quai André Citroën
métro: Javel-A. Citroën

Located in a small plaza in front of Canal+ at the corner of rue Cauchy.

The dynamic energy expressed in *Day Star* is typical of Di Suvero's art. Though the reddish brown, steel I-beams make reference to the heavy structural supports used to stabilize modern buildings, here they are thrusting rhythms aggressively puncturing space. As in many works deriving from the aesthetics that emerged in the 1960s, this sculpture defies refinement standards in favor of weathered rawness. But the nearby Eiffel Tower reveals that this aesthetic is hardly new. Di Suvero's sculpture even shares its splayed, three-legged stance with the famous Paris monument.

La Ribière Housing and Office Complex

architects: ARCHITECTURE STUDIO, 1993–98
13–17 rue de Cauchy, 75015
métro: Javel-A. Citroën

In this project (situated behind the Canal+ building), Architecture Studio has created an efficient, unusual layout by doubling a line of apartments facing the Seine with a row of offices. Despite the use of tender colors, the design is anything but bland. Sheathed in metal, the building's "helmets make one think that a little army of Samurai had been left there by a Japanese tour bus driver."

Parc André Citroën

landscape architects: Gilles CLEMENT, Alain PROVOST, 1988–92
architects: Patrick BERGER, Jean-Paul VIGUIER, Jean-François JODRY
quai André Citroën and rue Balard, 75015
Mon–Fri: 7:30–7:30; Sat–Sun, 9–7:30
métro: Javel-A. Citroën, Balard

When a huge Citroën auto plant on this site (the site where André Citroën built his first factory) moved to the suburbs in 1970, half of the land was designated for housing and offices. Not until 1984 did a conference determine that the other half—a sprawling 35-acre plot—

Parc André Citroën

become a park. Two teams, Clément-Berger and Provost-Viguier-Jodry, won a competition in 1988 to develop it with their proposals for an extraordinary community park and botanical garden. The design is defined by a large expanse of lawn, intriguing architectural structures, small theme gardens and an abundance of water, ramps, walkways and plazas.

For the most part the park has a formal, geometric layout. However, one section—the Garden in Movement (located just inside the entrance from the quay)—is a kind of wild prairie, where plants evolve naturally and visitors can meander and picnic at will. Even where paths control pedestrian access elsewhere in the park, there are steps, platforms, ramps, tunnels, canals, ponds, grottos, look-out towers and bridges that encourage close observation and intimate contact with nature. It is a very visitor-friendly environment. This may well be the only park in Paris where people can legally walk and play on the grass, and where dogs are not permitted. (You don't have to watch where you step!)

On the far side of the Garden in Movement is the Garden of Metamorphoses—a row of imaginative settings separated by waterfalls. Each plot has a unique selection of plants (trees, shrubs, flowers, ground covers), and a dominant color that evokes one of the seven metals within the alchemical transmutation of lead into gold. Surprisingly, visitors can relax on lounge chairs and other available seating in some of the gardens. (Unlike the Tuileries and Luxembourg Garden, you sit for free here.)

Throughout the park architectural structures define and order the various sections or vegetation. The built elements are generally simple in form, at times curious in appearance, but never audacious or severe. The largest build-

ings are the two tall greenhouses at the end of the lawn expanse. Their style evokes ancient temples, albeit with a contemporary cast and unconventional elements—like the juxtaposition of glass walls and raw wood columns. Positioned between the two greenhouses are intermittently spurting water jets, conceptualized as an "aquatic peristyle." Though this ensemble and the surrounding plaza impart to the park an air of grandeur, an informal, leisure-time atmosphere prevails.

Should you like to indulge in people-watching, there are no cafés in the park but there are some incredibly designed viewing platforms along the far side of the lawn (the side opposite from the gardens). The platforms, conceived as star observatories, are part of an independent activity realm replete with a moat, grottos, waterfalls and water-lily patches.

A rock garden with sculpted stones for children to play on lies at the end of the park near the Seine. Behind the main park and more integrated into the urban landscape are two additional gardens. The White Garden, which has an open ambience, features a sports field and an area with vivacious plants and white flowers. The companion Shade Garden is a somber, densely planted labyrinth bordered by steps.

Since colors and smells change dramatically each season—and the designers have programmed this into the landscape—it is worth visiting the park more than once. Even for those who don't like gardens this is an amazing place. For those interested in city planning, landscape design or gardens, this is a must!

Grand Palais–
Villa La Roche

Grand Palais

🚃 3 avenue du Général Eisenhower,
75008
01-44-13-17-17
Mon–Tues, Thurs–Sun, 10–8;
Wed, 10–10; closed Tues
admission: 50/35F

The Grand Palais houses large, block-buster-type art exhibitions from all periods, including the 20th century though rarely the contemporary years. You will undoubtedly see posters advertising the current shows all over the city.

Musée d'Art Moderne de la Ville de Paris

🏛 11 avenue du Président Wilson
📖 (Palais de Tokyo), 75116
01-53-67-40-00 f: 01-47-23-35-98
Tues–Fri, 10–5:30; Sat–Sun, 10–7;
closed Mon
admission: 27/14.50F; additional
fee for special exhibitions and ARC
métro: léna, Alma-Marceau

The City Museum of Modern Art covers the same territory as the National Museum of Modern Art in the Pompidou Center, though it has been more adventurous in its contemporary art exhibitions. On a given visit, you often can see several shows featuring noteworthy emerging artists from France or elsewhere plus a major exhibition of innovative, midcareer figures.

The museum's dynamic contemporary art program is called ARC— Animation, Recherche, Confrontation. ARC began in 1968 and has always been independent from the "historic" realm of the museum. Although the whole museum deals with the 20th century, ARC focuses exclusively on artists who are still living. In its location on the top floor, ARC is easy to miss if you do not see the humdrum sign on the staircase next to the room with the giant Dufy mural, or if you can't find the elevators that go to the 4th floor. Also be aware that the 4th floor is divided into several sections—a gallery set back in the center almost at the top of the grand staircase, a passage space extending across the center, a large curving gallery and a group of rooms tangential to the far end of the curving gallery. The layout for ARC is as confusing as this description! Indeed, the entire museum is not easy to navigate. Galleries end abruptly or intersect one another unexpectedly. Some spaces seem like endless expanses whereas others are constricted or secluded. And floors change in midstream and diverge in odd directions.

Boltanski, *Portant,* 1996 (Musée d'Art Moderne de la Ville de Paris)

The ARC space is usually divided into three one-person exhibits that run simultaneously. These show work by young (under 35) artists whose creations and ideas tend to be experimental and against the grain, if not conspicuously eccentric. Complementing these are large-scale monographic exhibits of more established artists and group or thematic shows. (These sometimes are in other galleries within the museum.) Exhibitions are typically accompanied by public conversations with the artists, lectures or conferences. With all of them there is some sort of publication— be it a modest brochure or an impressive catalogue. Introductory wall texts, which are usually quite simple and helpful, also introduce the artists and projects to visitors. Recent exhibitions: *Martine Aballea*, *Elizabeth Ballet*, *Michel Blazy*, *Christian Boltanski*, *Willie Doherty*, *Paul-Armand Gette and Lucius Burckhardt*, *Gilbert & George*, *Dominique Gonzalez-Foerster*, *Felix Gonzalez-Torres*, *Carsten Höller*, *Rebecca Horn*, *Pierre Huyghe*, *Fabrice Hybert*, *Donald Judd*, *Per Kirkeby*, *Ange Leccia*, *Gabriel Orozco*, *Philippe Pareno*, *Sigmar Polke*, *Gerhard Richter*, *Pipiloti Rist*, *Gregor Schneider*, *Rosemarie Trockel*, *15 Contemporary Artists from Scandinavia*.

The museum's collection of contemporary art is located in the center galleries on the ground floor and the curving galleries below. The installation begins with the 1960s and follows a loose chronological path to the present. A given room or suite of rooms displays the art of a particular movement or stylistic orientation. Groupings include Nouveau Réalisme, new figurative art from the 1970s, Supports-Surfaces, abstract art with a minimalist character, the Italian movement Arte Povera, a selection of exemplary works from the 1980s, a large-scale installation from 1974 by Gasiorowski, and a potpourri of recent work by a broad range of artists. There is also a small room for photographs and a video room.

The contemporary collection does not claim to be comprehensive and indeed it is not an international survey. (The lack of German art is most apparent.) Without being excessively nationalistic, the display presents impressive works by French artists many who will be discoveries for foreigners. It is, however, frustrating to see only one, totally decontextualized work by an artist. Brief informational labels would be welcome.

If you are not exhausted, you should go through the collection galleries of early-20th-century art. These encompass Fauvism to kinetic art and include many pivotal works from the modern era. Paintings by Robert Delaunay, Matisse's mural *La Danse*, Dufy's *Spirit of Electricity* and the Art Deco furniture collection are popular favorites. Should there be a special exhibition of modern (as distinguished from contemporary) art, be sure to see it. These shows are typically well conceived and filled with treasures not often on public view. One last advisory: save time for the bookstore. It's a small, jam-packed space across from the café on the lower level. The selection to superb for books and magazines on art and related subjects.

Martial Raysse

Sol et colombe, 1989–92
Conseil Economique et Sociale,
place d'Iéna, 75016
métro: Iéna

Raysse, one of France's celebrated artists, created the mural *Ground and Dove* with the assistance of the mosaic craftsman Luigi Guardigli. Its 11 panels create a decorative frieze above the entrance of an austere government building. In contrast to the grim facade, Raysse presents fanciful scenes suggestive of a universe shaped by mythical events. Only three of the panels are in color and all are very spare to the point of being evocatively ambiguous. From left to right, the images show a global sphere with an animal climbing on it; a man throwing a ball in the air; a man and woman touching hands; a man, woman and child; a giant rocklike form and a small figure; an empty space with a sphere flanked by two figures and a crowd of people watching in front; a man and woman sitting atop a large pink cube; the sun and a dancing figure reaching for a bird; radiating lines and babies playing; a line of seven figures with joined hands walking or dancing forward; a man flying in the air surrounded by stars.

Jean-Pierre Raynaud

Untitled, 1989/94
Centre National de la Recherche Scientifique (CNRS), 3 rue Michelange, 75016
métro: Michelange-Auteuil

Located in the courtyard just inside the street entrance.

Raynaud, Untitled

Raynaud created this monumental stele in honor of the 50th anniversary of CNRS. Its "inscription" takes the form of hardware from laboratory equipment scattered across the front and back of the monolith. The shiny chrome of the components reiterates the slick, white-tiles of the base though the curious, irregular shapes of the former contrast sharply with the uniform grid pattern and flat surface of the latter. Steles are a recurring theme in Raynaud's art, symbolizing memory, marking space and enshrining quotidian debris.

Villa La Roche

architects: LE CORBUSIER with Pierre JEANNERET, 1923–25
10 impasse du Docteur Blanche, 75016
01-42-88-41-53
Mon–Thurs, 10–12:30 and 1:30–6; Fri, 10–12:30 and 1:30–5. Closed during August
admission: 15/10F
métro: Jasmin

From the métro, walk down avenue Mozart; turn right at the first street, rue Henri Heine; turn left at the corner onto rue Docteur Blanche; almost immediately, turn left into the tiny street variously called impasse or square du Docteur Blanche.

If you want to see a building by one of the most innovative, influential architects of the 20th century, here is a perfect, very convenient opportunity. You'll actually get to see the exterior of two Le Corbusier houses, since Villa La Roche adjoins Maison Jeanneret (8 impasse de Docteur Blanche), a more modest dwelling built for the architect's brother and now used for the administrative offices, library and archives of the Fondation Le Corbusier.

Le Corbusier designed the villa as a place where Raoul La Roche, a Swiss banker and art collector, could display works in his collection and entertain when he came to Paris. Though the house may seem simple at first glance, it is a prime, sophisticated example of modernism. It also gives early evidence of Le Corbusier's famous "five points for modern architecture"—open facade free of all posts and beams, long window, structural posts (pilotis) that free the ground level, floor plan free of all interior partitions and roof terrace. In Villa La Roche, Le Corbusier had to deal with a small lot and yet, by using his five-point design elements, he produced a roomy dwelling. Raising the building off the ground was particularly useful here in increasing the amount of natural light in the living areas while simultaneously providing a covered area for car parking.

The entrance hall is a tall, airy space creatively linking the two wings of the house and three levels with a footbridge, staircases and balconies. The large living room (or gallery) on the main level is another amazing space. It features a ramp to the upper level and an expansive, curving window wall that looks out on an adjacent sitting terrace. A second terrace, designated as a roof garden, is on the upper level. As in most Le Corbusier buildings, the roof becomes functional as a garden-outdoor space, where residents can enjoy nature in the privacy of their own homes even in the middle of the city. Throughout the house, walls are unadorned, planar surfaces, and furnishings like bookcases, shelves, light fixtures and fireplace mantels are built in. You get a good sense of Le Corbusier's purist, minimalist aesthetic from the omnipresent light fixture—an exposed bulb at the end of a pole attached to the ceiling. More intriguing but equally spare is the black marble-topped table with one pair of legs configured as a black-tile panel and the other as a V delineated in chrome. Most

of the chairs, tables and other movable pieces currently in the rooms as well as the paintings are by Le Corbusier.

Unlike the multitude of modern buildings that have adapted Le Corbusier's style, Villa La Roche is not at all a monolithic box reduced to a simplistic structure and geometric repetitiveness. On the contrary, each space is unique and all component parts are precisely scaled and positioned in accordance with human proportions. For instance, the size and shape of windows as well as the amount of light and angle of shadow were critical factors. Similarly, a layout plan had to be inventive in terms of an interplay of volumes and perspectives from room to room. And though white walls are pervasive, the addition of a muted color (turquoise, brown, umber, beige, gray or rose) on one wall, floor, door or radiator served to articulate the space. It's as though Le Corbusier treated each room and the entire structure as an abstract composition in which all elements coexist in harmonious balance.

Etoile–Gare Saint-Lazare

Centre National de la Photographie (CNP)

Hôtel Salomon de Rothschild, 11 rue Berryer (corner of avenue de Friedland), 75008
01-53-76-12-32 f: 01-53-76-12-33
Mon, Wed–Sun, 12–7; closed Tues
admission: 30/15F
métro: Etoile

CNP is without a doubt the best place to see high-quality contemporary photography in Paris. The location in an elegant old mansion is a bit surreal since you first climb a grand baroque staircase and then enter barren, somewhat shabby rooms with unconventional artworks hanging on the walls or deposited on the floors. Despite the initial impression and the oddities of room sizes and shapes, the galleries are flexible enough to accommodate the varied scale of contemporary photographs as well as photo-installation and video-projection projects.

Exhibitions feature work by emerging artists, often presented for the first time in France or Europe. On a single visit you may see several one-person shows or a group show that brings together diverse creations under the umbrella of a timely and original theme. Typically the art is impressive and innovative in concept, technique and format. Since CNP does not have a permanent collection, all works are on loan or are temporary creations made on-site specifically for an exhibition. Some work is also the result of a residency or experimental project sponsored by the center. Recent exhibitions: *Peter Beard, Anna and Bernhard Blume, Sophie Calle, Hannah Collins, Pascal Convert, Wyn Geleynse, Anthony Hernandez, Manfred Jade, Henrik Plenge Jakobsen, Valérie Jouve, Andréa Keen, Carl de Keyzer, Zoe Leonard, Ryuji Miyamoto, Eric Poitevin, Olivier Rebufa, Eugène Richards, Thomas Ruff, Sam Samore, Patrick Tosani, Contemporary Austrian Photographers*. CNP publishes many catalogues associated with its exhibitions and an informative quarterly journal with articles on current exhibitions and essays on notable people or relevant topics.

Galerie Lelong

13 rue de Téhéran, 75008
01-45-63-13-19 f: 01-42-89-34-33
Tues–Fri, 10:30–6; Sat, 2–6:30;
closed Mon
métro: Miromesnil

This revered gallery shows blue-chip artists from the early and mid-20th century as well as some midcareer contemporary artists. The roster includes both European and American artists. Having spacious exhibition rooms, the gallery can present large works advantageously. Artists: Valerio Adami, Pierre Alechinsky, Karel Appel, James Brown, Alexander Calder, Anthony Caro, Marc Chagall, Eduardo Chillida, Walter de Maria, Jan Dibbets, Claude Garache, Ferran García Sevilla, Alberto Giacometti, Andy Goldsworthy, Donald Judd, Konrad Klapheck, Jiri Kolár, Jannis Kounellis, Alberto Magnelli, Henri Michaux, Joan Miró, Jacques Monory, Bernard Pagés, Edouard Pignon-Ernest, Paul Rebeyrolle, Jean-Paul Riopelle, Antonio Saura, Sean Scully, Susanna Solano, Saul Steinberg, Antonio Tàpies, Gérard Titus-Carmel, Jan Voss.

Galerie Jérôme de Noirmont

38 avenue Matignon, 75008
01-42-89-89-00 f: 01-42-89-89-03
Mon–Sat, 10–1 and 2:30–7;
closed Mon
métro: Franklin D. Roosevelt

This gallery roster includes established artists who are very chic and popular within the international art circuit. However, many of them have had little exposure in Paris. Even if you know the artist's work, exhibitions are well done and you'll probably see some unfamiliar images. Artists: Miguel Barcelo, Jean-Michel Basquiat, Ben, Francesco Clemente, Robert Combas, Tony Cragg, Keith Haring, Jeff Koons, McDermott & McGough, David Mach, Cady Noland, A. R. Penck, Andy Warhol.

Arman

L'heure de tous, 1985
cour de Havre, Gare Saint-Lazare,
75008
métro: Saint-Lazare

Located in front of the main entrance to the station in the courtyard on the right side.

The Hour of Everything is typical of the witty assemblage sculptures of the French artist Arman. As evinced in this tower of clocks (cast in bronze), a collection of common objects functions as both the material and the subject matter. This particular work is perfect for a railroad station—a place where people are always fighting against time no matter how many clocks are available for them to consult.

Arman

Consigne à vie, 1985
cour de Rome, Gare Saint-Lazare,
75008
métro: Saint-Lazare

Located in front of the main entrance to the station in the courtyard on the left side.

The title *Consigned for Life* gives a humorous twist to the pile of suitcases (cast in bronze) by referring to the plight of travelers who are burdened with too much baggage.

Montmartre

Théâtre des Abbesses

architect: Charles VANDENHOVE,
1996
31 rue des Abbesses, 75018
métro: Abbesses

Located just across from rue Ravignan (the street where Picasso lived when he first came to Paris).

With its classically attuned postmodern design, enhanced by contributions from five contemporary artists, Théâtre des Abbesses is a visually rich building. It was established as a smaller, sister hall to the Théâtre de la Ville, offering contemporary dance, music from various cultures of the world, avant-garde plays and pocket opera. Even before you arrive at its doors, look above the rooftops of neighboring buildings. You will see a curious wall painting of three giant coral-toned circles and stripes set within and behind arch and cornice structures. It is so distinctive a design that it effectively serves as a landmark for the theater, which is located in the cluster of buildings alongside. The painting is yet another exceptional outdoor artwork by Daniel BUREN.

It was crucial that the new 420-seat hall be sensitively integrated into the historic Montmartre neighborhood. Vandenhove produced an interesting solution by constructing a block of apartments at street-side, whose scale and curving zinc roofs fit nicely with the nearby architecture. The theater is hidden from view behind these units, though its presence is manifested by an oversized entryway in the facade of the apartment block. It leads into a courtyard that doubles as an outdoor lobby and stageset for the theater. The coral-toned colonnaded facade and neoclassical pediment have both a starkly modern and a historical appearance. You can again see the Buren painting, now more visibly referenced to the theater's exterior. Also notable, albeit barely perceptible, are the scattered words printed on the facade in blocks letters: IMAGINER, DESIRER, OBJET, C'EST SUR (it's certain), INATTENDU (unexpected), etc. This is the creation of the conceptual artist Robert BARRY. The words are meant to suggest actions and ideas common to theatrical productions. Echoes of the motifs of both Barry and Buren recur in the theater's interior: words are engraved in the frosted glass of the staircase balustrade, and stripes appear on furniture and balcony parapets. The hall is also enhanced by Olivier DEBRE's design for the stage curtains and fabric used in the side balconies and by Loïc LE GROUMELLEC's drawings of houses and figures on glazed metal panels in the bar, foyer and dance studios.

In addition to the theater and apartments, the complex includes a dance academy. Jean-Charles BLAIS created serigraphs as large plinths for this building, and Patrick CORILLON decorated the basement corridors with imagery of geological strata arranged in horizontal bands and overlaid with words relating to the basement environment—*plancher* (floor), *béton* (concrete), *vide ventilé* (ventilated void), *marne gypseuse* (marl with gypsum).

La Villette

Parc de la Villette

architect: Bernard TSCHUMI, 1987–91
211 avenue Jean Jaurès, 75019
métro: Porte de Pantin, Porte de la Villette

Located on about 74 acres of land bordered by avenue Jean Jaurès, boulevard Sérurier, boulevard Macdonald and avenue Corentin Cariou. An information center, in the red building to the left of the main entrance, is open everyday 10–7.

Parc de la Villette is a unique culture, leisure, sports, entertainment and people environment used by a widely diverse public with varying interests. A mix of hands-on activities (gardening, workshops, boating . . .), exhibitions (art, science, music, film . . .) and events (outdoor jazz, rock, carnivals, flower markets . . .) are available nearly round-the-clock for an audience of children, adolescents, adults and the elderly—blue-collar to silver-spoon inclusive. There's lots of open space traversed by walkways and punctuated by play areas and whimsical structures. Indeed, the park itself is a catalyst for laughter and pleasure. But unlike the typical city park conceived as an escape from the everyday world into a quiet, romanticized vision of nature, it aimed to be an "urban park." According to its designer, Bernard Tschumi, it is "a 21st-century park devoted to activity rather than the rest and relaxation goals of 18th- and 19th-century parks." Be advised that it's a gigantic spread of land with lots to see and do, so plan to spend a fair amount of time meandering around.

Until the early 1970s, the site contained a cattle market and slaughterhouses. Thereafter, the whole area rapidly declined, becoming an ugly wasteland. The first sign of revival occurred in 1979 when President Giscard d'Estaing announced plans to locate the Museum of Science and Industry in one of the old buildings. Three years later, President François Mitterand elaborated the project into an ambitious redevelopment program involving major new construction. Tschumi (a Swiss-born American resi-

Tschumi, folly

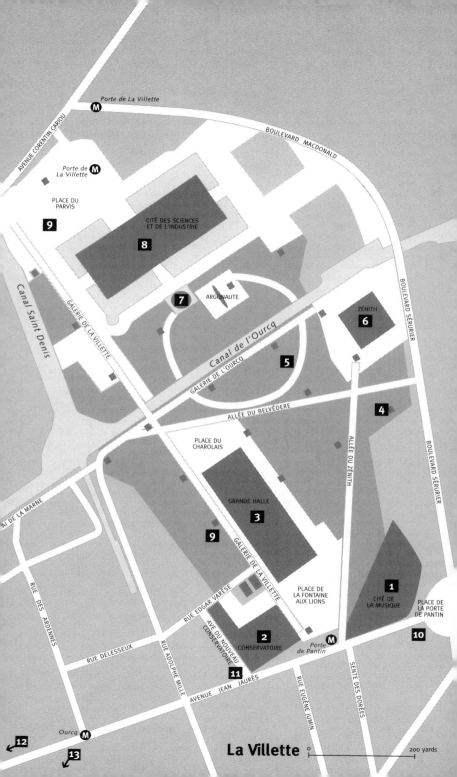

La Villette

dent) won the international competition (1983) to design the park, ultimately producing an internationally acclaimed setting. His plan relates to a view of contemporary life as an assemblage of disparate elements with fragmentation, disunity and absurdity being pervasive conditions. This contrasts with historical notions of stability, logic and order. In addition, he sees architectural structures as generators of movement and activity, as stimuli of the imagination. And this greatly elevates the role of people and human interactions.

Tschumi developed an open plan for the park with points of interest— "follies"—placed at regular intervals as determined by an underlying grid. The follies are eccentric, enigmatic, witty, oddly shaped, red-steel structures. They may seem like purely autonomous configurations yet each serves a function or houses a service—information center, snack bar, medical station, observatory, kiosk, concert stage, exhibit, clock and barometer, video, ticket office, children's theater, etc. Though there is a precedent for follies in the 18th-century romantic tradition, the 25 creations at La Villette are distinctive in their blatantly geometric, assertive, antihistorical forms. Their cubic cores with void and planar sides sprout cylinders, ramps, stairs, canopies, towers and all sorts of weird appendages.

A canal cuts through the center of the park on an east-west axis intersecting with a covered walkway (the strange-looking black industrial frame and white wavy-roof structure called "Galerie de la Villette") aligned as a north-south axis joining the métro stations at the two main entrances. Tschumi further organizes the park with a circular and a triangular tree-lined path and a winding promenade that curves around a succession of theme gardens. The gardens of mirrors, dunes, clouds, trellises, bamboo, equilibrium,

childish fears, flying trapezes and islands are without question extraordinary, but the grand finale, superspectacular dragon garden with its incredible slide sculpture is not to be missed. In keeping with his conceptual orientation, each garden is not only a particularized setting with a different ambience but also an activity area.

Philippe Starck

Furnishings and fixtures

Parc de la Villette, located here and there.

Be sure to sit in one of the inventively designed "park benches"—aluminum swivel chairs secured to the ground in small groupings. The ever-chic Philippe Starck also created the park lights and other fixtures that strikingly combine function with elegant form.

1 Cité de la Musique

architect: Christian de PORTZAMPARC, 1985–95
221 avenue Jean Jaurès,
Parc de la Villette, 75019
01-44-84-44-84
Tues–Thurs, Sat, 12–6; Fri, 12–9:30; Sun, 10–6; closed Mon
métro: Porte de Pantin

Located to the right (east) of the main entrance to La Villette Park.

This extraordinary Music Center is an award-winning design (Equerre d'Argent, 1995) by one of the most acclaimed, talented architects of his generation, Christian de Portzamparc (holder of the prestigious Pritzger Prize). It is a formidable project composed of two building clusters: a grand concert hall, music museum, center for organ studies, shops, instruction institute, documentation centers, and residential units (east); and a multifaceted conservatory (west). What is exceptional in Portzamparc's plan is his treatment of both clusters as

Portzamparc, Cité de la Musique

villages. The villages are assemblages of integral, heterogeneous parts housing a variety of particularized activities. But the differentiated elements are joined by a circulation network—the community streets and village squares—that provides open, interactivity space and harmonizes the whole. Metaphorically, the architectural plan is like a symphony, where a multitude of diverse instruments and sounds come together to articulate an ensemble.

Though the name "Cité de la Musique" officially refers to both sectors of the project, it has become synonymous with the more public, east sector as distinguished from the "Conservatory," the west sector. The entrance to the Cité is marked by one of Tschumi's red follies. After entering, you walk down a long passageway. The high wall on the left provides the leitmotif for all that follows: a precise, geometric schema of alternating solids and voids, lines and planes, darks and lights, horizontals and verticals, recessions and

projections. Natural light streams down from above. Unlike many contemporary buildings, the architecture is shaped by alluring harmonies and playful contrasts, not methodical repetitions or jarring oppositions. This isn't a cold, dehumanized environment. Instead, it's one that makes you feel enlivened, even awestruck. Once inside the main lobby (another spacious area), you can turn right toward the main concert hall—located within its own spherical structure—or you can turn left and arrive at the Musée de la Musique. The lobby, which truly feels like an outdoor plaza with buildings and walkways extending back from it, sweeps around in the rear, climbing up around the central core, while also giving access to a number of other services (dance and music archives, etc.) and buildings. As in a well-designed plaza, there are places to sit, a café, a street display of intriguing objects, announcement placards, separate facades and inviting entryways, and a confluence of activities and people.

Conservatoire Nationale Supérieure de Musique et de Danse de Paris

2

architect: Christian de PORTZAM-
PARC 1989–92
209 avenue Jean-Jaurès,
Parc de la Villette, 75019
01-40-40-46-46 f: 01-40-40-45-00
métro: Porte de Pantin

Located to the left (west) of the main entrance to La Villette Park. The officious guards at the door will probably tell you that you can't go inside unless you're a registered student. Try to latch onto a friendly student or ask to see the information officer and explain (use theatrical gestures if your French is limited) that you just want to walk through the courtyard and public areas on the ground and lower levels. Make yourself sound important, exaggerate your desperation and persevere relentlessly. The place has some incredible features, and it's a joy to meander around the build-ings, especially if you're an enthusiast of contemporary architecture.

The Conservatory is an advanced teaching institute for music and dance. Its several publicly accessible auditoriums are also the site of day and evening concerts of classical and contemporary dance and ancient, classical, contemporary, jazz and improvised music.

Before trying to get inside, look around the enclave of buildings in the Conservatory complex from the outside. On avenue Jean Jaurès, you will see a moat-like stretch of pebbles and walkways in front of an alignment of four discrete building blocks. A broad, upward-slanting roof gives the facade a unifying, continuous line, and inset windows punctuate the walls. Around the corner, the temperate block design recurs, but farther down the side facing the park you see the full flair of Portzamparc's rich vocabulary and architectural ingenuity. Here again he has designed the whole as an assemblage of self-defined units with walkways

Portzamparc, Conservatoire Nationale Supérieure

throughout and an open plaza in the middle. Among the most striking images visible from the park are an asymmetrical, nearly windowless, truncated-cone structure; and a sweeping arch with a cutout hole in its middle suspended over a passageway.

The interior of the main building has a long central corridor that opens up to sunlit atriums and a sunken lounge area. Bright colors on sections of the ceiling or walls, shifts in materials, hollow openings and changes in dimension enliven the space. A commissioned artwork by Pierre BURAGLIO, *R. F.* (1991) adds another eye-catching feature. Located on the white tile wall of a stairway going down to a patio, its red and blue irregular geometric shapes have the presence of signage, albeit in an abstract, reductive language that is universal and personal. Another art project, installed in a café-meeting room off the entrance corridor, comprises panels derived from a collage of printed images by Yann de PORTZAMPARC (1991). Several more works (all procured under the 1%-for-art law) are located around the large theater where public performances take place. Hanging on the concrete wall outside the orchestra level on the left side is *Blue Note* (1991) by BURAGLIO. It consists of a rhythmic, strategically arranged sequence of four tiny blue squares (enameled sheetmetal) and one upside-down T-shape. Above a nearby doorway, *The Black Rider* (1991), an abstract, monochrome painting by Georges NOEL, reiterates the reductive orientation of the environment; and a pair of black-and-white paintings (Untitled, 1991) by Antonio SEMERARO (located on the floor below in a corridor near the patio) conveys a similar orientation.

Be sure to walk outside the main building into the inner courtyard. You will experience a wondrous maze of open space and closed structures, sunken areas and raised platforms, elevated walkways, balconies, suspended staircases, curves and angles. Vistas and spatial interplays keep emerging but the layout never seems chaotic or flamboyant. If you have the time, go to an upper plaza to see reverberations of Portzamparc's mode of developing spatial interplay. And don't miss walking all the way down the courtyard to note how the lower-level grass patio (the one adjacent to the theater) extends beyond, passes under a bridge, then becomes an exuberant, cloistered garden with trees, bushes and benches.

As is obvious, the Conservatory is a giant conglomerate of units. It is also a mega-institution encompassing 80 music and dance practice studios, orchestral stages, a multimedia library, 3 concert halls open to the public, offices, residential quarters, a gymnasium, restaurant, cafeteria, infirmary, audiovisual center and public meeting rooms. In addition to the art mentioned above, there are minimalist paintings by Aurélie NEMOURS, titled *Rythme du millimétre* and *Plan pyramidal III* (1991)—in the lobby of the small performance hall; 10 sculpture-tabourets designed by Bernar VENET—placed all around; and an installation, *La réserve du conservatoire* (1991) by Christian BOLTANSKI, that presents an extensive, fictive archive of Conservatory materials stored in cardboard boxes piled on metal stands with related photographs hanging on the walls. To see the latter work, which Boltanski chose to locate in four basement storage rooms, you must get a key from the building's caretaker (the *gardien*).

3 | Grande Halle

renovation: Bernard REICHEN and Philippe ROBERT, 1985
Parc de la Villette, 75019

Located at the main entrance on the far side of the fountain plaza.

This mammoth building, previously the cattle market, is a classic example of 19th-century glass-and-iron architecture (it was constructed in 1867). In its current incarnation, it is a multipurpose hall used for conventions, concerts, exhibitions, music and theater festivals, trade fairs and almost any other gathering requiring a big space. The renovation respected the original structure, creating a flexible multileveled interior that can be restructured and subdivided.

4 | Hot Brass

architect: Bernard TSCHUMI
Parc de la Villette
01-42-00-14-14

Located at the eastern edge of the park just beyond the Jardin des Equilibres (Equilibrium Garden).

This folly structure is used for nightly live performances of jazz, acid jazz, hip-hop, swing or Latin music. There is dancing to DJ selections until early morning hours.

5 | Claes Oldenburg and Coosje van Bruggen

La bicyclette ensevelie, 1990
Prairie du Cercle, Parc de la Villette

In *The Buried Bicycle*, parts—the handlebar with a bell, a tire and a peddle—are enlarged to enormous size and made to appear as if sunk in the ground. At first it is difficult to recog-

nize the painted steel and aluminum parts and to identify the conglomerate as a bicycle. But as you walk around the individual segments and turn your head on an angle, you can begin to see the object and enjoy the humor and absurdity of such a gargantuan, mundane sculpture. As evinced by the number of children usually hanging and climbing all over it, the *Bicycle* is a clever, appealing work of public art.

7 | Le Zénith

architects: Philippe CHAIX and
Jean-Paul MOREL, 1983
Parc de la Villette, 75019
01-42-08-60-00

Located at the far east side of the park just before the canal.

The city initially built this hall to fill a void until a definitive rock-concert facility could be constructed. It was meant to be a temporary structure but proved so popular and appealing that it's still in use and is now permanent. Not only does the design by Chaix and Morel work well for a music hall with unobstructed views, but it was inexpensive and fast to put together (12 months from drawing board to final nail). The building, which can seat 6,300, is a squarish shape with a metal framework and silvery polyester covering. The concrete mast at the entrance was once a silo containing fodder for animals in the former La Villette slaughterhouse. Now it is topped by an airplane, the logo for Le Zénith and, according to the architects, a symbol of "new ways of creating architecture . . . [the search for] an approach surpassing high-tech."

7 | La Géode

architect: Adrien FAINSILBER, 1985
Parc de la Villette, 75019
01-40-05-12-12
Tues–Sun, 10–7; closed Mon
admission: 57/44F (no reductions

Oldenburg and van Bruggen, *La Bicyclette ensevelie*

2–5 and Sat, Sun)
métro: Porte de la Villette

With its polished steel surface reflecting changing skies and the surrounding landscape, this colossal geodesic sphere bears witness to the universe as an ever-active environment shaped by nature and contemporary technology. The structure sits within a pool of water and marks the main entrance to the Center of Science and Industry. Its interior is an independent reinforced-concrete structure containing a movie theater featuring a vast, hemispherical screen suspended under the building's dome. The curving screen envelops spectators in an all-around sound-space, and films, projected by the Omnimax system, enhanced with holograms and lasers, offer spectacular images of the planet's natural beauty. Although you'll miss the cinematic experience, you can see some of the structural complexity of the building from inside the lobby.

Cité des Sciences et
8 de l'Industrie

architect: Adrien FAINSILBER, 1980–86
30 avenue Corentin Cariou, Parc de la Villette, 75019
01-36-68-29-30
Tues–Sat, 10–6; Sun, 10–5; closed Mon
admission: 50/35F
métro: Porte de la Villette

This high-tech tour de force is another of Paris's monumental edifices of late-20th-century vintage. It lays claim to be the world's largest science complex—not a museum but an interactive, discovery facility with a mission of making science accessible, exciting and culturally relevant. With its sophisticated glass-and-steel design, the building itself signifies advanced technological creativity.

The imposing volume that now forms the core of the Science Center is actually a space adapted from a cattle slaughter house and auction hall, begun and left unfinished in the 1960s. Taking this as his point of departure, the architect Adrien Fainsilber created a framework of granite-clad towers, steel trusses—exposed and painted cobalt blue—and glass sheathing—a continuous surface of transparent walls. Three bioclimatic greenhouses, shaped as cubic mega-towers, add verdant nature to the south facade (fronting the park) at the same time as they collect daylight and store solar energy for use throughout the interior. (On last inspection, the greenhouses were poor exemplars of science in action since two of them were empty and the third housed dead trees!) The building is also surrounded by multi-leveled walkways and water-filled moats with bridge crossings. These architectural features enhance the majestic aura of the design even as they promote awareness of the three dominant themes within the Science Center's program: water, vegetation and light.

In the interior, a high and seemingly boundless central atrium reiterates the monumental scale of the exterior. Activity abounds as visitors crowd onto the banks of escalators—the prominent image in the grand entrance hall—and try out the multitude of exhibits on the mezzanine or upper levels. The space is largely wide open, enclosed when and where desired by modular cells. Overhead, another example of architectural technology appears in the form of two rotating, Teflon-covered cupolas supported by suspension cables and set inside domes with robot-operated mirrors. The mechanism brings natural light into the atrium.

As is apparent in any section of the center, no one just watches or studies a display. There is a kind of contagious wild energy and excitement that affects visitors of all ages as they get hooked and become challenged by some scientific principle or technological device. (Anyone who has been to the Exploratorium in San Francisco will recognize the syndrome. Art museum professionals should take note.) Within the Science Center there are temporary and permanent exhibitions (Explora), a special discovery hall for children, a convention center, a multimedia library, restaurants, a planetarium, aquarium and movie theater. The center also operates three other outposts nearby in La Villette Park: La Géode, Argonaute (a fighter submarine containing an exhibit on submersibles) and Cinaxe (The Simulator—a cinema in motion having seats set on hydraulic jacks to effect the experience of a space flight, speed-car racing, etc.).

Maison de la Villette and Pavillon Paul Delouvrier

9

Parc de la Villette, 75019
Wed–Sun, 1–7; closed Mon–Tues
admission: 30/25F

Maison—located at the far northwest end of the park. Pavillon—located to the west of the Grande Halle.

These two exhibition spaces present temporary shows based on themes relating to world cultures, the city and society. Often these include sophisticated documentary photographs, and occasionally the subject directly treats contemporary art, architecture or design.

Pierre Buraglio

11

Cross, 1995
Eglise Paroissiale de Sainte-Claire, avenue Jean Jaurès (corner of boulevard Sérurier), 75019
métro: Porte de Pantin

Located between the church and the Holiday Inn.

Christian de Portzamparc, who restored and enlarged this modest parish church (he also designed the adjacent Holiday Inn), asked Buraglio, an artist whose minimalist work he favored, to create a cross for the exterior. The very tall, utterly unembellished gray cross fabricated by Buraglio marks the entrance to the church. Though the cross serves as a Christian symbol, here it also becomes an urban sign, a place marker in the midst of a renovated neighborhood. Moreover, Buraglio conceived the cross, not in terms of a crucifix laden with the body of Christ, but as a "monument to the birds." Related to this, he painted a small section at the very top as a setting appropriate for birds—a sky blue field with a few clouds. Perhaps it is why he also designed the ladder, which leans against the cross, with missing and oddly spaced rungs. This form is nonfunctional for people but perfect as a bird perch. In its extreme starkness, Buraglio's cross is a haunting, enigmatic

Buraglio, Cross

object. It even becomes surreal due to its location: seemingly attached to a Holiday Inn and alongside an unusual, bulbous charcoal-gray form (Portzamparc's extension to the old church).

Public Housing and Post-Office Complex

11

architect: Aldo ROSSI, 1991
avenue du Nouveau Conservatoire
and avenue Jean Jaurès, 75019
métro: Porte de Pantin.
Located behind the Conservatory.

Just when you think you've left folly behind as you walk away from Parc de la Villette, you see a quirky, cylindrical blue metal tower patterned by windows. It sits alone boxed into a corner space between two brick walls and wears a yellow band indicating the presence of a post office. Customer service facilities are actually down the side street, occupying shop space on the ground floor of a housing complex which, like the tower, was designed by the esteemed architect Aldo Rossi. Whereas the tower is an object of fantasy, the housing, with its precise alignments of repeating elements, conveys an impression of utter rationality. Embracing one of the trademark aspects of postmodernism, Rossi borrowed design features from the past. He took the buildings facing the Tuileries on rue de Rivoli as his source, duplicating their sidewalk arcades, continuous stone facades, dormer windows and zinc mansard roofs. The tower, too, has roots in Paris, recalling the decorative cupolas and elaborate rotundas of buildings along the grand Hausmannian boulevards. In Rossi's classical hands, however, the architectural source has been radically and satirically altered.

Louise Lawler

12

Birdcalls II, 1990
18–34 avenue Jean Jaurès, 75019
performs daily on the hour, 9–6
métro: Jean Jaurès
Located at the La Fayette traffic circle.

This public artwork is a three-minute sound piece placed under a corner passageway in front of a France Telecom building. The sounds are a succession of artists' names voiced by Lawler in imitation of birdcalls. They are directed to a plaque in the ground engraved with the names of the revered 20th-century artists who made Paris great (Matisse, Picasso, Braque, Brancusi, Duchamp . . .). Although the work cleverly pokes fun at fame and recognition within the art world, the street noise surrounding the site makes it impossible to hear the birdcalls and even more difficult to realize that names are being spoken. Moreover, as with many sound and video public art projects, the mechanics are often out of order.

Ben, Jean Le Gac, Marie Bourget and Jean-Max Albert

13

Plaza art project
corner of rue de Belleville and rue
Julien Lacroix
métro: Pyrenées, Belleville
Located in the Belleville neighborhood, close to the south end of La Villette.

Four artists created works for this site, thereby changing a vacant lot with two blind walls into a notable place in the neighborhood. Near the top of one wall, Ben (an artist associated with the Fluxus movement) has situated two sculptures of workmen: one sits on the roof edge looking down and the other stands on a scaffold holding up the bottom of a giant black painting that is being installed. The painting bears the

Ben, Le Gac, Bourget, Albert, plaza art project

handwritten inscription—"il faut se méfier des mots" (beware of words). The idea of hanging a framed painting outdoors as if it were a billboard, the substitution of a written message for a visual image in a painting and the use of a canvas to issue a warning about language are typical ploys in the satiric, idiosyncratic, paradoxical art of Ben.

Using a realist style, Jean Le Gac has created a very different sort of imagery on the second large wall, though it too is suffused with humor. The depiction centers on a kneeling, perplexed man who holds a piece of paper with a cross drawn on it. As in many of this artist's compositions, the man is a detective and the scene suggests a pivotal moment in a story of police intrigue. Newspaper clippings, painted behind the figure, form an enigmatic background. A plaque, placed at the bottom of the mural, serves as a pseudo-explanation: "Accustomed to the allusive

style of painting, the young detective understands that the message tells him to continue his pursuit on the rue Julien Lacroix."

For her contribution to the site, Marie Bourget has situated a cone-shaped metal structure in the far corner where two walls intersect. Though the cone image appears to extend from the white form on top all the way down to the ground, only the upper section is sculptural. The rest is painted on the walls. When light shines down from the top cone (a light fixture is enclosed inside) it increases the spatial illusion of the work by producing a luminous white volume in the angle of the walls.

By placing bands of white marble all around the site, Jean-Max Albert not only outlines the periphery but also defines and unifies the space. Although his line remains continuous because it embraces some obstacles (like a pillar and light pole) and passes behind others (like the utility box and telephone booth), it hardly contains the site within a rigid boxlike enclosure. On the contrary, it slants upward and downward on the two street sides, becoming an element of movement that makes the site appear like a lozenge rather than a rectangular shape.

Although each artist uses a different mode of creativity, all deal with some form of illusionism—correspondences between what is seen, known and actually present.

Bercy

Ministère de l'Economie et des Finances

1

 architects: Paul CHEMETOV and Borja HUIDOBRO, 1982–89
1 boulevard de Bercy, 75012
métro: Bercy

When President Mitterand decided to expand the Louvre Museum, the Finance Ministry had to move from its cherished offices in the Palais du Louvre. The creation of a new building to house several ministers, 4,700 civil servants, a multitude of meeting rooms, social spaces, a data-processing center, etc. was not an easy task—especially since the chosen waterfront site was not large enough for the structure to be placed in the classic way, parallel to the river. Taking an unusual approach, the architects turned the ministry perpendicular to the Seine with one end crossing over a bordering street (rue de Bercy) and the other bridging the highway along the quay and continuing out over the water, its end supported by river-based piers. Because of its extreme length, its titanic dimensions and its aquatic mooring, the building is popu-

larly referred to as the "steamboat."

Though eccentric, the design accommodated the spatial needs of the project and still manages not to look massive. The accentuation on length was a big factor in reducing the bulk, and this was exaggerated by design features on the long side of the building. These include the horizontal bands of windows in the upper section and the straight-edged aqueduct motif on the lower levels (with recessed walls of dark-toned windows replacing the voids). Unfortunately, the interior did not profit from original solutions. Instead, its design adheres to the inhuman convention of office alignments with endless corridors in between.

Palais Omnisports de Paris-Bercy

2

 architects: Michel ANDRAULT, Pierre PARAT, Aydin GUVAN, 1980–84
2 boulevard de Bercy, 75012
métro: Bercy

Seeking to defy the massive appearance and industrial harshness of concrete buildings, the architectural team for the indoor sports hall in Bercy designed a structure shaped like a truncated pyramid and covered it with grass. By lowering the playing area and seating into the ground, they further scaled down the exterior form. And by cutting into the slanted grass sides with mastabalike stairs, mirror-glass surfaces and a circumferential walkway, they divided the large mound into segments.

A steel framework on the roof—designed by the revered architectural engineer Jean PROUVE—provides a key structural component and an ingenious system for irrigating, seeding and cutting the grass, ensuring that it is always green. Indeed, the whole building is outfitted with complex technical equipment that can be moved all around the hall to accommodate 17,000 spectators

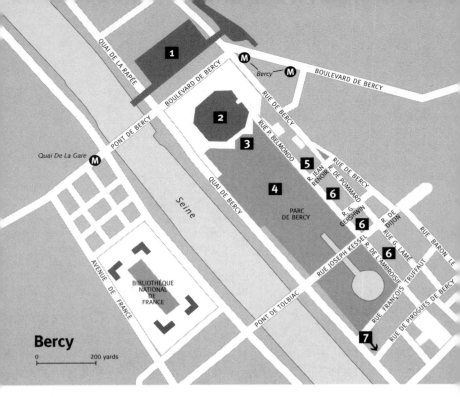

and 24 different kinds of sporting events, including swim meets. The building is also used for music performances from rock to opera.

3 | Gérard Singer

Canyoneaustrate, 1988
Parc de Bercy, 75012
métro: Bercy

The sculpture, *Canyonwaterstrata*, is part of a shallow pool connecting Palais Omnisports with Bercy Park. Its scalloped layers of molded concrete suggest strata. They form the sides of a deep canyon fed by water cascading gently down its steep slopes into narrow rivulets far below. You can walk along a serpentine path into the midst of the canyon environment.

4 | Parc de Bercy

architects: Bernard HUET, Marylène FERRAND, Jean-Pierre FEUGAS, Bernard LEROY
landscape architects: Ian LE CAISNE and Philippe RAQUIN, 1993–97
quai de Bercy, 75012
enclosed gardens, summer:
Mon–Fri, 8 am–9:30 pm, Sat–Sun, 8 am–9 pm. winter: daily, 8–5:30
metro: Bercy, Dugommier

Bercy Park is one of the largest of the more than 100 new garden-parks opened in Paris during recent years. It is a centerpiece of the redevelopment zone encompassing the previously nondescript, easternmost end of the city's Right Bank. Combining old formal aesthetics with people-friendly lawns (you can walk, sit and play sports on them) and a gardening-ecology center, Bercy Park has tried to accommodate the

Parc de Bercy

socio-cultural lifestyle of the 1990s. For serious horticulturists, Sunday putterers or anyone just wanting a place to relax and enjoy a quiet hour or two, this is a site to visit. City planners might also like to see how the designers have incorporated some of the old winding streets, cobblestone paths and rail tracks used to take wine and wine barrels from barges on the Seine to warehouses formerly located on the site.

The park is divided into three sections with wide paths providing perspective views from one end to another. If you enter from Palais Omnisports, you first come upon a vast expanse of grass. In contrast to the openness of this section, the next area is rigorously organized into a maze of square flower beds, each with a specific identity. You'll find a vegetable garden, orchard, rose garden, trellised vineyard, aromatic plants, bulb garden, labyrinth of yews and four kiosks (located at the cardinal points) denoting the four seasons and related colors. There are also three pavilions with handsome architectonic designs. A mound with an entrance cut in one side signifies water. A brick chimney stack in the midst of a brick-walled garden signifies fire. And a tight circle of white marble columns centered on a black pole topped with tiny weather vanes signifies air. An earth pavilion seems to be lacking, but perhaps the entire park is meant to take its place.

Whereas the middle section of the park has been designed as a French garden, the far section is a romantic, English-style garden. Its landscape of gently rolling hills and hardwood trees contains a canal, small lake, archaeological ruins and two Japanese-style footbridges that connect two sides of the park otherwise separated by a road. The public Gardening Center, housed in an old building formerly used to collect wine taxes, is also located here.

5 | La Maison du Cinéma

architect: Frank GEHRY, 1994

51 rue de Bercy, 75012

métro: Bercy or Dugommier

This dramatic building by the architect celebrated for his Guggenheim Museum in Bilbao, was designed to house the American Center. But financial and management problems within the organization mushroomed, and the center had to close in 1996. The building lay dormant for two years until the French government purchased it for use as a film center. When it opens at the end of the year 2000, it will be the new home of the celebrated Cinémathèque Française and Musée du Cinéma (relocated from their former location in the Palais de Chaillot) and a film library. By creating a high profile film center, France sought to advance the stature of a cultural industry considered a significant part of the country's heritage. It also fashioned a stellar command post for the impassioned, multitudinous population of French cineasts. Activities at the center will include historic and contemporary film showings, educational programs and international and documentary projects.

From the side facing the street, Gehry's building looks calm and classically Parisian. Like others in the neighborhood, it has orderly rows of windows, a rectangular shape and stone facing. When you move around to the sides facing the park, however, you see a more typical Gehry design, one that is free-form, exuberant and unconstrained by past conventions or context. The structure is a cacophony of oddly shaped, sharply angled, curvaceous, intersecting, overlapping, skewed parts centered on a steeply sloped, curving zinc roof that hangs over an entrance spilling out into a terrace café. In its bold, eccentric facade, the building expresses the kind of artistic freedom

and vanguard energy that was to have been characteristic of the activities and programs of the now defunct American Center.

Housing alongside
6 | Parc de Bercy

project head: Jean-Pierre BUFFI, 1989–96
architects: Franck HAMMOUTENE, 45–47 rue de Pommard (1994); Philippe CHAIX and Jean-Paul MOREL, 37–43 rue de Pommard (1993); Fernando MONTES, school, 33 rue de Pommard (1993); Yves LION, 4–5 rue Georges Gershwin (1994); Henri CIRIANI, 27 rue de l'Ambroisie (1994); Christian de PORTZAMPARC, 25 rue de l'Ambroisie (1994)
métro: Dugommier

Complementing the construction of Bercy Park and the development of a new neighborhood for the east end of Paris was the design of a prime alignment of housing bordering the long (north) side of the park. Not wanting to end up with either a hodgepodge or a barrier-like mass of humdrum, cookie-cutter facades, the city appointed a planning coordinator. He then established ground rules for the six architects selected to design the constituent buildings. The idea was to promote a modicum of order and unity while encouraging individual expression and diversity. As coordinator, Jean-Pierre Buffi determined that each apartment block would have a park and a street facade, a garden courtyard in between and side sections fronting cross streets—the latter ensuring easy neighborhood access to the park. Since a single architect would design a given sector comprising all frontages, there would be an unusual kind of wraparound unity as well as diversity within the outer street and park alignments. In addition, the roofs had to be made habitable with penthouses; the scale had to be reduced by adding balconies or verandas on every other floor; and unity was to be achieved through white stone facing on the park, gray on the cross streets and a common black-enameled steel railing—designed by Buffi—on all balconies and verandas.

Within the realm of city planning, the plan was an interesting experiment that did in fact produce varied designs (even each courtyard has a distinctive character) with unifying threads. The very choice of six different architects, instead of a single designer (or construction company/developer) is remarkable.

Centre Commercial
7 Bercy

architects: Renzo PIANO with Jean-François BLASSEL, 1987–90
place de l'Europe and quai de Bercy, Charenton-le-Pont
métro: Liberté

Located at one of the busiest traffic nodes on the border of Paris, where the boulevard Péripherique intersects the N4 highway.

Like most of Piano's work (he co-created Centre Pompidou), this mega-shopping center gives evidence of a highly original approach to design and love of high-tech architecture. The building is gargantuan, appearing all the more so because its form is one smooth, continuous curve of satinized stainless steel. Terms like "hypertrophic car bumper" and "huge zeppelin" have been used to describe it—not at all to the dismay of Piano who designed it "to attract the attention of cars speeding by." He even tilted the exterior tiles upward to maximize the surface sheen. (This meant putting an impermeable skin, supplied with its own drainage system, underneath!) Despite all the attention to technology, the building has not fared

well. In 1997 (and perhaps still), it had to be covered with fishnet to protect pedestrians and vehicles from falling steel tiles.

The framework, which is completely visible in the interior, is made of curved plywood resting on concrete supports. To the architect, it has the appearance of a wrecked ship's hull. But don't worry about the oddity of this metaphor for a public space—to wit a shopping center, since Piano has created a complementary image, a "haven of peace," in the form of a tree-planted "valley" situated in the central atrium.

Musée National des Arts d'Afrique et d'Océanie

293 avenue Dausmesnil, 75012
01-44-74-84-80 f: 01-43-43-27-53
Mon, Wed–Fri, 10–12 and
1:30–5:30; Sat–Sun, 12:30–6;
closed Tues
admission: 38/28F
métro: Porte Dorée

Located alongside the Bois de Vincennes at the edge of the city.

The museum's building, an Art Deco palace, dates from the Colonial Exhibition of 1931. In addition to its permanent collection, temporary exhibitions that span the centuries and many different art forms are ongoing. Some exhibitions feature contemporary work, either with an indigenous or vanguard character, by artists from African or Oceanic countries. At times, work by French artists bearing a connection to Africa or Oceania is also presented. For example, recent shows have highlighted paintings by Chéri Samba from Zaire; a joint project by Romuald Hazoumé and Hervé Di Rosa; and a wall in Marrakech by Annette Messager.

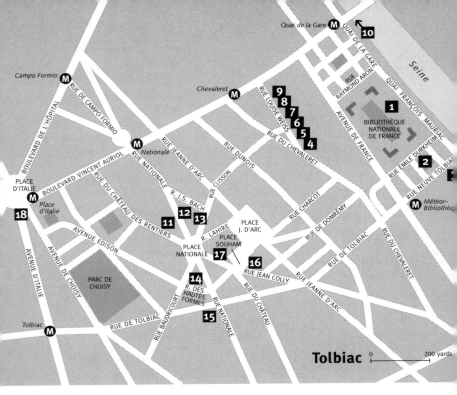

Tolbiac

Bibliothèque Nationale de France

1

architect: Dominique PERRAULT, 1996

11 quai François Mauriac (or quai de la Gare), 75706
01-53-79-59-59
Tues–Sat, 10–7; Sun, 12–6; closed Mon
métro: Bibliothèque, Quai de la Gare

Sometimes referred to as the TGB—Très Grande Bibliothèque (Very Big Library) —or the Bibliothèque Tolbiac, this building, which opened December 1996, replaced the former, long-revered, Bibliothèque Nationale on rue de Richelieu. The new library, located on a 17-acre site between the Seine and rail-road tracks of the Gare d'Austerlitz (now underground), provides state-of-the-art services and expanded space, but its design has been very controversial.

The architect, Dominique Perrault, sought to give the library a visual presence within the Paris skyline and simultaneously to avoid making it appear too massive. He therefore created a design in which four L-shaped towers ("open books"), sheathed in glass, stand at the corners of a sunken courtyard and in the midst of a monumental esplanade. To reach the towers and courtyard—or even the esplanade—you first have to climb steep steps set into surrounding embankment walls. It's like mounting the stairs of a Greek or Mayan temple, though devoid of any spiritual or historical aura. The steps and esplanade—which doubles as a terrace—are covered in an odd kind of wood having an unusual whitish tone. The wood is actually an exotic variety but there's nothing exotic about the bleak, austere environment confronting you. The forked-pole lights, similar to those on highways, don't help the ambience, and the encaged trees all along the perimeter establish a new standard for unnatural severity. (Supposedly the cages are meant to control the size and shape of the trees so they don't interfere with the exactingly geometric appearance of the site.)

From the vantage point of the esplanade, you can see the library's design more fully. The center space, conceived as an enormous monastic courtyard, is planted with a forest of ginkgo trees. Although these are visible from the surrounding reading rooms, the courtyard is totally inaccessible. Again, nature is enclosed and made into a specimen to be looked at from afar. The towers also present an image of hermetic existence. Originally, Perrault's design sought to emphasize the transparency and reflectiveness of the glass. But this idea met with harsh criticism because of potential sun damage to the books. As a result, protective walls of wooden shutters were installed inside the windows.

After you've climbed up to the esplanade, you must take an escalator down to reach the entrance door. There are two symmetrically placed escalators, one on each of the short sides of the rectangular courtyard, but often only one is in use. Surprisingly, the interior has a very different character from the exterior. Though still restrained, it seems almost lavish by comparison. Fine wood paneling, red carpets and soft lighting make the humanly scaled spaces comfortable and refined. The public area contains an auditorium, lecture hall, six lecture rooms, two exhibition areas, a restaurant, cafeterias, shops, a bank, post office and other amenities—in addition to the books and reading rooms. Unlike the previous library, which was a research center for scholars, off-limits to the general public, the new library accommodates a broader patron base in its policies and services. However, the two groups have separate work areas: scholars use the lower level (rez-de-jardin), furnished with 2,000 places; and others use the discipline-based rooms on the upper level (haut-de-jardin) containing 1,600 places. An encyclopedic selection of books is openly accessible, and a periodical reading room and audiovisual center are also available. Interestingly, two-thirds of the 12 million books stored in the library are housed on the two lower levels. The four towers only have books on the top 11 floors, the lower seven being occupied by offices.

The presentation of historically rich exhibitions, which sometimes show art from the modern and contemporary period, was an appealing part of the old library's program and that practice has continued in the new BNF. For example, Portraits, singulier pluriel (1997), featured telltale images of ordinary people from the current era by 11 contemporary photographers; and Artists' Books, 1960–80 (1998), had marvelous, unique examples of an increasingly important contemporary art form. The Galerie d'Exposition is open Tues–Sat, 10–7; Sun, 12–6; closed Mon. Admission: 35/24F.

Using the 1%-for-art provision associated with public construction, the library became the beneficiary of four commissions now located in the reading rooms. Jean-Pierre BERTRAND created a work about rhythm; Claude VIALLAT made a painting with color and movement as its focus; Gérard GAROUSTE used the tree of knowledge as the theme of his three-part composition with forged-iron reliefs, titled Les indiennes; and Martial RAYSSE developed an allegory of reading, writing and speaking in his painting.

In addition, commissions awarded to

Roy LICHTENSTEIN and Louise BOUR-GEOIS produced monumental works for the entrance lobby. *Les nymphéas* (*Water Lilies*), 1996, by Lichtenstein (located in the east lobby) is a large tapestry created in the comic-book mode the artist developed as his signature. Using repetitive bold black strokes and dots plus flat areas of blue, yellow, marbled green and a few red accents, Lichtenstein depicts the lilies floating in water. Though the water-lily subject pays homage to the French painter Claude Monet, the Lichtenstein version has none of the seductive, soft tones and lush sensibility of its impressionist antecedent. Dreamy romanticism has given way to a style associated with simple, direct, rapid communication and vibrant expression.

In *Toi et moi* (*You and Me*), 1997, the talented French-born American sculptor Louise BOURGEOIS, has produced a dazzling relief of cast and polished aluminum, shined to a mirror finish. It takes full command of the rear corner of the west lobby. Extending out from a wall in a hemispheric shape composed of convex, reflective scallops, the sculpture adds an expressive potency to the otherwise subdued, restrained lobby. Leave it to this nonagenarian to create a work overflowing with seductive forms and sensuous surfaces for a place that is the symbol of high intellectualism and propriety.

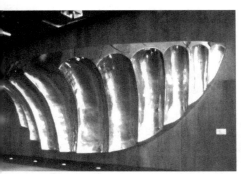
Bourgeois, *Toi et moi*

Paris Rive Gauche Development Plan

The new National Library of France is at the center of and integrated into "Paris Left Bank"—a major urban rejuvenation effort encompassing the surrounding Tolbiac-Masséna-Austerlitz districts. Previously the neighborhood was covered with streams of railroad tracks and full of abandoned factories. Now the area immediately adjacent to the library alone includes or will soon include: numerous large-scale apartment and office buildings, businesses, artist studios, schools, a university campus, a church, film theaters, shops, two public gardens, open spaces (pedestrians only), a huge métro-RER complex (météor), a pedestrian promenade along the river, a new bridge and foot-bridge across the Seine, and "Avenue de France"—a grand roadway, replete with a tree-lined walkway as its center spine, situated above the railroad tracks that have been relocated underground.

A second comprehensive development is also taking place around the Grands Moulins de Paris (the giant old mills) in the Masséna neighborhood (located between rue de Tolbiac and boulevard Masséna). Christian de PORTZAMPARC is the planning coordinator here. This part of the program was stalled for several years because of public outcries for the need for more green spaces and for a halt in the destruction of old buildings. The current statement of intent speaks of a move away from monolithic architecture toward the creation of a diversity and plurality of spaces, forms, functions and buildings. (The southwest region of these very districts still contains 28—some now empty—of the most horrific, assembly-line block towers and cement plazas built for social housing in the

1960s–70s.) The aim is to create neighborhoods within neighborhoods, public squares and green spaces and, as is traditional in Paris, to integrate shops and public services with housing.

Considering all the construction and development activities in the Paris Rive Gauche projects on one side of the Seine plus those in Bercy on the other side, the east end of Paris will have a totally new look and character in the 21st century. It's quite amazing to see spanking new districts in a classic old city like Paris and to observe the results of French-style urban planning. Try to save time to wander around the streets and courtyards and plan to people-watch in a café.

2 | Housing

architect: Francis SOLER, 1997
rue Emile Durkheim, 75013
métro (météor): Bibliothèque
Located across the street from the east side of the National Library.

Soler defied one of the sacrosanct tenets of modernism in this apartment building: he fashioned a decorative facade. But unlike previous modes of decor, typically sculptural and architectonic, he enveloped the entire building in glass screened with images from the 16th-century frescoes by Guilio Romano in the Palazzo del Te in Mantua. The imagery adds color and animation to the structure's stark geometric shape and industrial materials. On the one hand, the screened depictions set up a curious dialogue with the library—a depository of historical and cultural products. On the other, they suggest an ironic infiltration of Warhol's mass-production aesthetic into the domain of French architecture.

3 | Le Frigo

91 quai Panhard-Levasor, 75013
métro: Bibliothèque

"Le Frigo" was a community of 250 artists living in a complex of three buildings, originally constructed in 1919 as refrigerated warehouses and ice factories. Beginning around 1986, years before "Paris Rive Gauche" set up shop, the artists had established live-work space in the abandoned structures. They occupied less than one-third of the total square footage and sought to remain in residence there. But the development plan called for the destruction of one building and renovation of the other two so they would be better integrated with the new environment. The artists appealed their case and even paid rent to SNCF (the national railroad, owners of the property). Their efforts, which included public demonstrations and considerable press coverage, were to no avail. The hopelessness of their situation increased when a fire destroyed the building's roof in September 1997.

Scène Est

20–30 rue Louise Weiss, 75013
métro: Chevaleret
Located between boulevard Vincent Auriol and rue du Chevaleret in the area behind the new library on the other side of avenue de France. The galleries form a row of six storefronts along the covered walkway on the ground floor of large office buildings.

Despite all the planning and construction of new buildings and neighborhoods, it isn't easy to create communities or to add flavor and liveliness. In the case of the Tolbiac district—in particular a section where offices and bureaucrats abound—the head honchos wanted to add prestige and a bit of pizzazz to the area. To accomplish this, they enticed art galleries to move in by offering them low rent and appealing deals. Some had previously operated at other locations in Paris or in other cities, and some were starting from scratch. All are run by adventurous directors and tend to concentrate on emerging and highly unconventional artists. They also show work that is little known in France by young artists who are at the forefront of attention elsewhere. In contrast to the usual autonomy of art galleries, the Louise Weiss group works collaboratively to coordinate aspects of their programs and to organize openings as one multifaceted joint event. A spirit of comradery—not often found in the art world—is discernible. Of course these galleries are a considerable distance from the dominant art zones in Paris and need to make the East Scene an art phenomenon if they are to succeed. Time will tell, but for now be sure to include the six galleries on rue Louise Weiss if you really want to see what's happening in contemporary art in France. (The grand inauguration was in the spring of 1997.)

4 | Galerie Jennifer Flay

20 rue Louise Weiss, 75013
01-44-06-73-60 f: 01-44-06-73-66
Tues–Sat, 11–7; closed Mon
métro: Chevaleret

With display space in three rooms on two levels, the gallery has the opportunity to show several different projects of a single artist, or several artists at once. In its previous location in the Marais district, Galerie Jennifer Flay earned a reputation as a showplace for exciting work by emerging artists. The exhibitions presented thus far in Tolbiac suggest that the always intriguing if not controversial selection of art and artists will continue. Artists: Richard Billingham, Claude Closky, Melanie Counsell, John Currin, Willie Doherty,

Michel François, Dominique Gonzalez-Foerster, Felix Gonzalez-Torres, Ann Veronica Janssens, Sean Landers, Liz Larner, Zoe Leonard, Christian Marclay, Matthew McCaslin, Lisa Milroy, Cathy de Monchaux, Rei Naito, Marylène Negro, Jean-Jacques Rullier, Mariella Simoni, Georges Toby Stoll, Felice Varini, Xavier Veilhan.

5 | Galerie Almine Rech

24 rue Louise Weiss, 75013
01-45-83-71-90 f: 01-45-70-91-30
Tues–Sat, 11–7; closed Mon
métro: Chevaleret

While showing a variety of art styles and media, the gallery has a tendency to favor photographic work. It's not just mild-mannered imagery taken with a camera, however: it's challenging subjects and unconventional ways of treating or displaying images and prints. Artists: Merry Alpern, Rebecca Bournigault, Willie Cole, Liam Gillick, Fabrice Hybert, Johannes Kahrs, Ugo Rondinone, Sam Samore, Bojan Sarcevic, Annelies Strba, Jock Sturges.

Galerie
6 | Praz–Delavallade

28 rue Louise Weiss, 75013
01-45-86-20-00 f: 01-45-86-20-10
Tues–Sat, 2–7; closed Mon
métro: Chevaleret

The work shown here often has a satiric or social commentary edge, and the gallery has a penchant for Americans. Artists: Alain Balzac, Roderick Buchanan, Andrea Busto, Marc Couturier, Meg Cranston, Bruno Delavallade, Maria Hahnenkamp, Matthias Herrmann, Jim Isermann, Cameron Jamie, Erika Rothenberg, Yvan Salomone, Jim Shaw, Jeffrey Vallance, Erwin Wurm.

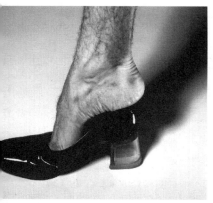

Matthias Herrmann, Untitled, 1998 (Galerie Praz–Delavallade)

Galerie
7 | Emmanuel Perrotin

30 rue Louise Weiss, 75013
01-42-16-79-79 f: 01-42-16-79-74
Tues–Fri, 2–7; Sat, 11–7;
closed Mon
métro: Chevaleret

The artists here span many different cultural perspectives and often the work has a decorative or mass culture flair. Artists: Maurizio Cattelan, Lucky De Bellevue, Diadji Diop, Eric Duykaerts, Efiaimbelo, Noritoshi Hirakawa, Henrik Plenge Jakobsen & Jes Brinch, Guy Limone, Mariele Neudecker, Adrien Qezaris, Alain Séchas.

8 | Air de Paris

32 rue Louise Weiss, 75013
01-44-23-02-77 f: 01-53-61-22-84
Tues–Sat, 2–7; closed Mon
métro: Chevaleret

In addition to its regular exhibition program, Air de Paris hosts a room with continuously changing shows, a free-access video library and the Silver Space—a tiny gallery within the gallery that presents surprises, photographs, erotica and fetishes. Artists: Christophe Berdaguer, Cindy Bernard, Henry Bond, Piort Dluzniewski, Liam Gillick, Joseph Grigely, Svetlana Neger & Plamen Dejanov, Carsten Höller, Pierre Joseph, Stephane Magnin, Monica Majoli, Paul McCarthy, Marie Eve Mestre, Philippe Parreno, Marie Pejus, Taddeus Strode, Elise Tak, Lily van der Stokker, Jan van Oost, Jean-Luc Verna.

9 | Art : Concept

34 rue Louise Weiss, 75013
01-53-60-90-30 f: 01-53-60-90-31
Tues–Fri, 2–7; Sat, 11–7
closed Mon
métro: Chevaleret

Art:Concept often has eccentric thematic exhibitions that include artists not in the gallery roster. The gallery has its roots in Nice and a history of giving artists their first exhibitions or first showings in France. Artists: Biefer/Zgraggen, Jean-Luc Blanc, Michel Blazy, Denis Castellas, Jeremy Deller, Richard Fauguet, Douglas Kolk, Stéphane Magnin, Max Mohr, Philippe Perrot, Roman Signer, Niek van de Steeg, David Zérah.

10 | Valerio Adami

Le matin and Le soir, 1985–87
Gare Austerlitz
métro: Gare Austerlitz

Located in the central lobby (also called the departure hall) of the train station.

These two murals depict a voyage to Persia with mythic heroes. In Le matin (Morning), a figure wearing shorts and sandals rests in a sunrise landscape and a bird flies near as if to awaken him. In Le soir (Evening), the fallen head of Medusa, other figures, a horse and train are set in a landscape. Appropriately, both paintings deal with the theme of departure and travel. Though Adami—an artist who emerged as a leading painter in France during the 1970s—works in a figurative, narrative mode, he delineates images abstractly using flat planes of bright, intense color and black outlines.

11 Artist studios, offices, and audiovisual center

 architect: Christian de PORTZAM-
PARC
121 rue Nationale (at place
Nationale), 75013
métro: Nationale

This striking building is composed of two huge cubes placed atop one another at a skewed angle and a base wrapping around the central core. To add to the oddities of the form, the top cube is white, the bottom is a mustard tone, and each side of both cubes has a different window pattern or no windows at all. In fact, function has played a big part in determining the design and window pattern. The ground floor has audiovisual workshops and an auditorium; the lower cube—with transparent and opaque, single frame or strip windows—contains offices; and the top cube—with a window wall on the north side and a shell of black steel on the south—accommodates nine duplex studios for artists.

12 Housing

 architect: Georges PENCREAC'H
rue Nationale, 75013
métro: Nationale

Located across the street from the Portzamparc building.

This eye-catching white-tiled structure exemplifies high-style modernism. Features like the shift from verticality to horizontality, the combination of planar elements with recessed voids, the grayish brick wall with porthole windows and the sleek rounded corner all serve to embolden the building without giving it a decorative appearance. By carefully determining the form, scale and orientation of each constituent element, Pencréac'h created a precisely balanced, refined facade. This building

is actually part of a housing complex that covers much of the area behind and around the corner.

13 Public Housing Complex

architect: Georges PENCREAC'H,
1990–94
66–74 rue Clisson and 1–5 rue
Jean Sebastien Bach, 75013
métro: Nationale

Several apartment buildings, each different but related, and a spacious garden plaza in the middle constitute this ample residential cluster. Like the Pencréac'h design around the corner on rue Nationale, the structures have angled, projecting and recessed balconies as well as windows articulating the surface with circular, horizontal and vertical forms. Because all the elements are judiciously arranged, the diversity does not create a visual onslaught. This is particularly true of the white, red and gray facings demarcating the various sections of the whole complex. As urban housing—especially public housing—this is an attractive alternative to the more typical block structures shaped by a mass-mentality aesthetic.

A grandiose tile mural on the street facade at the corner of rue Clisson and rue J. S. Bach, adds a bit of pictorial wit to the building and a focal point for the whole neighborhood. It is a sparse composition with only a few blue and green elements on a vast white field. The image has the semblance of enlarged brushstrokes or giant plant leaves. But when read with reference to a vertical strip of windows at the bottom, it takes the shape of an imposing portal leading into a citadel or castle. Perhaps its grand scale is an intentional bit of irony since the painted "gateway" is exaggerated and conspicuous while the actual entryway into the complex is an unassuming space between two walls gated by a common metal fence.

(Be sure to look at the overtly humorous and figurative murals on rue Clisson, across the street from the Pencréac'h housing.)

14 Public Housing

 architects: Christian de PORTZAM-PARC with Georgia BENAMO, 1979
rue des Hautes-Formes, 75013
métro: Nationale

Initially, the city planned to construct two tower blocks for public housing on this site. The architects, however, challenged the inhumanity of monotonous, assembly-line buildings, proposing instead a conglomerate of eight individualized structures (209 units) set around a modest courtyard. Although only a small urban redevelopment project, the housing ensemble gave preeminence to the postmodern generation in France, causing a revitalization in architectural design on a scale not seen since pre–World War II days

From the street, the dramatic half-circle and rectangle cut into the white facades and inset with bricks betray a blatant lack of conformity to a regularized, conventional design. More egregious deviations occur on the buildings turned toward the inner courtyard. They are different heights and odd shapes; spaces between the structures and juxtapositions are eccentric; windows are various sizes and diverse designs; flat surfaces are punctured with voids and recessed elements; and isolated arches and lintels hang in the air high above passageways. The rhythmic play of elements cuts the scale even as it animates the environment. These are not fancy structures and the courtyard is quite small. Nevertheless, the spatial refinements and people-orientation make them very appealing and distinctive.

15 Médiathèque Jean-Pierre Melville

 architects: Daniel and Patrick RUBIN—Canal, 1989
93 rue de Tolbiac, 75013
métro: Tolbiac, Nationale

From the exterior, the curved glass wall of the front facade of this multimedia library is striking. It's like a giant shopwindow allowing passersby to see that this public institution doesn't have the pompous, intimidating aura of a traditional French library. The reading area is a comfortable, open space, and even the five floors in the back section are totally unenclosed. It is clearly apparent that visitors have free access to a range of audiovisual equipment and the collection stacks. A white spiral staircase enlivens the interior with a sculptural element that is functional and yet symbolic of the spinning form of tapes and films.

Complementing the glass wall on the front is a colossal picture frame on the side wall (rue Nationale) containing a semitransparent photo. On the outside, it signifies high-tech and new media. On the inside, it provides subdued lighting within the viewing rooms. It is telling that the city decided to built this free, multimedia library—the first of its kind in Paris—in the midst of a multiethnic neighborhood. It instantly became popular and has been a major cultural resource for the community.

16 Housing

 architects: ARCHITECTURE STUDIO 1985–87
106 rue du Château des Rentiers, 75013
métro: Nationale, Tolbiac

Located at the corner of rue Jean Colly at place Souham

This 25-unit public-housing building unabashedly displays a raw industrial aesthetic and vanguard creativity. In addition, it stands as a kind of proto-type for construction on a "leftover," difficult site. The facade on one side is sheathed in gray tile with a white grid pattern. Recessed windows disappear within the grid. A second facade angles back sharply from the corner, where an open structural frame denotes the entrance. This frame is actually part of an imaginative crane the architects had

Architecture Studio, rue du Château des Rentiers

to develop to construct the building, since the narrow, wedge-shaped plot wouldn't accommodate an ordinary crane. Not only did the architects leave the crane as part of the building but they conspicuously exposed it at both the ground and roof levels as a focal design element. They draw further

attention to the building by transform-ing the entire left facade into a tiled street-métro-bus map showing the exact location of the building in relation to the surrounding area. The mural is so captivating, with white diagonal lines crisscrossing in all directions, that you hardly see the orderly rows of windows immersed within.

17 | Housing for the Elderly

 architect: Christian de PORTZAM-PARC, 1984
120 rue du Château des Rentiers, 75013
métro: Nationale, Tolbiac

This building sits between two mam-moth apartment buildings of the type created during the 1960s–70s. Portzamparc establishes correspon-dences with them by echoing in reverse the curve of one and creating a tall box-like void next to the other in homage to its height. More important, he counters their block structure by designing a building of modest size and human scale with individualized features. Indeed, the form he has developed—one curving segment extending out of another—and his use of diversely sized windows contrast sharply with the repetitive, inexpressive facades on either side.

18 | Grand Ecran

 architects: Kenzo TANGE with Michel MACARY and Xavier MENU, 1991
30 place d'Italie, 75013
métro: Place d'Italie

From a distance, the strange tower on this building attracts attention and it becomes even more curious from close-up. Its lower part is a glass-enclosed ele-vator shaft connecting walkways (also enclosed in glass) to an office building.

The upper part becomes an open cube continuing the steel framework from below but having additional beams extend in all directions. These beams, suspended in space by cables, are accompanied by floating glass boxes containing flaglike panels. Although you might expect the main building to be equally extreme in design and constructed of industrial materials, it is a large stone-covered structure with window-grid facades. On place d'Italie, however, a vast area of the curved front wall is covered with glass—the Grand Ecran (Big Screen) for which the building is named. Appropriately, two movie theaters lie just inside. In addition, there is a multipurpose auditorium, hotel, offices, garden and shopping center.

Tange, Grand Ecran

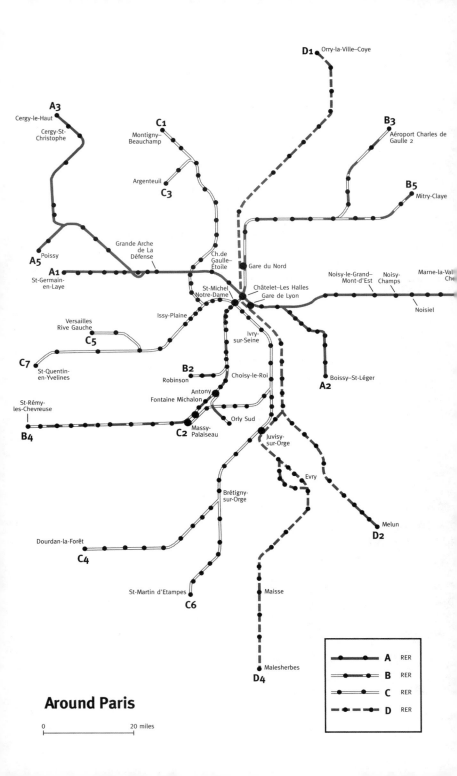

D1 Orry-la-Ville–Coye

A3 Cergy-le-Haut
Cergy-St-Christophe

C1 Montigny-Beauchamp

B3 Aéroport Charles de Gaulle 2

Argenteuil
C3

B5 Mitry-Claye

Poissy
A5

Grande Arche de La Défense

Ch.de Gaulle–Étoile

Gare du Nord

A1 St-Germain-en-Laye

St-Michel Notre-Dame

Châtelet–Les Halles

Noisy-le-Grand–Mont-d'Est

Noisy-Champs

Marne-la-Val Che

Issy-Plaine

Gare de Lyon

Noisiel

Ivry-sur-Seine

Versailles Rive Gauche
C5

C7 St-Quentin-en-Yvelines

B2 Robinson

Choisy-le-Roi

Boissy–St-Léger
A2

St-Rémy-les-Chevreuse

Antony
Fontaine Michalon

Orly Sud

B4

C2 Massy-Palaiseau

Juvisy-sur-Orge

Evry

Brétigny-sur-Orge

Melun
D2

Dourdan-la-Forêt

C4

St-Martin d'Etampes
C6

Maisse

Malesherbes
D4

Around Paris

0   20 miles

A RER
B RER
C RER
D RER

day trips from paris

Marne-La-Vallée

Marne-la-Vallée is one of the five *villes nouvelles* (new towns) developed on the outskirts of Paris as part of a decentralization effort begun in the 1960s. Transformation of the site from a rural area with many small villages and a few old châteaux into a string of 26 municipalities has advanced rapidly since 1972. Located to the east of Paris, the region is well served by the A4 line of the RER, the TGV from Charles de Gaulle airport and the A4 highway. It also lies along the Paris-Nancy-Strasbourg-Reims corridor.

Although only 20–45 min. from Paris, the Marne-la-Vallée satellite was structured as an autonomous, urbanized zone, itself composed of various differentiated centers. The master program formulated a mixture of residential, commercial and industrial developments in order to establish heterogeneity and to prevent the growth of a massive suburbia populated by commuters living in bedroom communities. Indeed, Marne-la-Vallée is the home to many corporate headquarters, a university campus, a pioneering art center, EuroDisney and much more.

Here, as in other new towns, the impetus for experimentation was strong. This resulted in the participation of some prominent, international architects and the creation of challenging, innovative projects. The area is filled with new buildings, landscaped terrains, recreational parks, business and community centers, neighborhood plazas and shopping malls. Predictably, the range of design prowess extends from lackluster to trendy, to adventurous, to bedazzling. If you're not really interested, but maybe just a little curious, you can readily get a taste by walking around one of the town centers and taking a ride on a local bus going through the area from center to center.

Mont-d'Est

Noisy-le-Grand/Mont-Est is the most urbanized of the town centers within the Marne-la-Vallée region. Its many office buildings and corporate headquarters make it an axis for business activity and development.

Palacio d'Abraxas

 Architect: Ricardo BOFILL, 1979–83
boulevard du Mont d'Est at
rue du Centre
RER: A4, Noisy-le-Grand/Mont d'Est

When you exit from the train you will be inside of a multileveled, American-style shopping mall (*Les Arcades*). Walk down the main axis toward the huge Carrefour store and continue past the adjacent parking garage. Ahead to your left is *Palacio d'Abraxas*.

Bofill built this enormous public housing project at the same time as *Les Echelles du Baroque* in Paris. Although they both display his penchant for constructing monumental buildings with facades in pseudo-historical styles, each has a distinctive ambience and appearance. If you like architecture with theatrical panache and an egregiously surreal, baroque flavor, this is a site not to be missed. Even if you prefer something more refined, a visit here will reveal a venturesome challenge to many of the ills of generic public housing.

The project contains 600 units spread among various structures (some 19 stories high) arranged as an enclosed community. First impression from outside is of brutality and monumentality, largely a response to the bleak cast concrete and the overwhelming scale of the buildings. The starkness and incongruity of the housing in its location exaggerate this response. On one side the complex is tightly backed up against neighboring business, office and parking structures, and on the other it appears like an island in the midst of scruffy, undeveloped land with a boulevard passing by. The buildings invoke Wall Street, but here you are in an environment just beginning to be urbanized, where new buildings are modernistic not fortress-like with classical columns, cornices and the like. The *Palace*'s architecture—an intimidating mode associated with banks, corporate empires, courts and government edifices—seems out of place, particularly since this is housing.

Of course, these oddities are all part of Bofill's postmodern strategy. He even declares this up front by titling the complex *Palace of Abraxas* in honor of the magician who invented the nonsense expression "abracadabra." Looking closely at the buildings, it's not long before you realize the design is completely based on artful illusions, sleight of hand, camouflage, befuddlement, disorientation and fantasy. Pilasters with "negative" segments in midstream, six-story-high inhabited entablatures with windows, mix-and-match borrowings from diverse historical styles and periods, street lamps hidden inside pseudo-capitals atop columnlike voids, immense doorways, gargantuan fluted columns encasing elevators, a courtyard forest with trees carefully aligned in rows, upside-down and phantom pediments, and the prefabrication of faux-marble facade parts out of concrete are but a few of the disjunctive, idiosyncratic features.

Three architectural entities shape the interior space and character of the overall project. The largest is the U-shaped *Palace*, a perimeter structure divided into numerous subsections each with its own entry and circulation system. Unlike most mass housing, and contrary to the exterior impression, here this layout and the creation of unit clusters configured around a common, nearly private hallway, deflates the aura of aggregate living.

Extending out from the *Palace* is the *Theater*—a grand, semicircular building easily identified by a ring of fluted, glazed columns, nine stories high. (They double as bay windows on the inside.) A grass amphitheater occupies the center, providing a serene, sequestered, open space. Again, the design aims to provide a deluxe public space and to counter the actuality of saturated density in the population within the complex.

The third architectural entity is a grand, cubic Arch located as a kind of centerpiece between the Palace and Theater. Sheathed in terra cotta and impressively tall, it recalls historic triumphal arch structures, except that this one is fully habitable. Like all the buildings in the complex, it has a rooftop terrace. Unfortunately the cypress trees that were to have landscaped the roofs have not survived well, but residents still enjoy the space, especially on Sundays. In fact, residents give the housing high marks overall. They particularly like the fact that apartments come in many different layouts, contrary to the conformity of most public housing and more like customized construction. The duplex form of many units and their general spaciousness are also very appealing. Interestingly, residential satisfaction is at odds with the comments of critics who have voiced great hostility to the complex, largely due to scale and density issues.

Pavé-Neuf

Les Arènes de Picasso

 architect: Manolo NUNEZ, 1980–84
place Pablo Picasso
RER: A4, Noisy-le Grand/Mont d'Est
This housing complex is a short walk from the Bofill complex. Take rue du Centre back toward the center of town, turn left on boulevard du Levant, then

right into allée Pablo Neruda—the first entrance into the expansive housing sector just ahead. Pass by place Georges Pompidou and go down the tree-lined pedestrian street (mail Victor Jarra) until you reach place Pablo Picasso.

Picasso's Arenas is a parody of a roman-tic-classical design by Etienne-Louis Boullée from the late-18th century. Borrowing from his predecessor, Nuñez creates a flat-surfaced, geometric shape of megalomaniac scale, decorated with repetitive, eclectic features. As you approach the building, its grandiose cir-cular wall looms large. The eccentricity of its size and shape is exaggerated by the unusual overlay of concrete, pat-terned by a grid of cutout circles and squares with crossed mullions adding another grid behind. The panoply of motifs covering an undersurface of win-dows proliferates when you cross into the central courtyard, faced on all sides by buildings of differing heights. Extending buttress "legs" with an Art Deco flavor create an encircling arcade, and a second megadisk structure, locat-ed opposite the first, exaggerates the geometric, repetitive character of the architecture. But Nuñez adds variation to repetition by using a different pattern design on each level of the facades. Like Bofill, he sought to break with the dull-ness of modernist block housing while retaining the advantages of mass-production construction.

Nuñez, *Les Arènes de Picasso*

Noisy-Champy

Housing

architect: Henri CIRIANI, 1977–80
allée de la Noiseraie
RER: A4, Noisy-Champs

Take the ramp walkway leading south from the RER station in the direction of buildings with a pronounced red-and-white grid facade. It's off the rue de la Butte Verte and the promenade Michel Simon.

Ciriani's housing complex is a remark-ably nonregimented ensemble of 300 apartment units. Without taking on the typically boring, garden-apartment aura or succumbing to the institutional, mass-production aesthetic, his low-bud-get housing presents a humanistic alter-native for high-density living. The archi-tecture, with its notable variations, is visually extraordinary. Each section is distinctive, with design and pragmatic features accommodating individual needs and tastes. Like Le Corbusier's apartment villas, which serve as a model for the basic concept applied here, the buildings are constructed in concrete, albeit with a light-toned, softly pat-terned surface. Most appealing is the arrangement of the apartments within a compact space. Situated on either side of a pedestrian path, the stepped-back architecture gives the units an open-air character. Hanging vines bring nature into the environment and enliven the facades. On the one hand, the front ter-races produced by this design also give residents a leisure place with privacy. On the other, they, and the close link between the public path and housing, contribute to social interactions and a sense of community. In contrast to much of the social housing within the new towns, this complex is in excellent condition, devoid of disturbing signs of age and wear-and-tear. Be sure to make time to see this complex if you are interested in multiunit, urban housing.

Cité Descartes

Cité Descartes was developed as a Parc Scientifique—a science and technology center. In less than a decade, it has earned stature within high-tech and computer circles for its advanced teaching and research facilities.

Ecole Supérieure d'Ingénieurs en Electronique et Electrotechnique (ESIEE)

 architect: Dominique PERRAULT, 1984–87
2 avenue Blaise Pascal, Université de Marne-la-Vallée
RER: A4, Noisy-Champs

From the RER station, go east alongside the tracks on boulevard Newton, turn right at the first main road, avenue Ampère.

As you proceed down avenue Ampère, you will begin to see an expansive, white aluminum plane sloping up to the right and stretching off into the distance. By any definition, this 1,000-foot-long futuristic-looking structure is enormous. And yet, quite amazingly, its size does not overwhelm people or the surrounding nature, largely because the slanting, luminous exterior diminishes the intensity of its massiveness. As you walk along the front, a staccato rhythm of voids and cuts (air vents and windows) adds an almost capricious tone to the otherwise unembellished, planar surface. The building has been described as a colossal computer keyboard and a humongous airplane wing. Appropriately, it houses a prestigious

engineering school and is the centerpiece of a community devoted to science and technology.

The drama of the exterior hardly prepares you for the elegant but casual, sun-drenched interior featuring a spacious esplanade with various nodes for meeting and activity. A glass-walled library sits at one end of the covered esplanade, and bridges connect it to a series of research and classroom buildings located behind and perpendicular to the main structure. All around, glass and white walls sustain the open-air ambience conducive to human interactions and relaxation. Even office blocks enhance the atmosphere by being situated like islands, shaped with seductively curving contours and enclosed with walls of transparent and opaque materials arranged in horizontal stripes. Perrault's creativity and use of innovative materials are further evident in his choice of fabric for a false ceiling and his unique skylight design, described as a series of "double bowstring strutted lenses." Contrary to the industrial ambience that prevails in many new buildings, here the high-tech construction and artificial, reflective surfaces have a buoyant gracefulness. The skillful, inventive design is especially impressive since this was the architect's first major commission. What a shame that he didn't achieve such outstanding results with the National Library of France, a recent, even larger project. Don't miss this site!

Piotr Kowalski

L'axe de la terre, 1992
carrefour Descartes
RER: A4, Noisy-Champs

The monumental sculpture *Axis of the Earth* is directly in front of the main entrance to ESIEE, situated in the middle of a traffic circle where the major streets of Cité Descartes converge. This intersection has also been designated as the strategic center of a future technopolis, the helm of the entire region east of Paris. The sculpture is a shiny, elongated, needlelike form emerging from a ground surface of volcanic lava. Its diagonal axis rises quite high and points toward the pole star (also called the North Star)—the celestial marker used for directional orientation.

Kowalski, *L'axe de la terre*; Perrault ESIEE (behind)

Ecole Nationale des Ponts et Chaussées (ENPC) and Ecole Nationale des Sciences Géographiques (ENSG)

architects: Philippe CHAIX and Jean-Paul MOREL, 1989–96
6 and 8 avenue Blaise Pascal, Université de Marne-la-Vallée
RER: A4, Noisy-Champs

The architecture of the National School of Bridges and Roads and the National School of Geographic Sciences is another inventive glass-and-steel design. A high-tech articulation is prominently manifest on the exterior in the exposed structural system of steel cables. Even if your engineering appetite is not whetted, and even though the long, glazed wall of the front facade may not seem too intriguing, do go inside. You will find yourself in a light, airy, spacious

atrium. It is a wondrous environment providing a clear orientation to the atypical layout of the building. Stairways go down to a terrace below, where you can enter two majestic, curved-roof spaces that give access to three side buildings, each five stories high, housing laboratories, classrooms and research facilities. The soft-toned gray of the steel and the screened panels over the omnipresent glass create a subdued quality throughout—this, despite the fact that the architecture is constructed of cold, raw industrial materials.

Noisiel

Housing

architect: Christian de PORTZAMPARC, 1982–88
allée des Bois
RER: A4, Noisiel

Located behind the RER station along the east side of the pedestrian street between allée Jean-Paul Sartre and avenue Pierre Mendès-France.

Once again the architect Portzamparc has created simple but impressive housing that injects class, style and privacy into apartment living. The housing occupies one side of an entire street—the major north-south axis and pedestrian passageway through the community. But Portzamparc avoids a monotonous, repetitive alignment by alternating six- and two-story segments and developing the facades as a dynamic sequence of shapes and rhythms that play off one another. Deep voids contrast with flat surfaces, and quarter-circle and porthole windows confront cubic forms and sharp angles. A bold geometric rigor tempered by a playfulness prevails throughout. Though the complex fronts a "street" that is actually a grassy garden mall, Portzamparc enhances the environment by modifying the straight edge into a gentle crescent.

Pol Bury

Untitled, 1981
avenue Pierre Mendès-France and
allée des Bois
RER: A4, Noisiel

Located in front of the Lycée Technique René Cassin.

This stainless-steel sculpture that pairs two geometric configurations harmonizes well with both the modern architecture of the school behind and the two silos around the corner. The sculptures—upright cones topped by mirror-polished spheres with sliced-out wedges —look like slick, machine-made figures even to the degree that the "heads" tilt this way and that with reflections constantly changing their surface expression.

Totem

south end of allée des Bois
RER: A4, Noisiel

On the borderline between the developed part of the township and land designated as open space, two silos remain. Located behind a school and as the terminal points of tree alignments, they appear as reminders of the farms that formerly dominated the region. One of the silos has been decorated with horizontal bands and geometric designs in colors that echo those in the surrounding landscape. If you look closely, you will see that the patterning defines a delightful figure of a boy wearing a wide-brimmed (farm?) hat. The image—a totem—thus forms an interface between past and present, man and nature.

La Ferme du Buisson-Centre d'Art et de Culture de Marne-la-Vallée

renovation: Antoine GRUMBACH,
Bernard HUET, 1990–
allée de la Ferme, 77437
01-64-62-77-00 f: 01-64-62-77-99
RER: A4, Noisiel

It's about a 10-min. walk from the silos to Buisson Farm. Go back down allée des Bois, turn right on allée Jean-Paul Sartre (immediately after crossing over the train tracks), turn left at boulevard Salvador Allendé, turn right at cours du Buisson, go past the library and veer to the right onto allée de la Ferme. Enter through the gated brick wall.

This site is a treasure, well worth the 25-min. train ride from Paris. The farm was established in the late 19th century as a complement to the Menier family's chocolate factory (now Nestlé). Inspired by utopian ideas circulating at the turn of the century, the property was developed as a model farm. Chestnut trees were planted on 5 acres of land, and two vast structures of brick and metal were built alongside an 18th-century barn. The site remained agricultural until the 1960s, thereafter deteriorating into an industrial wasteland. In 1979 a proposal to create a Center of Art and Culture (CAC) was sanctioned as part of the regional Marne-la-Vallée development, but not until 1990, when the Buisson Farm was declared a historic monument, warranting preservation as an exceptional example of 19th century architecture, did it become the art center's home. Renovation of the complex of buildings began and is still ongoing.

The ensemble currently includes a theater with 800 seats, two film halls, a bar-restaurant, an art exhibition gallery and a dance rehearsal studio. Further renovation will add a small theater, a public library and residential studios for artists. As a multidisciplinary center involved with music, dance, theater, film and the visual arts, The Farm is unusual in France. It not only brings together buildings equipped to present contemporary creativity in many different art forms, but it also is set up to encourage collaborations, conferences and an experimental atmosphere not constrained by the cultural pressures of a big city like Paris. In addition, The Farm energizes its programs through partnerships and exchanges with regional, national and international institutions. Success can readily be measured by the amazing theater and dance productions that have taken place in less than a decade of operation; by the inventive sets and costumes created by artists such as Judith Barry, Christian Boltanski, Pier Paolo Calzolari, Richard Deacon, Dan Graham, Jean-Michel Othoniel and Richard Serra; and by the annual jazz festival, popular with critics and public alike. One might say The Farm is returning to its utopian past by providing a place for artists to work in isolation but within a stimulating environment, where encounters with others are nourishing and supportive.

Though the exteriors of the old farm buildings and the interior spaces have been largely retained, some of the interior design renovations are dramatic and unexpected. This is particularly true of the Grand Théâtre (the core building of the complex, previously a granary). The decoratively patterned brick exterior and the surrounding farm ambience do not prepare you for the shiny marble walls and majestic stairway that confront you when you enter the building. The shift is tempered by correspondences in the horizontal stripes in reddish brown and cream tones, and solid and void articulations, but the extraordinary contrast remains. Indeed, the reno-

vation design itself effectively asserts the spirit of change and innovation underlying all activities at The Farm. (If you can attend a performance or get inside the theater itself you will see another extraordinary renovation and incredible space.)

Sol LeWitt

Wall Drawing, no. 649, 1990
Grand Théâtre, La Ferme du Buisson

LeWitt's richly colored murals cover the walls of the entrance lobby. Rather than produce a continuous design, the artist has divided his work into segments, each with a different, self-contained, spatially dynamic image. The images are either perspectival constructions with each triangulated wedge colored diversely, or they are multitoned, geometric forms expressed as solid volumes (some with cutout openings in a corner or side) and isolated on a single-hued ground plane. Typical of LeWitt's conceptual orientation, the segments confound the spatial logic of the whole even as they assert rational systems within the independent parts. LeWitt in fact formulates the concept for his creations in detailed statements, but then has his assistants produce the paintings on the walls. By this method, for which he is well known, he reorients the artistic process, foregrounding the idea over the making. The method also allows for variations to emerge when the written ideas and systems are translated into images and forms. Although the murals are rooted in an intellectual rigor and an austere imagery, their intense, dark and bright tones and their nuanced surface textures make them tantalizing if not seductive. As the decor for a theater lobby, they are superb. And yet, it is unfortunate that they are set claustrophobically beneath balcony overhangs and painted on walls that do not continue up the full height of the building. Their presence in and integration into the space thus seem somewhat compromised.

Centre d'Art Contemporain

La Ferme du Buisson
01-64-62-77-41
Tues–Sun, 2–6; closed Mon
admission: free

Located in the front left corner of the property in a former barn.

Buisson Farm's Contemporary Art Center has one of the most impressive, cutting-edge exhibition programs in France. Four major shows are presented each year, and often these are multi-room installations or experimental media projects. Although many exhibitions feature young, as-yet-unknown artists, the quality is very high. Most significantly, a fearless sense of creativity prevails as the artists explore new territories, awaken new ideas and derange habitual sensitivies. For example, Francisco Ruiz de Infante (1997) completely restructured the large, open space of the gallery and used sound, lighting, objects and manipulations of scale and form to produce a labyrinthine, experiential work. Explorations of space, a dominant mission of The Farm, often underlie art projects. Recent exhibitions: *Christophe Cuzin*, *Véronique Joumard*, *Joachim Mogarra*, *Daniel Schlier*, *Michael Snow*, *Loïc Touze*, *Apart* (a joint investigation of space-time by four dancers and eight sculptors—Colette Brunschwig, Jean Degottex, Betty Goodwin, Rebecca Horn, Emmanuel Saulnier, Sarkis, Jana Sterbak, Sarah Stevenson).

To facilitate travel from Paris, the center has free buses making the round-trip drive to The Farm for exhibition openings. (Call for required reservations.)

Château d'Eau

 architect: Christian de PORTZAM-PARC, 1971–74
rond point des Quartre Pavés
RER: A4, Noisiel

You can catch a local bus from The Farm (or RER) to the tower, or walk the distance in about 15 min. The best pedestrian route is north down allée des Bois until it ends, then right onto cours du Château. You will see the tower in the middle of a big traffic circle just ahead.

Water Tower, also called La Tour Verte (Green Tower) was the first major work of the now-famous architect Christian de Portzamparc and one of the initial construction projects in Marne-la-Vallée. It was designed both as a technical facility for the new town and as a community landmark. Situated at a busy intersection—the crossroads between the old village of Noisiel (site of the main offices of Nestlé), a public park and the new center of Noisiel—it embodies Le Corbusier's idea about creating urban megastructures at the juncture of major roadways.

What is intriguing in Portzamparc's design is the way he camouflages a big, unaesthetic infrastructure object by placing it inside a shell decorated by nature and by reconfiguring its form. More specifically, he surrounded the monumental water tower with chain-link fence, using it like a trellis to support vines. But the fencing is affixed to rectangular frames arranged to spiral up the tower's side. The weighty, firmly grounded object thus acquires a flowing line and a more graceful, polygonal shape. Sparkles of light shining through openings in the vine and trellis cover also animate the tower. Of course, the winding spiral image invokes the Tower of Babel, adding a touch of myth and satire.

Should you wonder about the plants, which now appear quite sparse and fee-

Portzamparc, Château d'Eau

This hotel and recreation area located adjacent to Disneyland Park, aimed to adapt the principles of design and administration from the Disney parks in Florida and California to the climate of the Ile-de-France. The first phase of development, now complete, includes a group of fantasy hotels, each signifying an aspect of American culture and each with the appearance of a different time and place. According to the project's director, it's not nostalgia for a lost past but intentionally fake images borrowed from the past, modernized and presented as stimuli for dreams and settings for the imagination. The theme park idea seeps into the architecture of each hotel, permeating little details as well as the atmosphere both inside and out. Three of the hotels occupy sites around an artificial lake, two others are a stone's throw behind and one serves as the entrance to Disneyland. An entertainment center, also on the lakefront and similarly presenting an image of American culture, amplifies the storybook ambience of the hotels.

You can go to any or all of the hotels on free shuttle buses that run continuously from a platform alongside the train station. A walk around the lake on the boardwalk is a great way to visit the site. You might also want to extend your visit until it's dark to see how lighting has been used as an important design element by some of the architects.

ble, they have suffered the fate of human, governmental error. Three years after the structure was completed, in 1974, municipal authorities failed to flush the automatic watering system during the winter months. As a result, the pipes burst and most of the original plants died. Unfortunately, they have yet to be replaced. Even without the greenery, the tower is quite an engaging design, well worth the trip to see.

Parc Disneyland

EuroDisney Resort Complex

 architectural director: Robert STERN, 1992–97
Marne-la-Vallée
RER: A4, Marne-la-Vallée—Chessy

Hôtel New York

 architect: Michael GRAVES

Here the theme is Manhattan in the 1930s. Images of skyscrapers, town houses, Wall Street, the Downtown Athletic Club, Rockefeller Center and other icons appear as a romanticized but somewhat sterile conglomerate. Although design elements are reminiscent of the styles from the past, the exterior appears very ersatz, like a cardboard model of a generic composite. The decor borrows strongly from Art Deco in its effusive use of bold outlines, rectilinear forms and cool, saccharine colors.

Sequoia Lodge

 architect: Antoine GRUMBACH

The setting and architecture of this hotel suggest the rustic ambience of outdoor life in the western United States. Echos of a Rocky Mountain lodge or a cabin in Montana derive from the bare stone and rough-hewn wood, though the redwood style of Greene and Greene (the celebrated team of early-20th-century California architects) is also pervasive. The buildings are complemented by a scenic landscape of evergreens designed to convey the spirit of America's national parks.

Newport Bay Club

 architect: Robert STERN

The sumptuous, refined (and decadent) atmosphere of a seaside summer resort in New England characterizes this mammoth building and its lakefront environment. Authenticizing details and a pseudo-obsession with an aristocratic, Americana lifestyle subsumes everything, making guests dressed in casual jeans and T-shirts seem oddly out of place. If you want to get a taste of the way patricians indulge themselves, or if you want to see an elite milieu replicated by the appropriation mind-set of a top-notch postmodernist, a.k.a. Robert Stern, be sure to visit this site.

Disney Village Entertainment Center

 architect: Frank GEHRY, 1997

Located just across from the train station and a few minutes' walk from the entrance to the Disneyland Park, this recent addition to EuroDisney has already become a major attraction for both visitors and area residents. (It is open all day and all night.) The true ambience of the village is only apparent at night when everything is lit up and kids of all ages fill the streets, shops, restaurants, clubs, movie theaters, video-game palace and concert hall. Complementing the hotel themes, the center has the folkloric character of Main Street USA, combining favorite places from both past and present. Planet Hollywood competes with a wild-west show, and a multiplex cinema with the latest films is as much of an attraction as the 1950s pink Cadillac and Corvette parked in front of Annette's Diner. Gehry's red-and-white striped towers that line the streets and mark the skyline serve as zany magnets drawing visitors toward the village. Within the village, the towers almost get lost among the circus of signs, bright colors, oversized image reproductions and palm trees. And these elements share center stage with an eccentric architecture featuring sharp angles, sweeping curves, geometric volumes, disjunctive forms and all sorts of shiny industrial materials. The whole is a visual cacophony usually accompanied by sounds creating an equally vivid sensory overload.

Gehry, Disney Village

111

Hôtel Cheyenne

 architect: Robert STERN
Desperado Road

This hotel has 14 separate structures designed to recall the frontier towns of the American West. There's a saloon restaurant, buildings dedicated to Billy the Kid, Sitting Bull and Wyatt Earp, hitching posts, white picket fences, dust-ridden unpaved streets and all sorts of artificial accouterments. The environment tells a story about a frontier town, but it's presented as a television or movie set: scenic facades along the streets and nondescript box structures behind.

Hôtel Sante Fe

 architect: Antoine Predock

Here, as in the Cheyenne Hotel, guest rooms are spread among separate buildings situated within an ambient setting. In this case, there are 42 "pueblos" in an ersatz Indian village dotted with giant cacti. The scene is meant to evoke the banks of the Rio Grande, with walkways resembling desert trails and a mountain in the form of a volcano. A classic cowboy smoking a cigar greets you from a gigantic billboard at the entrance. Though the soft-toned cubic buildings here try to look like exotic southwest dwellings, they could easily be mistaken for upscale housing in a suburban development.

Hôtel Disneyland

 architect: Robert STERN, 1990

Located in front of the main entrance to Parc Disneyland.

This hotel was part of the initial development of EuroDisney. Unlike the other hotels, which convey the character of a specific place in America, this structure is pure fantasy. It has the appearance of a fairy-tale palace with some borrowings

from Second Empire style. A lush garden landscape further sets the mood for imagination and pleasure—the mood that Disney sought to program into all aspects of the natural and built environment.

Environs to the South

Ivry-sur-Seine

Located just outside Paris on its southeast border, Ivry has long been a place where artists live. Many government-owned studios are located here, and the community, largely working class, has supported artist projects. For example, every other September, Ivry has an open studio event, complemented by other art-related programs and exhibitions. Artists also organize large-scale thematic shows or special projects in various city buildings. Though uneven, these are engaging exhibitions, often containing fascinating work by emerging artists.

CREDAC

 93 avenue Georges Gosnat, 94200
01-49-60-25-06 f: 01-49-60-25-07
Tues–Sat, 2–7; Sun, 11–6;
closed Mon.
admission: free
métro: Mairie d'Ivry or RER: C6,
Ivry-sur-Seine

This art center with a baffling double name, is situated in a shopping-apartment complex on one of Ivry's main streets. It is actually two institutions: a municipal art space, called Galerie Fernand Léger; and a national Center for Research, Exchange and Diffusion of Contemporary Art (CREDAC). Within the center there are three different exhibition spaces and each presents the work of a different artist. The program includes a mix of young artists at the start of their careers who have already received some recognition, and mature artists whose work warrants another look.

In its resident-artist program, CREDAC invites a foreign artist to come for 6–12 months to work on a specific project, which then becomes the subject of an exhibition. An award giving an artist an exhibition and a commission to create a public artwork for the city is also part of the center's program. Ongoing are a full range of activities— performance, lecture, film, video and dance events plus interchanges between artists and art historians, writers and philosophers. Since Ivry is only a métro stop away from Paris, attending an event here is an easy way for you to meet artists in their milieu and scratch below the surface of the French art world. Recent exhibitions: *Bernard Calet*, *Patrick Corillon*, *François Daireaux*, *Valérie Favre*, *Alan Fleischer*, *Stéphane Le Mercier*, *Tania Mouraud*, *Slimane Raïs*, *Philippe Richard*, *Ute Richter*, *Christian Sindou*.

Jeanne Hachette, Casanova and Voltaire Housing

architects: Jean Renaudie and Nina Schuch
avenue Georges Cosnat and surrounding area
métro: Mairie d'Ivry or RER: C6, Ivry-sur-Seine

You can't help but take note of the striking architecture all around CREDAC. These buildings stand out because of their thrusting terraces and explosion of angular forms. Constructed of poured concrete, they have a decidedly brutalist character except that they also embrace a naturalist mode by making outdoor living space and plants dominant parts of the structure. Renaudie and Schuch called this kind of design and planning "organic integration." These buildings have been variously dismissed as decorative bombast and called the most innovative work of the 1960s generation in France. Regardless of which may be true, they give bold evidence of the rebellion against rationality, pure form and object making that emerged after World War II.

La Manufacture des Oeillets

25–29 rue Raspail, 94200
01-46-71-71-10
Wed–Sun, 2–7
métro: Mairie d'Ivry or RER: C6, Ivry-sur-Seine

Located a few blocks away from CREDAC.

This group of former factories houses studios and is a site for theater, filmmaking and contemporary art exhibitions. Artists themselves organize showings of their work, special projects, performances and other activities here.

Brétigny-sur-Orge

Espace Jules Verne

rue Henri Douard, 91224
01-60-85-20-85 f: 01-60-84-22-55
Tues–Fri, 9–12 and 2–6; Sat, 9–12 and 2–5; closed Mon
admission: free
RER: C4 or C6, Brétigny-sur-Orge

From the train station turn left onto rue de la République; walk through the center of town (several blocks) to the intersection with rue Danielle Casanova; turn right and then take the first left onto rue Henri Douard. Espace Jules Verne is just ahead on the left. The walk takes about 15 min.

Espace Jules Verne houses an art exhibition space, library and theater for dance, drama and music performances. Although this is a community center, its programs are hardly on an amateur level. They attract the attention of both locals, Paris professionals and arts afficionados. The art center, for example, has an impressive history of challenging shows by innovative young artists. Recent shows have favored video and installation projects, conceptually based work and photography. Despite the gallery's irregular space, with its narrow, long and lofty shape bordered by a window wall along one side, artists have taken advantage of the situation by creating works or installations acutely attuned to the placement and juxtaposition of objects. To encourage appreciation and understanding, the public is invited to open conversations with the artist and curator or special performances on the first Monday evening of each month. For these events as well as for openings, the center provides free bus service from Paris. The gallery also publishes a catalogue for each of the four exhibitions it organizes annually. Recent exhibitions: *Michel Blazy*, *Maurizio Cattelan*, *Guillaume Janot*, *Liza-May Post*, *David Renaud*, *Franck Scurti*, *Roman Signer*, *Transrévélateurs*.

Evry

In 1965 Evry became the seat for the newly created Department of Essonne. Its population has since mushroomed, and it is now one of the dynamic administrative and economic centers along the ringroad, the Francilienne—a highway linking the five "new towns" within a 20-mile radius of Paris, of which Evry is one. The construction of a modernized town center, though not yet completed, has strongly affected the appearance of and attitude toward Evry. The project includes a new train station, pedestrian streets, housing, shops, hotels, a theater, skating rink, cinema and bowling complex, swimming pool, indoor sport and concert hall, library, National School of Music and Dance and a ceremonial plaza faced by a new city hall, cathedral and the Chamber of Commerce and Industry building for the region of Essonne.

Cathédrale de la Résurrection

architect: Mario BOTTA, 1992–95
place des Droits de l'Homme, Evry
Centre, 91007
01-64-97-93-55
RER: D4, Evry

The Evry cathedral—the first cathedral built in France during the 20th century —has a dominant place, both geographically and aesthetically, in the new town center. Its use of brick and the boldness of the solid-and-void contrasts, the irregular fenestration and presence of pronounced circular and rectilinear shapes have clearly influenced other projects in the surrounding area. Nevertheless, its circular form topped by an unusual slanted glass roof lined with trees gives it singular distinction. This is especially true at night, when the encircling, hollow groove just below the rooftop is illuminated. The light, combined with the majestic cylindrical form, endows the building with a magical or spiritual aura like the soaring spires of Gothic cathedrals.

The brick exterior—which is patterned and delineated with narrow and wide bands—has also become a signature element of the cathedral. Unlike most contemporary buildings that have an industrial appearance from their aus-

Botta, Cathédrale de la Réssurection

tere steel, glass, and concrete facades, here the brick sheathing gives evidence of skilled craftsmanship and Botta's own attention to exacting detail and surface design. Indeed, the brickwork, which is in turn interrupted by recessed windows with pronounced geometric shapes, and the windows create an emphatic counterpoint to the otherwise flat, regularized surface of the edifice. Projecting elements—the scaffoldlike campanile of black-painted steel topped by an elongated cross, the detached ceremonial entry stairs and the walkway bridge—further upset the sense of order and coherence that at first seems to rule the building's design.

In the interior of the cathedral, Botta has used the patterning of the brick-work and the curvature of the walls to mark the positioning of the altar and to create a sweeping movement up toward the skylight. Somewhat surprisingly, the skylight roof on the inside has a complex structure, composed of slits, glass planes and exposed steel pipes in a cubic framework. The open display of the building's structure in this area is, however, not at all characteristic of the interior design. More typical (and a Botta trademark) are markings of opulence like the pink and black marble along the walls of the encircling corridors and stairways. In addition, the simple beauty of the cutouts in the brick walls contributes to an overall refinement.

On one side, the cathedral fronts the ceremonial city plaza, and on a second side it opens onto streets and a small shopping zone. It also is attached to a housing complex designed by Botta (unfinished in 1998). Like the cathedral, the latter is sheathed in patterned brick, but its rectilinear forms and its alignments of big square and slit windows set at regular intervals are clearly different. Taken together, there is a purposeful harmony between the two projects that gives them an appealing and necessary cohesiveness.

(Anyone who has seen the San Francisco Museum of Modern Art, also designed by Botta, will recognize it as the kissing cousin to the Evry cathedral.)

Milly-la-Forêt

Jean Tinguely with Niki de Saint-Phalle

Le cyclop, 1969–94
Milly-la-Forêt, 91490
01-64-98-83-17 f: 01-64-98-94-80
May–Oct only. Fri, 10:15–1 and 2–4:45; Sat, 11–1 and 2–5:30; Sun, 11–1 and 2–6:15. In Oct, the last visit is at 4:15
admission: 35/30/20/5F—
reservations are advisable

Milly-la-Forêt is a village in the Fontainebleau Forest, about 40 mi (65 km) from Paris. The sculpture site is impossible to reach by public transportation, but you can get close to it by taking the RER, D4 to Maisse. You will then have to walk (over 4 mi, 7 km) or call a taxi to go to the sculpture. The route is direct, just follow the road (D837) to Milly-la-Forêt and turn left into an unmarked exit just after the turnoff for Milly. By car from Paris, take A6 south; exit at Cély-Milly onto N372 in the direction of Milly; at the Milly traffic circle take D837 in the direction of Etampes; go 1/8 mi (200 m) and turn right into the forest along an inconspicuous road that may have an arrow saying *Le cyclop*. From the parking area, you walk down the road until you come to a pedestrian path on the left, which leads to the sculpture. Visitors are formed into small groups to tour the interior of the sculpture with a guide.

The idea for *Le cyclop* dates back to discussions Tinguely had in 1969 with friends, fellow Swiss artists Bernhard Luginbühl and Daniel Spoerri. For years, he worked secretly on the project with Niki de Saint-Phalle, his longtime collaborator, and various assistants. When he died in 1991, the monumental head, configured for visitors to enter and climb around, was 75 1/2 feet tall and included some 300 tons of metal. Equipped with all sorts of animated parts and sounds, it also incorporates contributions from many artist-friends. As an art object it is nothing short of mind-boggling. To some it may appear as a fun-filled, imaginary extravaganza. To others it is a scary, decapitated head from a mythic colossus. And it can also be viewed as a one-eyed mechanized monster plagued by menacing thoughts deriving from socio-political-cultural realities. No matter how you respond, a visit to this site is an experience you won't forget.

As you walk through the forest to get to the sculpture, you leave the everyday world of real time and defined space and enter unfamiliar, indeterminate territory. One of the first things you see when you arrive at the clearing is a glittering, golden iris and oscillating pupil firmly embedded within an ocular-shaped crater dead center in the middle of a massive, bulbous face with reflective mirror-mosaic skin. Below the eye, a hollow area takes on the appearance of a gaping mouth displaying two phallic teeth, a thick upper lip and an extended tongue in the form of a long water slide. Visible behind are tumbling metal parts, many of which are rusted. The sight is so eccentric and packed with numerous different parts, that you walk around and around, hoping somehow to put it all together and have it make sense. Forget this; it won't ever happen. You'll have to settle for an accumulation of fragments and nonsequential provocations.

Tinguely & Saint–Phalle, *Le cyclop*

So, return to the front for a closer look at Niki de Saint-Phalle's gaudy face, and to the back for further inspection of Tinguely's so-called *tour éphémère* (ephemeral tower) with its zillions of wheels, pulleys and assortment of extraneous junk. When you least expect it, the wheels will start turning in a chaos of different speeds, and the head will emit a cacophony of squeaks, bangs, clacks and screeches. At the center of the noise and movement are aluminum balls (with a 14 in. diameter) darting in and out of the structure along wire tracks. The performance conveys a sense of erratic life (or thought) kept going by fits, spurts and eruptions. There can be no smooth sailing here, for the head is a discombobulated arrangement of zigzagging levels, scattered stairways, platforms, balconies and terraces. In addition, there's the incongruous presence of a carefully built brick base and four thriving oak trees nestled near the ear.

Before going inside the cyclop's head, be sure to look at the object elements on the ground level. These include a crushed metal sculpture by CESAR; a very tall meter stick made to order for measuring the height of an oversized head, by Jean-Pierre RAYNAUD; Rico WEBER's presentation of 10 identical white plaster casts of himself lying saintlike but wearing rubber boots; Tinguely's *Hommage à Duchamp* (a steel chocolate grinder); and Bernhard LUGINBÜHL's giant listening ear, steel pinball machine, and black relief assemblage, *Hommage à Louise Nevelson*. There is also a video interview with Tinguely and Saint-Phalle that gives a historical context and shows some of their other fantasy projects.

You enter at the base of the skull, climbing though heavy round doors, like those on fortified châteaux or bank vaults (by Luginbühl). You then pass by a checkerboard-tile wall with mirrors and an electricity control panel in which switches are named for the artists who contributed to *Le cyclop*. In a nearby alcove, a maquette with molecular shaped elements represents the unity of art and science. The work is titled *Hommage à RU486* (the controversial abortion pill—or morning-after birth control pill—developed in France but not available in the U.S.). These works and the colorful mosaic column greeting you on the next level are all by Saint-Phalle. (The column is from *Tarot Garden*, an ongoing outdoor project in Tuscany.)

Across from the column is *Pénétrable sonore*, a sound-object by Jesus-Rafaël SOTO. Composed of long aluminum rods, hanging 28 rows deep and 28 rows across, it produces a symphony of gongs and jingles when activated by the wind or a person walking through it. Above, the glass-covered case filled with work gloves—gloves used in making *Le cyclop*—is an *Accumulation* by ARMAN.

As you climb on up, you are next confronted by a gold mirror-mosaic skull with red eyes and silver teeth (by Saint-Phalle), set in the center of radiating black steel bars and suspended inside a giant upside-down air tube. (A castoff from the Centre Pompidou.) The latter image, a Tinguely apparatus, has become known as the "suicide funnel." Evoking the death theme, it recalls the artist's famous performance sculpture, *Homage to New York* (1960), a work that destroyed itself in the garden of the Museum of Modern Art. However, unlike his earlier work, *Le cyclop* is a mechanized creation that keeps revitalizing itself, thus refusing to commit suicide.

The stairway to the next floor is lined with little flea-market assemblages each set in its own vitrine. The collection—*Piccolo museo* (*Little Museum*)—is by the self-taught, Art Brut artist, Giovanni PODESTA. By displaying these nicely framed objects in the midst of his conglomerate, junk-laden sculpture, Tinguely underscores the difficulty and absurdity of defining art and artists.

In the theater, which is the next feature in *Le cyclop*, each chair is distinctive and faces a different direction. The only one occupied is *Le banc* (*The Bench*). However, the blue spotted dog and black man reading a newspaper who are seated on it are oblivious to the nonstop performance on stage: "L'amour," a violent drama in which an immense hammer keeps crushing a bottle. Nearby, you encounter *Barricades, Homage to May '68*, a layered Plexiglas construction by Larry RIVERS, and *Piège* (*Trap*) by Daniel SPOERRI, a facsimile assemblage of a small restaurant decorated with a clutter of pinups on its walls. A second work by Spoerri, *La chambre de bonne* (*Maid's Room*), perfectly replicates the tiny attic room where the artist lived in 1952 when a student in Paris. Because the room is turned sideways 90 degrees, objects seem to float in space, and a dizzying, claustrophobic sensation prevails.

Along the stairs to the top, Sepp IMHOF (the professional welder who helped build the entire head) installed a black metal relief, *Meta-Merz-Bau*, in homage to the famous construction accretions of Kurt Schwitters, and at the top, Tinguely has created *Hommage à Yves Klein*. This work, an eye-level square pool of indeterminate depth with a smooth, reflective surface having an immaterial quality, makes reference to Klein's famous installation, *The Void*. (The pool is actually only 2 in. deep and composed of black tar.) The top terrace also includes a room filled with word and phrase paintings by BEN. From the vantage point at the top, you encounter the grand finale of *Le cyclop*—a railroad car suspended in space on ungrounded tracks. But this is not just any car, it's a French train car like those used to deport Jews to concentration camps during World War II. Making the image even more disconcerting are the eerie figures inside—40 limp beings clinging to one another, all dressed in black and all with ghostly white faces. The work, *Hommage aux déportés* (1974), is by Eva AEPPLI. At the end of the descent there is one more object to experience. It's an invisible "water painting" titled *Tableau générique* by Philippe BOUVERET. You won't see anything here but water until an aspirin is added and the emitted fizz brings to visibility a plaque commemorating the formal inauguration (1994) of *Le cyclop*. As noted in the inscription, President Mitterand and the Minister of Culture, Jacques Toulon, were in attendance.

Antony

If you want to see some intriguing, low-budget design projects by one of France's leading architects, you should visit this quiet, tidy, suburban community to the south of Paris.

Centre de Loisirs Paul Roze

architect: Jean NOUVEL, 1982
RER: B4, Antony

From the RER station take bus 196; or walk up rue Maurice Labrousse, turn left at avenue du Bois de Verrières, continue until you reach rue Camille Pelletan, turn left and you'll find the center just ahead on the left, next door to a primary school.

The center, also called Les Godets, is part playground and part adventure park for children. But this is not your typical slick, designer creation. The landscape has been left as untouched scrub, and the buildings—which consist of a series of small boxes connected to one another in a simple alignment sloping down a hill—are rugged and unpretentious. The structures serve a range of functions: meeting places, locker rooms, reception areas, caretaker's house, auditorium, darkroom, kitchen, offices, etc. Although they are constructed of industrial materials, they have eccentric, playful features that offset the hard-edged, cold, impersonal aura of corrugated aluminum, glass and concrete. Each building is different and distinctive because of its materials and design. Nouvel's clever vocabulary includes a cupola, barrel vault and glass miter roof-peak; juxtapositions of curved, block and angled shapes; solid and transparent wall surfaces; recessed and projecting elements; idiosyncratic color panels; skewed positionings of windows; and a building that has plantlike designs on glass on one side and geometric patterns on the other. Despite the array of diversity, the whole holds together quite well and is not at all chaotic or overbearing.

Anne Franck Collège

architect: Jean NOUVEL, 1978–80
rue Adolphe Pajeaud
RER: B4, Fontaine-Michalon

From the RER station, take bus Palatin 3; or walk along rue Prosper Legoute, turn left onto Adolphe Pajeaud, continue until you reach the school (right side of street). If you are coming from the Centre de Loisirs, you can walk through a nice stretch of park and ponds to rue Georges Suant, which then intersects with rue Adolphe Pajeaud (20 minutes).

A modular plan and industrial materials of government issue (cinder blocks, small glass panes, etc.) had to be used in the construction of this middle school. Nouvel's design adapts to the requirements even as it enlivens and satirizes the inherently bleak, regimented, institutional appearance that is the typical result of such restrictions. For

example, the architect availed himself of the modular system, promoted for its great flexibility. But then he blatantly nullified and ridiculed the essential premise of flexibility by creating a humdrum beam structure that supports nothing, by delineating the floor with a grid that runs haywire in corridors beyond the entrance hall and by developing a monotonous facade into which color panels are haphazardly inserted to upset the otherwise repetitive regularity. Nouvel also situates chain-link walls with dense jungles of vines cascading down, perpendicular to one section of the facade. The dramatic contrast of the plant masses with the grid pattern on the facade rebukes the modular system in yet another way.

Within the interior of the school, ornamental and absurdly out-of-sync trimmings further disrupt the code of rational order. They moreover unsettle the stereotypic, boring appearance of a public school. Most notable are the displacement of gym-floor markings to classroom hallways, the nonsensical series of numbers and zigzags in colored neon, the incongruous classical columns set here and there, and the draped statues.

(As in most French schools, there is a guardian at the door who will probably tell you that you can't enter. If you are exceedingly polite and ask to speak to the *directeur*, you should be able to get permission at least to walk through the ground floor. It's worth the effort.)

Choisy-le-Roi

Louise Bourgeois

Les bienvenus, 1996
Parc de la Mairie
RER: C, Choisy-le Roi

From the train station, walk through the adjacent park, go around the building (city hall) to its front, keep walking until you are get to the tree just inside the entrance gate.

If you look up into the designated tree, you will see the sculpture. It may not be immediately visible amid the tree branches and leaves, especially if it's spring or summer when the foliage is most plentiful. The unusual, amusing location is classic Bourgeois—a wonderful way to catch people unawares and make them look twice at the work. There are actually two sculptures hanging side by side, seemingly floating in air, their cast aluminum forms shining brightly. Each is a mass of tightly entwined components suggestively looking like a coil of appendages in an endless, protective, comforting embrace. To be sure, the work's placement in a tree also suggests the image of a bird's nest, adding the connotation of a family dwelling and shelter composed of layers of collected materials.

According to the artist, *Les bienvenus* (*The Welcomed Ones*), also titled *Le nid d'amour* (*The Love Nest*), "gives us a new way to see, to communicate, and a new way to love." The work has particular significance due to its location in front of a city hall, the site where marriage licences are issued and weddings take place. Moreover, Choisy-le-Roi was the place where Bourgeois lived as a child, where she developed a fascination for the nests of warblers. They were perched high in trees and made from a leaf folded back on itself with its edges carefully sewn together. Their half-organic, half-geometric form incarnated the perfect image of a shelter. Turning back to this source is not surprising for the artist who has readily admitted: "All my inspiration comes from my childhood, my education, from France at a certain moment of my life."

Issy-les-Moulineaux

Jean Dubuffet

La tour aux figures, 1986–88
Ile Saint-Germain
RER: C5 or C7, Issy-Plaine

From the RER walk across the short bridge (Pont d'Issy) to Saint-Germain Island. May–Sept, Wed and Sun afternoons, visitors can enter into the sculpture. (Don't be surprised if the keeper of the key doesn't show up to open the door.)

Situated on top of a hill at the east end of the island, Dubuffet's monumental sculpture-tower (over 78 ft high) hovers over a favored leisure park where Parisian families go to play sports and relax. The image follows in the path of other Dubuffet projects: his designs for "buildings" from the late 1960s, his construction of habitats in the 1970s and his many figures for *Hourloupe*, the utopian world he invented. Like these, the tower is covered with a maze of red, white and blue interlocking shapes with bold black outlines. Inside, the meandering layout of rooms, stairs, landings, niches and a winding stairway to the top not only reiterates the twists, turns, crevices, planes and deep hollows of the exterior surface but allows for the entangling movements to be experienced in real time and space.

Dubuffet envisioned his *gastrovolve*, or "climbing habitat," as a place of meditation illuminated by traces overlapping one another according to the dream-walks you take when lost in thought. For him, it is a monument promoting the rights of the imagination.

Saint-Quentin -en-Yvelines

This is one of the new towns, located just pass Versailles, 12 1/2 mi (20 km) from Paris. Designed largely as a residential and commercial community, it has become a thriving economic center, home to many corporations and banks. In contrast to the typical French mode of urban planning, where housing and shops are integrated into small neighborhoods, here the layout is more like the cliché American suburb with office buildings, services, markets and most of the shops gathered in the center of town surrounded by spreads of garden apartments and single-family houses, each with its own patch of grass. There are also large shopping centers on outer roadways. An important difference, however, is the integration of numerous outdoor recreational areas, acres of green space and natural waterways within the city proper and throughout the region. If you plan a visit, be sure to spend time exploring the parks and wandering around the downtown area to see its delightful intertwines of canals and pedestrian streets.

Nissim Merkado

Meta, 1988–92
rue des Coquelicotis
RER: C7, Saint-Quentin-en-Yvelines
From the RER station, walk along avenue des Prés. After you cross avenue des Sources de la Bièvre, you'll be at the uppermost edge of a park. The sculpture is just ahead (10 minutes).

Meta is an environmental sculpture located at the head of a canal crossing the city. Likened to a meteorite, it is a large, mirror-polished black granite disk (82 1/2 ft diameter) seemingly floating just above the ground in an inclined position. Its surface is cut by a slit positioned as if to mark 12:00. Beneath the disk is a kind of sound environment resembling a classical temple. Twelve support pillars of graduating heights, together with the lines of light shining through the slit and the narrow opening around the circumference, define the space. Concrete stepping squares precisely placed in the water allow you to walk around and experience the markers and effects from different vantage points.

The inaccessible glass chamber at the top of the disk counters the infinitely simple measuring aspects of the sculpture with the infinitely complex. Sheltered within the transparent room is a blue neon "needle" associated with hidden and uncertain dimensions, such as the light conveyed by the TGV or the depth of the underground water level.

Les Arcades du Lac, Le Viaduc, Le Temple, La Colonnade, Les Pavillons

architect: Ricardo BOFILL, 1972–81
bordered by boulevard Descartes and route de Guyancourt in the Voisins and Montigny le Bretonneux neighborhoods
RER: C7, Saint-Quentin-en-Yvelines, then bus 14 to Les Arcades du Lac
Caution: bus 14 doesn't run on Sundays and it's a long walk from the train station.

Of all the Bofill complexes around Paris, this is the most diversified and upscale, though it is still public housing shaped by prefabricated reinforced-concrete construction designed with satiric appropriations from classical architecture. As usual, the ensemble (actually there are three ensembles) comprises megastructures, except that here there are no high-rises. The grand scale is nevertheless glaring since the architecture poses such a dramatic contrast to the modest suburban dwellings (mainly garden-apartment developments) of the surrounding area. Quite purposefully, Bofill has situated his buildings in the midst of a wide-open flat space on the shoreline of a lake (man made) to give them the semblance of majestic palaces of overwhelming magnitude—like nearby Versailles. He even nicknamed one part of the project "Versailles for the people."

Underlying all the surface pizzazz, was Bofill's intention to create an apartment conglomerate with communal space and to break with the rationalist fundamentals of architecture—a virtual gospel set forth in the 1920s and still dominant in the 1970s when the Saint-Quentin housing came into being. As much as his obsession with community comes through in the spatial layout, it is curious that there are no group amenities like meeting rooms, child-care centers, laundries, exercise or health facilities, convenience stores—not even the ubiquitous French bakery or café. Underground parking is available and does serve to keep cars out of sight, thereby making the grounds friendly to pedestrians and children. But here again, Bofill effectively discourages communal gatherings and virtually inhibits outdoor play by omitting seating in most of the plazas and by covering public spaces with paving or formal "keep-off-the-grass" landscaping.

The ensemble called Les Arcades du Lac, conceptualized as a "garden city" with each structure being one of the elements in a formal French garden, was the initial segment (1972–75) of Bofill's Saint-Quentin village. This rigorous, compact plan of organization—translated into square city blocks, narrow and wide pedestrian streets, covered arcades, inner courtyards and a circular plaza centered on an anomalous pseudo-shrine—is apparent as soon as you enter the complex. And just as large formal gardens become enveloping labyrinths, one has the sense that this is a labyrinth, too. A repetition of common elements—mainly classical motifs presented in a reductive, unadorned form and mass-produced in low-cost industrial materials—stands out. But so too does the diversity of terra cotta and concrete; grid, stripe and smooth surfaces; dark and light; reddish brown, gray and white tones; rectangular and curved shapes; and vertical and horizontal rhythms. Moreover, everything is in human scale, and there's lots of natural light and private spaces. In a strange way, these "urban gardens" are both attractive and bleak, a good alternative to conventional mass housing and yet so impersonal and machinelike as to be macabre.

Le Viaduc is clearly one of the most surreal designs you'll find in 20th-century housing. As its name suggests, the image is a series of narrow, reinforced concrete arches and high supporting piers. But whereas viaducts normally are bridges over obstructions in the landscape, this one is itself an obstruction, existing as a solitary oddity extending from the shoreline (in front of Les Arcades du Lac) out into the lake. In fact, it has apartment units in its six five-story-high piers, a central passage running through at ground (water) level and terraces behind the capricious, mirrored pediments atop the arches.

At the opposite end of the lake, stretching across the entire shoreline like a royal château, is a monumental, symmetrical, classically styled, white marble-looking ensemble that denies all pretense of being an apartment complex. Le Temple—a rectangular building of considerable stature and volume—occupies the central position, jutting all the way forward to be slightly over the water's edge, and all the way back to flank the city street. On either side, La

Bofill, *Le Temple, La Colonnade, Les Pavillons*

Colonnade—a grandiose crescent with an unvarying facade made to look like a stately peristyle—curves around to *Les Pavillons*—two independent square buildings echoing the basic design of *Le Temple* in a greatly condensed form. As ever with Bofill's architecture, what you see at first glance is not what it seems to be. Two-story buildings are made to look one-story high (*Colonnade*), and four-story buildings (*Temple* and *Pavillons*) appear to have only two stories because windows extend across floor divisions. Moreover, windows on the ground level almost invisibly double as entry doors. The facades thus give the illusion that the whole is a single dwelling with regal, high-ceilinged rooms. Bofill clearly sought to aggrandize the external impression; however, the constituent apartments are actually quite luxurious—despite being prefabricated concrete constructions. Almost all are duplexes with private or semiprivate entrances, and all have extraordinary views and sunlit rooms. The taller structures have hollow centers formed into interior grass courtyards, and the pediments are fronts for airy penthouses.

Thus Bofill again achieves a curious merger between a blatant adoption of mass-production, cost-saving, quantity uniformity and depersonalized grandeur, and an acute sensitivity to privacy and residential comfort.

La Défense

The vast area called La Défense is located just outside Paris to the northwest, lying across the Seine river between Courbevoie and Puteaux. In 1958 the state designated the land for development as a new modern office district. Its name derived from a monument on the site commemorating the defense of Paris against the Prussians in 1871. The plan—housing units plus industrial and artisan establishments—called for the total destruction of old neighborhoods. In their place, new construction would create a very long, very wide central esplanade with skyscrapers all around and transportation networks underground. It was a gigantic undertaking with radical socio-economic and cultural implications. Moreover, the organizational setup—a development agency overseeing the plan and selling construction rights to investors—was a new approach to urban planning in France. It introduced a capitalist-inspired form of laissez-faire spatial configuration and design.

The result—an unpleasant environment dominated by blocklike towers of excessive height, extreme density and architectural mediocrity—was intensely criticized. Hard times and stagnation befell La Défense even as pressure built to institute dramatic changes in the original plan. A second wave of construction began during the 1978–88 decade. An international design competition for the Grande Arche, launched by President François Mitterand, also helped by establishing a monument that would not only endow La Défense with a trademark image but also create an axial alignment between the new district and important sites in Paris.

Today La Défense is still dominated by corporate skyscrapers (48 in 1998). But low-rise housing units, a mammoth commercial center (with shops, restaurants, leisure-activity areas, nine cinemas and three department stores), outdoor plazas, an automobile museum, exhibitions, open-air concerts, festivals and a central esplanade sprinkled with fountains and public seating—not to mention a car-free environment serviced by the métro, RER, 20 bus routes, two train lines, huge parking lots and a direct link to the national highway system—have made La Défense a bustling hub, tourist site and the largest business park in Europe. Nevertheless, many people still view La Défense as a dehumanized, denaturalized city such as might be found in a futuristic horror film. Concrete walkways, escalators and staircases pass around a maze of monolithic skyscrapers, and trees—if present at all—are aligned in geometric boxes like artificial objects within a sovereign grid. Even on a sunny day when people sit at the outdoor cafés and throngs of businessmen move about, they are so out of scale with the surroundings, and so out of sync with the glass, steel and stone, that they—the humans—appear as oddities from a bygone era.

If you've never been to La Défense or haven't been back in the past decade, do take the short métro ride and visit. But don't approach it as an all-purpose community. View it instead as a business park or the office center of a capital city (like the Avenue of the Americas in New York). With this mind-set, you'll really appreciate its lively atmosphere and refusal to be either a suburbanized, countrified island or a dense, traffic-choked urban zone.

The esplanade and subsidiary areas near housing and office towers include over 70 artworks. Many are monumental in scale and most were specially commissioned for the site. Unfortunately, with a few exceptions, the work is fairly mediocre. In the main, projects are oversized, weak clones of styles or concepts developed by celebrated international artists.

La Grande Arche

 architect: Otto VON SPRECKELSEN, 1982–89
1 parvis de la Défense, 92060
01-49-07-27-57
daily, 10–7
admission (elevator to the top): 40/30F
métro/RER: Grande Arche de la Défense

Though it's called an arch, it's really a colossal hollow cube. The design was determined by an international competition (with 422 entries) seeking a contemporary monument that would continue and terminate the world's most famous urban axis—the path connecting the Louvre's Cour Carrée, Arc de

Triomphe du Carrousel, place de la Concorde and Arc de Triomphe. The winning proposal by von Spreckelsen, a Danish architect, called for ending the axis with a pure, geometric form—an open portal or window to the world. As a decidedly 20th-century structure using the traditional framework of a triumphal arch, it conveys technological prowess born from power and heroic strides.

The structure, which houses offices and a rooftop visitors' center and viewing terraces, was indeed an engineering feat. It is an immensely tall form (301 ft high) weighing some 300,000 tons but supported by only six pillars on each side. Four exterior speed elevators provide direct access to the top, and a canvas "cloud" lies suspended in space above the ground pavilion. Carrara marble, gray granite and reflective glass give the exterior a glistening, smooth surface.

Should you decide to go to the top, be sure to peruse the small bookstore there. It has an unexpectedly good selection on architecture in France.

Jean-Pierre Raynaud

La carte du ciel, 1989
top of the Grande Arche

On the ground surface of the four rooftop patios, Raynaud has created a *Map of Heaven* to relate the architecture to the celestial realm above. The imagery extends the sense of the axial, land orientation of the arch and its image as a open gateway. By also including zodiac motifs from the cosmological order, the map asserts a mythical alliance between earth and sky. Using his familiar aesthetic, Raynaud has imbued the map with an austere and elegant aura delineating a square grid and circular dial with black granite lines, numbers and signs on a white marble base. The designation of east as the

zero degree and Ram sign orients the building as in ancient civilizations.

Takis

Signaux lumineux sur miroir d'eau, 1974–88
esplanade, behind the Grande Arche
métro/RER: Grande Arche de la Défense

Luminous Signals on a Mirror of Water includes 49 painted steel poles topped by fanciful, geometric shapes and colored lights flashing on and off according to an intermittent and random system. There are two groups of these sculptures, each set in a shallow pool at either end of the esplanade.

La Pacific, Japan Tower

 architect: Kiso KUROKAWA, 1992
Valmy district, La Défense 7
métro/RER: Grande Arche de la Défense

Japan Tower is one of the newest buildings at La Défense. It's located across the major highway that marks the frontier of Paris, in an area where the business complex is extending westward beyond the Grande Arche. Kurokawa's design explicitly embraces the location by placing a grand staircase and enormous portal in the center of his building. The passage connects with a red pedestrian bridge—curved and narrow like traditional Japanese bridges—that spans the highway going in the direction of the arch and esplanade. The back of the building also follows the curve of the highway. In front, the curve encompasses an expanse designed for theater performances with the steps serving as seats for the audience.

As much as Japan Tower is a high-tech design, Kurokawa derived inspiration from traditional Japanese sources.

The shape bears witness to "Chu Mon"—the symbolic gate marking the entrance to the room where the tea ceremony takes place. The glass facade, which leaves a second internal wall visible, is "a re-working in steel and translucent plastic of the 'shoji,' the traditional sliding door of paper with a wooden frame." There is also a Japanese rock garden on the roof. Housing offices and exhibition rooms, *La Pacific* was conceived as a business center where two economic communities (France and Japan) could come together, and as a cultural center with an ambassadorial outlook. Indeed, the monumental doorway in the middle of the building metaphorically suggests this even as it establishes a link to the Grande Arche.

Piotr Kowalski

Place des degrés, 1982–89
porte Sud, La Défense 7
métro/RER: Grande Arche de la Défense

Located at the foot of the Pascal and Voltaire skyscrapers.

Conceptualized as an "urban landscape" providing a pedestrian path across a sloping terrain, this three-tiered stone, steel and concrete plaza features two eccentrically shaped stairways and a series of emphatically angled objects. At the lowest level, an angle of steel painted dark blue sits on the ground. Its open end faces a red double-angle attached to a tall pole imbedded in the terrace of the upper level. In between are three red open-sided shapes, cube-like except for their slanting tops, a cascade of cubes containing plants and a white stone form suggestive of a rising turbulent wave. The ensemble of disparate, enigmatic elements structures the space and calls attention to the extreme geometricization of the surrounding environment.

CNIT

architects: Bernard ZEHRFUSS, Robert CAMELOT and Jean de MAILLY, 1958
le Parvis
métro/RER: Grande Arche de la Défense

CNIT (Centre National de l'Industrie et Technologie)—a giant exhibition hall—was the first major building at La Défense. With its distinctive form—a triangular-shaped structure with a vaulted concrete roof resting on three points and window-wall facades—it stood out in an environment of mushrooming skyscrapers. At the time, the design exemplified advanced technological know-how. The vault was the largest in the world, and its structure, composed of two separate layers with space in between and steel cables linking the three base supports, was highly innovative. However, the vast, open interior, suited for large conventions, proved unprofitable. Finally, in 1989, a renovation divided the building into smaller display and meeting spaces, a hotel, shops and services. Now CNIT is like a World Trade Center and international business forum.

César

Pouce, 1994
place Carpeaux
métro/RER: Grande Arche de la Défense

On the left side of CNIT.

This giant bronze *Thumb* emerging from the plaza adds a touch of humor to its surroundings.

Joan Miró

Bleu, jaune, et rouge, 1977
place de la Défense
métro/RER: Grande Arche de la Défense

Located in front of Les Quatre Temps shopping center.

These two oddly shaped, fantasy figures with bright blue, yellow and red markings convey the creative imagination of Miró, the Catalan artist who lived in Paris between the wars. They almost seem to mock the stiff, monolithic skyscrapers in the surrounding environment.

Christine O'Loughlin

Art déplacé
place de la Défense
métro/RER: Grande Arche de la Défense

Adopting the spirit of earthworks developed during the 1970s, O'Loughlin has delineated a large circle on an expanse of grass. But the circumferential band does not merely define the shape; it becomes a force all its own, widening and narrowing and changing from a positive to a negative element in relation to the grass. Unfortunately, barriers have been set up to prevent walking on and around the work, so you can't get a very good sense of its concept and form. Considering all the tall window-wall buildings in the area, however, *Displaced Art* has added value since it can be viewed from above.

Alexander Calder

Red Spider, 1976
place de la Défense
métro/RER: Grande Arche de la Défense

With its dynamic integration of form and space, this red-legged sculpture is a classic work by one of the masters of 20th-century public art.

Yaacov Agam

Fontaine monumentale, 1973–75/77
esplanade du Général de Gaulle
métro/RER: Grande Arche de la Défense

Extending across the middle of the esplanade near the Atlantique skyscraper.

Using the optical aesthetic he developed in the 1960s, Agam has imbued a pool and waterfall wall with a vibrant composition of alternating color blocks. Sixty-six jets of water move up and down in staccato rhythm, accompanied by taped music.

Guy-Rachel Grataloup

Trois arbres, 1988
esplanade du Général de Gaulle
métro/RER: Grande Arche de la Défense

Near the Ariane skyscraper.

Satirically, perhaps, the mosaic tower *Three Trees*, with its imagery of intertwined tree branches, calls attention to the substitution of a man-made environment for trees and nature.

Bernar Venet

Deux lignes indéterminées, 1988
cours Michelet, La Défense 10
métro/RER: Grande Arche de la Défense

Two Undetermined Lines typifies Venet's mode of turning the image of drawn lines into a monumental bronze sculpture.

François Morellet

La défonce, 1989–91
esplanade du Général de Gaulle
métro/RER: Grande Arche de la Défense

In front of the Ariane skyscraper

Smashed In is one of the most eccentric and adventurous sculptures at La Défense. Taking a parallelepiped as his imagery, the artist has delineated it with steel beams placed in a skewed, only half-visible position wrapped around the FNAC building and then suggestively disappearing into the ground. The architecture of FNAC (National Collection of Contemporary Art) is itself odd since the visible part, situated in the middle of the esplanade, is a one-story rectangular box, and the rest—the part used for art storage—is underground. Morellet thus plays with the idea of art that is shown and hidden in terms of both his own sculpture and the FNAC collection. His work is also an ironic comment on the idea of integrating architecture into the environment. Rather than relating to the triumphant spirit of La Défense, the sculpture *La défonse* becomes an object of disruption and disequilibrium. As in many of his works, Morellet uses imbalance and angularity to produce tension between walls and lines.

Bezons

This working-class suburb is northwest of Paris.

Centre d'Hemodialyse and Polyclinique du Plateau

 architect: Jean NOUVEL, 1978–80
rue Robespierre
RER: Grande Arch de la Défense; then bus 272 to Bezons, exit Albert 1e (15 min).

It's a short walk from the bus stop to the clinic. Cross boulevard Gabriel Peri, walk down rue Albert 1e until rue de Sartrouville, turn right for a short block, then left into rue Robespierre.

When the Val Notre-Dame Medical Clinic needed to expand its old, sandstone building, it decided to add a radical design by the young, rising-star architect Jean Nouvel. Taking a contextual approach based on a creative use of symbolism and cultural images, he sought to arouse strong responses to his adoption of industrial materials and high-tech construction. Knowing that the new clinic would be a place where patients stayed for short-term treat-

ments or convalescence, Nouvel conceived of it as a place of transit, an identity that he expressed by incorporating into his structure archetypal elements from hotels, boats and trains. Immediately apparent on the exterior is the corrugated metal sheathing—reminiscent of international trains—and the masts, footbridges, railings and portholes—virtually synonymous with steamers and cruise ships. On the interior, the gnarled wooden doors, curved ceilings of the corridors, rounded contours of the furniture, and vertical and circular neon lights suggest nautical fittings or sleeping-car compartments. Besides contextualizing the building with the transit theme, the uniqueness and lighthearted humor in the design relieve the somberness of sickness and the sterile aura of most clinics.

Poissy

Villa Savoye

 architects: LE CORBUSIER with Pierre JEANNERET, 1928–31
82 rue de Villiers, 78300
01-39-65-01-06 f: 01-39-65-19-33
Apr–Oct: Mon, Wed–Sun,
9:30–12:30 and 1:30–6; closed Tues. Nov–Mar: Mon, Wed–Sun,
9:30–12:30 and 1:30–4:30;
closed Tues
admission: 25/15F
RER: A5, Poissy, then bus 50, direction La Coudray, exit Lycée Corbusier. By car: A14 west to exit N184; then NI90 west to Poissy; from Poissy center D30 west to rue de la Maladrerie; turn right (rue de Villiers) just past the water tower at the fork with an island in the intersection. The villa is behind a stone wall.

This structure, classified as a national monument in 1965 (and totally reconditioned in the mid-1990s), is a must-see for anyone interested in 20th-century art or design. Built as a summer house for Pierre Savoye and his wife, it is an exemplar of the white villas Le Corbusier designed for rich private clients during the 1920s. On the one hand, it is an autonomous, floating cube isolated in a grass lawn and unequivocally revealing the architect's passion for pure form and geometric rigor. On the other hand, the "suspended garden" on the rooftop and wraparound band of windows facing out in all four directions—which insert "domestic life . . . into a Virgilian dream"—indicate a deep concern with the relationship between architecture and the environment.

Before going inside the house, note how the trees surrounding the lawn are purposefully taller than the house to shield it from the sight of neighbors or passersby and to provide the residents with a forestlike vista. Also note how the architect averts extreme reductivism and humdrum similitude by having points of emphasis and contrast. For example, the exterior is stark white—a signature feature of Le Corbusier—and yet, a section on the ground level is green and the windows are outlined in brown. The prominent angularity of the dwelling is also both emphasized and

subdued by the curving walls on the ground and roof levels.

You enter from the rear and can go up into and through the house via either a ramp or a circular staircase. It is somewhat odd to find a sink in the entrance hall, and somewhat discomforting to enter a room that is dark and cold. But, as is typical of Le Corbusier, the ground floor is a maintenance area containing parking for cars, living quarters for household help and service rooms. Residential functions are situated on the next floor up. Of primary importance is the spacious living room, designed with a horizontal line of windows along its rear wall, a pink wall, a light blue wall and a window wall opening to an interior courtyard. The room contains a small white-brick fireplace and waist-high shelves, some of which are enclosed behind stainless-steel doors. On the ceiling, extending the whole length of the room, is a curved and angled stainless-steel form covering fixtures for indirect lighting. Everything is precise and functional. This is also evident in the chrome chairs with leather or horsehide seats and the glass-top tables—furniture designed by Le Corbusier for the historic Esprit Nouveau pavilion at the Decorative Arts exhibition of 1925.

Just off the living room is the kitchen, furnished with three sinks, numerous cabinets (again with stainless-steel sliding doors) and lots of work space with white-tile countertops. The impression of efficiency and simplicity is omnipresent. This is also true in the bedrooms with their geometric, multisided room dividers housing closets, sinks, toilets and dressers. In the rooms and corridors, white walls are juxtaposed with a single colored wall (orange-rust, black, deep blue, brown, rose, light gray or pink); curved walls appear as counterpoints to the sharp angularity of the boxlike volumes; and

Le Corbusier, Villa Savoye

interconnections between spaces are ingeniously designed to provide fluidity, privacy and openness. Le Corbusier has also taken special care to create an amazing master bathroom with a sunken turquoise-tiled tub and a tiled lounge platform shaped to follow the curves of the body.

Throughout the house, windows give views inward to the central courtyard or outward to surrounding nature. There are also skylights that greatly increase the amount of sunlight and airiness in the rooms. A trademark feature of the house is the habitable roof with its patio and curved-wall solarium (a sunroom with plants). Seeing all the care taken to make even the smallest details conform with a functionalist, purist order, one can make better sense of Le Corbusier's famous statement: "A house is a machine to live in." The idea is not to create mechanized dwellings for human automatons but to conceive of houses as perfected tools placed at the service of their occupants.

Cergy-Pontoise

Located 15 1/2 mi (25 km) northwest of Paris in the valley of the Oise river, Cergy-Pontoise is another of the new towns created as a satellite city around the capital. Planned as a residential, commercial and industrial development, it has become a university center and is rapidly expanding its potential for recreational activities associated with the river.

Cergy Saint-Christophe

When Saint-Christophe laid out its development plans, it sought to revive the tradition of plazas and streets making separate circulation paths for pedestrians and cars. You immediately get a sense of this when you emerge from the spacious RER station and find yourself in an eye-catching passageway covered with a glazed barrel roof and with a huge clock at its end. (With its nearly 40-ft diameter this clock is the largest in Europe.) The area around the station forms a small plaza opening onto the main street—a pedestrian-only avenue lined with shops, offices, markets and the city hall. Along the way, you pass through several other plazas and ultimately come to one of Bofill's monumental apartment complexes and Karavan's grand axis project. The latter in particular is a site well worth seeing if you have any interest in land-use planning or public art, or if you just want to see one of the most ambitious works of contemporary creativity.

Place des Colonnes

 architect: Ricardo BOFILL, 1981–85
place de la Tour Belvédère
RER: A3, Cergy Saint-Christophe

Place des Colonnes (Plaza of Columns) is the last of the four grandiose housing projects Bofill created in or around Paris. Located at the interface between the town center and the esplanade to the river, the architecture relates to both even as it asserts itself as an independent entity. As you come upon the housing from the town, it clearly stands out because of its stark whiteness (the surface looks like stone but is concrete) and the flagrantly urban, classical, uniform character of its facades. In contrast, most town buildings are brick with modernist, undecorated facades and a more low-key, nonmetropolis appearance. Yet Bofill coheres his housing with the height of adjacent buildings (four stories) along the periphery where they meet and exaggerates a connection with the town by setting his rigorously symmetrical layout in alignment with the main street. On the side fronting the town, Bofill has also made his buildings congenial by bordering them with a stepped pedestrian walkway and some shops.

If you walk straight ahead through the center, you will enter a modest-sized, cross-shaped courtyard surrounded by buildings having the same facades as on the exterior. Any sense of monotony is, however, overwhelmed (or at least relocated) when you pass into the next courtyard. In dramatic opposition to the angularity and human scale of the previous courtyard, this is a gigantic semicircular space surrounded by a continuous facade featuring a six-story-high, pseudo-classical colonnade with intervening walls of tinted glass. It is a setting of absurd hyperbole and crazed theatricality despite (or because of) its references to the classical—a refined, tempered order associated with civility, class and power. Bofill not only caricatures the style itself but mocks the idea that an architectural style carries with it symbolic assumptions, especially socio-economic pretensions. Don't forget, these buildings with their look of imperial grandeur and authoritarian bravado are mere apartments—to boot, subsidized public housing.

Although this immense courtyard offers little in the way of human scale, if you go into the square courtyards of the side buildings—located alongside the other four-story structures and entered from the crescent through a supersized portal—you will find an almost intimate space, albeit still surrounded by austere, formal facades. Alternatively, if you exit the crescent on the side facing the valley, the monumentality of the architecture is more than equaled by the majesty of the vistas and landscape.

Dani Karavan

L'axe majeur, 1980–
RER: A3, Cergy Saint-Christophe

This is an ambitious environmental project consisting of a 3.2-km (almost 2 mi) axis across the Oise valley organized into 12 stations. It forms a conceptual continuation of the celebrated Paris axis extending from the Louvre to the Grande Arche at La Défense. By creating a project of urban scale in a still-emerging cityscape, Karavan promotes the importance of Cergy-Pontoise while contextualizing the district with reference to Paris.

La tour belvédère (1985), located in the center of Bofill's *Place des Colonnes*, is the starting point of L'axe majeur. This unornamented square-shaped tower is itself a beacon as well as a place to view the entire axis project and get a panorama of the whole region. (Go to the mayor's office in city hall for the door key.) Don't be alarmed if you sense a list in the tower; it was purposefully constructed to lean slightly in the direction of *L'axe majeur*. At ground level, it is perfectly aligned with a narrow opening in the colonnade hemicycle—the opening in turn frames the axis and the tower. At night the tower emits *Le laser*, a blue laser beam demarcating the full path of the axis.

As you walk away from the tower, you pass through the third station, *Le verger des impressionnistes—Camille Pissarro*, an orchard that bears witness to the agricultural past of the region and to the landscape favored by impressionist painters like Pissarro. Just beyond, *L'esplanade de Paris*, a vast open stretch of land paved into a flat field, presents a very different frame of reference. Instead of having a base in nature and a pastoral sensibility, it is geared to urban life and a mass sensibility. Karavan conceived of the esplanade as a grand public square where crowds would gather for all sorts of events and ceremonies. By embellishing the threshold area with a semicircle inset created of gray-rose paving stones formerly part of the Napoleon Courtyard in the Louvre, he also imbued it with an illustrious lineage. Getting into the act, the citizens of Cergy-Pontoise chose to build a geyser fountain (a boxlike platform with a hole in the middle) in the center of the main walkway to raise awareness of the site's importance as a source of geothermic energy.

The next station, *Les 12 colonnes*, is a bold architectural display marking the boundary between the plateau and the hill beyond. Because of the exacting alignment, you can see only the front row of four columns as you approach along Karavan's axial walkway. Quite suddenly as you get close, not only does the whole riveting set of 12 come into view, but a wondrous perspective of the surrounding landscape opens up. It's one of those amazing sites that gives you a timeless sensation. Contributing strongly to this impression is the resonant power of the columns. Although they are utterly simple, polar forms arranged in a compact cluster, they convey enigmatic allusions to past and future, stability, cohesiveness and loss. Here again, Karavan gives the columns a historic citation by making the dimensions of the space they occupy equal to those of the Arc de Triomphe du Carrousel in Paris.

After descending some stairs, you pass through the next station, *Les jardins des droits de l'homme (The Gardens of the Rights of Man)*—Pierre Mendès France, which connects the inhabited area of Cergy Saint-Christophe with the Oise valley. Olive trees will eventually form a border around a still-undeveloped garden area in the middle. Karavan specifically selected the symbolic olive tree originat-

ing in the da Vinci hills of Italy, and President Mitterand further distinguished this part of the project when he planted the first tree on October 18, 1990. At the bottom of the garden, another segment waiting to be built is *L'amphithéâtre Gérard Philippe*. This structure curved into the shoreline and facing both the Oise river and the leisure lake beyond will provide a viewing area for water shows and other attractions being developed as part of the region's summer program.

Karavan also plans to construct *La passerelle*—a walking bridge. It will connect the axial walkway leading to the amphitheater with a small, man-made island, *L'île astronomique*, located not far from the shoreline of the lake. The island and *La pyramide*—a concrete structure built on the water alongside the island—are both conceived as orientation settings, or poetic observatories, for measuring time and situating oneself in the universe. By cutting a cavity out of the stepped pyramid, Karavan increases the play of sunlight and wind on and around the pyramid. Of course, the pyramid itself invokes the spirit of contemporary Paris, calling to mind the fact that I. M. Pei's recent addition to the Louvre established a new marker along the historic axis in the capital city.

The final station is *Carrefour de Ham*, a cloverleaf traffic hub, located in the open countryside across the lake, about 1 mi (1.5 km) from the island. When the beam of *Le laser* illuminates the path of *L'axe majeur*, it extends to this point, a distance of about 2 mi (3.2 km) from the tower. According to Karavan, the laser beam represents science and a view toward the 21st century.

As is often the case with contemporary art that appears totally abstract, reductive and inexplicable, the work takes on a deeper, unseen dimensions when the artist (architect or historian) discusses it in terms of underlying references or formative meanings. Though these enhancements can greatly enrich appreciation, in successful works they never substitute for the direct, personal experience of the art itself. Here, for example, the incredible succession of spatial, visual experiences is itself extraordinary. It stands on its own. Karavan's contextual, historical associations only add icing to the cake and suggest alternative flavors and additional layers.

Housing

architect: Christian de PORTZAM-PARC, 1983
allée du Vif Argent
RER: A3, Cergy Saint-Christophe

As you walk back up Karavan's axial path, veer off to the left when you reach the orchard. The alignment of small apartment buildings (eight units in each structure) fronting the grass area is by the renowned French architect Portzamparc. The front facades have some of his signature markings—the void and planar combinations, circular and rectangular shaped elements—but basically the buildings lack the quirky elements and energizing tensions of his other work. Moreover, the structures are not aging well. The effects of time and/or poor care and construction are evident even though the buildings are less than 20 years old.

Cergy-le-Haut

This zone only began to be developed as a neighborhood within Cergy-Pontoise in the mid-1990s. If you are lucky enough to visit on a nice day, you will experience the unbelievable Pontoise light that attracted artists in the 19th century. You might even catch a glimpse of clouds that actually have silver linings.

Jean-Michel Alberola

Ceux qui attendent, 1993–96
RER station, platforms
RER: A3, Cergy-le-Haut

The national railroad corporation and district of Cergy-Pontoise commissioned *Those Who Wait*, a series of steel relief murals, to enliven the train platforms of the new RER station in Cergy-le-Haut. Given the context of the site, Alberola, a celebrated French artist known for his narrative and mythological paintings, centered the project on the theme of travel. Specifically concentrating on the aspect of displacement that is so much a part of the travel experience, he developed 13 cutout stencil compositions in steel to be located in long, arc-shaped spaces (*arcatures*) on the walls behind the train tracks facing two platforms. The full ensemble of murals stretches all along the platforms, but the individual parts (each a self-contained mural) are visible to "those who wait" for a train going in either direction.

For his subject, Alberola chose 17 sites classified by Unesco as world heritage treasures: Mont Saint-Michel, Temple of Angkor, Giza Pyramid, Statue of Liberty, Machu Picchu, Great Wall of China, Teotihuacán, Parthenon, etc. He then used a computer to manipulate promotional photos of these sites to the point where their identities were almost unrecognizable. When the images were subsequently made into monochrome

Alberola, *Ceux qui attendent*

133

silhouettes (some are two-toned in rust-red and black) with some interior cutout details, they became even more difficult to decipher. But Alberola added the name of the site (written as perforated lettering) to the depictions. He thus aids and accelerates perception, though shifting the visual experience, with the name as a point of departure, from recognition to discovery, from cliché exactitude to imagination. The results are evocative and the art is extremely compatible with the design of the architecture and the train setting.

Alberola dedicated the entire project to the impressionist painter Camille Pissarro. (A commemorative plaque in the station denotes this.) He chose Pissarro not just because he lived and worked in the Oise valley, but because he painted untitled, archetypal landscapes that were actually existing places depicted in a kind of blurred abstraction.

Lycée Jules Verne

architects: ARCHITECTURE STUDIO, 1991–93
rue Michel Strogoff and boulevard des Explorateurs
RER: A3, Cergy-le-Haut

Located in front of the Mirapolis Amusement Park, a short walk from the train station.

This gigantic, high-tech school building would be startling anywhere, but it appears especially out of place situated next to barren farmland on one side and a barely developed community on the other. As with much of the city planning for the *villes nouvelles*, future projections, not actualities, determine the size and nature of building projects.

As you come upon the school from the front, you first see a concrete-block building painted with bold red stripes. This rudimentary, bleak structure, which provides housing for teachers, unfortunately gives a poor introduction to the project. It is even more unfortunate that guards and school administrators rudely deny visitors access to the school property. You can therefore only view it from behind a cyclone fence. Nevertheless, you'll be able to appreciate the extraordinary design of the project.

The facility has a dramatic, futuristic appearance. Not surprising, given that the dynamic form of the main structure was inspired by the design of the high-speed TGV train. This source is most evident from the back of the building, where length is mind-boggling, and the image is a seamless curvature of polished metal beginning at ground level and sweeping upward and over with no separation between side wall and roof. Before you walk to get a view of the back, however, take note of the design in front. Here the curvature appears as a striking overhang with a prominent semicircular cutout in its midst that embraces a blue-and-white striped office building—another circular form. Exposed structural elements give the building an industrial, high-tech appearance even as the repetitive design of the glass-and-concrete facades hark back to a modernist model. Stripes and bright colors, as well as eccentric shapes and contrasting forms, further enhance the lively character of the architecture.

Although the perception of the school from the front suggests a campuslike complex with various units connected by bridges, a walk around the

Architecture Studio, Lycée Jules Verne

school indicates two very long buildings, bordered by perimeter streets and fitting tightly into a triangular plot that narrows to an acute angle. Considering the limitations of such an oddly shaped parcel of land, the creativity of the design is all the more amazing. It would have been nice, however, to find some landscaping incorporated into the design or the surroundings. And since the project was restricted by a tight budget, sadly there is already conspicuous evidence (faded and splotchy colors on the concrete walls) of very premature aging!

Amiens

Train from Paris (Gare du Nord) to Amiens (Gare Routière), 1 1/2–2 hr.

Sol LeWitt

Wall Drawing, no. 711, 1992
Musée de Picardie, 48 rue de la
République, 80000
03-22-91-36-44 f: 03-22-92-51-88
Tues–Sun, 10–12:30 and 2–6;
closed Mon
admission: 20/10F

Go left from the station toward the tower (tour Perret); turn right onto rue de Noyon, which then becomes rue des Trois-Cailloux; at place Gambetta turn left onto rue de la République; continue ahead for several blocks and you'll come to the museum's stately building on the right (10–15 min).

Although the Musée de Picardie does not have a major 20th-century focus, it welcomed the creation of a permanent "mural" by a vanguard American artist Sol LeWitt. The work, located in a rotunda at the rear of the main gallery, was seen as a complement to the 19th-century murals by Puvis de Chavannes that decorate the walls around the grand staircase at the front of the

museum. For his part, LeWitt created one of his signature wall drawings, conceptualizing his design specifically for the space in which it appears.

Using the octagonal rotunda as his point of departure, LeWitt developed a composition to encompass the walls, vaulted doorways, coffered-ceiling and semicircular stairway that perfectly integrates with the architecture and decor of the original and recently restored museum. Four colors (red, blue, yellow, gray) dominate the polychrome design. It is rich in tonal variations and each element interplays with the color, form and placement of the others. The artist also uses outlines to emphasize a form or to expand its size and expressive impact. Taken as a whole, LeWitt's design radically transforms a space that otherwise is a passageway into a focus of attention. Appropriately, it is both vibrantly contemporary and classical.

Stephan Balkenhol

Untitled (3 sculptures), 1993
Pont de la Dodane area, Saint-Leu

It's an easy walk to Saint-Leu, the oldest neighborhood in Amiens, and in the process you'll pass through the center of the city and see one of the most majestic Gothic monuments—the Cathédral Notre-Dame. From place Gambetta take rue Dusevel; turn right on rue Cormont; at place Saint-Michel turn left onto rue de Metz-l'Evêque; continue down the hill (the street becomes rue des Cornes) until you reach the Somme river canal; turn left onto place Parmentier; you will soon come to a bridge (Pont de la Dodane). Now, look into the water in front of the bridge.

The painted wood figure of a man standing on a buoy in the middle of the river is Balkenhol's sculpture. The strangeness of the location is magnified by the figure's banality, for he is dressed

Balkenhol, Untitled

FRAC de Picardie

45 rue Pointin, 80041
03-22-91-66-00 f: 03-22-92-97-84
Tues–Sat, 2–6; closed Mon
admission: free

From the plaza in front of the train station, turn left at the first street, rue Vulfran; go up the hill and turn left onto rue Pointin at the traffic light (5 min).

In addition to being a regional collecting and educational organization, the Picardie FRAC also has its own exhibition space. It is moreover unique in concentrating its collection on drawings. However, the term "drawing" is very loosely defined to include all sorts of works—even sculptures and installations—with a graphic or linear character. Indeed, the collection, which has works from an international spectrum of famous and unfamiliar artists, contains some extraordinary works that truly push the idea of drawing in intriguing directions.

The main gallery, located in the center of a new office building, is a huge, unencumbered room with skylights. Thematic and monographic exhibitions presented here are either displays of works in the collection or projects that take collection objects as the point of departure. There is also a small gallery that shows the work of young, emerging artists. This art center is a very professional, well-run operation with an exhibition history that is impressive and distinctive.

in ordinary clothes and seems quite nonchalant. If you now turn away from the river, you will see two figures, a man and a woman, set high on the front gable walls of houses located opposite one another at the front of the square, place du Don. Here, too, the figures are dressed simply and stand upright in an unassuming posture with their hands at their sides.

The German artist Balkenhol has made wood figures, roughly carved and wearing everyday dress, the subject of his art since 1983. They invariably have a primitivistic aura and yet they seem poised and confident. Using a strategy of displacement, the artist aims to make us think about customary assumptions and all we take for granted in the non-spectacular world in which we live.

Reims

Train from Paris (Gare de l'Est), 1 1/2 hr.

Le Collège—FRAC Champagne-Ardenne

1 place Museux, 51100
03-26-05-78-32 f: 03-26-05-13-80
Tues–Sun, 2–6; closed Mon
bus A or G, place Museux/Le Collège

To walk (15 min): from the cathedral plaza take rue Libergier; turn left almost immediately onto rue Chanzy; pass straight through place des 6 Cadrans; continue on along rue Gambetta until rue des Moulins. On this corner, there is a small plaza (place Museux) in front of a church and an old building. Enter the building—a former Jesuit school—turn right, walk across the courtyard and look for a sign designating the FRAC exhibition space.

Should you plan a trip to the Gothic cathedral in Reims—one of the finest in Europe, the site of coronations for French kings, with stained-glass replacement windows by Marc Chagall (1974)—or a tasting tour in the region's wineries (Reims is the City of Champagne), be sure to allot time to visit this exhibition space. Le Collège—FRAC organizes four exhibitions each year and presents works from its collection in a fifth. It has a strong program, exemplified by recent showings of such artists as Chris Burden, Jimmie Durham, Jefs Geys, Christian Lapie, Rainer Oldendorf, Patrick van Caeckenbergh, Franz West and emerging artists from the region. A good percentage of the artists come to Reims to develop special projects for an exhibition.

Bourges

This delightful city with a medieval cathedral, magnificent public garden, elegant palace and pedestrianized center is a nice place to spend a day. Train from Paris (Gare Austerlitz), 2 hr; from Nevers, 1 hr.

La Box

9 rue Edouard Branly, 18006
tel/fax: 02-48-24-78-70
Mon–Sat, 3–7; closed July–Oct
admission: free

The name "La Box" derives from the site's previous use for boxing. The space is quite small and compact, but as is true of other galleries associated with national schools of fine arts, this one has an adventurous of-the-minute program. Although basically a one-person operation with lots of help from students, La Box presents an impressive program of nine exhibitions each year, most of which are accompanied by informative catalogues. The work shown represents a broad spectrum of art, especially fresh ideas from young talents. Often artists create an installation or special project on site.

Three exhibitions each year feature artists who have been jointly invited by the school and gallery to be in residence for a minimum of three months. In addition, the June exhibition presents the work of a sculptor who has allied his or her art with sound or music. (This show is coordinated with Bourges's annual International Festival of Electronic and Synthesizer Music.) Recent exhibitions: *John Armleder, Pascal Broccolichi, Alec de Busschère, Delphine Coindet, Peter Downsbrough, Liliane Moro, Bernard Piffaretti, Christian Robert-Tissot, Elmar Trenkwalder, Yoon Ja & Paul Devautour, Drawing in Process.*

Nevers

Train from Paris (Gare de Lyon), 2 hr; from Bourges, 1 hr.

Jean-Michel Alberola, Gottfried Honneger, François Rouan, Claude Viallat, Raoul Ubac

Stained-glass windows
Cathédrale Saint-Cyr et Sainte-Julitte
rue de la Cathédrale

During World War II, a bombing raid on the night of July 16, 1944, destroyed part of this medieval cathedral, including the original stained-glass windows. Although reconstruction plans initially proposed that Sam Francis and Simon Hantaï, two young abstract artists, be commissioned to create new windows, there were no materials available for the project. It was not until 1977–83 that the first replacements were fabricated. They were bright red, yellow and blue wave-pattern abstractions created by Raoul Ubac for the circular and arch windows in the apse at the back of the church. Since then, many additional windows, designed by four contemporary artists, have been installed and others are in various stages of development.

For his decoration of the narrow arch windows on the back walls (the Romanesque section of the building), Alberola derived inspiration from prophesies recounted in the Apocalypse. Biblical references merge with abstract forms, a personal vocabulary and citations from a German stained-glass window of the 11th century to produce rhythmic, resplendent depictions. They echo the lush color and figuration of their medieval forebearers, but totally reshape the presentational mode, proposing a contemporary vision of the Apocalypse theme and new stained-glass techniques.

Following a different, more reductive tendency, Honneger has created utterly spare designs for the sequence of clerestory (upper level) windows along the nave. His blue and red monochrome fields have a single autonomous, elementary curved line in their midst—a line that reiterates (often in reverse) the architectural contour of the window and vault. Rouan, who will be developing the lower windows along the nave, has already produced the stained glass for the nave chapels. They are kaleidoscopic compositions of black, white and gray with bright red, blue or yellow. The patterns are fragmented and animated even as they exude tranquility by ultimately turning in on themselves.

At the front of the cathedral, Viallat produces a vibrant symphony of color and light in the double tier windows around the apse. Using his signature patchlike shapes and repetitive patterning as a format, he embraces the potency of stained glass by superimposing tones and enmeshing layers of space and form. An additional group of stained-glass windows, designed by Alberola, will eventually be installed in the apse chapels. With all the new windows, the Nevers cathedral is an unusual synthesis of Romanesque and Gothic architecture and 20th-century art.

Rouan, stained glass

Eglise Sainte-Bernadette du Banlay

architects: Claude PARENT and Paul
VIRILIO, 1963–66
rue de Banlay
03-86-57-32-90
Apr–Sept: daily, 7–7:30. Oct–Mar:
7–12 and 1:30–7

Located on the northeast border of
Nevers, just off the traffic circle, rond-
point Georges Pompidou, an easy 15-
min walk from the city center. Once on
rue de Banlay, after you cross the second street, rue Emile Zola, you'll see
#29. The church is on the plot behind
the fence. The church is often closed
but if you call ahead you'll have no
problem getting the key.

If you are curious about French architectural history, this is a site to visit. The
building was at the forefront of postwar
construction in raw, cast concrete, a
style often labeled brutalism. It followed
in the footsteps of Le Corbusier (especially the Ronchamp chapel, 1955) and
paralleled the work of Peter and Alison
Smithson in England. If you walk
around the exterior of the building, you
can readily see how the architects
shaped the whole using a few enormous, severe forms that brutally abut
and interrupt each other. In particular,
the two steeply inclined segments (the
front and back blocks), converging and
rising up as overhangs suspended above
the ground exemplify the "oblique
function" formulated by Parent and
Virilio. The contrast between extreme
solidity and exaggerated discontinuity
gives the structure its brute power.
Despite its compact, massive structure
(inspired in part by military bunkers),
the interior has a spiritual aura owing to
the majestic volume of the space and
diffuse luminosity. There are no views to
the outside and little color to relieve the
austere gray of the concrete, but the
skylight running the full width of the
building, uniting the fractured, dark,
sloping segments, serves as an actual
and symbolic source of light.

Tourcoing
Lille
Amiens
Reims
Strasbourg
PARIS
Bignan
Rennes
Orléans
Ronchamp
Nantes
Tours
Blois
Chenonceaux
Bourges
Dijon
Oiron
Nevers
Chagny
Rochechoart
Limoges
Thiers
Lyon
Angoulême
Vassivière
Villeurbanne
Ussel
St-Etienne
Meymac
Bordeaux
Grenoble
Crestet
Figeac
Digne
Plieux
Cahors
Vence
St-Paul-de-V
Lectoure
Mouans-
Biot
Nîmes
Arles
Sartoux
Nice
Toulouse
Montpellier
Marseille
Vallauris
Antîbes
Castres

excursions to the provinces

Lille Region

The amazing speed of the TGV makes it possible to go north from Paris to Lille in one hour. You can therefore go back and forth in the same day if you just want to get a quick look. Far more preferable is a short excursion or week-end with time to visit sites in Villeneuve d'Ascq and Tourcoign. If you're taking the Chunnel to London, you can also stop on the way since the route (car and train) passes through Lille.

Lille

Palais des Beaux-Arts

renovation: Jean-Marc IBOS and Myrto VITART, 1997
18 bis rue de Valmy, 59000
03-20-06-78-00 f: 03-20-06-78-15
Mon, 2–6; Wed–Thurs, Sat–Sun, 12–6; Fri, 12–8; closed Tues
admission: 30/20F, under 25 free

From the Lilles Flandres train station it's a 10-min walk along rue du Molinel, or you can take the métro to République.

As part of its renovation program, the architects constructed a new, stream-lined building behind the existing museum built in the late 19th century. Most significantly, they designed its inner facade as a wall of glass and created a garden plaza, largely occupied by a shallow pool (temporary exhibition galleries lie underneath) in the space between the two buildings. The elaborate, fanciful shape from a past era thus becomes a wondrous image reflected across the surface of the high-tech edifice from the present. But the reflected image is hardly an exact replica since a geometric composition in red and gold—painted on corridor walls paralleling the window wall of the new building—adds a modernist overlay. The effect is dazzling.

Commissions for two monumental works of contemporary art were also part of the renovation. Though the museum is renowned for its historic collection and does not show or collect contemporary art, it aimed to signify its modernity and future by given prominence to these works from the current era.

Guilio Paolini

Exposition universelle, 1994–97
atrium, Palais des Beaux-Arts

The revival of the museum's grand atrium as a public space was a major aspect of the recent renovation. For his part, Paolini created an installation—composed of 48 one-meter (about 3 1/4 ft) square glass cubes and a mirrored sphere—that echos and arouses awareness of the atrium. In accordance with his typical mode of creativity, the artist doesn't restate the obvious, however. He confounds all sorts of ideas about form and perception. To begin with, all his sculptural elements are three-dimensional objects yet they are nearly invisible and seemingly volumeless since they are made of transparent and reflective materials. Thus, the conventional notion that an artwork has its own character and attracts attention to itself (in contrast to deflecting attention to its surroundings) doesn't apply here at all.

Half the transparent cubes form a rectangle around the periphery of the atrium, reiterating the position of columns and pillars in the architecture. A serigraph printed on top of each shows a ground plan of the space with a portion darkened to denote the angle of vision of someone located in the middle of the atrium looking toward the particular cube. The 24 remaining cubes are set together as a conglomerate unit, like a table, in the center of the atrium. Here the printed image is an ensemble across all the cube tops. It presents a view of the glazed roof above as if seen by someone standing in the very center of the atrium. It's like a photo taken with a wide-angle lens. The image is not only confusing in its perspective but complicated further by the grid pattern of the cube tops and the grid delineations in the skylight overhead reflected on the surfaces of the cubes. (These grids are quite noticeable if you look down from the balconies on the second floor.) Complexity notwithstanding, Paolini adds yet another view—a view of the atrium in its totality, or globality (albeit distorted), captured in a mirrored ball suspended midway between floor and ceiling in the middle of the atrium.

Like various other conceptual and site-oriented artworks, Paolini's installation challenges the idea of a fixed image by revealing that seeing is a composite of reality, knowledge, remembered experience and representations. The work suggests that a place is largely imaginary, formed by successive, partial and reflected visions, each conditioned by the particularities of a given perspective at a moment in time. Admittedly, this type of mind-teasing sculpture does not have instant or widespread appeal. But if you lay aside your customary orientations to art and proceed more as a sleuth trying to put the parts together, you will surely experience discovery in the work, and maybe even pleasure.

Gaëtano Pesce

L'élairage 1994–97
entrance lobby, Palais des
Beaux-Arts

If the Paolini was too cerebral for your taste, the work by Gaëtano Pesce will surely redress the balance. The artist, a celebrated designer born in Italy and residing in France, sought to restore a forthright sign of opulence and welcome to the museum's entrance hall. He therefore designed two chandeliers displaying an unfettered expression of visual exuberance. Placed at either end of the lobby, they are gargantuan, curving forms whose fullness of volume is more than matched by their radiance of color. Composed of 12,500 glass tiles with a metal structure underneath and a fishnetlike web on the exterior, they hang down from the cathedral ceiling to about 12 ft off the ground. Beyond functioning as light fixtures, they are dominant presences in the setting and luminous objects in space. Because Pesce has treated the surfaces like an abstract painting with cascading and merging fields of white, yellow, green, red, blue and black, the chandeliers also stand out as works of contemporary art.

Euralille

 Master planner: Rem KOOLHAAS, 1989–2004

"Euralille" is the name of the grand development project within the city of Lille. Unlike other planning efforts geared to revitalize and restructure an urban center, here the aim was to construct, virtually from scratch, a dense zone of international convergence. Euralille was conceptualized as the nexus of ground transportation systems in northern Europe, a major business hub for the European Community and a megalopolis for the 21st century. The site, 300 acres of marginal land between Lille and its outlying suburbs, was deemed to be ideal. The location was roughly equidistant from Paris and London and a pivotal point for the Paris-London-Brussels triangle. It was thus perfectly situated to become a dominant station within the extended TGV network (a multinational undertaking) and the point of convergence for trains and highways headed toward the newly sanctioned (1986) Chunnel. Moreover, Lille was a provincial city in the midst of an economically distressed, industrial region sorely in need of "metropoli-tanization." Hopes were high for this million-dollar, future-oriented enter-prise, and Rem Koolhaas, a star of the new generation of city theorists who based his ideas on "Bigness" and "cultural congestion," seemed like the perfect project director. (He expounds on these topics in his renowned books *Delirious New York* and *SMLXL*.) With completion of the first phase in 1996, it is possible to see some results.

Initial concentration was on the train station, a commercial and office complex and a convention-exhibition-entertainment center. To say that each of these is gigantic severely underestimates their size. True to his theories, Koolhaas encouraged the creation of high-density, monumental structures. He favored buildings that were like containers with neutral exteriors (coverings) and open interiors having an unlimited potential for rearrangement. As much as they reveal his embrace of new engineering technologies and industrial low-tech components, they convey his scorn for aesthetic and contextual concerns.

The dramatic contrast between Euralille and historic Lille is unquestion-ably jarring but from Koolhaas's perspective effective in heightening intensity and heterogeneity. Similarly, he considers Euralille's lack of planned order and cohesion desirable, for it generates activity, tension and instability—features deemed integral to the dynamics of urbanism. Indeed, Euralille is unique among postmodern cities in France in that it doesn't privilege pedestrians, external public spaces, neighbor-hoods or nature. Quite the contrary, it reestablishes a skyline of boxlike towers and a landscape of multilane express-ways, train-track pastures, concrete pathways and perpetual congestion. When you walk around outdoors, you readily get the impression of a disparate assemblage of huge structures—gray objects in a gray environment.

In fairness to Koolhaas, many key features of the original plan were scrapped along the way or so modified by political and economic decisions that they no longer are conceptually or architecturally recognizable. This hasn't made Euralille any less controversial; it remains the subject of heated discus-sions regarding past, present and future urban planning. You may not like what you'll see, but you'll never know until you see it.

Centre Euralille

architect: Jean NOUVEL, 1991–94
avenue Le Corbusier, 59777
Mon–Sat, 10–8; closed Sun

This shopping-office-housing-entertain-ment-hotel megastructure dominates the triangle of land between the old train station—Gare Lille Flandres—and the new Gare Lille Europe. For all the hoopla about Euralille's radicality, you may think you're in the wrong place when you stand at the corner of place des Buisses and survey the converging facades of Nouvel's edifice. It looks a lot like 1960s-style, glass-and-steel block architecture sensationalized by an entrance whose thrusting, bombastic overhang and barrage of signage comes right out of Times Square. On closer inspection, the architecture does pre-sent some uncommon features, not the least of which is the discrepancy between spatial expectations derived from the exterior and the spatial reality inside the shopping mall.

Walking to the right down avenue Willy Brandt, the structure seems to extend endlessly. It is composed of a long, multistoried platform with three intermittently placed residential-office towers (five were planned). A suspended walkway creates a horizontal line of continuity and awninglike projection below which are an array of entrances, zigzagging staircases and balconies. The bleak darkness—omnipresent shade plus gray-tinted glass in a grid defined by charcoal-toned steel—and prevalence of industrial metal on the lower facade were to have been enlivened by hanging vines, but few have survived the lack of sun and the harsh northern climate. More successful are the accents of bright red in the form of hingelike color bars placed at edges and corners across the entire facade.

The most ambitious scheme, however, is Nouvel's implementation of an electronic system, commonly used in Japan to create animated patterns along a glass facade. The process entails computerizing a photograph onto holographic films which are then screened as a repetitive sequence onto a window wall. When seen in sunlight, the image—in Euralille one was a banal depiction of carts in a supermarket parking lot—is dramatically transformed into iridescent colors, textures and volumetric forms. It's also cinematic: images seem to move with you as you pass in front of them. However, this side of the building, across the street from postal loading docks and leading to the freeway, has very little pedestrian traffic. Moreover, the imagery is not very visible or colorful on sunless or overcast days, of which there are many in Lille.

The side of Centre Euralille bordering allée de Liège and facing avenue Le Corbusier begins with a blue hotel building and follows with residential buildings in which apartments can easily be converted to offices. The entire facade is a continuous, 10-story-high, flat surface. Articulation comes from horizontal lines of colored louver boards alternating with rows of windows. Nouvel sought to animate this side as he did the south facade by arranging the colors in a syncopated order. The effect, however, has been weakened by the substitution of subdued tones for the bright hues called for in the architect's plan.

Enormous shopping malls are still somewhat unusual in France so Nouvel's development of the interior of Centre Euralille as a small city covered by a roof had a double impact. From the main entrance you pass into a central street lined with storefronts set in a stepped-back pattern. It crosses diagonally through the building to another major entryway at place de l'Europe and the new train station. A second street intersects the first and the same layout recurs on all three levels. Near the middle, an island provides escalator circulation and opens up views to the bottom of the underground parking and all levels in between. What makes the space distinctive, giving it the look of an ultra-modern vessel or an underwater cave, is the reflecting aluminum roof positioned at an oblique angle. It hovers overhead unattached to the shopping realm though connecting on the sides with equally shiny stainless-steel walls. Not only does the roof assert the volume of the whole but it also adds lively design elements—slats painted red in one direction and big glazed cutouts that bring natural light into the interior.

Espace Croisé

101 Centre Euralille, 59777
03-20-06-98-19 f: 03-20-06-67-42
Tues–Sat, 1–7; closed Mon
admission: free

Located in the back of Centre Euralille, on the top level, left of the escalators going down to place de l'Europe.

Judging by its location in a chic, bourgeois shopping mall, you might expect this art center to have a similar orientation. Not so. This is one of the most free-wheeling exhibition and activity centers in France—not because it shows avant-garde art objects but because it deals almost exclusively with new media, new technology and design. It produces and shows Internet creations, runs a multimedia space and has a refreshing program of exhibitions, video and experimental films, debates and conferences. When you get tired of looking at all the trendy products in the neighboring shops, stop in here and feast on a different kind of dazzle. Recent exhibitions: *Eric Duyckaerts, Pierrick Sorin, Robotic Forum, Video: A Kind of Irony* (*Peter Campus, Marie-Ange Guilleminot, Joan Jonas, Bruce Nauman, Nam June Paik, Pipilotti Rist, Bill Viola . . .*), *For Example, Berlin: Six New Architectural Projects, A Century of Avant-Garde German Cinema.*

Gare Lille Europe

 architect: Jean-Marie DUTHILLEUL
place de l'Europe

Unlike the heavy stone enclosure walls around most train stations, here the glass sheathing makes the edifice virtually transparent. Urban space connects directly with people traveling in the trains, standing on the platforms or sitting in waiting areas. Conversely, the TGV and other trains are visibly part of the Euralille environment. Adding to the sense of openness are the curving roof hovering over but never touching the side walls (it's been called a "flying carpet") and the roadway (avenue Le Corbusier) running right through the building. There are also two office towers (see below) spanning the station on bridgeways.

As seems apparent from the exterior and is verified when you try to find the train you need, the interior is a baffling, Piranesian space. Streams of nonconnecting, diagonal circulation paths crisscross its entire length leading to multiple railway lines, a range of city exits and numerous links to adjacent parking garages and buildings. You are

therefore subject to near entrapment in the wrong place or lengthy backtracking should you make one wrong move. If train travel weren't disorienting enough, here's a station structured to enhance distress and confusion!

Tour Crédit Lyonnais

 architect: Christian de PORTZAMPARC
place de l'Europe

Located above the TGV station facing the rear entrance to Centre Euralille.

This incredibly unusual high-rise by Portzamparc, the architect of Cité de la Musique and other celebrated projects in Paris, will undoubtedly leave a lasting impression. Dramatically shaped like a ski boot or high-backed chair, its 20-story mass seems to float in space, proudly asserting command of the skyline even as its slanting sides and sharply angled form reinforce uncertainty about its structure. Unlike static

Portzamparc. Tour Crédit Lyonnais

buildings with vertical walls and horizontal roofs, this one has vitality, appearing as if it might get up and go. (An appropriate image for an edifice straddling a train station.) Its characteristics also change radically from front, side and back perspectives.

The glazed front of the tower gives all offices a panoramic view of the city and a maximum amount of natural light. Having a green sunscreen, the window wall is a nuanced surface variously toned green, blue or gray depending on the weather. In contrast, Portzamparc has sheathed the back facade with gray stone (except for a central green-glass panel) and perforated it with trapezoidal windows that progressively widen in consonance with the building's shape. Yet another rhythmic pattern occurs on the sides, where alternating, horizontal bands of green glass and gray stone create a steady flow across the surface.

Entrance halls for the tower are in the elongated, tapered base. To arrive at this level, however, you must take an elevator, passing through a series of spaces. From place de l'Europe, the location of the elevator is extremely understated, it being in a small white structure hidden behind an equally innocuous window-faced structure. This mismatched pair, set at a skewed angle to the base platform above, seems a meager appendage for the main building though it cleverly brings the massive high-rise down to human scale at ground level.

Tour Lilleurope

architects: Claude VASCONI with
Jean-Claude BURDESE
parvis de Rotterdam

Located above the TGV station parallel to the Crédit Lyonnais Tower.

Suffering from juxtaposition with an eccentric building, this tower falls by the wayside as a generic gray block. Though not extraordinary, its positioning of a cable-and-steel frame around but separated from the glazed facade does give the high-rise a less massive appearance on the outside and a more flexible interior space. Splitting the tower in two horizontally also provides a point of accent in an otherwise repetitive, monolithic surface.

Originally the Euralille master plan called for six towers to be built over the train station. Because construction over the tracks is now unlikely, if not impossible, the two existing towers become even more forceful as silhouettes in space, and the station itself gains visual prominence.

Robert Cahen

Mur d'images, 1995
allée de Liège

Monitors are situated along the sidewalk, inserted in the supporting concrete wall of the viaduct Le Corbusier opposite the blue hotel building.

This real- and recorded-time video installation (*Wall of Images*) is an intriguing public artwork. But the lack of an ongoing repair and maintenance budget has made it a dead object, like many other mechanical and electronic projects situated in nonart spaces. Should it be revived, you would be able to experience a diversity of visual and acoustic passages on 29 differently sized monitors ("animated windows") spread like a landscape along the wall. Some images are historical snapshots assembled into a narrative and others are "living postcards" showing scenes in distant places visited by the artist during the past several years. Interspersed with these photo-collages are live projections being captured on the spot by cameras in the immediate vicinity. As you look at the spectrum of images, unforeseen connections emerge and boundaries between disparate times and places blur. Within a city where past and present so abruptly confront one another, such visions (or re-visions) have particular resonance.

Lille Grand Palais (Congrexpo)

architect: Rem KOOLHAAS, 1990–94
boulevard des Cités Unies, 59777

From place de la Gare take rue de Tournai to its end facing the peripheral highway; walk through the underground passage and you'll be in front of Congrexpo (5 min).

Within the field of architecture, Koolhaas's Grand Palais (also called Congrexpo) was greatly anticipated as the exemplar of his theories about an autonomous, container building with a functional open interior, all exuding "Bigness." By any definition, this mammoth complex is Big. It encompasses three entities, Zénith—a rock concert hall (left), Congrès—a multilevel conference center with three auditoriums, meeting rooms and a restaurant-banquet hall (center) and Expo—a convention-exhibition space (right). Yet the totality of its grand ovoid shape is lost since you can't get an overall perspective of it, and the front facade, which is visible, has been separated into parts, each with a different design and dissimilar materials. Though its architecture may well be noncontextual and autonomous, its location as an utterly isolated entity on the far (east) side of the peripheral highway, separated from both the old and new parts of the city as well as the suburbs, makes this issue fairly nonconsequential. If anything, its overt incorporation of harsh, industrial materials makes it blend into the bleak wasteland, railroad-track setting around it.

Unlike the spate of recent buildings with a coherent, refined industrial appearance, here the rubblelike treatment of the concrete on the exterior of Zénith, the brutalist, raw aspect of structures in the center area, and the green corrugated plastic and faux-stone surface of Expo give Koolhaas's edifice a cheap, tacky and alienating character. And the juxtaposition of light, transparent materials with heavy concrete engenders an idiosyncratic collage. There is, however, an alternative expression in the sweeping curves, so pronounced on the two side segments. Most impressive is the gentle undulation and outward tilt of the plastic wall in Expo and its independence from the curved shape of the roof. Likewise in Zénith, extreme curves shape the edge of the flat overhanging roof and the outer wall of the concert hall, which in turn has a sloping underside with roller-coaster waves. (The hall is raised on pylons leaving the ground area unenclosed.)

Among the major compromises that had to be made because of budget limitations and technical complications was the sectioning of the interior into three functionally separate, enclosed spaces. Since interior openness was a dominant element of Koolhaas's theory, this change greatly altered an essential feature of his design. There are still interconnections between the three units but walls between them prevent the kind of fluidity of spatial expansion and recreation described in the original proposal.

Villeneuve d'Ascq

Musée d'Art Moderne

🏛 1 allée du Musée, 59650
03-20-19-68-68 f: 03-20-19-68-99
Mon, Wed–Sun, 10–6; closed Tues
admission: 25/15F; free 10–2, first
Sun of the month
métro: line 1 to Pont de Bois, then
bus 41 to Parc Urbain-Musée; or
line 2 to Font de Mons, then bus
10 to Parc Urbain-Musée (15 min).
(If you have never ridden on a
high-tech subway system, this is a
perfect chance to do so. The trains
are driverless, fast, quiet and clean,
and underground platforms have
safety walls to separate the trains
and their noise from passengers.)

The museum, built in a large park, was
founded in 1983 to house the Masurel
collection of modern art, a gift to Lille.
Neither large nor comprehensive, the
collection nonetheless has significant
highlights in cubist works by Braque,
Henri Laurens and Picasso, and paintings by Derain, Léger, Miró, Modigliani
and Rouault. Since the museum would
not have been able to expand with new
purchases of early-20th-century art, it
decided to move into the realm of contemporary art. Its tendency has been to
favor works with a conceptual orientation. Among its holdings are objects by
Art & Language, Lewis Baltz, Victor
Burgin, Georges Chaissac, François
Dufrêne, Barry Flanagan, Dennis
Oppenheim, Gina Pane, Claude Rutault.
Special exhibitions, whether contemporary or not, enjoy a reputation of being
thorough and penetrating. Recent exhibitions: *Alighiero e Boetti*, *Allan
McCollum*, *Thomas Ruff*, *The Other
Side of the Decorative*, *Art Brut*,
American Art.

Several sculptures, mainly of a modernist vintage (Calder, Lipshitz, Picasso . . .)
are located on the park grounds. Most
prominent is Richard Deacon's *Between
Fiction and Fact* (1992). Set in a place of
honor in front of the museum, its bold,
curving, loop structure of gray-painted
steel creates an interesting contrast
with the assemblage of boxlike forms
constituting the museum's brick architecture.

With its enchanting setting and spacious building, the museum promises to
become a major exhibition and collecting site for contemporary art in the Lille
region. Even now with its limited collection, it's a delightful place to visit,
especially if you want to escape the
urban tempo for a few hours.

Tourcoing

TGV from Lille Flandres station to
Roubaix, 15 min; from Paris (Gare du
Nord), 1 1/2 hr. You can also go by tram
from Lille Europe or Lille Flandres, exit
Le Fresnoy. After 1999 an underground
train will link Tourcoing with Lille.

Le Fresnoy—Studio National des Arts Contemporains

🏛 architect: Bernard TSCHUMI,
1991–97
🎥 22 rue du Fresnoy, 59207
03-20-70-43-62 f: 03-20-26-44-62
exhibitions: Mon, Wed–Sat, 1–7;
Sun, 3–7; closed Tues
admission: 25/20F

It's a short walk from the TGV station. If
you took the tram from Lille, take bus
21, direction Blanc Seau, exit Le Fresnoy.

This is an exciting, new visual arts center
created for the 21st century. Its
approach toward art and its activities
are adventurous and unconventional.
Even a day trip from Paris just to visit

this site is a rewarding experience. You can wander through the mind-boggling building, see several exhibitions, observe work in progress, perhaps catch a lecture by a distinguished guest or a performance, see a new or historic film, browse through the media library and bookstore, chat with some of the students and artists in the café, and absorb some of the center's forward-thinking ideas about what constitutes and shapes "art."

Le Fresnoy, which opened in October 1997, is uniquely devoted to audiovisual and multimedia creation. It encompasses a postgraduate art school, audiovisual production center, cinema, exhibition space and faculty studio-apartments. Equipped with state-of-the-art technology and innovative work and display areas, the center encourages experimentation and crossovers between professionals working in different artistic disciplines—visual arts, film, photography, video, computer imagery, sound technology, music, architecture, performing arts, etc. Indeed, it has eliminated media-based classifications to expand the dialogue related to questions of theory, aesthetics and methods of presentation.

Artist-professors, invited for one year, pursue personal projects with the assistance and collaboration of students who in turn carry out their own projects. The emphasis is on production,

though guest scholars, critics, film directors and the like are invited to give lectures focused on the historical avant-gardes and the contemporary creative scene. The lecture series—held on Mondays and open to the public—also includes specialists from the realms of technology of interest to audiovisual and artistic creation. More than an art school for a circumscribed body of students, Le Fresnoy is an important resource center for the visual arts.

The exhibition program, like all else in the center, aims to break from established protocols. It uses its two theaters as commercial cinemas to present a full schedule of independent and experimental films, and it takes advantage of the large nave of the old hangar, now called the *Grande Nef* , and all adjoining spaces, including the *Entre-deux* (the space in between the old and new roofs) for formal exhibitions, installations, performances, site-specific projects, faculty presentations and in-process work. Recent exhibitions: *Voix, Voices, Veus* (an exploration of the human voice in works by Vito Acconci, Judith Barry, Geneviève Cadieux, Janet Cardiff, Jochen Gerz, Gary Hill, Pierre Huyghe, Kristin Oppenheim, Monique Toebosch), *Cross-Country* (a project about landscape comprising *The Second Promenade*—an installation by Jean-Louis Boissier, *Canal, Caravana Obscura*—photographs by Christine Felten and Véronique Massinger, *Igloolik Videos* by Zacharias Kunuk, and *Amsterdam, Global Village* —an installation by Johan Van der Keuken), *Projections: Transporting the Image* (film and video installations by Jean-Pierre Bertrand, Patrick Bokanowski & Christopher Cardoen, La Cellule Metamkine, Atom Egoyan, Alain Fleischer, Henri Foucault, Anne Marie Jugnet & Alain Clairet, Jozef Robakowski, Bill Seaman, Michael Snow) .

For the architecture, Tschumi created

Tschumi, Le Fresnoy

a startling complex, boldly conveying the spirit of unabashed openness that Le Fresnoy aimed to promote. His strategy shared a likeness with the famous surrealist image of "the chance meeting of a sewing machine and umbrella on an operating table." Defying the long-standing reverence for logic, unity and order associated with Bauhaus design, Tschumi juxtaposed "found" structures already on the site with new construction. Moreover, he embraced incongruity and egregious discontinuity.

For six decades up until the early 1970s, the site was a leisure palace popular with the working-class communities of Tourcoing and Roubaix. It was a neighborhood center offering movies, dancing, swimming, wrestling, roller-skating, pony rides and refreshment bars. After it went out of business, the old buildings lay abandoned and suffered major deterioration. Everyone assumed the structures would be torn down, but Tschumi decided to keep some of them as well as the former lay-out. (Apart from other considerations, this saved a considerable amount of money.) He put a huge roof over the entire complex and preserved such things as the main hangar with its spacious nave and large side area, the film theater bar, the grand access stairs and the pitched, tile roofs of four small buildings. He also added components and developed a staggering, multilayered, interconnecting system of ramps, bridges and stairways (colored royal blue) suspended in space by cables. (Some are at unbelievable heights.) New and old, enclosed zones and open spaces are each conspicuously self-assertive. There are crossovers but no attempt is made to create an overall unity or comprehensive logic. A staircase comes down from the roof and meets the ramp of an old building; parts of an old building hang outside the new roof; and dramatic collisions of scale are omnipresent. "Architecture of the event" is the term Tschumi has used to describe the montage of numerous layers, each with its own logic and independence, and the composite with surplus, undesigned spaces.

The exterior equals the interior in being audacious and distinctive. Notable at first glance is the lack of outer, enclosing walls! With no walls, the high roof—an expanse of curving metal with skylight cutouts in an array of large geometric shapes—becomes all the more dramatic. The design calls to mind the futuristic proposals of Buckminster Fuller for domed cities (1950s), which likewise covered a community with a floating roof. But in contrast to Fuller's homogeneous structures, Tschumi's repeatedly foregrounds the concept of heterogeneity. This is particularly obvious in the staircase at the front facade—a bipartite structure, one side a tapering path made of shiny, perforated metal and the other, rose-toned granite stairs proportioned to double as seating. With its extreme length, climbing in space from the ground to the third level, and its disparate parts, the main entrance overtly signifies the deregulated, polymorphous creativity of Le Fresnoy's program.

Partly responding to a tight budget, Tschumi used a wide range of industrial materials in his design. The list includes metal fencing, screens, concrete, glass and all kinds of steel. However, he imbued these materials with style though never succumbing to decorative, transformative practices. For example, he avoided a monotonous, severe wall of flat corrugated steel across the back of the center, a long stretch running parallel to a highway, by creasing the steel horizontally and punctuating it with a few eccentric window openings.

Loire Region

Orléans

Train from Paris (Gare Austerlitz), 1 hr; from Tours, 1 1/2 hr; from Blois, 35 min.

FRAC Centre

12 rue de la Tour Neuve, 45000
02-38-62-52-00 f: 02-38-62-21-80
Mon–Fri, 10–12 and 2–6
admission: free

The collection of this FRAC is unique in specializing on architecture. It's an amazingly comprehensive corpus of drawings, models, photographs, architectonic sculptures and multimedia designs associated with realized constructions, theoretical ideas and utopian creations. Included are works by a broad range of artists and architects from many different countries and diverse stylistic and conceptual orientations. The works reveal diverse attitudes toward form, function and space in buildings, cities, gardens, public monuments and independent projects. In addition, they give strong evidence of the mutually vitalizing dialogue that has been ongoing since the 1960s between the disciplines of art and architecture.

At any given time, you can see selections from the collection or a special exhibition in the FRAC gallery or elsewhere in the city. Recent exhibitions: *Mutations@morphes*; *Objectile*; *Silos— Robin Collyer, Andreas Gursky, Axel Hütte*; *Architectures in Games*; *François Roche*. Use a visit here as an excuse to spend a day wandering around historic and modern Orléans—or vice versa.

Blois

This picture-book old city has a château at its center and steep streets winding up and down its hilly terrain. Train from Paris (Gare Austerlitz), 1 1/2 hr; from Orléans, 35 min; from Tours, 40 min.

Musée de l'Objet

6 rue Franciade, 41000
02-54-78-87-26 f: 02-54-74-88-45
Wed, Sat–Sun, 2–7; closed
Mon–Tues, Thurs–Fri
admission: free

From the train station walk down avenue Jean Lalgret; go across the square Augustin Thierry; turn left on rue Gallois; when rue Gallois curves to the right, go straight ahead on rue Chambourdin; take a sharp right at the first crossing onto rue des Minimes; almost immediately turn left onto rue Franciade (15 min).

Inaugurated in 1996, this unusual museum is located in a former convent, now the city's Ecole des Beaux-Arts. Its mission is to track the dialogue between European artists and banal, everyday objects. As the museum reveals, artists of the last half century—following in the footsteps of Marcel Duchamp— have been strongly inspired by poetic, neutral, clinical, political, satiric, refined, kitsch, cruel and childish common objects. The resulting creations are not only fascinating but also provide a riveting history of contemporary culture. The display includes about 100 works by both international names (Boltanski, Broodthaers, Christo, Cragg, Polke . . .) and unknown artists. Most of the objects will probably be unfamiliar and there are many eye-openers that shed new light on artistic preoccupations. All the works come from the collection of Eric Fabre and are on a 15-year loan to the museum.

In addition to the collection galleries, there is a temporary exhibition space located in a small building in the middle of the interior courtyard. Special exhibitions—like *Piano Family of John Cage* and *Di Rosa and Modest Art*—are as unique and captivating as the collection. Don't skip this site or you'll miss an incredible, fun-filled experience.

Ben

Mur des mots, 1958–95
Ecole des Beaux-Arts,
rue de la Paix

Located in the back courtyard–parking lot of the Ecole des Beaux-Arts and Conservatoire National de Musique, facing rue de la Paix.

If you can't gain access to the courtyard through the gate (often locked) or by entering the building (around the corner to the left), the view through the gate is quite good. *Wall of Words* is a composite of 282 text paintings, created over a 37-year period, reproduced as 319 enamel panels and set together as a mural on the exterior wall of a building. It's typical of the work produced by Ben, a Fluxus artist who gained a reputation in Nice during the 1960s by creating paintings, installations, performances, manifestoes and a store focused on the absurdity and ambiguity of language. Often, as here, his work takes the form of a handwritten or printed single word or short phrase placed alone on a monochrome ground like a sign. The signs seem like cryptic messages, commandments or maxims, but usually they are merely provocations, highfalutin professions of faith, banal or indifferent statements or nonsense aphorisms. Examples are *Pas d'art sans verité* (No art without truth) and *je tourne en rond* (I turn in a circle). As a mural spread across an entire wall with variations in the size of the panels and the amount and size of the writing on each, and with a few color panels interspersed

among the black ones, Ben plays wittily with Mondrian's compositional format. His signs also create a nice counterpoint to the rows of windows with their diverse shapes and grid patterns.

Ben, *Mur des mots*

Jan Dibbets

Stained-glass windows
Cathédrale Saint-Louis,
place Saint Louis
sometimes closed noon–3
and after 6

Located in the center of the old city atop a hill looking over the countryside.

In 1992 Jan Dibbets, a celebrated Dutch conceptual artist, received the commission to create 32 stained-glass windows for the high and low bays of the cathedral in Blois. As of 1997 four were installed; the full sequence will be completed for celebrations in the year 2000. In his approach, Dibbets has adapted his habitual process of reordering a form or image to engender new perceptions and alternative ways of expressing space. Using near and distant views, displacement techniques and a sequential organization of space, he challenges customary modes of representation. He also reorients seeing and thinking.

As his point of departure in Blois, Dibbets used the lozenge shape, typical of Gothic stained glass, and the cames (lead rods used to hold the panes of glass). From these basic elements, he has designed geometric configurations and decorative graphics in harmony with the architecture. The compositions are utterly spare and simple with a limited range of very cool colors applied with extreme sparseness. "Content" derives from symbolic words referring to the traditional liturgy. But the words— Christe, Eleison, Kyrie, Gloria, Ite Baptizate, Sanctus—are envisioned in three different languages—Latin, Greek and Hebrew. Moreover, because they are so enveloped in the design and often split apart they become horizontal and vertical movements across space rather than linguistic signs.

In their austere, reductive appearance, Dibbets's designs contrast greatly with the vibrant, majestic windows in medieval cathedrals or even the lush stained-glass windows Matisse made in 1951 for the chapel in Vence. Evoking a serene, pure, light and airy sense of space, they affect a very different vision of the celestial aura. But without the luminous color reflections of traditional stained glass, they do little to enliven the cold, gray stone of the cathedral.

Dan Graham and Jeff Wall

Pavillon des Enfants

This work has been commissioned for the millennium celebration. Check with the tourist office for its location and details.

Tours

This charming, lively city in the center of a popular château region can be visited as a day trip or a weekend excursion including Oiron and other regional attractions. TGV from Paris (Gare Montparnasse), 70 min; train from Blois, 40 min; train from Orléans, 1 hr.

During the summer season, châteaux in the region sometimes host contemporary art exhibitions. To learn about current shows, check local media and tourist office listings.

Centre de Création Contemporaine (CCC)

53–55 rue Marcel Tribut, 37000
02-47-66-50-00 f: 02-47-61-60-24
Wed–Sun, 3–7; closed Mon–Tues
admission: free

From the train station, exit left onto rue Edouard Vaillant; not far ahead, turn left just opposite the Holiday Inn (designed by Christian de Portzamparc); this street angles into rue Marcel Tribut at the first crossing.

CCC—a noncollecting art enterprise— has a spacious, raw, flexible gallery designed to accommodate all sorts of exhibitions. Its impressive program consists of about four or five annual shows, either monographic exhibitions or installation-type projects specially created on the site. The selection of atypical artists who don't just produce unconventional work but explore new forms of artistic production has been a consistent aspect of the center's program. Professionalism permeates all activities and artistic experimentation and research is given a high priority. Most exhibitions are accompanied by informative, quality catalogues. From time to time, CCC presents art projects in outdoor locations within the city of Tours. Recent exhibitions: *Secret Noises*, *Basserode*, *Angela Bulloch*, *Christo*, *Pierre Joseph*, *Marin Kasimir*, *Tadashi Kawamata*, *Olivier Mosset*, *Richard Nonas*, *Julian Opie*, *Miguel Palma*, *Bernhard Rüdiger*, *Franck Scurti*, *Xavier Veilhan*.

As the administrator of the Fondation Atelier Calder, the CCC has an ongoing relationship with the international artists invited for residences at

Alexander Calder's studio in nearby Saché. The studio is closed to the public except for special events, such as an exhibition of work by the resident artist at the end of his/her tenure. Pier Paolo Calzolari, Jessica Stockholder and Allan Sekula were in residence most recently.

Alexander Calder

Untitled
place du Général Leclerc

Located in front of the train station near the Centre International de Congrès.

This stabile sculpture, commissioned by the University of Tours in the early 1970s, is the only monumental work by Calder (a longtime resident of the region) visible in Tours.

Centre International de Congrès

architect: Jean NOUVEL, 1993
boulevard Heurteloup

If you walk across the plaza in front of the train station, you will see an eye-catching glass building, fronted by a roof extension that looks like a baseball cap visor. It sits between a garden and the tourist office (also designed by Nouvel) on the corner of rue Bernard Palissy. This is the city's new convention center. Notably, it does not appear like a massive, imposing structure. Quite on the contrary, it fits well with the small shops lining the street alongside and the peaceful mood of the adjacent garden. Nouvel has achieved this integration by creating a building with a dramatically sloping roof and height adjusted to its surroundings. Its curving, glazed, reductive, streamlined form also lessens its presence as a large, distinctive shape even as these features establish the building as a vanguard design by one of the world's renowned architects of the contemporary era.

Horizontal lines of red, yellow and blue fluorescent tubes on the front facade, in the lobby and on upper-level walls accentuate continuity between exterior and interior spaces without being flamboyant. (This is most effective at night.) Be sure to walk inside, for here you will see greater evidence of the architect's extraordinary creativity in layout and design. A grand, open space greets you immediately as you look down from the top of the escalators into the main exhibition hall. Equal to the incredible expanse on the lower level is the amazing ceiling whose dramatic slope and black, reflective surface make the hall even more immeasurable and wondrous. The ceiling slant is, however, not a gratuitous feature. It actually corresponds with the floor gradation of an upper-level auditorium. Indeed, Nouvel has resourcefully positioned three auditoriums upstairs while simultaneously keeping the overall height of the building in check and constructing an unenclosed main hall.

Ecole Supérieure des Beaux–Arts

Jardin François I, 37011
02-47-05-72-88 f: 02-47-66-91-88
Mon–Fri, 1–7
admission: free

From the center city take rue Nationale toward the Loire river; cross rue du Commerce on the left; walk to the historic building in the center of a garden area; enter through the door on the right side facing rue Nationale.

Just to the left of the entrance, you will find the art school's exhibition space. The program here seems somewhat makeshift and informal though adventurous. It includes projects by guest faculty and resident artists, some of which—like the spectacular video installations by Beat Streuli (1997)—are far better than the more formal displays you'll see in museums. The space is well worth a visit even if you don't recognize the names of the featured artists.

Chenonceaux

Château de Chenonceau

22 mi (34 km) east of Tours

For the past several years, this château has held a contemporary art exhibition annually June–Nov. Miguel Barcelo and Enzo Cucchi were the featured artists in 1997 and 1998 respectively.

Oiron

This tiny rural village (population about 600) southwest of Tours is impossible to reach by public transportation. The closest you can get is by taking a train from Tours to Saumur with a bus connection to Thouars (1 1/2 hr). From Thouars it's about 7 1/2 mi (12 km) to Oiron.

Château d'Oiron

Oiron, 79100
05-49-96-51-25 f: 05-49-96-52-56
Apr 15–Sept: daily, 10:30–6:30.
Oct–Apr 14: Tues–Sun, 1:30–5:30.
Sept–May: closed Mon. Best to call to be sure of the schedule.
admission: 32/21F

Don't miss the conceptually rich, fanciful exhibition in this château situated in the enchanting setting of Oiron—a classic, old, country village. Making this site the highlight of a weekend away from Paris will be an unequaled experience you won't forget.

The château was built mainly during the 16th–17th century by the Gouffier family, whose lineage included high dignitaries within French royalty. It was especially Claude Gouffier, the grand squire for Henri II, whose interest in art prevailed in the decoration of the country estate. After the family's decline, the property deteriorated and was eventually purchased (1943) by the State and declared a historic monument. Indeed, the château is a grand, three-story edifice with a rare 16th-century gallery of frescoes and other notable accouterments from the past. Restoration of the building's illustrious structure is ongoing, and plans exist for replanting the gardens.

Interest in using the château as a site for contemporary art stirred in 1987 when it first housed an exhibition of recent art by vanguard artists. Several other exhibitions followed, and then, in 1993, Jean-Hubert Martin (a past director of the Musée National d'Art Moderne, Paris) put together a collection by commissioning artists to create works particularly for the château. The collection was inspired by the 16th-century idea of a cabinet of curiosities—an assortment of objects made by man (hence artificial) or found in nature (hence natural). Such collections (often considered as the prerational ancestors of museums) were assembled by cultivated princes who, in flattering themselves as being "curious" and scholarly, sought to explore new domains of knowledge and establish a more humanistic, less transcendent interpretation of the world. In the installations, objects were fastidiously placed to intermingle sensibility and knowledge. The five senses (seeing, hearing, smelling, tasting, touching), like the four elements (earth, air, fire, water), were common themes. Taxonomies were most often used as an organizational tool.

Oiron's contemporary cabinet of curiosities is imbued with similar themes. It occupies more than 32 rooms and locations in the historic château and includes the work of some 69

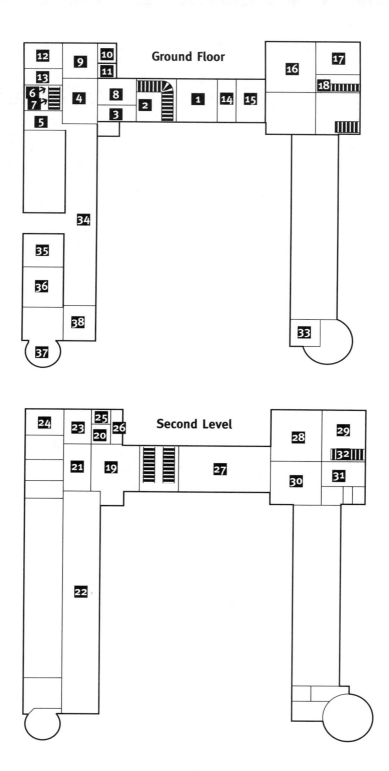

prominent international artists. New works have periodically been added to the collection, and occasionally special exhibitions are installed in the château.

In keeping with the spirit of cabinets of curiosities, most of the art projects on exhibit here are based on arcane references or unconventional propositions. Your visit will be greatly enhanced if you spend a fair amount of time viewing, unraveling, contemplating and, if possible, discussing each work with someone else. This isn't your typical museum exhibition. It requires a probing, discovery-oriented mind-set. Not to worry, however. This won't be a dull, didactic experience. There's lots to see and you undoubtedly will be captivated. The following commentaries provide background information to facilitate your appreciation of each project. (These are largely derived from descriptions by Jean-Hubert Martin in the *Beaux-Arts* publication on Oiron.) You may find some discrepancies between this list and the installation since the artwork is occasionally rearranged or removed from view.

1 Portrait Gallery. This entrance hall, remade into a room for hunting trophies in the 19th century, was remade again into a portrait gallery by Christian BOLTANSKI. But instead of displaying images of aristocrats and kings, Boltanski has honored current residents of Oiron. He has also defied the tradition of using a portrait gallery to legitimize a regal, ancestral heritage. Alternatively, he has created a democratic, future-oriented gallery showcasing photo portraits of all the children in the village school. You'll notice that the display contains photos from successive years since 1993. As with royalty, who had their portraits painted annually, Boltanski too traces the development of his subjects.

2 Renaissance Stairwell. *Unicorn Horn* by James Lee BYARS is located beneath the stairs on the ground floor in front of heraldic French arms framing the cellar door with figures of fools, a dog and a falcon. The horn—a tall, slender, pole-like object—sits atop its pedestal—a high, narrow block of pure white marble. In fact, the horn is a tooth from a real narwhale, long considered proof of the existence of the unicorn. Not only is the horn/tooth a veritable curiosity, but Byars's mode of displaying it reinforces its status as one of the most precious objects ever known.

3 Corridor of Illusions. In his work, Felice VARINI has created an optical game. To play, you must find the four points of view that permit you to inscribe four ellipses perfectly within a square mirror. The ellipses, painted in blue, are spread across the walls and ceiling, and the mirror is on the floor. The game thus reverses the widespread opinion that images we see in a mirror are deceptive. Here, in contrast, the mirror lets us grasp the truth by revealing the organization of the forms.

4 Map and Cosmology Room. This room includes works depicting different ways of perceiving the world. The Dutch artist Wim DELVOYE shows astonishing images that might delineate coastlines. Alain JACQUET indicates an impossible view of the globe, deformed into a doughnut with the aid of a computer. And in *Atlas*—for use by artists and the military—Marcel BROODTHAERS suggests the relative superficiality of countries by reducing them to silhouettes with minuscule dimensions.

A glass door off the Map Room will take you to the Alebrijes Room, where papier-mâché animals related to funerary rites are on display. They were created by the Linarès family in Mexico.

5 Downstairs Chapel or Cabinet of Formalin. Using the procedure of periphotography, Patrick Bailly-Maître-

GRAND has created a series, titled *Formalin's Band*, comprising 11 anamorphic (distorted optical image) prints. The depictions show cylindrical bottles of formalin containing animals with the whole surface rendered visible. In the flattened, stretched-out imagery that results, the misshapen animals end up looking like chimeras in a monstrous universe.

6 Wood staircase to mezzanine. As you climb the stairs, note the far-fetched models—*Paris-Nouvel, Italy, Germany Year 2000*—by Bodys KINGELEZ from Zaire.

7 Light Bulb Room. Bill CULBERT has installed his installation, *Small Glass, Pouring Light* (1983), in this small room. It consists solely of some two dozen glasses filled with red wine placed atop a very long table lit from above by three hanging lamps. An eerie, mystical aura prevails and becomes even more intense when you realize that the shadows cast by the glasses bear the image of light bulbs.

8 Dining Room. Table settings of 150 residents of Oiron line the walls of this room. Each ensemble, ingeniously personalized by Raoul MAREK, includes a plate adorned with an individual's profile, a crystal wineglass engraved with their initials and a linen napkin stamped with their handprint. In addition to the display, the artwork includes an annual June 30 dinner. It is a ritual meal wherein the residents gather in the château—a place of collective memory—and use their special table service. At the table, a video by Fabrice HYBERT explains the process of making *bonbons très bons* (very sweet sweets) from algae. These treats can be either taken internally or used externally, as edible treats or for a bubble bath. The room also contains a sideboard chock-full of a collection of Delft plates with stereotypic Dutch images. However, the plates are really a series of circular saws. It is a game of deceit, like the ones commonly found in historic cabinets of curiosities. Here the artist, Wim DELVOYE, applies his biting humor to assault a cliché of beauty revered in his homeland.

9 Space-Time Room. In his project, Stanley BROUWN confronts the space-time concept, which has become a cliché in art history discussions of Cubism and other early-20th-century art forms. He does so by elaborating the difference between measurements surmised by the body and the abstract measurement derived from the meter, a mathematical calculation. Similarly, the famous date paintings by On KAWARA play with paradoxical notions of abstract and concrete by making the date (a time concept) into a material object (a painting) and an image (a written construct).

10 Moon Room. Inspired by the mythic union of Diana and Neptune—moon and sea, Sara HOLT took long-exposure pictures aboard boats with her camera lens pointed at the moon. She particularly chose nights when the waters were choppy and undulating. As you can see in the display of photographs, the images, which emerged directly from nature, are drawings and writings with a supernatural character.

11 Room for *The Way Things Go*. The witty, pseudo-scientific video (from a 1986–87 film) by the Swiss team FISCHLI and WEISS is on view here. It is a series of ill-fated constructions made of common objects and arranged as a plodding, ludicrous chain reaction. If you've never seen this masterful creation, sit down and prepare to laugh and marvel through the entire production.

12 The Natural History Cabinet. For his project, Paul-Armand GETTE placed the scientific method in service of the imagination and poetry. He prepared an inventory of local resources—plants, insects, stones—calling special attention to the rich volcanic history of the

Baumgarten, mural

photograph of a painting by Bertrand LAVIER; and a sculpture by Yoon HEE, *Catastrophe intime*, showing the liquid state of a brass alloy and rare, unexpected colorings from the heating process.

16 Room of Rabelaisien Humanities or Room of the Cosmography of the Tours Region. Lothar BAUMGARTEN has adorned the walls of this room with names from *Animals of the Full Moon* and words and expressions from *Pantagruel* by Rabelais, the 16th-century humorist and satirist who lived about 22 miles from Oiron. The words—printed in block letters on brightly colored grounds of red, yellow, blue or white—are dispersed disjunctively, as in a suprematist composition, on the scruffy white surfaces of the walls or on black rectangular shapes painted on them. But here as elsewhere, Baumgarten is more concerned with shifting socio-territorial structures than with formalist issues. Indeed, his references to a Rabelaisian world merge with the evocation of a local ecosystem to suggest the trail of a fragile popular culture in the process of disappearing.

17 Sun Room. The exhibit here features the series *365 Solar Burnings*, made by Charles ROSS in New Mexico. Using an enormous magnifying lens, Ross concentrated the sun's rays on pieces of paper to produce these sun-fire drawings. He not only produced a burn image of the sun's intensity each day for a year but also recorded the daily angle of the sun's arc, which ultimately yields a depiction of the sun's path over the course of a year's time. The latter—a double spiral—becomes visible by putting all the daily burnings together end to end. Although this image is ignored by scientists, it plays a part in the iconography of the ancient Indians in Chaco Canyon.

18 Bottom of the stairs and above the door. The American Lawrence WEINER is

region as evidenced in fossils, ammonites and ancient rams' horns.

13 Room of Mutants. Giuseppe PENONE, an Italian artist associated with the Arte Povera movement, has here arranged snake skins vertically to suggest the body posture associated with humans. As a result, he disorients and transforms customary perceptions about the animal species and the adaptation of waste materials for art.

14 Room with Faïence. Anne and Patrick POIRIER, renowned for their art dealing with found and created remnants from the past, have installed *Memoria mundi*—an assortment of stones and inscribed landscape drawings—in this room with faïence floor tiles from the 18th century.

15 Room of the Ultimate Painting. On display in this room are some radical paintings in which artists have substituted austere forms, a concern with material, humor or meditative perception for images. Included are a work by the Japanese artist Kazuo SHIRAGA who has painted with his feet since the 1950s; a metamatic art machine by Jean TINGUELY (on the fireplace); imprints of a paintbrush—the smallest gesture possible with the most fundamental marking tool used in painting—by Niele TORONI; monochrome paintings exactly matched to the gray color of the wall by Claude RUTAULT; a painted-over known for his word paintings, usually produced directly on walls, in which the texts offer a poetic evocation of the environment. Here he uses the château's motto, "Hic Terminus Haeret" (Here Is the End), appropriated by Claude Gouffier from Virgil in 1570. His print style also duplicates the typography of the old inscriptions on the facade and elsewhere in the château.

19 Harlequin's Room or Emigrants Room. This room formerly contained many paintings from the large collection amassed by the Gouffier family. Now it is the site of four amateur copies, created by André RAFFRAY, of 20th-century French masterpieces: Picasso's *Demoiselles d'Avignon*, Henri Rousseau's *Sleeping Gypsy*, Matisse's *Dance*, Duchamp's *Nude Descending a Staircase*. These paintings were all made in France and yet each is now owned by a museum in a foreign country. Raffray's colored-pencil reproductions call attention to the emigration of art and to how this especially affects amateur artists who no longer have access to originals for their production of copies.

20 Chapel. The eagle and lobster coffins by Kane KWEI from Ghana are African versions of European tombstones. The images correspond to a person's profession or social position.

21 Room of Aeolus (God of the Wind) and Flying Things. In his taxidermic sculpture of a winged unicorn (inspired by images of Pegasus and unicorns in the 16th-century mythological paintings in the grand gallery just ahead), Thomas GRUNFELD relates to a dominant human curiosity: flight and airspace. Annette MESSAGER offers a different perspective on the aerial theme in her vitrine displaying dead birds dressed in little knit coats. The coats suggest a vain attempt to revive the birds even as they evoke a surreal human-animal juncture. Alternatively, PANAMARENKO's hybrid creature tries to reconstitute the

archaeopteryx—ancestor of all birds, thought to be mythic until its fossil was discovered in Bavaria in the 19th century. His image has wings and feathers as well as reptilian characteristics in its teeth, long tail and free fingers with anterior limbs. By adding battery power, Panamarenko has attempted to revive the skeleton's capacities of movement.

Dealing with air in terms of floating and equilibrium, Wolfgang NESTLER fabricates a balance resting on the point of a pin so fragile it seems to defy the laws of physics. Even the slightest impulse disturbs its poise, in turn upsetting the undulating movement of a large gliding wing.

22 The Painting Gallery. These paintings were made between 1546 and 1549 by Noël Jallier, and, as noted in the inscription, the gallery was dedicated to François I. Beginning at the right of the chimney is a cycle of representations of the Trojan War, followed by scenes from the *Aeneid*. The paintings above the door allegorically celebrate the king's glory.

23 Mama W's Bedroom. By the 17th century cabinets of curiosities often seemed ridiculous, prized only for their sentimental, pretentious value. Those enamored of rationality mocked them as an amusement for women. This was the case with a decadent version, the collection of the so-called Mama W assembled by Madame de Wendelstadt in Darmstadt during the 1870s. Daniel SPOERRI has regrouped the objects in this collection, combining them with notes about their provenance duly certified by their donors. (Originally the collection was in an inlaid box but now the objects are in frames made by a peasant from the Bernese Alps during the long winter months.) Among the curiosities are a bullet found in the Waterloo battlefield; a weeping willow branch that grew alongside the tomb of Napoleon at Saint-Helena; a piece of the first

German flag that flew over the Strasbourg cathedral in 1870; and an amber amulet found in a Scythian tumulus.

24 Cabinet of Monsters. During the Age of Enlightenment when a new epistemology was emerging, the fabulous animals and monsters of the cabinets of curiosities became the subject of study and controversy and caused them to be further discredited. These legendary beasts, whose existence in ancient texts could not be questioned, had excited curiosity and covetous desire. Some travelers who claimed to have seen them even provided detailed descriptions, but the morphology varied in each case. In addition, forgers fabricated them. Still today the tradition lives on with the *Volpertingers*—animal fetishes of Bavarian hunters. The invented hybridizations created by Thomas GRUNFELD also partake of this history. Of course, we now can view his wondrous taxidermic creatures—like the one with a bird's head and fish's body—as mythological, extinct species or futuristic products of genetic manipulation.

In the adjoining room, Joan FONTCU-BERTA elaborates on the monster theme by relating the extraordinary discovery of a cocatrix—a sort of amphibious horse whose remains were found and dredged up by Dr. Ducroquet from ditches in the basement of the château. Drawings by the Nigerian artist Bruly BOUABRE, hanging in a nearby corridor, take yet another approach to the theme.

25 Rooms of Discovered—or Exposed—Chefs. This little rooms pays ironic homage to *chefs* (the word can refer to a cook, head or chief) and *couvre-chefs* (a humorous word for headdresses). In the first room, the anagrammist YPUDU (Jean DUPUY) has set up a clever scheme for examining your own head as seen by pigeons. Don't forget to leave a trace of your sweat on a piece of paper. The imprints of the first 5,000 visitors are displayed on the wall.

26 Room of Musical Flies. In keeping with his usual mode of artistic creation, Ilya KABAKOV uses the appearance of an abandoned place to evoke feelings about the life of its former residents. Here he focuses attention on the old bathrooms.

27 King's Room or Hall of Armor. Formerly, the piers between the windows of this majestic grand hall bore larger-than-life portraits of men dressed as warriors. This history, and the fact that every cabinet of curiosities had to have a section devoted to the martial arts, inspired Daniel SPOERRI to create 12 macabre *Bodies Chopped into Pieces*. Made from found objects carrying their own mysterious histories, his figures convey the diversity of the world and organized chaos. They bear witness to torture, salvation, survival, heroism, conquest, invention, sexuality, culture, nature and myriad other themes.

28 King's Bedroom. Restored to a semblance of its former splendor, the bedroom now features Claude RUTAULT's reductive circular and rectangular canvases set into the wall and colored with the same red-orange of the surrounding surface. Although these nearly invisible artworks are in marked contrast to the ornate 16th-century decor, their overwrought silhouettes aim to evoke the variety of painting genres (history, portrait, still life, landscape) in ostentatious collection displays. Another curiosity in this room is the log by Jean-Charles BLANC in the fireplace. It is a tree from a Caribbean island that has grown around a motorbike. The black leather armchairs in front of the fireplace (and elsewhere in the château) are designs by John ARMLEDER. Each chair is marked in a different place by a sign—a colored line and/or geometric shapes. The signs refer to Suprematism, a source of strong influence on the artist and a modern movement (rooted in Russia and strongly associated with Malevich) setting forth a new visual language and new perspective of the world. Appropriately, as objects in a cabinet of curiosities, the armchairs are conduits for tactile sensations. (Sit down and enjoy the experience.)

29 Cabinet of Muses. This is a rare example showing the taste for rich, excessive decor at the beginning of the 17th century. The paintings present Apollo, Minerva and Mercury guiding the nine muses, six of whom carry musical instruments instead of their traditional attributes. On the wall between the windows, Diana receives the spoils of her hunt from some nymphs.

30 Room of Peasant Uprisings. In his trilogy, Braco DIMITRIJEVIC, originally from Sarajevo, calls attention to the peasant wars that were legion during the 16th century when the Gouffiers lived extravagantly in their grand château. *Triptychos post historicus: The Last Battle of Paolo Uccello* is a denunciation of fratricide wars. It represents the elite culture by three portrait paintings of aristocrats, including one of the Sun King dressed as a Roman emperor. Opposing them is the culture of the populace, represented by pitchforks, vehemently thrust into the walls, and coconuts, imported from Africa and symbolizing cannon balls.

31 Room of Waves. This is a room dedicated to water, a source of the marvelous. On display is a parallelepiped constructed from eels submerged in a matrix of polyester. This object by Toni GRAND relates to the never-ending discussion about the presence of geometry in nature. In this case, the issue centers on the assertion that eels are rarely the same length, hence always providing only a proximate, indeterminable sense of their geometry. A second wave object by Pascal CONVERT, deals with the principle of analogical correspondence, a

Shannon, *Decenter Acenter*

keystone of 16th-century thought. It satirically suggests the resemblance between the convolutions of a piece of coral, imprinted on copper, and a brain.

A third example focuses on trichoptera, the larvae from butterflies that live in streams and build their houses out of elements found in their surroundings. Capturing the industrious ingenuity of the butterflies, Hubert DUPRAT has fabricated some incredible facsimile casings made of gold encrusted with pearls and precious stones. Clearly, his designs are much more appropriate for breeding trichoptera in an aquarium in a sumptuous château. Also in this room is Daniel SPOERRI's *Breton Pharmacy*, a cabinet filled with 117 flasks of water taken from springs and fountains in Brittany, an area whose water is well known for its healing power.

32 Staircase rooms. The small wood staircase beside the Room of Waves gives access to the Room of Geometric Figures. Its walls are covered with soft-toned wall designs painted from a conceptual program created by Sol LEWITT. Farther on, a tiny room off the stairs contains the *Cabinet de Claude Gouffier* by Guillaume BIJL. Here the cabinet is a closet filled with clothing such as a 16th-century gentleman might have worn.

33 Tower of Waves—added to the château by Mme de Montespan in the 18th century. The tower, which has never been lived in, contains art devoted to meditation and contemplation.

In the Levitation Room, the spacious, light-filled rotunda of the tower (1st level), Tom SHANNON has created a mesmerizing object. *Decenter Acenter* includes a huge aluminum disk suspended by wire cables in space and perfectly aligned with the circularity of the room. Exactly in the center of the disk is a glistening sphere. Bisected horizontally, it floats on its own in space, its upper half seeming to levitate. This wondrous image—actually based on hidden magnetic forces—presents an allegory about earth and the cosmos.

In the Room of the Queen's Workers (also 1st level), Wolfgang LAIB fabricated a wall with one of his favorite materials, beeswax. The powerful smell awakens the senses even as the wax recalls many different workers: those who served the queen bee, those who constructed the wall with Laib, those who built the château and those who served royals during the centuries when the château was inhabited.

At the very top of the tower in the Room of Minerals and Sleeping Beauty (a meditation room), Marina ABRAMOVIC has installed a bed and a chair. You are invited to relax in them, and when you do your back and neck will make contact with the energizing powers of quartz.

Abramovic, relaxation bed

34 Gothic Gallery of Horses. In creating a work for this covered arcade, the German artist Georg ETTL took into consideration the old ocher plaster still on the walls and the inscription over a door: "Here are horses, naturally removed [because of age] from the most renowned group owned by King Henry. Second in rank, they were in his stable at the time of his accession to the throne." Using ground charcoal applied with a brush, Ettl drew profiles of horses in harmony with the scattered marks left from the previous images. His figures have powerful necks and rumps but elegant legs, exquisitely poised for prancing. All drawn from a single model, with some slight differences, they form a procession leading from the central part of the château along the length of the north wing to the front tower.

35 Old Kitchens (17th century) or Music Room. In this space, you will hear sound compositions by Gavin BRYARS. Each was written for a different room in the château.

36 Old Kitchens (17th century) or Room of Anamorphoses. Games of visual deception were especially popular in cabinets of curiosities. In these, you must find the exact viewpoint to be able to decipher the images. Markus RAETZ is a renowned specialist of distorted optical imagery and clever layouts based on strategies geared to disconcert the observer. His silhouette presents a sort of Janus figure forced to hide its ambiguity. The bust never reveals its two faces at the same time, except with the aid of a mirror that magically shows the absent segment. In another anamorphic game, Piotr KOWALSKI introduces a coded image from which he produces a geometric version in a hologram. The latter is an illusion making three spheres of different dimensions appear as if they are the same size.

37 Tower of the Sword (16th century) or Vanity Room for the Stonemasons. Place your back to the window and you will see the earth disk by Gloria FRIEDMANN. Its form has resulted from wear and tear over time to piles of bones and stones.

38 Steward's Room or Battle Room. Although battles were central to the life of the 16th-century château proprietors, the Scottish artist Ian Hamilton FINLEY makes reference to the 1942 air-and-sea battle of Midway, waged between Americans and Japanese. At first, the humming of industrious bees rejoining their hives in rosebushes suggests a bucolic setting. But this doesn't reveal their murderous side, seen in the photographs of bombardiers affixed to the walls. Idyllic landscape or terrible battlefield? The simultaneity of perspectives refers to a temperament where beauty and crime can triumph together.

Bretagne–Nantes

Rennes

This lively city that's easy to enjoy has a charming old section of town, now pedestrianized, a university center and a picture-perfect, indoor French market (Halles Centrales). TGV from Paris (Gare Montparnasse), 2 1/4 hr; train from Nantes, 2 hr.

Galerie du TNB

1 rue Saint-Hélier, 35000
02-99-31-55-33
Tues–Sat, 2–8; Sun, 2–7;
closed Mon
admission: free

Located a short distance from the train station. Walk down avenue Jean Janvier, turn right at rue Saint-Hélier and off the corner on the left is the theater (5 min).

The gallery is a string of rooms, just off the lobby on the upper level of the popular Théâtre National de la Bretagne. You can visit the space even if you're not attending a performance. It presents changing exhibitions of contemporary art, most of which are gleaned from the FRAC collection of the Brittany region. It's not a great space but a stop here will give you a chance to see recognized artists who may or may not be part of the international circuit.

La Criée—Halle d'Art Contemporain

Halles Centrales, place Honoré
Commeurec, 35000
02-99-78-18-20
Tues–Sat, 2–7; closed Mon
admission: free

The central market hall (originally an auction house for gross sales of fish, then of fruits and vegetables) is in the midst of a busy commercial area between rue Vasselot, rue de Nemours, boulevard de la Liberté and rue Jules Simon. The art center is in a wing of the market's enormous brick building (1920s), accessible from an entrance off a small triangular plaza facing rue Vasselot.

La Criée has developed a remarkable interchange with its local neighborhood, the larger city, the university and art school in Rennes, the art history departments in the region, FRAC Bretagne and other art centers. It has also earned a reputation for its ambitious program that has highlighted the work of adventurous, conceptually rigorous artists from Europe and the U.S. Using its two modest-sized rooms to the fullest, its exhibitions are both object and project oriented. Recent exhibitions: *Vito Acconci*, *Pier Paolo Calzolari*, *Jean-Gabriel Coignet*, *David Diao*, *Günter Förg*, *Gloria Friedmann*, *Gary Hill*, *Thomas Huber*, *Fabrice Hybert*, *Ilya Kabakov*, *John Knight*, *Eugène Leroy*, *Gilles Mahé*, *Haim Steinbach*, *Felice Varini*, *Jacques Villeglé*, *Large-Scale Work*, *The Time of the Marquise—A Contemporary Evocation of the 17th Century*, *The Sea is Not the Earth (Tacita Dean, Yvon Salomone, Allan Sekula)*.

Peter Downsbrough

Unité-De-La . . . , 1990
rue de Nemours at boulevard
de la Liberté

This mural, located on a wall just behind the central market and La Criée is a simple but compelling and witty design. The imagery plays with the concept of unity and disunity by showing the frame of a rectangle (suggestively the same proportions as the side wall) sliding off the building, taking with it half the letters of the word UNITE, the other half remaining in place on the wall.

Marta Pan

Fountain
5 rue Martenot, patio of Conseil
Régional

Located on the north side of La Vilaine canal, near rue Victor Hugo.

This work is a serene, refined design composed of a wall of water and elements of gray granite. But it is oddly crammed between an iron fence at the property line (bordering the sidewalk) and the back of the Regional Council's building. Moreover, it is situated on a tiny plot below a driveway, totally secluded from those with access to the grounds, and so obscured by the barrier fence that pedestrians walking on the adjacent sidewalk can hardly see it. The site is a travesty for any artwork, but particularly in this case since this is a virtuoso fountain design! Despite the difficulties of viewing it, don't hesitate to track it down if you are in Rennes.

Galerie Art & Essai

Université de Rennes 2, 6 avenue
Gaston Berger, 35043
02-99-14-11-42

This university gallery has a varied program of art connected to many different disciplines. It's worth a visit since the exhibitions often include off-beat, conceptually rich and experimental work. Recent exhibitions: *Absalon*, *Sadie Benning*, *Richard Billingham*, *Homo Zapiens Zapiens*, *69/96: Doublings and Self-Portraits by Proxy*, *Play with Your*

Friends (French and Irish Art), *100 Years of French Film Sets*, *Electronic Encounters*, *Murmurs from the Streets*.

Bignan

Bignan is not accessible by public transportation. The nearest you can get by train is Vannes, 15 1/2 mi (25 km) to the south. By car from Vannes, take D767 north toward Pontivy; exit Locminé; take D123 in the direction of Bignan. Train to Vannes from Nantes, 1 1/4 hr; from Rennes, 1 1/4 hr; from Paris (Gare Montparnasse), 5 1/2 hr.

Domaine de Kerguéhennec, Centre d'Art Contemporain

Bignan, 56500
02-97-60-44-44 f: 02-97-60-44-00
sculpture park: year-round, daily, 10–6
admission: free
exhibitions: Tues–Sun, closed Mon.
Apr–June 14 and Sept 16–Dec, 10–6; June 15–Sept 15, 10–7
admission: 25/15F

Kerguéhennec is a 420-acre estate with a grand 18th-century château, model farm, 27-acre lake and an extensive park (including an arboretum with rare species) landscaped by the famous Bühler brothers in 1872. The property has been open to the public since 1986 and now houses indoor exhibition spaces (mainly in the old stables and château); a café, library, studios and housing units for resident artists and art history interns; the Regional Workshop for Restoration (specializing in polychrome wood sculpture); an agricultural training center; and an impressive collection of sculpture distinguished by many works specifically related to the natural surroundings or history of the site and region.

Kerguéhennec is, moreover, a meeting place where creative minds in many fields get together to formulate, research and exchange ideas. Be sure to ask about ongoing pursuits and check the schedule of special events. Be aware that the interior and exterior areas are still being refurbished or developed, so information is subject to change. This is especially true with respect to the sculpture park, where new sculptures are regularly created on site as temporary or permanent installations. Ask about the latest additions.

Although the sculpture park is a main attraction, the indoor exhibitions warrant equal attention. They are well-conceived, fascinating projects typically featuring amazing works of art by known and unknown, emerging and established artists from all over the world. If this sounds too good to be true, just check it out for yourself. Most particularly, don't miss the thematic group exhibitions. These projects often embrace ideas and objects from realms like archaeology, ethnology, history, or other artistic expressions like film, video, literature, theater, the circus, music and dance. Performances are a regular part of the activity at Kerguéhennec, and they are typically adventurous and spectacular. If you can schedule or change your visit to attend an event, chances are you'll see something special. If nothing else, you can participate in or listen to discussions with resident artists every Sunday during the summer season at 5:30. Recent exhibitions: *Density or the Unimaginable Museum*, *Insomnia*, *Synaxis*, *Praxis*, *Hand to Head—the Theoretical Object*, *The Domain of the Diaphanous*, *Pier Paolo Calzolari*, *Gérard Collin-Thiébaut*, *Geoffrey James*, *Harold Klingelhöller*, *Eugène Leroy*, *Mario and Marisa Merz*, *Yves Oppenheim*.

Even with a map (available at the

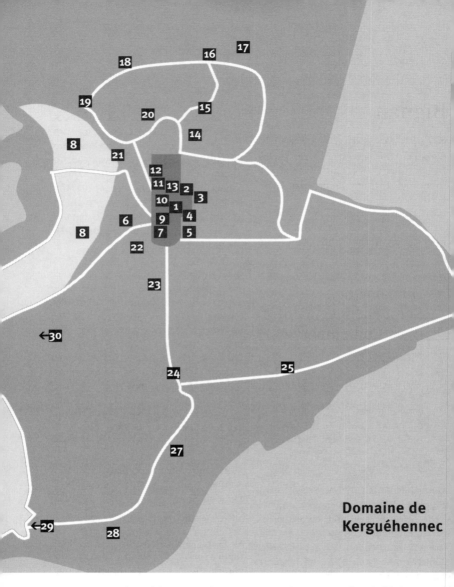

Domaine de Kerguéhennec

entrance or in the café), you may have a hard time finding the sculptures in the park. They are located throughout the grounds and because some are meant to be well integrated with the natural setting, they are hard to see and off the beaten track. Ask about the possibility of having an intern serve as your guide, if only to help you locate the art. There's lots to see, so reserve a whole day to enjoy the visit. It will probably be one of the great highlights of your travels. Sculptures in the park include:

1 Alighiero e BOETTI, *Pallacorda* (*Rope Ball*), 1968–95. At first this may seem like a minimalist sculpture, but on closer inspection you will see that it is a mind-teasing object. The ball sits atop a column seemingly formed by a coiling cable emitted from the ground below and the ball above. Beginning and end, solid and void, line and plane, pedestal and object are thus vividly manifest as shifting, incongruous dualities.

Boetti, *Pallacorda*

2 Maria NORDMAN, *Fragment d'une cité nouvelle* (*Fragment of a New City*), 1987. Using the ruins of a former structure, the artist has re-envisioned it as an emergent site. But the setting and the elementary components she has added have a haunting character, especially since light and shadow play games with our perceptions. The same image appearing as a positive and negative configuration, and our position as viewers who are kept outside of spaces that are simultaneously open and closed arouse feelings of ambiguity and uncertainty.

3 Matt MULLICAN, *Divisé par cinq—en énumérant sur une verrière verte* (*Divided by Five—Counting on a Green Glass*), 1995. Outlining a formulation with numbers, signs, symbols and words, Mullican focuses attention on the complexity and specificity of communication. Despite careful delineations and the adoption of some universal codes, meaning is not necessarily conveyed in the same way or at all to everyone. The particularities of the inscriptions here relate to archaeological theories about Neolithic Breton objects owned by the nearby Société Polymathique du Morbihan.

4 Jean-Pierre RAYNAUD, *1,000 pots bétonnés peints pour une serre ancienne* (*1,000 Painted Cement Pots for an Old Greenhouse*), 1986. The artist has satirically filled the estate's huge 19th-century greenhouse with bright red flowerpots. Not only do the pots replace the flourishing plants that typically occupy a greenhouse, but these pots are solid cement. Raynaud thus exemplifies a not uncommon situation in which an assembly line of mass-produced, identical objects designed by man, made by machine and that are even nonfunctional displace diversity and nature.

5 Thanassis TOTSIKAS, Untitled, 1992. This sculpture derived its shape from a public performance in which fire was used to recall primordial energy and the clash between nature's creative and destructive powers.

6 Dan GRAHAM, *Deux cubes, l'un tourné à 45°* (*Two Cubes, One Turned at 45°*), 1986. The hallmark disorientation caused by Graham's juxtaposition of transparent, darkened and mirror walls is here increased by his creation of an irregular, intersecting cubic structure. As

Graham, *Deux cubes, l'un tourné à 45°*

you move within the glass units, your physical and visual orientation to your own body and the immediate surroundings is simultaneously and alternatively blocked, unveiled, confounded and simplified.

7 Toni GRAND, Untitled, 1988. With the luminous white surface, modulated rhythms and upward thrust of his pole sculpture, Grand aims to capture the movement of fish in water at the same time as he suggests the finite and infinite distance between earth and sky.

8 Marta PAN, *Structures flottantes* (*Floating Structures*), 1986. From the field alongside the château and from the paths farther north, you will get the best views of the two red configurations that Pan has set in the middle of the lake. Their abstract, geometric forms swirl around or angle up above the waterline emphasizing the flow of the current and the forces of nature.

9 Franz WEST, *Auditorium*, 1992. By placing his carpet-covered lounges in front of the château, the artist instigates a situation in which you view the treasured edifice and its surroundings even as you become aware of your dual roles as spectator and participant in an ongoing history. You effectively become an actor sitting on a work of art. In that the 72 oriental rugs come from various countries and refer to a range of cultural traditions, West also conflates the actuality of place and immediate experience with references to external or imagined realities.

10 Pedro Cabrita REIS, Untitled, 1994. This zany, ersatz bicycle wagon has the appearance of something Charlie Chaplin might have concocted to carry a dead body in a funeral procession. The box was actually used to catch an escaped horse during an experimental theater production developed jointly by a group of circus performers and sculptors who were in residence at Kerquéhennec during the summer of 1994.

11 Malachi FARRELL, *Bubbles* (*air survival*), 1993. Located in the courtyard fountain.

12 Harald KLINGELHOLLER, *Injustice crie* (*Injustice Cries*), 1995.

13 Louise BOURGEOIS, *Twosome*, 1991. To see this amazing mechanized sculpture, located in a room of the old stable, you must get the assistance of a staff member or guide. The work is spectacular and should not be missed! As in many of her projects, Bourgeois infuses common forms or subjects with sexual, feminist overtones. Here the imagery and sounds share a likeness with a train moving down a railroad track, a giant bullet emerging from a gun barrel and a rocket releasing a concealed weapon.

14 Carel VISSER, *L'oiseau phénix* (*The Phoenix Bird*), 1989. Appropriating old parts of farm machinery, Visser has created an assemblage configured like a bird.

15 Ian Hamilton FINLAY, *Names on Plaques, Names on Trees*, 1985–86. The artist fabricated 10 classically engraved travertine plaques and affixed these to the trunks of trees. There are five rectangular plaques with the Latin name of each tree and five oval plaques identifying lovers from literature who carved their names on a tree or rock. Nature and culture, science and romance are thus signified as equivalent aspects of an exacting, categorizing, contrived, reductive, aloof system.

16 Ulrich RUCKRIEM, *Bild Stock* (*Wayside Shrine*), 1985. Embracing the raw, cut and finished qualities of granite, the artist has constructed a volumetric block with the presence of a shrine or tombstone. But there are no relics or inscriptions, only framelike cavities opening to the interior and exposing an utterly blank, polished surface.

17 François BOUILLON, *Cène d'extérieur* (*Last Supper Outdoors*), 1987. In a clearing of a wooded area, Bouillon has arranged a group of shardlike units in a circle. Although each bears a label, neither it nor the image clarifies meaning or identification. By pushing metaphoric and mythic associations to the point where individualized responses takes over, the artist sought to substitute seeing for knowing. He wanted the art object to remain ephemeral, a simple sign without a fixed meaning.

18 Richard LONG, *Un cercle en Bretagne, Domaine de Kerguéhennec*, 1986. The circular pile of reddish slate-like stones from nearby Saint-Just is similar to many other stone sculptures Long has created to commemorate walks he has taken in wilderness regions all over the world.

19 Gilberto ZORIO, *Canöe*, 1985. Suspended above a path and situated amid tree branches, this long, narrow sculpture looks like a racing scull. But its propulsive, wooden form is broken in two and reassembled with the curve of one section opposing and overlapping the other. The javelin piercing the juncture of the two sections reiterates the semblance of brutal assault conveyed by the fractured structure, yet it also functions, paradoxically, as the element holding the parts together.

20 Markus RAETZ, *Mimi*, 1979–86. This winsome, 40-foot-long stick figure casually reclines on a grass field with arms behind its head and knees raised. The image, which aggrandizes a small-scale model made with matchsticks, captures the playful spirit and structural skill of the original design while adding boldness by using squared granite beams. Characteristically, Raetz underscores the figurative power of the most simple, unembellished mark or form seen isolated and together in a grouping of like marks or forms.

21 Germaine RICHIER, Untitled. This bronze figure by an artist of the mid-century generation, though out of synch with the rest of the sculptures in

Rückriem, *Bild Stock*

the park, does serve as a valuable comparison. With its plantlike form, the image suggests a harmonious unity between man and nature. It therefore lacks the potency of disorientation and challenge that has preoccupied artists of recent generations.

22 Keith SONNIER, *Porte-vue* (*Viewing Portal*), 1987. Recalling the prehistoric dolmen structures of Brittany, Sonnier has constructed a simple stone sculpture with the image of an entry passage. Placed on the crest of the lawn fronting the château and sweeping down to the lake, *Viewing Portal* shapes several perspectives of the estate. The doorway itself serves as one frame with two mutually exclusive orientations, and portholes cut in each of the supporting posts provide alternative views.

23 Giuseppe PENONE, *Sentier de charme* (*Trail of a Hornbeam Tree*), 1986. In a most enchanting way, Penone has created an inventive, animate symbiosis between man and nature. A hornbeam tree (birch family genus) grows inside an open-bodied female figure depicted in the process of walking forward. The intertwine of human anatomy with leaves, branches and trunk is thus coupled with divergent directional movements. The flowing tracks on the ground behind the figure in turn become enmeshed with the vitality of plant growth. One can imagine that eventually nature will totally overwhelm the figure, its tracks—and the art object (culture). Nature will then reclaim its preeminent place in—and as—the landscape.

24 Etienne HAJDU, *Sept colonnes à Stéphane Mallarmé* (*Seven Columns for Stéphane Mallarmé*), 1971. Like Richier, Hadju is a midcentury artist rooted in conventions of poetic metaphor. His mode of abstraction, inspired by ancient Cycladic sculpture, is characterized by reductive, curving forms with decorative surfaces.

25 Thomas BAUMANN and Filippo di GIOVANNI, *Espaces—Intervalles—Ahar* (*Spaces—Intervals—Ahar*), 1994. In this work, the artists confound the imagined construction of buildings, based on the delineation of perimeters and door openings, by having spaces intersect one another and by collapsing rational distances between elements. The inclusion of a tablelike object in one unit and two exterior columns topped by tall, white panels further skews the framework by confounding relationships and adding consideration of interior and exterior space.

26 Mario MERZ, *L'autre côté de la lune* (*The Other Side of the Moon*), 1984–92. This sculpture bears the signature spiral form often used by Merz to signify infinite movement in and out of a center.

27 Elisabeth BALLET, *Trait pour trait* (*Line for Line*), 1993. Illusion is the primary feature of Ballet's architectural sculpture. Her circular structure is both visible and invisible, depending on the light and your distance from the work. It is an enclosed space, segregated from its surroundings but also a transparent, open framework that blends with the landscape. As you approach, moreover, you will probably have difficulty determining whether various trees lie inside or outside the enclosure.

28 Pat STEIR, *Cascades*, 1992. Expanding her waterfall paintings, in this case Steir places a waterfall image in a real landscape. She does so by depicting the image on a transparent sheet of plastic and then hanging it in a forested area so it blends seamlessly with its surroundings. You'll have to look closely for this work, since it is located at a distance from the viewing path and its image gets lost in the trees.

29 François MORELLET, *Le naufrage de Malevitch* (*Malevich's Shipwreck*), 1990. Morellet plays with systems, particularly the geometric plane of a surface and the geometry of the plane in space. Here he takes the famous white square of Malevich, breaks it into three fragments and scatters the parts near the shoreline of the lake, setting them on skewed angles as if they were sinking from view into the water. Not only does the work literally destroy the integrity and purity of the white square but it metaphorically declares a virulent rupture with the conceptual, formalist theories of Suprematism—a revered exemplar of modern art.

30 Max NEUHAUS, Untitled (sound installation), 1986. Using synthesizers, Neuhaus has created an almost imperceptible, high-pitched, cricketlike drone, derived from La Monte Young's atonal music. The sounds emanate from two unseen sources facing each other across the lake. Ostensibly the sound creates a sonic net to catch the park's birdsongs, dominated by a cuckoo. You can only find the sound if shown exactly where to stand.

Nantes

TGV from Paris (Gare Montparnasse), 2 1/4 hr; train from Tours, 1 3/4 hr; from Vannes, 1 1/4 hr.

François Morellet

Portail 0°–90°, Portail 8°–98°, 1987
Médiathèque, quai de la Fosse
tram: Médiathèque

This site sculpture serves as the entry gate into the small plaza fronting the city's lively Médiathèque complex. With its two gigantic, open-grid doorway structures, it also acts as an icon marking the location and signifying an open-door spirit of welcome.

Dan Graham

Nouveau labyrinthe pour Nantes, 1994
place du Commandant l'Herminier
tram: Chantiers Navals

Located at Pont Anne Bretagne, a short walk from the Morellet sculpture along quai de la Fosse.

This plaza design or, in Graham's terminology, "sculpture/architecture," is a labyrinth structured by passages, minimalist balustrades, benches and walls of glass and mirror. Although the walls—which produce a confounding view, blocking or exposing you to your own image and/or your immediate surroundings—are the dominant feature of the design, they are judiciously spread out and nicely integrated with the other elements. In his signature way, Graham provides a contemplative setting that forces you to become aware of yourself both as a body perceiving your own image and as a person devoid of an identity, lacking a clearly defined sense of place, time and social context. "Throughout my work . . . geometrical forms are inhabited and activated by the presence of the viewer; an impression of unease and psychological alienation results from a constant movement between inclusion and exclusion."

Apartment buildings face the plaza on three sides, and the river—with a tram line and major roadway in between—runs along its main border. There is also a busy tram stop directly in front, and streets fan out from the sides. The site (formerly used for parking) is thus much more than the location for a work of art. Indeed, it also functions as a meeting and relaxation place for neighborhood residents, a pedestrian intersection and a waiting zone for tram passengers. Graham's design, with its right-angle positioning of walls and balustrades, creates welcome private spaces. But his labyrinthine plan, with its indirect circulation paths, does not take the habits and needs of users into account. The city has therefore constructed an ugly wooden staircase and walkway through the center of the plaza and over its front wall. It also installed some benches, which are a welcome addition but unappealing in design and inadequate in number. What could have been a wonderful work of public art, connecting conceptual issues, context and social needs, has instead become a travesty—an injustice to art, artist and the public.

FRAC Pays de la Loire

7 rue Frédéric Kulmann (ancien passage Lavoisier), 44100
02-40-69-87-87 f: 20-40-69-15-57
Tues–Sun, 2–6; closed Mon
admission: free
tram: Chantiers Navals

From the Graham sculpture, exit onto rue Brunellière, cross place Bouhier to boulevard de Laynay, take the first left onto rue Lavoisier, at the end of this street turn right onto rue Frédéric Kulmann.

After several moves in recent years, this FRAC finally found a permanent home with spacious quarters in an old warehouse at the west end of the city. The space is well suited to the center's varied, energetic program that includes performances, installation projects, displays of art from the collection and exhibitions of work by young and prominent international artists working in traditional and new media. Over the years, this FRAC has amassed a superb collection, revealing a strong sense of the innovative directions that have emerged during the past few decades.

It has become a summer tradition for the FRAC des Pays de la Loire to invite 5–20 artists to participate in a two-month "international studios" program. Artists are encouraged to explore a mode of production different from that which they normally use, to draw from the local context or collaborate with a person or institution in the area. Each fall, the results are shown in an exhibition (accompanied by a conference and informative catalogue) at a site in the Nantes region. Recent exhibitions: *Olga Boldyreff*, *Sylvie Bossu*, *Pierre Buraglio*, *Wim Delvoye*, *Paul Armand Gette*, *Raymond Hains*, *Claude Lévêque*, *Yves Oppenheim*, *Chaude Rutault*, *Sarkis*, *Vassiliki Tsekoura*, *Krzysztof Wodiczko*, *Troel Wörsel*.

Musée des Beaux-Arts

🏛 | 10 rue Georges Clemenceau, 44000
01-40-41-65-65 f: 02-40-41-67-90
Mon, Wed–Thurs, Sat, 10–6; Fri, 10–9; Sun, 11–6; closed Tues
admission: 20/10F, additional fee for special exhibitions

From the train station, walk down rue Stanislas Baudry alongside the Jardin des Plantes (if you like flowers, be sure to make a major detour in this renowned botanical garden), turn left at rue Georges Clemenceau and you'll see the museum in the middle of the block on the left side (10 min).

The contemporary art galleries in this museum offer a good overview of the major movements and artists of the French postwar generation. You will see classic examples of Nouveau Réalisme, Supports-Surfaces, B.M.P.T. and Figuration Libre. Art from the postwar period is also featured in temporary exhibitions from time to time—*Tony Cragg*, *Barry Flanagan*, *Paul Armand-Gette*, *Per Kirkeby*, *Claude Rutault*, *Sarkis*, *Pierrick Sorin*. For more current work, be sure to check out *La salle blanche* (The White Room), just off the main lobby to the right. This space presents solo shows of emerging artists, and the choices are excellent. For example, a 1997 exhibition introduced a very compelling installation of obtuse portraits of individuals and families—the production of an emerging British artist of note, James Rielly. Other recent exhibitions: *Philip Cognée*, *Orshi Drozdik*, *Olav Christopher Jenssen*, *Antoine de La Boulaye*, *Yves Oppenheim*, *Seton Smith*, *Jana Sterbak*, *Jessica Stockholder*, *Rosemarie Trockel*, *Luc Tuymans*, *Troels Wörsel*.

Limoges Region

Train from Paris (Gare d'Austerlitz), 3 hr. A visit to the Limoges region will get you away from big-city hustle and the frenetic pace of being a tourist. This is an area where you can easily enjoy the pleasures of French country life and unspoiled nature. If your destination is the sculpture park at Vassivière, be sure to combine this with visits to contemporary art sites in the delightful, old villages in nearby rural Meymac and Ussel.

Limoges

Gilberto Zorio

Canoa, 1987
Gare des Bénédictins,
avenue de la Gare

This soaring, daggerlike sculpture is suspended from the dome in the entrance hall of the train station. Quite similar to the canoe Zorio created at the Domaine de Kerquéhennec (Brittany), this version is an elongated, sleek form comprising two overlapping segments with a dart piercing the center at the juncture point. On the one hand, the image has a primordial character expressing a pragmatic and creative spirit tempered by unfettered intuition. On the other hand, the image seems futuristic, like some sort of vehicle or weapon allied to space ventures.

FRAC Limousin— Les Coopérateurs

impasse des Charentes, 87100
05-55-77-08-98 f: 05-55-77-90-70
Tues–Fri, 12–7; Sat, 2–7;
closed Mon
admission: 10/5F

From place Denis Dussoubs in the center of the city, take rue François Chenieux to avenue G. et V. Lemoine; turn left; in the middle of the block turn left again at impasse des Charentes, a tiny, dead-end street. You can also take bus 1–9 and exit at Coopérateurs.

The site, a 19th-century industrial building, was formerly a wine storehouse and then a warehouse for a grocery chain called Les Coopérateurs. Within the site, the center is at the back of the building, at the bottom of a steep slope, on the sub-basement level totally closed off from natural light. The aura of a crypt is pervasive. You will experience this immediately as you enter and face a long hall with arches receding into the distance. Both this central passageway and the 28 symmetrical rooms that flank it are constructed of stone with vaulted ceilings. The space is clearly a challenge for displaying contemporary art and yet there is a pleasing intimacy within the small, separated galleries.

This FRAC is both a collecting agency and an exhibition center. The collection focuses primarily on avant-garde photography—especially work having a conceptual or text-image orientation—and sculpture. The exhibitions, either one-person shows or selections from the collection, tend to feature art with a conceptual edge. Recent exhibitions: *Martine Aballéa, Lynne Cohen, Bill Culbert, Hubert Duprat, Toni Grand, Asta Gröting, Douglas Huebler, Richard Monnier, Steven Pippin, Allen Ruppersberg, Elmar Trenkwalder, Boyd Webb, William Wegman.*

Ile de Vassivière, Beaumont du Lac

This forested island in the midst of a region favored by the French for vacations centered on fishing, camping and outdoor summer sports lies about 37 mi (60 km) east of Limoges. (Alternatively, it is 74 1/2 mi or 120 km west of Clermont-Ferrand.) It lies within one of the largest lakes in France, a man-made body of water formed as part of a dam project undertaken in 1951 by Electricité de France. The island, which is also sizeable, is a natural preserve containing botanical walks, deer park, farm with animals, meteorological station, tourist bureau, art center and sculpture park. There is no public transportation to the island. The nearest you can get is Eymoutiers–Lac de Vassivière, a 50-min train ride from Limoges. You may be able to find a taxi to take you the short distance (about 9 mi or 15 km) the rest of the way, but don't count on it. It's best to call or fax the art center to arrange taxi service in advance. From May to Sept, you can also take Le Petit Train—an old steam engine conveyance operated for tourists (13F). It will take you to the pedestrian bridge crossing to the island. The train adds charm but is slow and infrequent. Your best bet is to rent a car in Limoges. (Since Rochechouart —see below—also requires a car, you should consider a multiday rental if you plan to visit several sites in the area.)

Centre d'Art Contemporain de Vassivière en Limousin

architects: Aldo ROSSI with Xavier FABRE, 1988–91
Ile de Vassivière, Beaumont du Lac, 87120
05-55-69-27-27 f: 05-55-69-29-31
sculpture park: year-round, daily
admission: free
exhibitions: Apr–Oct, daily, 11–7.
Nov–Dec and Feb–Mar, Tues–Sun,
11–1 and 2–6; closed Mon and
during Jan
admission: 15/5F

During the 1980s, community efforts to create a cultural/art center on Vassivière Island resulted in the formation of a sculpture park and the construction of a new building for the center. Going all-out to capture the imagination of the public, the organizers of the project hired the esteemed Italian architect Aldo Rossi. The unconventional, impressive edifice he created is itself one of the highlights of a visit to this site. Located on the summit of the island, the project consists of a cone-shaped tower resembling a lighthouse with a catwalk on top, and a long, narrow building extending into the landscape like a bridge or jetty. Both parts are aus-

tere, simple shapes of brick and granite, though not at all intimidating. On the contrary, the classic, metaphoric forms are harmoniously related to the setting though they are also bold presences— intriguing objects of contemporary design.

Without even thinking, you are drawn to the center and animated by an urge to explore both its exterior and interior. Like the outside, the inside is quite engaging. Of special note is the idiosyncratic play of space, form and scale at the entrance; the curved wood ceiling, cable support system, faux-clerestory row of half-circle windows and cathedral space in the main gallery; the horizontal layout of the little theater; the observation corridor looking down into the artist's studio (a disaster for artists since they become specimens on display, but a treat for visitors who are given the rare chance to watch an artist at work); the idyllic views of the environment perfectly framed by well-positioned windows; the gargantuan side-door openings, each a different height; and the awesome, dramatic space of the tower. As appealing as aspects of the architecture are visually, the building—like many museums designed by celebrated architects— does not provide the best conditions for viewing or exhibiting art. Its theatricality and irregularities compete for attention and make amenable installations of contemporary art—which is itself often eccentric—difficult.

In its galleries, the center shows a diversity of creative orientations and media. At any one time, you will usually see the work of a different artist in each gallery, and exhibitions tend to focus on a specific body of work or an on-site project. Be sure to look at the display in the tower, a high, cone-shaped space that has inspired many artists to produce formidable works. If you're not too overwhelmed by the

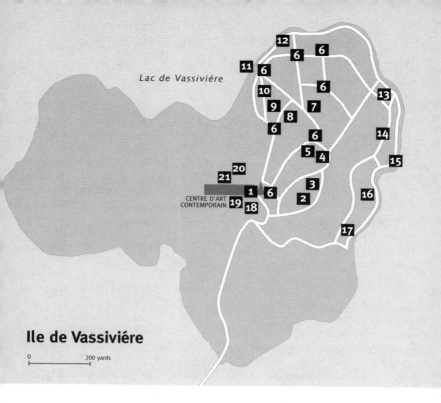

Lac de Vassiviére

CENTRE D'ART
CONTEMPORAIN

Ile de Vassiviére

0   200 yards

height, you can climb the steep, spiral staircase winding up the inner wall and get a spectacular view of the environment.

Don't be surprised if a staff member gives you a personal introduction to an artist's work or even accompanies you around a gallery. You will also find signage, leaflets and attractive catalogues with helpful (nondidactic) information. Emphasis here is on making visitors feel welcome and less alienated from the contemporary art on display. Recent exhibitions: *Catherine Beaugrand, Bertholin, Sylvie Blocher, Etienne Bossut, Shane Cullen, Thomas Demand, Noël Dolla, Bernadette Genée & Alain Le Borgne, Claire-Jeanne Jézéquel, Joan Jonas, Erik Levine, Ana Mendieta, Bernard Pagès, Carmen Perrin, Michelangelo Pistoletto, Thomas Rentmeister, Moniek Toebosch.*

In addition to exhibition galleries, the center houses a theater-video space, library, bookstore, education area, café-restaurant, artist's apartment and the aforementioned artist's studio. From the start, the plan included a major work area for use by a resident artist. The production of art, as well as contact between the artist and public, are primary components of the center's program. During a residency, an artist typically develops a sculpture for the park and/or creates work for the indoor exhibition spaces. Initially, priority was given to art related to nature. The use of granite, a material indigenous to the region, was also favored. Over time, attitudes have loosened and now the main criteria is that artists be sensitive to concepts of architecture and landscape.

Prepare to spend a full day at Vassivière so that you can enjoy the building and exhibitions and also have enough time to walk leisurely around the island to see the sculptures and relax in the quietude of the setting. The outdoor projects, specifically sited by the artists, are located in the depths of the forest, in open meadows or at the water's edge. There is no one path linking them all, and some sculptures are multipartite or unobtrusive objects that are not easy to see or find. Don't get discouraged, the hunt is part of the experience!

Vassivière is an incredible setting and great place to visit. The collection includes a range of sculpture, largely by artists with little exposure outside Europe. The work is well suited to the environment, especially as it echoes a tone of harmony and tranquility. You won't find the monumental industrial sculptures of 1960s vintage or politically-conscious art raising strident challenges to the relationship between human activity, landscape, history, ecology and land use. Instead, most all the objects have a poetic tone and deal metaphorically with concepts of growth, renewal, decay, survival, memory, space, time and seeing.

Sculptures currently installed in the park in the area behind the tower include:

1 Alain KIRILI, *Ariane messagère des dieux* (*Ariadne, Messenger of the Gods*), 1991. Installed at the entrance to the art center, this torsolike image, formed of concrete, leans forward suggesting that it—like the mythic Ariadne —is poised to give you the thread by which you might find your way out of the labyrinth (mental and physical) you are about to enter.

2 Dominique BAILLY, Untitled, 1990. Here and there in a rock-strewn clearing in the forest, the artist has positioned oak blocks tempered by scuff marks and punctures, and cut to blend with the time-worn stones that are naturally part of the setting.

3 David NASH, *Charred Wood and Green Moss*, 1989. A sense of unease is aroused when you come upon the clearing where pieces of charred, hewn wood give evidence of logging activity and a fire. At the same time, there is a beauty in the blackened surfaces of the burnt debris, which have been enriched over time by a velvety coat of green moss. In his characteristic manner, Nash has appropriated elements from nature, arranged and adjusted them to cause transformation and revival in a different form.

4 Kimio TSUCHIYA, *Eternity*, 1990. The young Japanese artist Tsuchiya evokes the idea of eternity, not by a perfect, unbroken, stable form, but by a semicircular wall constructed from old, irregularly shaped stones of many different sizes interlaced by a few dominant beams of burnt wood and held together by nothing more than an amazing ordering of the disparate parts. As if this frontal image were not wondrous enough, Tsuchiya has created a totally different arrangement on the back. Similarly, it is an assemblage of stones collected from the region, but instead of wood beams as marks of accentuation, here an old, tattered window frame set in the middle of the wall evokes the image of a ancient shelter.

Tsuchiya, *Eternity*

5 Kimio TSUCHIYA, *Ever*, 1990. This tall pear-shaped object, composed of gently curving, variously shaped sheets of steel that overlap and interweave, sits like an immutable, dominant presence, strangely stalwart and autonomous in the midst of the forest.

6 Michelangelo PISTOLETTO, *Art Sign*, 1993–94. The artist has installed seven cruciforms made from volcanic rock at the intersections of paths within the sculpture park. By using the cross—a timeless, universal sign with particular currency in art history—and lava—a material associated with the chain of volcanoes in the nearby Auvergne region—Pistoletto allies his sculpture directly with the setting. Spreading the work out as recurring images that you come upon at each crossroad also creates continuity and remembrance as factors of time and space. These are prominent themes in Pistoletto's art.

7 Bernard CALET, Untitled, 1990. As you approach this work, its smooth, reflective plane of polished black granite seems like an incredibly still surface of water. On closer inspection, the stone surface becomes a mirror, allowing a majestic perspective of the trees and sky even as it reveals the fallen leaves and buds swept about by the wind. The gloss of a utopian vision is thus interjected with traces of reality.

8 Anne Marie JUGNET, *erreurs-exact*, 1994. High above eye level, floating amid the trees, are two light yellow neon signs. One is the word *erreurs* the other the word *exact*. Though their color makes the words blend with natural light reflections, as you walk along the path you suddenly are caught off-guard by the sight of a totally out of context, isolated neon sign with a message that is perplexing and enigmatic. What errors does it refer to? What's a neon sign doing in the middle of a forest? Still contemplating the first sign, you come upon the second, which is

Jugnet, *erreurs–exact*

equally inexplicable. (At only one particular point on the path can you see both signs together.) Even if you link the words together (*exact errors*) they make no sense. In fact, they become an oxymoron since it's possible to have an exact error unless, of course, it's a planned error and then it's not really an error. However, if you just consider the words grammatically (in French), you could perhaps claim an example of an exact error since the adjective *exact* doesn't agree with the plural, feminine noun *erreurs*. Metaphorically, you might consider the neon signs' intrusion into a peaceful, natural environment as a far bigger exact error.

9 Marc COUTURIER, *Nadir*, 1990. By placing his sculpture at the top of a sloping glade, Couturier transforms a low wall of glass and aluminum panels depicting the top section of a circular shape into the suggestive image of a sun or moon rising or setting over the horizon. Here again, the artist does not so much represent an element in nature as evoke a changing, captivating force of nature.

10 Bernd LOHAUS, *Essai/Par toi/Traces*, 1986–92. Like finding a penny on the sidewalk when you happen to look down, this work has that sense of an unexpected surprise causing a shift in mood. Composed of three weathered stepping stones, placed alongside a path and inscribed with the words "Attempt," (or "Essay") "By You" and

"Traces," it directly poses a challenge for you to move into a realm of memory, to take notice of traces. Its enigmatic, disjunctive message serves as a catalyst to poetic revery.

11 Frédéric OLLEREAU, *La maison de laine* (*The House of Wool*), 1997. The sculpture consists of a granite block in the form of a schematic house the size of the artist seated with his body folded in on itself. Sheathing the form is a black, wool cover woven on each side with a skeletal bone—the skull, two arms, two legs and the torso. In time, the cloth will disintegrate and reveal the stone structure—another skeleton, now totally unprotected and vulnerable. As outer and inner layers displace one another, images of the house as shelter, the body as imprisoned form and anonymous existense come to the forefront

12 Andy GOLDSWORTHY, Untitled, 1992. A stone wall curves near the shore of the lake, climbs out of the water, moves as a tall barrier line on the land, breaks as it jumps across a path and then forms another big circular shape enclosing some trees in the midst of the forest. The full shape is like a figure 8 with small openings at both ends. Depending on the water level, sometimes the outermost part of the figure sinks below the lake's surface and the wall rises up dramatically from below, appearing even more like an unnatural presence and inexplicable borderline. In fact, Goldsworthy constructed his wall on the remains of a wall that had once defined a field in what had been the open valley land prior to the creation of the dam. Now the wall itself is a boundary, contrasting and enclosing two different environments—water and woods. This work, one of the most impressive at Vassivière, recalls *Spiral Jetty*, the influential sculpture by Robert Smithson that effectively initiated the earth-art direction in sculpture, especially in terms of minimalist images and references to some human act of intervention in nature.

13 Per BARCLAY, *Water House*, 1995. Barclay has created a small wooden cabin with windows of the same size placed opposite one another on the four walls. The house is filled with water up to the lower window frames. When you look inside the cabin you see the surrounding landscape through the opposite window as well as its reflection in the water. The sculpture thus merges and confounds exterior and interior space as well as perceptions of surface and volume. In addition, Barclay makes reference to the houses of the seven small villages flooded in the Maulde valley when the dam was built.

14 Veit STRATMANN, Untitled (*Piece for Hellerau*), 1996. Originally created for Hellerau, a Russian military hospital in Berlin, this work addresses issues regarding public and private space and the ways in which architecture and simple apparatus modify and control our patterns of movement. For his sculpture, Stratmann developed a structural frame in the form of a pseudo-pathway with converging orthogonal sides. It is made from common steel tubing, painted a banal reddish brown color. The shape, open on its narrow end, invites you inside its boundaries only to block your course with a barrier at its opposite end. From the outside, the interior seems like an enticing, private space,

Goldsworthy, Untitled

but when you are inside, the space entraps you in a seemingly no-exit situation. Even if you don't move inside the frame, the sculpture itself, situated in the midst of a narrow woodland path, becomes a barrier to your movement. Its zooming orthogonals, moreover, distort spatial perspective and judgments of distance.

15 Jean-Pierre UHLEN, *Steinland* (*Stone Land*), 1990. The components of this sculpture—a red-painted steel element shaped as a door frame, a slanted red-steel plank propped up by rocks, three steel girders joined at right angles and set on the ground atop stones—are positioned as an ensemble on a small grass clearing overlooking the lake. The geometric industrial character of the work contrasts sharply with the natural surroundings even as the imagery suggests openings and entrances into the space beyond. The juxtaposition of steel and stone also offers comparison and contrast between past and present, natural and man-made structural materials. Even stronger is the reference to indigenous granite stones, plentiful within the confines of the sculpture but invisible within the territory now covered by the lake.

16 David NASH, *Descending Vessel*, 1989. Using the canting trunk of a fir tree, still rooted in the ground but chopped off on top, Nash carves flat sides on the exterior and a cavity in the interior. The image of a dugout boat results, but the vertical position is utterly incongruous with this suggestion. As in many of his sculptures formed of destroyed or dead tree fragments found in the immediate setting, Nash devises an odd mode of recycling in a topsy-turvy world.

17 David JONES, *Green Place with Red Ants*, 1988. Jones marks his own serpentine path in the forest by setting long cylindrical iron beams, cast to look like tree trunks, atop granite supports.

Some of the stones have geometrically carved shapes and others have been left in an irregular, untouched state. The work expresses a conflation of accidental and intentional order, real and artificial, natural and man-made.

18 Roland COGNET, Untitled, 1995. Lying on the lawn in front of the art center are two logs cut from the trunk of a sequoia tree. In fact, these are not actual logs, but facsimiles cast in concrete. By conflating natural and industrial materials, the artist sought to suggest a parallel with the relationship between Rossi's architecture and the island's environment. There is symmetry and duality in both pairings.

19 Marylène NEGRO, *Sport France*, 1995–98. The seven exercise stations placed around the lawn are actual pieces of equipment sold by Sport France. However, they usually have instruction panels telling you how to use them. By omitting the instructions, Negro takes the authoritarian voice out of physical exercise, inviting you to jump, run, balance or just play as you please.

20 Vladimir SKODA, Untitled, 1996. This steel and bronze sphere set on a circular base embedded into the lawn is an utterly reduced, geometric form and yet it appears like a planetary body because of the outdoor, open space context.

21 Bernard PAGES, *Point de vue* (*Point of View*), 1997. It his characteristic manner, the artist has constructed an assemblage of industrial materials, some painted in acidic tones, to explore the concept of balance. He places the heaviest element—a concrete block—atop a non-volumetric base of twisted steel bars that looks like it's both collapsing under the weight and swirling about as windswept ribbons.

Meymac

This picturesque, hilltop hamlet with winding streets and Old World flavor is situated just to the west of Ussel, equidistant between Limoges and Clermont-Ferrand. Train from Limoges, 1 3/4 hr; from Ussel, 15 min.

Abbaye Saint-André —Centre d'Art Contemporain

place du Bûcher, 19250
tel/fax: 05-55-95-23-30
Mar–June and Sept–Dec: Mon, Wed–Fri, 2–6; Sat–Sun, 10–12 and 2–6; closed Tues. July–Aug: Mon, Wed–Sun, 10–1 and 2–7; closed Tues
admission: 20/10F

From the train station, it is a 20-min walk to the village center.

With its founding and subsequent expansion, the art center has been instrumental in the restoration of the badly deteriorating, old Benedictine abbey in the heart of the town. It now occupies the entire west wing and corner tower of the building, devoting four floors of large and small rooms to exhibition galleries. For a small operation, it has not only a sizeable space but also an ambitious program. Unlike most of the urban-based centers of contemporary art, this one serves a rural community of 3,000 residents. In line with its mission —to provide the local public with indispensable keys for understanding the evolution and complexity of contemporary art—its program combines thematic group exhibitions related to the major creative movements of the last half century, retrospectives of established artists and showings of young French artists. Catalogues accompany most projects. Recent exhibitions: *Anne Barbier*, *Basserode*, *Glen Baxter*, *Sylvie Blocher*,

Etienne Bossut, *Henri Cueco*, *Eric Duyckaerts*, *Christian Eckart*, *Jörg Immendorff*, *Albert Irvin*, *Saverio Lucariello*, *Markus Lupertz*, *Didier Marcel*, *Gilles Noaillac*, *Rob Scholte*, *Andreas Schulze*.

Robert Jacobsen

Untitled, 1991

Located on the side lawn of the Abbaye Saint-André, this monumental steel work by one of Denmark's leading sculptors serves as a landmark for the Contemporary Art Center. Its rectangular cagelike structure delimits an open space. Two extraneous elements—an arc and a slanted plane—puncture the interior space, countering the right-angled core of the sculpture with directional thrusts. Characteristically, Jacobsen produces a field of forces held in tension within a stable structural frame.

Ussel

This old rural village with roots in the 15–17th century is situated to the east of Meymac. Train from Meymac, 12 min; from Limoges, 1 3/4 hr.

Braco Dimitrijevic

Satire post historicus, 1987
Musée du Pays, garden

Located in the garden behind the city museum. It's a short walk from the train station to boulevard Clemenceau in the center of town. Turn right after the Gendarmerie Nationale (police station) onto a small street, rue François Grabié. Just ahead on the left you will find a small garden-park. The sculpture is alongside the path leading to the back door of the museum.

At first the six bronze busts on marble pedestals seem like conventional portraits honoring illustrious persons. But when you read the labels identifying the figures, you begin to realize that this is not your usual commemorative sculpture. Half the names—Michelangelo, Leonardo da Vinci, Albrecht Dürer—are familiar, famous persons. The other three—Mario Orsini, Jules Bailly, Dieter Koch—are unknowns with ordinary names. (Actually the names derive from three passersby the artist met by chance.) The explanation for the odd grouping lies in the story inscribed on a plaque set in front of the busts: "There were once two painters who lived far from the cities and towns. One day the King lost his dog while hunting in the vicinity. He found it in the garden of one of the two painters and invited him to his château. The name of this painter was Leonardo. The name of the other one has disappeared forever in human memory."

This work is part of an ongoing pantheon of busts created by Dimitrijevic to raise consciousness about how history can cause people to move from the status of anonymity to notoriety and vice versa. Indeed, history is not an absolute or fixed condition, but something shaped and continuously reshaped by those in positions of power. Having grown up in Zagreb, Yugoslavia, the artist had experienced the situation in which huge photographic portraits suddenly appeared on the facades of the main city square and everyone instantly viewed them as freshly installed effigies, the members of a new government.

Rochechouart

A turreted castle (mainly 15th century) located on a promontory rock identifies this town, about 22 mi (35 km) west of Limoges. Since there is no train service to Rochechouart and bus service does not permit a return trip the same day, a visit here is best made by car.

Musée Départemental d'Art Contemporain

Château de Rochechouart, place du Château, 87600
05-55-03-77-77 f: 05-55-79-49-94
spring and fall: Wed–Sun, 2–6; closed Mon–Tues. June–Sept: Mon, Wed–Sun, 10–12:30 and 1:30–6; closed Tues and during the winter. Days and hours vary according to the temporary exhibition schedule so be sure to call in advance.
admission: 15/10F

Here again, the region and city decided to make use of and renovate a historic building to coincide with the creation of a contemporary art center. Despite its limited, quirky exhibition space, the museum has a world-class exhibition program and collection. Not only does

Lafont exhibition (Musée Départemental, Rochechouart)

the list of artists represent an impressive cross section of contemporary art but the selection of work is also notable for its high quality. Recent exhibitions: *Crossed Singularities*, *Love Boat*, *The Earth Is Not Round—New Narration*, *Pep Agut*, *Stephan Balkenhol*, *Jean-Marc Bustamante*, *Geneviève Cadieux*, *Tony Cragg*, *Grenville Davey*, *Richard Deacon*, *Wim Delvoye*, *Patrick Faigenbaum*, *Douglas Gordon*, *Rodney Graham*, *Gary Hill*, *Fabrice Hybert*, *Thierry Kuntzel*, *Suzanne Lafont*, *Gabriel Orozco*, *Javier Perez*, *Michelangelo Pistoletto*, *Hermann Pitz*, *Jason Rhoades*, *Wiebke Siem*, *James Welling*.

In addition to its contemporary focus, the museum houses the Raoul Hausmann Estate, comprising 135 artworks and archives. A room devoted to Hausmann shows changing exhibitions of his art and writings, including photomontages and phonetic poems from his Dada years in Berlin.

Be sure to see Richard LONG's *Ligne vivante* or *Rochechouart Line* (1990), specifically commissioned for the château and located in the east wing in the Salle des Fresques d'Hercule. Since the 1960s, Long has been creating art that sets up a dialogue between the open countryside—nature—and an exhibition site—culture; between time measured in a walk outdoors and time suspended in an art object. Here, his 62-ft-long, 3-ft-wide line of stones bears witness to walks he made in the area around Rochechouart. By placing the line in a room with 15th-century frescos describing the works of Hercules, the sculpture also arouses comparisons between real, remembered and mythic activity; sublime, mundane and heroic experience.

Located in the garden in front of the courtyard at the entrance to the museum, is a second commissioned work, the sculpture *Arbre* (1985–86) by Giuseppe PENONE. In addition to being literally intertwined with a tree, Penone's granite *Tree* shares its form with the spiral-twist columns of the courtyard architecture, the curvaceous shape of a woman's body, the winding movement of a snake and the planar surface of a leaf.

Angoulême

This charming hilltop city with narrow streets and café-laden plazas is known as the "capital of the comic strip." Train from Limoges, 1 1/2 hrs; TGV from Bordeaux, 45 min; TGV from Paris (Gare Montparnasse), 2 1/4 hr.

FRAC Poitou-Charentes

Hôtel Saint-Simon, 15 rue de la Cloche Verte, 16000
05-45-92-87-01 f: 05-45-95-94-16
Tues–Sat, 10–12 and 1:30–7;
closed Mon
admission: free

Rue de la Cloche Verte is one of the narrow streets in front of place des Halles at the eastern end of the old city.

Don't think you're at the wrong place when you come to the address. The center is located in a Renaissance town house with an ornate facade. To get to the galleries, walk through the small courtyard inside the street gate, enter the modest door to the left and then climb the narrow, curving staircase. The exhibition spaces are in the upstairs rooms of the house, and the program is mainly selections from the collection of this and other regions. It's all pretty low-key but the displays typically include significant works by notable artists, many whose names are not yet familiar outside Europe.

Centre National de la Bande Dessinée et de l'Image—CNBDI

🏛 architects: Roland CASTRO with
🏢 Jean REMOND, 1987–90
121 rue de Bordeaux, 16000
🎥 05-45-38-65-65 f: 05-45-38-65-66
May–Sept: Tues–Fri, 10–7; Sat–Sun,
2–7; closed Mon. Oct–Apr: Tues–Fri,
10–6; Sat–Sun, 2–6; closed Mon
admission: 30/20F

If you walk down avenue de Cognac along the city wall, near the bottom of the hill you will come to the back of the CNBDI. You can take the side stairway to the front entrance or continue on the street to the intersection and turn right onto rue de Bordeaux. The latter path is preferable since you will then take in the full force of the facade when you approach the site.

Located at the foot of the northern ramparts of the city, on the side of a steep slope leading down to the Charente river, this site was originally (beginning in the 6th century) home to a Benedictine abbey. From the time of the French Revolution (1791) until 1973, its use was industrial, first as a paper workshop and then as a brewery. In its most recent reincarnation, the building has been radically reconstructed and the site is now a striking, multi-faceted center dedicated to comics. The rubric "comics" encompasses cartoon images, comic strips, comic books, animation and silicon graphics.

Even before you enter the building, its eccentric, fantasy design offers a taste (or rather a blitzkrieg) of the comic-book spirit. Conceived as a "terrain of adventure" and designed "to inspire fiction," the architecture takes full advantage of its dramatic, romantic, preposterous site. The facade moves in and out, up and down from space to space. It's a disjunctive collage of vestiges from previous structures, ruins, reflective mirror walls—including a theatrical concave segment in the center—stairs and bridges of industrial steel suspended at vertiginous heights, terraces and lightwells, cuts and abysses. As an additional dynamic, the center has converted the esplanade in front of the building into an outdoor museum called *Le parvis des Etoiles* (The Plaza of the Stars). It contains "drawings" made in one-meter-square slabs of cement by renown comic-strip artists who come to visit. As of 1997, there were 37 slabs, including a Tarzan by Burne Hogarth and a Spirit by Will Eisner (two U.S. artists).

Inside, you will find a museum, temporary exhibitions, a bookstore, small projection room, large movie theater (with a full-scale cinemathèque program), library, conference rooms, production and teaching laboratories and cybercafé. For anyone interested in experiencing an outstanding museum installation that is visitor-friendly and enriched with easy-to-digest bits of contextual, historic and artistic information, the museum is not to be missed. The display features selections from the permanent collection of over 4,000 original comics that trace the history of the medium from 1830 to the present. Although the emphasis is on Franco-Belgian work, there's a special section devoted to American comics. The exhi-

Castro, CNBDI

bition space is one giant open hall with labyrinthine subsections curving around and paths extending in various directions up and down several levels. Within this space, comics are arranged in small groupings and placed in slanted cases fitted with rails to lean on or accompanied by chairs to relax in. Optimal viewing conditions prevail and great attention is paid to your comfort. Enjoyment and appreciation is further heightened by the sketches, prints, scenarios, artist-interview recordings, sculptures of famous comic-book figures, derivative objects and multimedia presentations (videos, slides, audiotapes) interspersed with the comics throughout the hall. Even if you're not a big comic-book fan, you will undoubtedly have fun at this site. It's totally unique!

Festival of the Comic Strip

This popular event occurs annually the last weekend in January in sites throughout the city. When the festival celebrated its 25th anniversary in 1998, over 160,000 visitors converged on Angoulême, overwhelming its resident population of 47,000.

Bordeaux–Toulouse

Bordeaux

This city is rich in cultural initiatives and support of contemporary art. During the summer months, many of the grand châteaux in the region are the sites of excellent contemporary art exhibitions. Since 1987 Mécénart Aquitaine (a patronage association) has also sponsored a large biennial exhibition in one or more of the wine-growing properties. The programs and locations of these summer activities vary annually, so you will need to check the local media or the free leaflet, *Calendrier*, for relevant details. TGV from Paris (Gare Montparnasse), 3 hr; train from Toulouse, 2 1/2 hr.

capcMusée d'Art Contemporain

Entrepôt, 7 rue Ferrère, 33000
05-56-00-81-50 f: 05-56-44-12-07
Tues, Thurs–Sun, 12–6; Wed, 12–10; closed Mon
admission: 30/20F for temporary exhibitions; 20/10F for collection; free on Wed
bus: 1 to Lainé; 7, 8 to Quinconces

The museum is located at the north end of the city, just off quai Louis XVIII near the port area of the Garonne river. It's a nice walk from the center city and if you're a landscape or flower lover, you might want to combine your museum visit with a tour of the Botanical and Public Gardens, a stone's throw away.

"capc" (Centre d'Art Plastiques Contemporains) began in 1973 as a center for contemporary art. It rapidly emerged as a premier exhibition site within both France and Europe. When it moved (1979) into its present location—Entrepôt Lainé, a converted 19th-century warehouse used for storing exotic goods from France's colonies—it acquired a site of monumental size and character. You experience the monumentality as soon as you enter the striking and spacious, spare and yet majestic main hall, or Great Nave (*Grande nef*), as it is called. Constructed in stone and surrounded by arched side aisles on the ground floor with an arched mezzanine above, the architecture has an openness and grandeur—a double-edged sword for displaying art. In addition to the central hall, there are many galleries to the sides on two levels. Throughout its history, the museum has encouraged artists to deal with the space by developing art and installations specifically allied with its scale and scope. Recent exhibitions: *Vito Acconci, Laurie Anderson, Richard Baquié, George Baselitz, Louise Bourgeois, Daniel Buren, Marie-Ange Guilleminot, Simon Hantaï, Fabrice Hybert, Anish Kapoor, Anselm Kiefer, Jannis Kounellis, Wolfgang Laib, Sol LeWitt, Mario Merz, Annette Messager, Tony Oursler, Jack Pierson, Jean-Pierre Raynaud, Richard Serra, Cindy Sherman, Frank Stella, Niele Toroni, Luc Tuymans, Claude Viallat, Andy Warhol.* The exhibition program is renowned throughout the art world for showing the cream of the international vanguard. What has made it especially distinctive is the fact that it has developed major shows of these artists before other museums in France, Europe or even internationally, and has consistently created remarkable exhibitions.

For the first 20 years, one director (Jean-Louis Froment) shaped the direction and ambitions of the museum. A new management team, in place since 1996–97, has sought to build on the past, shifting a bit by adding more thematic exhibitions and art from Asia. Exemplifying this, was *Cities on the Move: Art and Architecture in Asia* (1998), a project that also is notable for being a joint venture of the Art Museum and Architecture Center at Entrepôt. A space devoted to projects by young artists has also become an ongoing aspect of the museum's program.

When capc became an official museum in 1984, it began devoting serious attention to building a collection. By 1997 it had acquired about 600 works. Included are major examples representing most facets of international, vanguard experimentation from the 1970s to the present. French painting from the 1970s, English land art, American conceptual art, Italian Arte Povera, painting from the 1980s and current work are areas of particular strength. Selections from the collection are usually displayed on the second level and upper terrace. Be sure not to miss the rooftop installation of a Richard LONG stone line, the Keith HARING elevator wall and the Max NEUHAUS sound installation in the stairwells of the south wing. Because the focus has been European and American art, this is an excellent place to see and compare work from various countries who have been at the forefront in the late 20th century. You will probably find some unfamiliar names and finally get to see work previously known only from photos and descriptions.

Lectures, conferences, artist presentations, special events, concerts, dance performances, poetry readings, classes for children and adults, videos and catalogues accompany most exhibitions. If there is an event scheduled when you visit, its well-worth trying to attend. Perusing the bookstore, library and café are also enjoyable ways to expand your visit.

Bourgeois, *Spider*, 1996 (capcMusée d'Art Contemporain)

Arc en Rêve– Centre d'Architecture

⌨ Entrepôt, 7 rue Ferrère, 33000
05-56-52-78-36 f: 05-56-81-51-49
Tues, Thurs–Sun, 12–6; Wed,
12–10; closed Mon
admission: 30/20F, free on Wed

Also located in Entrepôt, to the right and up the stairs from the main entrance.

This is one of a handful of art centers focused exclusively on architecture, urbanism and design. Its exhibitions feature models of both sites and buildings, drawings, plans, photographs, installations, videos, furniture, all sorts of handmade and manufactured objects and graphic design projects by both renowned, established figures and the experimental, emerging vanguard. Coverage is international and extremely diverse in terms of stylistic and theoretical approaches. Displays not only give you access to some of the most interesting or provocative work from the past and present but also present hypothetical and fantasy designs for the future. Even if you're not involved with the field of architecture, a visit to this center will strengthen your take on contemporary creativity and culture. Catalogues and free brochures are excellent. Recent exhibitions: *New Architecture in Flanders*, *Expressions/ Impressions: Graphic Artists in Aquitaine*, *BLOC—the Fractured Monolith*, *Young British Architecture*, *Warchitecture: Urbicide—Sarajevo*, *36 Models for Private Homes*, *Transarchitecture*, *Yves Brunier* (landscape architect), *Elizabeth Diller & Ricardo Scofidio*, *April Greiman* (graphic designer), *Stephen Holl*, *Rem Koolhaas, Bruce Mau, Jean Nouvel*.

Ecole des Beaux-Arts de Bordeaux

⌨ architect: Massimiliano FUKSAS,
1993–94
Université Michel de Montaigne,
Talence, 33405
Bus 30, G, 81, U from place de la
Victoire, exit Fac de Lettres,
Esplanade des Antilles, Talence.

This art school (5 mi from Bordeaux) brings together training in the visual arts, theater, music, dance, film, radio and various other disciplines. The building, clad in oxidized copper, has a bold, exacting appearance. It is a long, green box with an encircling horizontal slit (recessed windows) and two large vertical shafts on each of its long sides (recessed entrances below and window walls above). These few elements are the only openings or design features on the exterior. In reality, some small windows interrupt the continuous planes, but folding green shutters covering them make them blend perfectly into the facades. One additional element, also a box form (a radio studio), sits atop one corner of the roof. Actually it's two attached boxes, one with window walls, which actually rests on the roof, and the other sheathed in wood, which floats over the roof and extends beyond the edge of the building below.

The interior, which is surprisingly well lit, has many different types of spaces, diversely scaled and punctuated by rigorously shaped, geometric openings. Indeed, all the component forms and articulations, as well as the building itself, are extremely severe and reductive, comparable to those found in minimalist sculpture. This correspondence is not an accident, for Fuksas strongly advocates a renewal of architecture's identity as an art form. In his view, buildings should emphasize their presence and image as sculptural entities, yet still be functional. If you want to see a striking work of contemporary architecture that doesn't just pretend to be different, this is it.

Mutations urbaines

Special exhibition, June–Oct 2000

Bordeaux will celebrate the millennium with a grand project organized by Arc-en-Rêve and directed by the dynamic, controversial architect Rem KOOLHAAS. Held in the city's big esplanade, place Quinconces, it will illustrate great urban disorder "from European cities to American megalopolises to Asian conurbations."

Toulouse

As a major high-tech and aerospace center, Toulouse is one of the fastest growing cities in France. Its historic, Visigoth past and its venerable university (dating back to the 13th century) add a traditional and intellectual dimension, though its large student population (83,000) vibrantly energizes the urban ambience. Indeed, the city is a friendly, upbeat place. It's easy to walk around the center city or you can use the new métro system. During the summer months, many of the towns and villages in the southwest region of France, not far from Toulouse, host contemporary art exhibitions. Here again, you can get information about these from local tourist offices, posters and mass media publications. Train from Bordeaux, 2 1/4 hr; from Montpellier, 2 1/2 hr; TGV from Paris (Gare Montparnasse) via Bordeaux, 5 1/2 hr.

Galerie Municipale du Château d'Eau

1 place Laganne, 31300
05-61-77-09-40 f: 05-61-42-02-70
Mon, Wed–Sun, 1–7; closed Tues
admission: 15/10F—reduced rate
for everyone on Sun
métro: Saint-Cyprien/République

Château d'Eau is a short walk from place du Capitole, the city's main square. It's just across the Pont Neuf on the west (left) bank of the Garonne river.

This art center, founded in 1974, focuses exclusively on photography. It has a unique location (a favorite tourist attraction) in a renovated brick water tower with an additional exhibition gallery and documentation center situated alongside, under an access arch of the 17th-century Pont Neuf. During the course of its history, the center has organized an amazing number of exhibitions and produced a rich archive of related catalogues, posters and postcards. It also has amassed a significant collection of original photographs and photography equipment, as well as a substantial book and video library (open to the public). Historic and contemporary, fine art and documentary photography are all within the center's scope, though the more vanguard mixed-media, conceptual or technically experimental art/photo projects of recent decades have not been included.

Virtually all the photography seen here is classic in its orientation to process, and it tends to be figurative, narrative or surreal in its approach to imagery. However, the typical "high art" attitude does not apply. You will therefore see Neo-Realist Italian film posters, science photos, world press photos, jazz images, sports photos, magazine covers and the like. In addition, the displays present work from countries outside the mainstream—like Haiti, Cuba, Ukraine, Taiwan, Argentina, Chile, Bulgaria—by photographers who are unknown and who probably would not identify themselves as "artists." The quality is uneven but the breadth of the span is admirable. Recent exhibitions: *Paul Caponigro*, *Robert Doisneau*, *Frantisek Drtikol*, *Elliot Erwitt*, *Walker Evans*, *Graciela Iturbide*, *Carl de Keyser*, *Josef Koudelka*, *Dorothea Lange*, *Duane Michals*, *Jan Saudek*, *Maurice Tabard*, *Shoji Ueda*.

Both the water tower and underarch space are captivating sites but very poor environments for exhibiting art. Especially in the tower, the narrow corridorlike galleries and intrusion of the old water mill and sales displays make viewing difficult. Unprofessional hanging and lighting are also problematic.

Espace d'Art Moderne et Contemporain de Toulouse et Midi–Pyrénées

renovation: Antoine STINCO and Rémi PAPILLAULT
76 allées Charles de Fitte, 31300
05-61-59-99-96 f: 05-6159-38-67
métro: Saint-Cyprien/République.

Located on the left bank, just past the major intersection where rue de la République meets the stately, tree-lined allées Charles de Fitte.

This is the latest in a series of amazing contemporary art centers that have sprung up during the past several decades in the French provinces. Among these, Art Space is unique in being a conglomerate, formed by joining the city's Museum of Modern Art, the regional Contemporary Art Center (previously situated in Labège), the FRAC de Midi-Pyrénées and the Art History Annex of the Municipal Library of Toulouse. As was the case with La

Villette Park in Paris, the site in Toulouse was previously occupied by the city's slaughterhouses. (Strange coincidence that culture centers are replacing slaughterhouses!) The main building, a grandiose structure designed by Urbain Vitry in 1827 to echo the form and proportions of Toulouse's historic Saint-Sernin basilica, has been handsomely renovated by Stinco-Papillault. It opened to the public in the fall of 1998.

Retaining much of the exterior design and interior division of space from the former structure, the art center has at its disposal a large central hall surrounded by wide, arcaded aisles, a rear hemicycle, multistory rooms on the sides, and a vast area in the front. In addition to the galleries, the building houses a bookstore, café-restaurant, auditorium, library and youth club. Complementing the building is the spectacular landscaped setting. Arranged as garden courts, the property is bounded on one side by a resurrected Gallo-Roman wall and in the back by a monumental staircase leading to a belvedere and walkways overlooking the Garonne river.

The permanent collection and temporary exhibitions are presented in the central hall of the main building. Of note is a special Picasso room highlighted by an incredible stage curtain, *Composition with Minotaur* (1936). Also on display are works from the collection donated by Daniel Cordier, which concentrates on art from 1950 to 1955, and paintings by Georges Mathieu, a postwar leader of gestural abstraction in France. Indeed, all modes of postwar art from various European countries, the United States and Japan (Gutai, a vanguard performance-oriented movement) are a strength of the permanent collection galleries. In recognition of its geographic location, special attention is also paid to recent art from the southwest region of France, Spain and Italy. Contemporary art is represented in the collection and major exhibitions, and plans call for establishing an experimental gallery in the hemicycle space. Performances, films and videos, installations, music and lectures—many deriving from collaborations with other cultural institutions in the city and region—are an ongoing part of the program.

Galerie Sollertis

12 rue des Régans, 31000
05-61-55-43-32 f: 05-61-25-34-13
Tues–Sat, 10–12 and 2–7; Mon,
2–7
métro: Esquirol

Located near the place des Carmes, between rue du Languedoc and rue Pharoan.

With its focus on photography, conceptual and minimal art, and its active participation in international art fairs, this gallery has played a strong role in bringing challenging contemporary art to Toulouse. Artists: John Armleder, Pierre Barès, Jean-Marc Bustamante, Sophie Calle, Paul-Armand Gette, Philippe Hortala, Alain Josseau, Bertrand Lavier, François Morellet, Olivier Mosset, Edda Renouf.

Michelangelo Pistoletto

Le génie du temps, 1985
Hôtel de Région Midi-Pyrénées,
boulevard Maréchal Juin

Located at the front entrance to the regional government building, just beyond the Saint-Michel bridge beside the roadway paralleling the river.

Standing upright on a pedestal, but missing a head and other body parts, the sculpture initially appears to be a dilapidated monument, a remnant of a traditional marble figure put in a public place as some sort of memorial. Yet, on

closer inspection, not only does the sculpture become totally enigmatic as an image, decidedly not a human figure and not a ruin, but the very idea of a commemorative image also becomes questionable if not absurd. With its ascending, swirling form, Pistoletto's eccentric configuration has the dynamic of an irrepressible, self-sustaining force. Its truncated, asymmetrical body carved with jagged cuts also suggests a long, stalwart existence that has weathered change, harmony and discord. The image thus evokes a spirit that deeply affects but extends beyond the particularities of person, place and historical moment. True to its title, it evokes *The Genie* (or *Genius*) *of Time.*

Cinémathèque de Toulouse

69 rue du Taur, 31080
05-62-30-30-10 f: 05-62-30-30-12
exhibitions: Tues–Fri, 10–10; Sat,
2–11; Sun, 2–8; closed Mon
admission: free (films: 28/25F)
métro: Capitole

This film center (located just off place Saint-Sernin in the center of the city) has an exhibition hall, large collection of French films, two screening rooms and library. It runs a substantial lecture and publication program as well as two–four film showings each day.

Métro

The new Toulouse subway system gives superb evidence of how the French can produce a technologically advanced, aesthetically superb, government-based project. Be sure to check it out, if only to look. It's clean, user-friendly, functional, efficient and quiet. A reductive approach to design prevails, though concern about appearance extends to all components—even to the métro officers who wear spiffy, gray checked jackets! Under the 1%-for-art requirement, 15 artists (most of whom lived or exhibited in the region) were chosen in 1992 to create works in each of the 15 stations being constructed. Many of the projects are installation oriented and some are both inside and outside the stations. The character of the designs is wide ranging and variable in artistic merit, but Toulouse stands out as being the first major city to commission art at the construction phase for every station in a new transportation network. You can see many of the works without paying to enter the métro system. Or, you can pay once and ride throughout the system stopping at, but not exiting, each station.

Giulio Paolini

Capitole métro station

Allying his design with the name of the station and main city square (a reference to city magistrates once known as "capitouls"), Paolini has created an installation of early dynastic, gray marble columns and wall drawings of columns. It is located in a corner space near the ticket machines. Though the columns are incongruous and functionless, they have a curious relationship with a huge column wrapped in stainless steel that is the functional, structural support in the vicinity. Indeed the capi-

Paolini, Capitole métro

tals atop Paolini's columns are all unadorned tubular designs, looking more like industrial tools than architectural decorations. As interesting as this project is, one has to wonder why the métro (or the artist) chose to put a "public" artwork in such an extraneous space totally unconnected to the pathways used by, or even seen by, passengers.

François Morellet

Saint-Cyprien/République métro station

By placing an architectonic, brick construction in the plaza and traffic island near the entrance to the station, Morellet integrates his work into the immediate environment and allies it with the historic use of brick in Toulouse. But in his characteristic mode, he wreaks havoc with logic by setting walls on diagonals and suspending them in space. He also creates an odd dualism between a plane of rippling water and a plane of air vents. Inside the station, in the area around the ticket booth, he skews the geometric pattern of the wall tiles, creating irregular, oddly angled shapes and sweeping, linear patterns.

Lectoure

One of the oldest villages in the region, situated about 56 mi (90 km) northwest of Toulouse between Auch and Agen on route N21. Train to Agen, 1 hr, then bus to Lectoure, about 40 min.

Centre de Photographie de Lectoure

5 rue Sainte Claire, 32700
05-62-68-83-72 f: 05-62-68-83-03
Tues–Fri, 9–12 and 2–6 (summer, 3–7); closed Mon
admission: free

The center shows an interesting cross section of adventurous international artists. During the summer, a veritable photo festival occurs with exhibitions at various sites within the city. *Photographic Memory in the Feminine* was the theme in 1996, the work of Jan Groover was a highlight of the 1997 season, and 1998 featured a group show with photographs by Jean-Marc Bustamante, Sophie Calle, Georges Rousse and others.

Plieux

About 6 mi (10km) east of Lectoure between Auch and Agen.

Château de Plieux

Plieux, 32340
05-62-28-62-92 f: 05-62-28-60-53
Mon, Wed–Sun, 3–7; closed Tues

In the summer the château presents an exhibition by a well-known contemporary artist. For example, Christian Boltanski created a site installation in 1997. During the year, the display is composed of works from the permanent collection, which includes modern and contemporary work by artists like Pierre Alechinsky, Karel Appel, Anthony Caro, Jannis Kounellis, Wifredo Lam, Joan Miró, Paul Rebeyrolle, Richard Serra, Antoni Tàpies.

Figeac

A quaint, pedestrianized village, easily reached by train from Toulouse, 2 1/4 hr, or Limoges, 1 1/2 hr. If you've never visited this region of France, be sure to spend time exploring the river valleys of the Dordogne, Lot and Tarn with their majestic cliffs, caves, grottos, prehistoric sites, charming hamlets and haute cuisine. Particular favorites are the spectac-ular, cliff-top village of Saint-Cirq Lapopie (bus from Figeac, 1 hr; from Cahors, 40 min) and the nearby Pech-Merle cave with its incredible stalagmites and wondrous Cro-Magnon paintings.

Joseph Kosuth

Ex libris, J.-F. Champollion, 1990
place des Ecritures

Located next to the Musée Champollion in a courtyard tucked away in the heart of the old city. Enter from rue des Frères or rue Seguier.

A cobblestone courtyard, bordered by the solid, sandstone walls of 13–14th century houses, serves as the site of this public art commission. (The back wall, which has windowlike openings for views down into the courtyard, shields an upper-level garden, accessible by a side staircase.) Not at all object-oriented or even sculptural in form, the work is a flat surface of shiny granite, spread across the ground plane of the courtyard. And, unlike most artworks that are designed to be looked at, this one is meant to be walked on. With its irregular contour shape and its surface divided into three sections, each engraved with a different type of iconic and phonetic writing, it has the image of the Rosetta stone. Indeed, it is an immense replica of the celebrated fragment of black basalt stone, found in 1799, bearing an inscription in hieroglyphics, demotic characters and Greek that provided clues to deciphering Egyptian hieroglyphics. Notably, it was Jean-François Champollion, a native son of Figeac, who was responsible for unraveling the complex graphics of the Rosetta stone in 1822.

For Kosuth, an artist preoccupied with the irrationalities and arbitrariness of language, especially the differences between words (written and spoken) and images (pictures and things), the stone has particular resonance. Here, he has created a situation in which viewers can vicariously discover the Rosetta stone and think about the mystery and magic of written communication. The placement of the work also invites consideration of the relationships between text, image, setting and context—ancient Egypt, Renaissance Figeac, 19th-century Europe and contemporary art.

Cahors

A lively, friendly little city, west of Figeac and north of Toulouse. Bus from Figeac, 1 3/4 hr; train from Toulouse, 1 1/4 hr.

Le Printemps de Cahors

05-65-22-07-32

As part of its annual spring festival held for several weeks in May or June, the city sponsors an exhibition devoted to photography and the visual arts. Organized by a guest curator, it typically includes a strong group of international artists. The location varies from year to year but some part tends to be in the Musée Municipal. There are often nighttime events in the streets—like video projections on walls of buildings. Artists in past festivals: Doug Aitken, Vanessa Beecroft, Danièle Buetti, Thomas Demand, Stan Douglas, Robert Filliou, Gary Hill, Dennis Hopper, Alfredo Jaar, Valérie Jouve, Jürgen Klauke, Joachim Koester, Mark Lewis, Tracey Moffat, Yasumasa Morimura, Philippe Parreno, Anne and Patrick Poirier, Seton Smith, Boyd Webb, Robert Wilson.

Castres

A pleasant, riverside town to the east of Toulouse. Train from Toulouse, 1 1/2 hr.

Centre d'Art Contemporain de Castres

35 rue Chambre-de-l'Edit, 81100
05-63-59-30-20 f: 05-63-72-50-94
July–Aug: daily, 10–12 and 2–6
Sept–June: Tues–Fri, 10–12 and 2–6; Sat–Mon, 3–6
admission: free

Located in the center of the city, a few blocks from the Musée Goya.

Occupying a ground-floor apartment and contiguous garden in a 17th-century building, this young art center has a substantial program. In addition to its regular activities, it has been actively engaged in displaying proposals for public art commissions in the local area. Exhibitions have presented the work of Pierre Antoniucci, Pierre Buraglio, Diller & Scofidio, Lüdger Gerdes, Paul-Armand Gette, Andy Goldsworthy, Alain Jacquet, Mark Luyten, Annette Messager, Jaume Plensa, Jürgen Schilling and others.

Montpellier– Provence

Montpellier

Punctuated with medieval walls, luxurious 17–18th century mansions and Greco-Roman-style monuments, this city also has the advantage of nice weather, an appealing location bordered by beaches on the Mediterranean, a university and office-research facilities for international electronics and media conglomerates. Moreover, Montpellier is in the midst of a veritable renaissance, spearheaded by major architectural and environmental

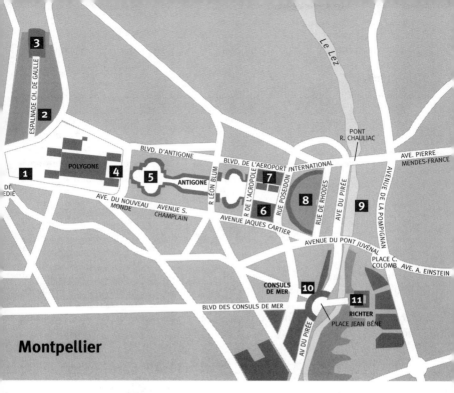

Montpellier

ventures that are in many ways comparable to the *grands projets* and urban development in and around Paris. Indeed, extraordinary neighborhood complexes and activity centers are radically transforming the character, appearance and expanse of the city.

A high level of creativity is in evidence throughout—not surprising, since Montpellier made a concerted effort to select world-renowned architects, urban planners and landscape designers. Teams under the direction of a master architect are developing autonomous sectors, but these and their constituent parts—housing, recreation units, businesses, office centers, open space, transportation, parks—are all integrated into a cohesive plan. Montpellier contends they are building "a new art of city living . . . where importance is placed on the quality of life and environment." They call it a Eurocity for the 21st century. In contrast

to futuristic thinking centered on technology, here emphasis is on "the right to beauty—for everybody," regardless of whether one lives in social or private housing, center city or suburb. Such things as the pedestrianization of the old center city as well as the new sectors and the coordination of work and play, private and public space have already had a marked effect. You can sense it in the infectious vibrancy in public places.

For anyone interested in urban planning (and contemporary architecture), or anyone wanting to experience an alternative mode of city life and different way of relating people to the built and natural environment, a visit to Montpellier is a must. This city is clearly one of France's biggest secrets. The greatest shame is the lack of artist involvement with all the new construction and the omission of innovative 1%-for-art projects or notable art commissions within the city. If you have time to explore all parts of the urban development projects, you will want to get complete, up-to-date information from the planning office in city hall (to the north side of Polygone). TGV from Paris (Gare de Lyon), 4 1/4 hr; train from Toulouse, 2 1/2 hr; from Nîmes, 1/2 hr; from Marseille, 2 hr.

For instant submersion in the lively ambience of Montpellier, go to the heart of the historic old city at place de la Comédie, an enormous, elongated public square (foot traffic only). At the front end, an elaborate 19th-century building (Opéra-Comédie) stands as a commanding presence, a keynote of cultural tradition. Alongside, a network of bustling, shop-laden walking streets converge on the plaza, bringing people into the open space. All around, cafés and restaurants set up their operations outdoors, many in the midst of the plaza itself. Stately facades add elegance to the perimeter, and the long wall-fountain, which dominates one span, emits rhythmic, soothing sounds. In the morning, when market tables and stalls take over a sector of the square, the atmosphere shifts to a commercial orientation. Later, in the afternoon or evening, a stage is at times set up for a music, dance or theater performance and the atmosphere shifts again. Even when there is no formal stage, street musicians and the like are a source of ongoing entertainment. And should you wander down the tree-lined boulevard (esplanade Charles de Gaulle), which extends diagonally off the far end of the plaza, or into the ever-crowded concourse (allée Jules Milhau) leading into Polygone—a mega-shopping mall—you will experience another range of ambient shifts. Taken all together, these ingredients—not to mention the nonstop socializing and people-watching of and by men, women and children who stand, walk about or sit wherever convenient—make the plaza a dynamic, magnetic center of city life.

The energy in the plaza also characterizes the city planning set in motion in 1977 when Montpellier decided to "reinvent itself." The mind-boggling strategy included a first stage of extending business, housing and leisure environments up to and slightly across the Lez river. A second stage developed the open spaces of sparsely inhabited land all the way east, just short of the Mediterranean beachfront. But unlike much urban expansion, here it did not just happen arbitrarily or piecemeal. It was planned and controlled with growth set at a manageable speed. The project also embraced the renovation and restoration of the long-neglected historic buildings and residential areas in the old city.

FRAC Languedoc–Roussillon

4 rue Rambaud, 34000
04-67-22-94-04 f: 04-67-58-49-80
Mon–Sat, 11–7
admission: free

From place Saint-Denis (just south of the old city), go down cours Gambetta; turn left onto rue de la Raffinerie—the street immediately after the huge Sécurité Sociale building; turn left at the first street, rue Toiras; turn right onto rue Rambaud and you will find #4 a few steps from the corner.

This art center presents an exhilarating program of cutting-edge exhibitions and projects. Free of a categorizing attitude, this FRAC focuses on creativity in lots of forms and gives strong support to artists and emerging ideas. (Be sure to check out the design in the announcements/posters.) Recent exhibitions: *Pep Agut, Christine Borland, Anke Doberauer, Eric Duyckaerts, Jacques*

Fournel, Nicolas Frespech, Rodney Graham, Lothar Hempel, Carsten Höller, Pierre Joseph, Matthieu Laurette, Joe Scanlan, Nedko Solakou, Rirkrit Tiravanija, Uri Tzaig, A Roof for the Whole World, Denature, The Future of the Past, Love—etc., New History.

Espace Pitot

 architects: Richard MEIER with Antoine GARCIA-DIAZ, 1989–92 rue Pitot and rue Carré du Roi

Located just beyond the fashionable rue Foch and Arc de Triomphe, to the right side and below place Royale de Peyrou.

This housing complex includes a public pool, gym, shops, a central plaza, offices for an administrative tribunal and parking garage. It's an odd plot of land squeezed up against rue Pitot—a noisy, narrow thoroughfare bordered by a stone wall, itself the boundary of a high plateau embellished by a promenade and picturesque sites with spectacular views of the region. You might say the location is on the wrong side of the street, literally in the shadow of an elevated status symbol—even more so since city law prevents buildings below the plateau from rising above the height of the wall. Meier's response to these limitations was to develop the tribunal building along a side street, facing away from the traffic and wall, and to create an internal plaza surrounded by housing and shops virtually hidden from and inaccessible to the outside world. By placing the pool, gym and parking underground, he also expanded the amount of square footage and natural light available to the housing and offices. The integration of the disparate components is quite masterful.

The design is classic Richard Meier—stark, white, geometric architecture in which balconies, windows and walkways are articulated as lines and planes, solids and voids, repetitions and divergences. Rectilinearity dominates though the tribunal structure has a pronounced circular segment at one end. Even objects in the courtyard—a small amphitheater, minimalist fountain, open-grid sculpture (a barrier between the offices and housing), air vents, elevator entrance—reiterate the reductive orientation. Despite its being a very private, quiet little neighborhood with a handsome, albeit austere appearance, Espace Pitot has suffered its share of criticism. The lack of greenery (an egregious omission in a Mediterranean climate) and the cloistered courtyard are especially controversial.

Banque de France

 architects: Odile DECQ and Benoît CORNETTE, 1996 avenue de Lodève

Located near the periphery of Montpellier, but only 10 min by bus 1 from the train station. Exit at Rabelais and walk a short distance up the street.

Don't look for your typical bank building or urban environment. It's an unimposing, low structure, set back behind trees and bushes in an almost pastoral setting. The wide driveway with automatic gates will signal its presence. To enter the property and the building, you will have to give a very convincing statement about your deep interest in architecture since high-security restrictions prevail. Alternatively, you can simply cash a traveler's check or use the ATM.

Pragmatic and security reasons dictated the bank's move from its previous location in the midst of the pedestrianized center city. Notably, it selected a young architectural team with a rapidly rising reputation to design a new, super-high-tech, state-of-the-art facility. The structure encompasses an elegant, long, sleek, "one-story" segment with glass, black and white marble walls; and a three-story segment with glazed and white concrete walls. The two segments abut one another at right angles. A third, very secluded building lies to the left. Quite skillfully, the architects have given the main building a residential appearance and scale, at least from the front perspective. In fact, it sits on the crest of a hill, and additional floors lie beneath the public space visible from the facade. Both the exterior and interior are exquisitely proportioned and reveal a fine sensitivity to materials. Although the reductive aesthetic bears witness to contemporary architecture with industrial leanings, it also follows in the footsteps of Mies van der Rohe's famous design for the Barcelona Exhibition (1929).

Jean-Marc Bourry, Alain Goetschy, 1 Gilles Vexlar

Wall Fountain with Three Young Men, 1990
place de la Comédie

This fountain is extremely well designed as a border for the city's grand plaza on one side and a focal point for a residential area on the other. In addition, the space is quite long, narrow and on different levels. Meeting the challenge of the site, Vexlar (designer) created a long wall coated with a moving stream of water on the facade oriented toward the plaza. Two rows of rhythmically shooting spurts lie behind the wall, and on a lower level, three theatrically posed bronzes of young men (by Bourry and Goetschy, sculptors) stand in a pool of water. From the residential area, the figures are seen from the waist up, but from the plaza, only their heads and upper torsos are visible. One figure touches the water, another has his hand on his head and the third raises his arm. Their gestures are humorously reminiscent of the Three Graces, though these three "beauties" proudly display masculine, muscle-bound bodies.

Pavillon du 2 Musée Fabre

esplanade Charles de Gaulle
Tues–Sun, 10–7; closed Mon

This pavilion is often used for art exhibitions that occasionally feature a figure from the contemporary era. For example, an excellent showing of recent works by Claude Viallat, the celebrated French artist who works with space, color and pattern dynamics, was held here during the summer of 1997.

3 CORUM

architect: Claude VASCONI, 1984–87
esplanade Charles de Gaulle

Conceived as a space for cultural and business exchanges, CORUM is a conglomerate edifice housing the Palais de Congrès (Convention Center), Opéra Berlioz, three auditoriums (2,010, 745, 318 seats), meeting and exhibition spaces, conference rooms, cafés, a brasserie (indoors and on a terrace) and parking garage. Although an enormous structure set on the edge of steep terrain on the boundary of the historic city, the architecture takes full advantage of the site to reduce the visual impact of its mass and integrate it with the surroundings. As you approach from the esplanade the building appears to be only two stories high (the same height as the trees lining the esplanade) and its widespread entrance stairs open out to join the walkway and envelop you in its midst. Vasconi has created an impressive, seamless continuity. Only when you walk around the corner or take the short path up to the belvedere rooftop, do you become aware of the monumental size of CORUM and the extraordinary steepness of the long slope from the esplanade down to the Nîmes highway at the bottom.

The building and landscaping on the

left side are tiered to accommodate the lay of the land. Terraces positioned at various levels provide side entrances and relaxation areas. They also subdivide and demarcate the component parts of the multifaceted facility. A shift from the predominant rose granite facade (delineated in horizontal bands that counter the vertical drop of the terrain) to window walls also links the interior and exterior environments.

On the inside, a grand lobby, extending across four levels, commands the central space and unifies the Opéra with the Convention Center and other activity areas. Escalators cascade down both sides; glazed wall and roof sections inundate the hall with natural light; rose granite surfaces and horizontal delineations harmonize the lobby with the facade; and bars, snack counters and numerous sitting areas make it people-friendly. What seems on paper to be an odd combination of functions has been given an architecture to make it work.

Antigone

 project head: Ricardo BOFILL, 1979–80

Antigone, the first stage of the grand urbanization plan, encompasses the area from Polygone to the far banks of the Lez river, previously an old military ground. The new neighborhood was conceived as an expansion toward the east that would balance the urban center (to the west) and integrate an embellished river into city life. Housing and civic buildings intermix along the pedestrian axis—a succession of communal plazas. The exaggerated perspective down the axial core ends at a grandiose triumphal arch, which is actually the Hôtel de Région (Regional Council Hall). This and other buildings share common elements, regulated by Bofill's district plan. A classical style (here given a Mediterranean flavor) and monumen-

tal-human scale—trademarks of Bofill's own architecture—create a neighborhood identity even as it links the new cityscape with place de la Comédie in Montpellier's historic center and the old monuments near promenade du Peyrou. Monotonous uniformity has, however, been forestalled by quirky architectural features and a masterful ground plan.

Les Echelles de la Ville

 architect: Ricardo BOFILL, 1988
place Paul Bec, Antigone

In a rather clever move, Bofill designed *Les Echelles de la Ville* (*City Ladders*) to camouflage the rear of the Polygone mall (Galerie Lafayette department store) and give the Antigone district an exalted entrance. The building is U-shaped with stepped facades forming two continuous terraces which, along with oversized windows, give the illusion of three stories of palatial proportions. A gargantuan classical doorway in the center, flanked by descending diagonal staircases crossing the entire span of the back wall, reinforces the grandeur. In fact, this is a six-story structure housing restaurants, offices, some design studios and a multimedia library. As is his custom, Bofill has enlivened the edifice by bordering the staircases and terraces with planters and has affected the look of expensive stone instead of economical, reinforced concrete and prefabricated parts. Classicism adopted in an ironic pose and monumental scale, as introduced here, will become dominant leitmotifs of Antigone.

Nombre d'Or

 architect: Ricardo BOFILL, 1982–84
place du Nombre d'Or, Antigone

The outside of this housing complex (*Golden Number*) has classically styled, individual units arranged in jagged clusters and forming a sprawling rim wall. Interspersed here and there are functionless, sky-high columns and architectural motifs configured to give the deceptive impression that the units are stately, three-story town houses. In contrast, the inside of the complex is a large plaza surrounded by a continuous window-and-pilaster facade, articulated as a sober, repetitive design except for the eccentric, curved cornice projecting from the roof as a detached overhang. Viewed from the plaza, the structure is clearly a seven-story apartment building.

Ground-floor shops and cafés spill into the courtyard, and a central tree-lined square, surrounded by concrete benches, provides a social and recreational space. Although this square is a regular geometric form, the plaza itself is shaped as a square with four half-circles bulging out from its sides. Characteristically, Bofill rigorously orders his design and layout but includes disjunctive oddities and confounding irregularities.

Place du Nombre d'Or has a small, freestanding, classical portal (another oddity) at its eastern end, which opens onto the axial street of Antigone.

6 | Piscine Olympique

 architect: Ricardo BOFILL, 1994–97
avenue Jacques Cartier, Antigone

As you walk down the main axis, which variously narrows and widens, you pass a continuum of apartment and government office buildings, all with classical-Mediterranean-styled facades, structured from sand-toned concrete. Then you cross rue de l'Acropole. Coming into view and unlike all else is a high-tech design, totally sheathed in glass with a steel framework painted white, visible behind the transparent walls and a white-tiled overhanging roof topped by curious cable-and-column structures looking like a row of

ships' masts or a suspension bridge. Like a magnet, this distinctive building draws you near and you can't help but enter. Once inside, you immediately feel your eyes pop as you take in the sheer grandeur and openness of the surroundings. It's mesmerizing. If there is a swimming pool paradise, this is it.

The main space is a vast, luminous area containing an Olympic-size pool flanked by tiered spectator seating, and a large leisure pool with a slide, rapids, two inset hot tubs and a wading pool for children alongside. Bofill has effectively created two zones—one for serious sport and the other for recreational pleasure. He separates the zones by placing them perpendicular to each other and on different levels. In between is a trapezoidal half-wall (concrete) shielding staircases—a superb design, and all around are a terrace and balcony configured as relaxation or viewing areas. Technological features—like the motorized sunroof above the leisure pool—further imbue each zone with an appropriate ambience. Also housed in the building are a gym, health and fitness club, solarium, restaurant, café (accessible to swimmers and visitors), three boutiques, press center, offices and a meeting hall.

7 | Bibliothèque Municipale

 architects: Paul CHEMETOV and
Borja HUIDOBRO, 1997–2000
rue de l'Acropole, Antigone

Across from the Olympic Pool is another high-tech public building, also grand in size and design with a half-glazed and half-enclosed structure. It is the Municipal Library, which also serves the region. Created by the architects who designed the Ministry of Finance in Paris, it is still in construction, scheduled to open in mid-2000.

8 | Port Juvénal Housing

architect: Ricardo BOFILL, 1989
l'esplanade de l'Europe, Antigone

Having walked through the sequence of plazas and buildings along Antigone's central axis, you experience a kind of monumentality brought down to human scale by details, juxtapositions, variations and polarities. When you cross avenue Poseidon and pass through a narrow opening between duplicate parts of a standard seven-story building, you are not prepared for the overwhelming, uninterrupted, utterly plain, green acreage—a "do-not-walk-on-the-lawn" plaza—and the surrounding, ultra-monumental, hemicycle building with a seemingly endless, repetitive facade. Like Bofill's *La Colonnade* in Saint-Quentin-en-Yvelines near Versailles, this apartment structure looks like a palatial peristyle. Configured with columns, glazed interstices and an entablature (which doubles as the top floor), it pushes the classical-modern, aristocratic-mass housing, serious-absurd conflation to an extreme. Beyond the bombastic facade, however, the layout with private entrances, no long corridors, sunlit rooms and a river view for everyone far exceeds the conditions of most high-rise and block apartment buildings regardless of cost.

9 | Hôtel de Région

architect: Ricardo BOFILL, 1985–87
avenue de la Pompignane and
Porte d'Occitanie, Antigone

The best view of the Regional Council Hall (at least for its west side) is from the restaurant and staircase terraces on the banks of the Lez river, just in front of the Port Juvénal apartments. From here you also get to see the extraordinary landscaping and recreational development along the riverfront. (Just a few years ago, this was a swampy riverbed!)

Conceived as a door open to the region, this tall building—the climax of Antigone's grand axis—dominates the landscape. The side fronting the Lez, with its Arc de Triomphe image translated into a glass-sheathed facade with enormous corner columns, is a perfect complement to the grandiose, pseudo-historical Port Juvénal building it faces. On the entrance side, where the section surrounding the center opening is a monumental, faux-stone portal with all the appropriate classical stylizations, the door symbolism also conveys stability, dignity, order and authority even as it oozes theatricality. In addition to government offices and the regional assembly room, the building houses museum rooms and a view-oriented reception hall on the top level. (In case you're wondering about the glass barrier with steel bars across the center space—the "open door" image—it's not a security shield but a windscreen.)

Bofill, Hôtel de Région

Port Marianne

The large area extending east from Antigone to the railroad tracks (site of a future TGV station), 5 mi (8 km) from the sea, constitutes the second stage of Montpellier's ambitious development project. Named Port Marianne, it will encompass five new residential neighborhoods, higher education and research centers, business parks, cultural and sporting facilities, a port, city park, new public transportation routes (including a tramway system) and landscaped or natural terrains. The goal is to "establish an equilibrium and compatibility between home, business and leisure."

10 | Consuls de Mer

project head: Rob KRIER, 1995– (60%, end of 1998)

This residential neighborhood, located just south of Antigone along the Lez river, was the first project constructed within Port Marianne. Krier, a well-respected architect from Luxembourg who places priority on livability and public spaces, organized the area into small islands with housing grouped around accessible gardens or courtyards. Conceived as city dwellings, the apartments—six stories high and a mix of social, midlevel and expensive housing—are close together but so interspersed with private spaces and oriented toward the river esplanade that a pastoral aspect prevails. The colored facades (peach, cream, white, gray, salmon) reinforce this while also serving to individualize each unit. Unlike the buildings in Antigone, premised on repetition and fabricated by a mass-production technique using concrete, here diversity within a reductive mode is the base and the material is masonry covered with plaster. Facades in Consuls de Mer (Sea

Consuls) are quite spare with unpretentious architectural accents.

Divergent symmetry is a good way to describe Krier's approach, and this is most evident in his organization of the housing span fronting the river. At either end are towers, though one is octagonal and the other round. The crescent in the middle similarly terminates in two towers, both square but each with unique surface detail, window patterning and rooftop design. Krier's overall plan for the district established the harmony among buildings designed by 11 different architects. The towers and structures in the first river block are his own creation.

Richter

project head: Adrien FAINSILBER, 1995– (80%, end of 1998)

Located across the Lez from Consuls de Mer, the Richter district contains university buildings including a large library open to everyone; student, faculty and urban housing; shops and businesses; and an urban park bordering the water and fanning out beyond the residential sector. The layout orients structures toward the river (those closest are all U-shaped) and designates three large public spaces for development as meeting sites where the paths of diverse sectors of the population will cross. A primary aim was to create a noninsular university, integrated with daily city life. The academic buildings (designed by René DOTTELDONDE) form a north-south alignment across the district with the Bibliothèque François Mitterand (library) —a prow-shaped structure in glass with one straight and one curved side— marking the entrance to the area. In contrast to the visible commonality among the buildings in Antigone and Consuls de Mer, here the architecture is extremely varied. Some structures have an industrial aesthetic, others have a more refined, high-tech image; some are primarily steel, others are sheathed in glass or concrete; and though some have prominent balconies and terraces, others have planar facades.

Blaise Pascal

 project head: Claude VASCONI (95%, end of 1998)

Located on the sides of the Millénaire business park, this residential neighborhood includes some social housing though many dwellings are upscale duplexes with large terraces and private gardens.

Jardins de la Lironde

 project head: Christian de PORTZAMPARC

Construction of this district has been put on hold but is scheduled to begin after3 2000. The plan calls for preserving the character of being in the country. Modest housing for various social levels will be around planted courtyards opening into the natural environment.

Nîmes

This is a delightful, upbeat city favored by throngs of tourists who come to see the ancient ruins and monuments or to attend concerts or bullfights in the superb Roman amphitheater, Arènes. In a blitz of activity in the late 1980s, the city commissioned a number of creative, public art projects and built an incredible culture center (museum-library). Thus Nîmes took its place on the international map of notable art world cities. Train from Montpellier, 30 min; from Marseille, 1 1/4 hr, TGV from Paris (Gare de Lyon), 4 1/2 hr.

1 | Carré d' Art

 architect: Norman FOSTER, 1993
place de la Maison Carrée, 30000

Located at the juncture of boulevards Victor Hugo and Alphonse Daudet across from the historic Maison Carrée, an incredibly preserved Roman temple.

Carré d'Art (Art Square), an elegant building that houses a contemporary art museum, regional art history documentation center and the city library, was designed by Norman Foster, a celebrated British architect. He conceived the edifice as a 20th-century complement to the neighboring Maison Carrée (Square House), built around 5 A.D. Amazingly, the two structures do complement one another, despite their extreme differences. On the most obvious level, the exterior glass walls of Carré d'Art make it a very open and inviting public space, whereas the windowless, marble walls of the Maison Carrée establish the setting of a private temple. In Foster's building, the breathtaking central atrium, which floods the building with natural light, the majestic staircase suspended in space and the glass-walled elevator reiterate the airiness of the transparent sheathing. Light—and art—were also important factors in the design of spacious art galleries with high ceilings and computerized shutter blinds and canvas screens. (The latter adjust light levels automatically to conform to specifications geared to protect the art.) Unlike many high-tech and late-20th-century buildings having a cold, industrial ambience, here the architecture is spare but comfortable. Taking its cues from the Maison Carrée, it articulates a classic order even as it embraces steel, glass, reinforced concrete and technology.

Because there were city height restrictions related to the ancient buildings, Foster developed his building

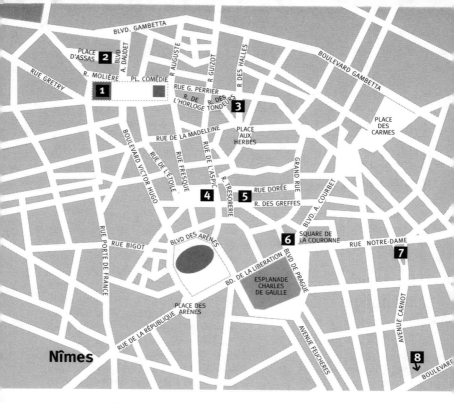

Nîmes

below ground level. But in order not to make the lower floors seem like basements, he made the atrium go through the entire building and created glazed or open spaces around the atrium wherever possible. He also designed the structure to enhance the conception of Carré d'Art as the meeting point of local and regional cultural life. Thus, there is a plaza in front of the building, a large entrance lobby and various other places where individuals and groups can chat or gather together. Indeed, all the public spaces are accessible and visually enticing from the atrium.

The libraries, offices and general service areas—including an auditorium, conference rooms, museum bookstore (a good selection of books and catalogues), lobby exhibition space, magazine-newspaper kiosk room (a great place to read the latest periodicals) and café—occupy the lower levels; the sec- ond floor houses the permanent collection galleries, and the top floor has a flexible space for temporary exhibitions as well as an extraordinary, terrace café-restaurant with a chic decor of fine wood and gray marble and a great view of the city and countryside. (The terrace floor extends out, becoming a protective awning over the front plaza.)

Within the museum, rooms are particularly appealing because they vary in size and proportion and move away from the whitebox phenomenon. Most unusual is the gallery with double-height segments along two walls, designed to accommodate oversized artwork. (The effectiveness of this feature in terms of viewing the art is debatable.)

Be sure to look at the two artworks in the lobby, commissioned as 1%-for-art-projects. *Gaul* (1993), a dark gray, planar sculpture with a slightly bowed, very vertical shape is a classic object by Ellsworth KELLY. It is reductive, yet hardly endowed with the stasis of a simple, geometric form. An oddly sensuous tension exists as its long edges stretch upward and curve outward against the pressure of containing contours and surrounding space. Although Kelly made this work specifically for this site, thinking its opacity would contrast with the transparency of the building, in actuality it barely stands out. Indeed, its neutral color and architectonic shape (it is almost as tall and narrow as the structural columns) make it blend into the setting. It shares the refined, precise appearance of Foster's architecture.

Located on a lengthy gray concrete wall to the right side of the lobby is *Mud Line* (1990–93) by Richard LONG. Here too the coloration of the work is closely related to the subdued tones of the building, but the splattered markings are noticeably different from the severe, staid lines of the architecture. Long's expression of the poetry of a remote, rugged landscape (always a specific place he traversed on a solitary walk) and the vitality of a banal, even odious material from nature is heightened by its displacement in a chic, urban, utterly man-made setting. By situating his precise mud prints on the border between order and chaos, nature and culture, he also upsets considerations about the form and meaning of art.

Carré d'Art—Musée d'Art Contemporain de Nîmes

1

🏛 | place de la Maison Carrée, 30000
04-66-76-35-70 f: 04-66-76-35-85
Tues–Sun, 10–6; closed Mon
admission: 24/18F

This is a well-respected institution with a rock-solid program of contemporary

art exhibitions and a first-rate permanent collection. Not only does the architecture contribute to an extraordinary viewing experience, but the exceptional care taken in the presentations makes for a memorable visit.

Albeit modest in size, the collection is composed of major works by intriguing artists who have or are challenging standards or reasserting important ideas of modernism. The collection spans the years from 1960 to the present and has three main orientations: art from the Mediterranean region (asserts Nîmes's location halfway between Spain and Italy); art from Anglo-Saxon countries (Germany, Britain, the United States); and art from France (work associated with significant movements like Nouveau Réalisme, Supports-Surfaces, B.M.P.T., Figuration Libre). The installation of the collection galleries indicates many of the dominant tendencies of individuals and groups included in the sphere of the museum's focus. It provides an excellent and distinctive overview of contemporary art from a European perspective. For American visitors who are probably not familiar with many of the artists and artworks, it is especially valuable. Unfortunately, the museum doesn't include brief, informational texts in the galleries, so you can't orient yourself to unfamiliar work. Within the display are works by Giovanni Anselmo, Richard Artschwager, Ross Bleckner, Alighiero e Boetti, Christian Boltanski, Jean-Marc Bustamante, Noël Dolla, Tony Cragg, Günther Förg, Bernard Frize, Toni Grand, Raymond Hains, Alan Kaprow, On Kawara, Jannis Kounellis, Yves Klein, Bertrand Lavier, Mario Merz, Annette Messager, Olivier Mosset, Juan Muñoz, Sigmar Polke, Martial Raysse, Gerhard Richter, Mimmo Rotella, Niele Toroni, Claude Viallat, Rachel Whiteread, Christopher Wool.

Special exhibitions are usually one-person shows of recognized, midcareer artists or thematic shows. Typically these are compelling, thoughtful presentations that reveal the general orientation and particularities of an artist. Recent exhibitions: *Absalon, Jean-Pierre Bertrand, Alan Charlton, Daniel Dezeuze, Juan Muñoz, Giuseppe Penone, Sigmar Polke, Martial Raysse, Gerhard Richter, Thomas Schütte, Thomas Struth, David Tremblett, Forms of Color, With the Passing of the Trace.*

2 | Martial Raysse

Place d'Assas, 1989

Located a block away from Carré d'Art, off boulevard rue Voltaire.

This plaza was given new life when Raysse (an artist from Nice who gained popularity in the 1960s) created an ensemble of mythological sculptures, fountains and elements from nature. He ordered the space by setting two large stone heads at the ends of a tiny canal running the length of the plaza. One head represents Némausa—a spring of water, the feminine principle; the other is Némausus—the city, the male force. (A spring, whose venerated guardian was named Némausus, gave rise to the city now called Nîmes.) In the middle of the plaza in a small round pool stands the centerpiece: four columns bearing a star emitting a jet of water. The pool also contains male and female bronze figures. Raysse has also constructed a hill of rocks and rare Mediterranean vegetation at the far end of the plaza. Some olive trees and the statue of an old man reading—symbol of wisdom—are atop the hill. In its totality, the plaza is an inviting, low-key ensemble of disparate elements, quiet and communal spaces unified by referential threads and interlocking pathways.

3 | Philippe Favier

In eminenti, 1990
près des Halles.

Près des Halles is a tiny street at the intersection of rues des Halles and rue Général Perrier, across from Les Halles.

This wall decoration is on the side wall of a three-story building. The wall faces a compressed space leading into a modest residential neighborhood at its rear and at its front opening onto a major shopping street in the center city. Favier captures the character of the situation in the small composition he placed in the center of the wall. It is formed of a circular sheet of glass with small bronze objects—ambiguous forms appearing a bit like little houses—lining the edge of the glass, though not completely since large empty spaces exist between various clusters and isolated objects. When the light is conducive to reflections, the image of the renovated, old stately buildings across the street intrudes on the circle of small objects (the little houses). As suggested by the title, the work refers to issues of eminent domain, raising questions about public and private rights, especially as they pertain to the intersection and overlap of business, historic and residential zones within a city. Favier's "mural" is an engaging, unusual public art project—a nice alternative to the ubiquitous painted murals or advertisements that usually fill city walls.

4 | Martial Raysse with V. Tongiani

Fountain, 1987
place du Marché

Located at the east end (the end near rue de l'Aspic) of the plaza. If it's a nice day, it may be difficult to find this work amid the café tables and frolicking children in this popular plaza.

A bronze crocodile chained to a palm tree, a bird (often missing since it is repeatedly stolen) and two broken marble columns constitute the imagery of this fountain. Derived from the city coat of arms, the elements symbolize the victory in Egypt over Antony and Cleopatra by Augustus and a troop of Roman legionnaires based in Nîmes. The crocodile and hawk—sign of Isis, the Egyptian nature goddess—evoke the Nile, and the columns memorialize the splendid buildings created during the centuries of Roman life in the city.

5 | Takis

Un signal
inner courtyard, Hôtel de Ville,
rue des Greffes

This tall spiral-enveloped pole topped by green disks and red and white blinking lights was the prototype for the sculptures Takis created for La Défense in Paris. With its nonvolumetric form, the sculpture is perfect here since it doesn't intrude on the compact space of the courtyard and the hurried streams of people who continuously traverse it. Yet it adds a lively, zany touch—a public sculpture posing as a pseudo–traffic signal.

6 | Claude Viallat and Jean–Michel Wilmotte

Interior decor, Quick restaurant, 1989
boulevard Amiral Courbet
Located at the corner of boulevard de la Libération, across from esplanade Charles de Gaulle.

Only the French would commission an artist celebrated for his brightly colored pattern paintings to create a public artwork as the decoration for a fast-food restaurant situated in a beautiful 19th-century building! Given all the advertising signage and architectural embellishments in the space, it is difficult to tell

where the art of Viallat (a native and resident of Nîmes) begins or ends. For sure, the wavy, repetitive design on the ceiling, and the two-tone blue coverings on the columns in the dining area are signature Viallat. He and the designer Wilmotte were also responsible for the flashy color scheme—sunshine yellow walls, royal blue tables, grass green chairs and lipstick red counters.

7 | Philippe Starck

Bus stop, 1987
traffic island, avenue Carnot,
corner of rue Notre-Dame

Inspired by the crocodile—the city symbol—Starck designed this bus stop as a long, winding line of dark green seats slithering out from the front and back ends of a monumental shelter. The seats are small, solid cubes, and the shelter is a covered, open-sided cube. Both are of crocodile green marble. All is pristine and simple, though the necessary accouterments—a bus schedule panel and public telephone—are incorporated

Starck, bus stop

into the pillars of the shelter. It's an attractive and functional design and a excellent exemplar of public art.

8 | Némausus

architects: Jean NOUVEL with Jean-Marc IBOS, 1981–87
avenue du Général Leclerc
bus 2, exit Némausus

To walk: from the train station go right on boulevard Talabot; turn right onto avenue du Général Leclerc—it angles back behind the station and then straightens out after a juncture with boulevard Natoire; continue down the street (5 min); the site is on the right.

If you're expecting a chic, upscale building, like Nouvel's Fondation Cartier in Paris, you'll undoubtedly think you have the wrong address. The location is an industrial district, the street is a busy truck route, and Némausus is the name for two exceedingly eccentric structures having the earmarks of cruise ships, jet hovercrafts or the viewing stands at a racetrack. They are nearly identical, situated parallel to each other and perpendicular to the street with a plot of land planted with sycamore trees in between. It won't take long to realize that these strange-looking forms are apartment buildings—144 units of public housing. Curiously, the city of Nîmes includes this site on its tourist maps but strangely lists it in the category "Leisure, Sports, Transportation!"

Commissioned by the socialist mayor of Nîmes, these long, six-story housing units are totally constructed from inexpensive, industrial materials: corrugated aluminum sheeting on the exterior and staircases; perforated and galvanized aluminum for the footbridges; and within the interior, office-type glazed room partitions, simple gray plastic flooring and bare concrete walls. Only the prototype for accordion garage doors, which form the entire facade on

the south side, can be called a luxury item. These were included because they opened the full width of the apartments, thereby extending the living area onto the terrace-balconies. Materials, like all else in the project, evolved from a refusal to accept the conventional restraints and inadequacies of public housing. Nouvel's top priority was to create the largest possible living space. He not only did this but also provided numerous features rarely found in public housing: cross ventilation, spacious balconies, large bathrooms, double-height living rooms and 17 different apartment types. The structures still look good, showing little wear and tear and no grafitti. What's more, the residents are enamored with their units.

The buildings are raised up on red-striped concrete pilotis, floating over a sunken, barely visible parking lot. Cantilevered roof screens act as sunshades for cantilevered terraces whose oblique angled walls are constructed with the same screening. The terraces ingeniously serve as walkways along the north facade and as private balconies on the sunny, south side. Because the walkways are wide and open, they function as convenient and safe play areas for kids. By placing them, as well as the stairs and elevators, on the outside, thus eliminating internal circulation

Nouvel, Némausus

areas, Nouvel was able to increase the square footage of the units by almost 30%.

Expanding on ideas set forth by Le Corbusier regarding mass housing, Nouvel has created "machines for living." Designed as a modern industrial object, they offer a very appealing alternative to block housing.

Crestet

Don't be surprised if you can't find this village on a map. It's a very, very tiny hamlet 29 mi (46.7 km) northeast of Avignon, at the foot of Mont Ventoux. It's also extremely difficult to visit without a car. The best you can do is to go by train to Orange and then by bus to Vaison-la-Romaine, but the connections are not very convenient. From Vaison-la-Romaine, its about 3 3/4 mi (6 km) to Crestet, but there's no public transportation. By car: take D975 from Orange (A7 and D977 from Avignon) to Vaison-la-Romaine; D938, direction Malaucène to Crestet; just past the main intersection in the village, turn right onto a steeply climbing road. At the top is a picturesque château overlooking oak and pine forests, vineyards, farms, medieval villas and Gallo-Roman ruins. It's classic Provence! The region is filled with artists, writers, burned-out academics on sabbaticals and wealthy Americans trying to duplicate experiences described by Peter Mayle in his best-selling books. Especially in the summer, there are amazing music, theater and dance festivals in the area, not to mention the gourmet restaurants and wineries. Archaeological sites and other places of interest also host exhibitions of contemporary art. For information on these, check the local press and tourist bureau. Be prepared for swarms of tourists.

Le Crestet, Centre d'Art

chemin de la Verrière, 84110
04-90-36-34-85 f: 04-90-36-36-20
July–Oct: daily, 11–7. Nov–June:
Mon–Fri, 10–12 and 1:30–5:30;
closed Sat–Sun
admission: free

Chemin de la Verrière branches off from the road in front of Crestet's hilltop château.

Being so isolated on a hilltop in the midst of a forest, the Crestet Art Center is a very peaceful, unusual site in which to view contemporary art. In high tourist season, it's a perfect respite from crowds. Don't be misled, however. It may be situated off the beaten track, and you may not read much about its activities in the international press, but Le Crestet has an impressive profile. Should you ask in-the-know museum professionals and gallery directors in Paris or budding French curators and critics, you'll find they keep apprised of what goes on here.

Despite its relative youth, the center has earned a reputation for being a place that welcomes new ideas and experimentation. It has an admirable record for giving young artists their first recognition and has sought to make itself a site for discussion, research and reflection. Some of this occurs as private investigation and some within exhibitions, conferences, seminars, performances and publications. The theme of all activities is "the new relationship that artists of our postindustrial civilization maintain with nature." But the theme is not at all construed narrowly. The center sees itself as a laboratory for exploring different facets of "art and nature, art in nature"; for encouraging new forms of sensibility; and for advancing "the will to make work that redefines each day as nature, landscape, environment."

A major component of the center is a residency program for artists, writers, philosophers, sociologists, botanists and landscape architects. (Dancers and musicians will soon be added.) Situated in the midst of an extraordinary landscape with nature as a focus, residents engage in communal thinking and collaborative projects. Each artist is invited to conceive a project directly related to the immediate setting and context. These projects are not geared toward formal exhibitions and are intended to last only the duration of the presentation. They have been variously produced as ephemeral objects, photographs, videos, installations, reflective texts and narratives. Recent residents: Ghada Amer, Basserode, Michel Blazy, Sylvie Blocher, Philippe Cazal, Patrick Corrillon, Marc Couturier, Bertrand Gadenne, Marie Legros, Frédéric Lormeau, Marc Quer, Erik Samakh, Seton Smith, Didier Trenet.

In addition to the residency program, the center organizes exhibitions. Here, too, a spirit of exploration prevails. Recent exhibitions: *Friendships and Other Catastrophes—the Map of Tenderness*, *Marc Couturier*, *Ulf Rollof*, *Gérard Traquandi*.

The main art center building, a concrete structure of geometric modules with interior patios and roof terraces, was constructed in 1969–72 as the house-studio for François Stahly. He, a sculptor, and his son Bruno, an architect, created the design. The property was purchased by the state (1983) and in 1988 became a site where artists were invited to install works in nature. By the time Le Crestet, Centre de l'Art was officially inaugurated in 1993, the emphasis had shifted from developing a sculpture park to being an art-nature laboratory. You can still walk around the land and see sculptures by early residents (Paul-Armand Gette, Dominique Bailly, Vincent Barré, Frans Kracjberg,

Nils Udo . . .). *Sky Space*, a new installation by James Turrell, will be added as part of the millennium celebrations in France.

Arles

Arles has a rich history as a Roman capital, medieval religious center and temporary residence of Vincent van Gogh. With its ancient ruins, winding pedestrian streets and incredible summer festivals, it earns its appeal as a favorite tourist destination. Since Arles is the site of the National School of Photography, this realm of art is well represented in the city. Train from Nîmes, 30 min; Marseille, 45 min; Montpellier, 1 hr.

Musée Réattu

🏛 | 10 rue du Grand-Prieuré, 13200
04-90-49-37-58
Tues–Sun, closed Mon. Apr–Sept: 9–12 and 2–7. Oct–Mar: 10–12 and 2–4:30.
admission: 15/9F; additional 5F for special exhibitions

The collection of contemporary art here is very limited but it does offer a sampling of abstraction and space-color, reductive art from the mid-1980s (mainly French). The display includes works by Roger Ackling, Pierre Alechinsky, Arman, Pierre Buraglio, Michel Duport, Toni Grand, Pascal Kern and François Morellet. These are worth taking a look at, especially if you want to grasp differences from and similarities with American minimal and process art. The museum also has 57 drawings by Picasso, some early-20th-century paintings and sculptures and a surprisingly good collection of photographs by Cecil Beaton, Brassaï, Jochen Gerz, André Kertész, Georges Rousse, Jerry Uelsmann, Edward Weston and others. (The museum's Weston holdings are especially extensive.)

The museum is set in two historic 15–17th-century buildings and little has been done to alter the original layout. To get to some of the galleries, you have to meander up and down stairs and in and out of all sorts of spaces and rooms. Don't be surprised if you get lost or miss what you're searching for. It's best to be proactive by repeatedly asking for help. (Other visitors are as helpful as guards).

Rencontres Internationale de la Photographie

04-90-93-77-05

This annual gathering in Arles of the International Photography Meetings is a major event for photographers. Each year there is a different director and theme. In 1998 it was *Ethics, Esthetics, Politics*; in 1997—*Twenty Years for Photography*; and in 1996—*The Real, the Fictions, the Virtual*. All facets of photography are represented: documentary, fine art, advertising, science, photojournalism, industrial aesthetics, etc. Apart from all the informal interchanges among venerated stars, midcareer figures, emerging talents and students in the field, the festival encompasses numerous exhibitions, theater performances, courses, workshops, debates, presentations, evening events and other activities. In 1997 the appearance of Henri Cartier-Bresson and Nan Goldin's showing of her *Ballad of Sexual Dependency* in the city's Roman amphitheater were main attractions. The exhibitions range from retrospectives to outrageously unconventional displays. They are held in all sorts of venues throughout the city. It's great fun and enlightening to see the full gamut of shows. Since Arles is a small, compact city, this is easy to do.

The major sessions and performances are usually held during the second week. Other activities and events span the period from July through mid-Aug. Advance tickets are sold for certain events.

Marseille

Marseille is the country's second most important center of contemporary art. It has a very lively art scene, numerous museums with refreshing exhibitions, unconventional galleries and alternative spaces, a sizeable artist community, art festivals, research and production centers and a down-to-earth attitude. There's a lot to see and do, but don't expect to function at a Parisian pace. Remember, this is a Mediterranean culture. People take their time here and don't always abide by the posted time schedules. TGV from Paris (Gare de Lyon), 4 1/2 hr; train from Arles, 45 min; from Nîmes, 1 1/4 hr; from Montpellier, 1 3/4 hr; from Nice, 2 1/2 hr.

Since 1985 all the city museums have been headed by one director. Moreover, the unusual consolidation was wed to an agreement assuring the director's commitment to contemporary art. The museums publish a free booklet, *Musées de Marseille*, with information on all their exhibitions. You can also pick up *Via Marseille*—an exhibition, event and opening list which is coordinated with a map—in most galleries, museums and other art sites.

During the past two decades, Marseille has become a mecca for artists. They come to live and work here because studios are relatively easy to find and inexpensive, and because the city actively supports contemporary art. Artists often organize exhibitions (individual or collective) in their studios or in rented spaces. The *vernissages* (openings) have become popular social gatherings for the local art world and good

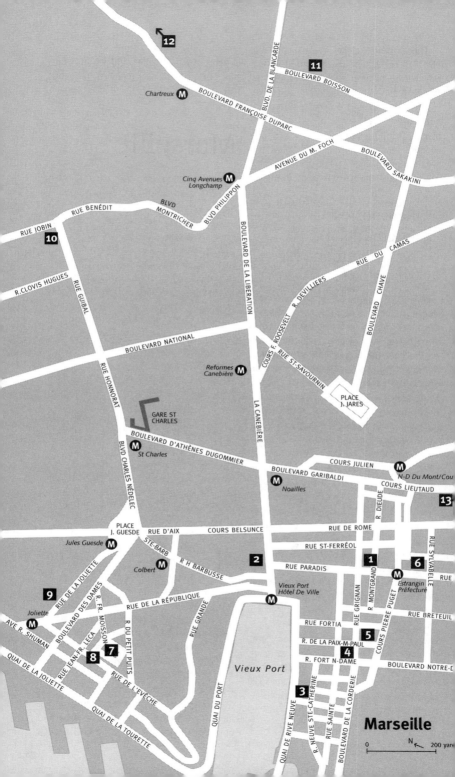

Marseille

0   N ← 200 yards

opportunities for artists to have their work seen by museum and gallery professionals. Since openings are often scheduled for the same night, they are usually crowded and the atmosphere is festive. You'll find many "artist associations" named as the sponsor of galleries and events. These "associations," which can be formed with just three members, can get funding, services and assistance from the city. Usually they present the work of local artists, but sometimes they invite artists from elsewhere (young as well as well-known figures) to exhibit or come to Marseille as a guest. Association activities and locations are listed in *Via Marseille*. Spaces with ongoing exhibitions include: Cargo, Casa Factori, Château de Servières, Galerie Porte Avion, Interface/MMM, Le Hors-Là, Le Laboratoire, Le Radeau, Les Grands Bains Douches de la Plaine/Art Cade, Les Poules Anonymes,]'OL[, Tohu Bohu, Triangle-France. You'll find exhibitions elsewhere as well—in cafés, theater lobbies, tourist offices, etc.

1 | Musée Cantini

🏛 | 19 rue Grignan, 13006
04-91-54-77-75 f: 04-91-14-58-81
Tues–Sun, closed Mon. June–Sept, 11–6; Oct–May, 10–5
admission: 10F; special exhibitions 15F
métro: Estrangin/Préfecture

Located in a 17th-century three-story mansion with natural light, large open rooms and a garden courtyard, this museum oozes aristocratic elegance. The sweeping staircase in the entrance hall sets the stage as soon as you enter. Surprisingly, the rooms, which still have the old architectural detail, provide good settings for 20th-century art. In fact, it's a joy to visit this museum since every room is different and all are human scale. The incredible diversity and its generally positive effect on the

art are totally unlike new museums with their empty shell, consistent, boxlike spaces. What's even more amazing in the Cantini Museum is that new galleries, contained within a recently constructed side wing, retain the spatial ambience of the mansion though the rooms have a decidedly contemporary design. There's one grand room with a high skylight and several others that are variously scaled. It's a very appealing place in which to see art. This was particularly apparent in a Carl Andre exhibition (1997), where his large installation pieces looked spectacular, assuming a resonance not manifest in most museum installations.

Until 1994, both modern and contemporary art were the province of the Cantini Museum. Since then, this museum focuses solely on pre-1960s modernism, and MAC (see below) deals with contemporary art. The lines are not precisely drawn, however. You therefore might find a special exhibition of 1960s–70s art at the Cantini Museum and some 1950s art at MAC. The permanent collection here begins with Post-Impressionism and moves through Fauvism, Cubism, Surrealism and abstraction with works by Bacon, Brauner, Derain, Dubuffet, Dufy, Ernst, Giacometti, Kandinsky, Kupka, Léger, Masson, Matisse, Miró, Picabia, Picasso and Riopelle. Included are many unique objects by admired figures as well as some lesser known artists. Despite expansion, space often can't accommodate both the collection and special exhibitions. This is most unfortunate when a big exhibition takes over the entire museum and none of the collection is visible. Recent exhibitions: *Antonin Artaud, Jean-Michel Basquiat, César, Juan Gris, Edward Hopper, Henri Michaux, László Moholy-Nagy, Oscar Schlemmer.*

A drawback of Cantini and other museums in Marseille is the extremely elitist, white-cube attitude. They provide no wall texts, brochures, extended labels or other materials to assist or orient visitors with the art.

2 | Musée de la Mode

🏛 Espace Mode Méditerranée,
11 la Canebière, 13001
04-91-56-59-57 f: 04-91-90-76-33
Tues–Sun, 12–7; closed Mon
admission: 15/7.50F
métro: Vieux Port

One of France's most prominent designers, Jean-Michel WILMOTTE renovated this building and furnished it with such things as the chairs in the lobby.

Even if you don't have a particular interest in fashion but are interested in contemporary culture or installation design, be sure to put this on your list of places to see. The space of the museum is small, which means that the large collection of post-1930s clothing (mostly couturier) and related materials is not on display. What you will see is a fascinating, expertly curated, thematic or one-person show composed mostly of loans from elsewhere. Moreover, the absolutely mind-boggling, albeit unpretentious display will make you realize how visually and conceptually weak installations in art museums usually are, and how much this affects your response to the work.

Take, for example, the exhibition *Unknown Closets of Known People: Actors* (1997), for which two incredible interior designers—Paul MATHIEU and Michel RAY—produced the ambience of a closet (or a series of closets) containing 30 outfits (by Chanel, Comme des Garçons, Jean-Paul Gaultier, Emanuel Ungaro, etc.) worn by actors (Brigitte Bardot, Catherine Deneuve, Madonna, Kristin Scott Thomas, etc.) in various films. The minimalist setting was completely white (floor, walls, ceiling, closets), and an alignment of open-faced, cubiclelike closets commanded the center of the gallery. Set side by side and back to back, the closets were simple frames. Each one contained an outfit hanging alone on a hanger suspended in space. The costumes thus appeared like silhouettes, devoid of the famous bodies associated with them, but with so much presence that they readily aroused thoughts about their history and character.

An almost imperceptible audiotape reinforced a sense of intimacy by providing a soundtrack of someone entering a closet and leisurely going through its contents. As a viewer you vicariously had a powerful sense of being inside the closet, not as a voyeur but as someone seeing clothes through the analytical eye of a sociologist, anthropologist or filmmaker. Indeed, the clothes became the actors, playing roles, hiding and divulging themselves. Since you could get quite close to the outfits and see the particulars of size, fabric, style and decorative details, the sensations were intensified. A small label gave basic information about each outfit, and a one-paragraph text, printed creatively in large letters and stretched across the length of a side wall, provided a general orientation to the exhibition. In a second room, vitrines contained magazine reviews, photographs, accessories, letters and an array of documentation about the development of the exhibition. Every part of the display was engaging and enjoyable on many different levels. Nothing was didactic, and you went away energized by a refreshing take on contemporary culture.

Other recent exhibitions: *Yves Saint Laurent—Exoticisms, Paco Rabanne, Peter Lindbergh—Photographs, Christian Lacroix and Theater, Man-Object, Body Fashion, Histories of the Mannequin.*

3 | Galerie Roger Pailhas

🔲 20 quai de Rive Neuve, 13007
04-91-54-02-22 f: 04-91-55-66-88
Tues–Sat, 11–1 and 2–6;
closed Mon
métro: Vieux Port

Located alongside the Old Port on the first floor (top of stairs) of a renovated warehouse.

This spacious, loftlike gallery presents a busy program of exhibitions, artist talks, discussion sessions, performances and conferences. Roger Pailhas has long been at the forefront in developing Marseille's contemporary art scene and bringing innovative, talented artists to the public's attention. His exhibitions show all kinds of art—including video, installation, photography and techno-mechanical creations. Artists: Eija-Liisa Ahtila, Michael Asher, Stephan Balkenhol, Bernard Bazile, Julien Blaine, Sylvie Blocher, Daniel Buren, Frédéric Coupet, Peter Fend, Fortuyn/O'Brien, Rainer Ganahi, Dan Graham, Pierre Huyghe, John Knight, Silvia Kolbowski, Langlands & Bell, Violetta Liagatchev, Haim Steinbach, Michèle Sylvander, Joep van Lieshout, Jeff Wall, Lawrence Weiner, Yoon Ja & Paul Devautour.

4 | Galerie Jean–François Meyer

🔲 43 rue Fort Notre-Dame, 13001
04-91-33-95-01
Mon–Sat, 3–7
métro: Vieux Port or Estrangin/Préfecture.

The space is modest and the work is by young artists. Much of what you see in this gallery is brash and unorthodox, but it reveals the fearlessness found in the best of emerging talents.

5 | Galerie Athanor

🔲 84–86 rue Grignan, 13001
04-91-33-83-46 f: 04-91-72-17-27
Tues–Sat, 2:30–7; closed Mon
métro: Estrangin/Préfecture

In its three exhibition rooms, the gallery can accommodate all sorts of projects. This a place where you can see the cream of the crop of artists from Marseille, including the emerging generation. The gallery is one of the mainstays in the city, respected for its encouragement to artists and collectors alike. Artists: Georges Autard, Vincent Bioulès, Jean Bellissen, Pierre Buraglio, Giuseppe Caccavalle, Jean-Jacques Ceccarelli, Dominique Cerf, Max Charvolen, Frédéric Clavère, Yvan Daumas, Jean-Louis Delbès, Daniel Dezeuze, Gérard Fabre, Anna Gérard, Yannick Gonzalez, Joël Kermarrec, Ernest Mela, François Mezzapelle, Judy Milner, Yves Reynier, Vladimir Skoda, Jean-Marc Simmonet, Jean-Jacques Surian, Claude Viallat.

6 | Galerie du Tableau

🔲 37 rue Sylvabelle, 13006
tel/fax: 04-91-57-05-34
Mon–Sat, 4–7
métro: Estrangin/Préfecture

This tiny gallery presents a new show of a young artist each week with openings every Monday night. The owner, Bernard Plasse, has kept this rigorous schedule alive since 1990, simply because he loves art and wants to help young artists. The work on display is not always terrific, but sometimes you'll catch a budding talent. Moreover, the gallery is a casual meeting place where information is exchanged and ideas are discussed. It's unique and indicative of the low-key, goodwill attitude that permeates Marseille's art community.

7 | Centre de la Vieille Charité

2 rue de la Charité, 13002
04-91-14-58-80 f: 04-91-14-58-81
Tues–Sun, closed Mon. June–Sept,
11–6; Oct–May, 10–5
admission: 15F (special exhibitions)
métro: Joliette

The amount of space encompassed in this complex of restored 17–18th-century buildings is striking. Architecturally, it includes a French baroque chapel in the center of a large, square courtyard bounded by a handsome procession of arcaded three-story structures. Originally built to shelter vagrants, orphans and the rural poor hoping to escape the plague (hence its name, Old Almshouse), it now houses a multitude of exhibition, research and conservation facilities and institutions. Foremost among them is the Museum of African, Oceanic and Amerindian Art and the Museum of Mediterranean Archaeology. Special exhibitions, organized by various city museums and usually presented in the chapel, are also a major attraction. Be sure to check current listings, since these often feature contemporary art. Recent exhibitions: *Carl Andre —Poetry*, *Trisha Brown—Drawings*, *Nan Goldin*, *Gabriel Orozco*.

A theater on the premises is frequently used for new or classic works by esteemed members of yesterday's vanguard, and experimental, often groundbreaking presentations by young artists. If a performance is scheduled during your visit, try to see it regardless of whether you recognize the name. Chances are good you'll catch something special. You can always play it safe and see a film in the Miroir theater. These are part of the cinéMAC program. (See MAC below.)

8 | FRAC PACA

1 place Francis Chirat, 13002
04-91-91-27-55 f: 04-91-90-28-50
Mon–Sat, 10–12:30 and 2–6
admission: free
métro: Joliette
Located off rue de l'Observatoire, just beside La Vieille Charité

In its two large rooms, FRAC PACA (Provence-Alpes-Côte d'Azur) presents exhibitions focused on artists in its collection. Although quite diverse, the collection tends to favor young artists, video and photography. For its one-person exhibitions, the center gives artists free rein to express their talents. Group shows develop a theme calling attention to common tendencies shared by various artists. Recent exhibitions: *Travels to Alexandria or the Passage of the Witness*, *Transatlantique Boat-Armoire*, *Gilles Barbier*, *Judith Bartolani & Claude Caillol*, *Sophie Calle*, *Frédéric Clavère*, *Elizabeth Creseveur*, *Valérie Jouve*, *Saverio Lucariello*, *Niek van de Steeg*, *Yoon Ja & Paul Devautour*.

9 | CIRVA

62 rue de la Joliette, 13002
04-91-56-11-50 f: 04-91-91-11-04

Artists (designers, architects, too) from all over the world come here to work with glass experts and use the state-of-the-art facilities and technology. They are not artists who customarily work in glass but those who want to do a specific project that requires glass. CIRVA— Centre International de Recherche sur le Verre et les Arts Plastiques (International Center for Research on Glass and Art)— is entirely devoted to the experimentation and artistic production with glass. Its mission is to give artists the time and means to explore a new medium carte blanche. This luxury has yielded some outstanding results. Not only have artists discovered new forms and ideas, but the collaborative process has led to advancements in glass relevant to artisans, industrial engineers and scientists. Among those who have worked at CIRVA are Larry Bell, Andrea Blum, Marie Bourget, James Lee Byars, Erik Dietman, Thomas Huber, Shiro Kuramata, Mario Merz, Robert Morris, Jean Nouvel, Jean-Michel Othoniel, Giuseppe Penone, Gaetano Pesce, Andrée Putman, David Rabinowitch, Tom Shannon, Vladimir Skoda, Pierre Soulages, Rosemarie Trockel, Claude Viallat, Robert Wilson, Terry Winters. Although the studio is closed to the public and has no exhibition space, it's useful to know about its existence within Marseille's multifaceted art domain.

10 | Friche la Belle de Mai

41 rue Jobin and 9 rue Guibal, 13003
04-91-11-42-43
Mon–Sat, 2–7 (during exhibitions)
métro: Saint-Charles

This huge, old warehouse (called "The May Beauty") behind the train station is now the site of numerous studios for artists, writers, musicians, experimental theater and dance companies. It's also an informal art world meeting place, where you can see exhibitions and performances. If you are in town during an open-studio event, it is worth attending. It will expose you to a good cross section of work being done by Marseille artists. Simultaneously, you'll get a chance to meet the locals. The same is true for exhibition openings at Friche, which are crowded, festive parties.

Ateliers d'Artistes de
11 | la Ville de Marseille

11–19 boulevard Boisson, 13004
04-91-85-42-78 f: 04-91-85-13-47
Tues–Sat, 2–7; closed Mon
métro: Cinq Avenues/Longchamp

From the métro, take boulevard de la Blancarde (north), then turn right onto boulevard Boisson.

In 1990 the city transformed this abandoned industrial building (and a second building at 1 place de Lorette), into 15 low-rent artist studios, two studio-residences, a production studio, a documentation center (with dossiers on artists living in Marseille), a small publishing operation, a supply depot and a large exhibition space. Artists are selected for a two-year period during which they have access to teaching sessions, individual critiques, lectures, seminars and open-studio events.

The exhibition program run by the Ateliers is dynamic and a vital component of the city's art scene. Shows are monographic, group and thematic projects or exchanges with other cities (Munich, Brussels, Venice, etc.). Sometimes critics and artists serve as guest curators and catalogue authors. For the solo exhibitions, artists are typically invited to come to Marseille for an extended period of time to create an installation in the gallery space. While in residence, many of them become part of the community by teaching in one of the region's art schools, giving public lectures or spearheading conferences. Recent exhibitions: *Stephen Craig*, *Thierry Kunzel*, *André Lützen*, *Johan Muyle*, *Marielle Paul*, *Huang Yong Ping*, *J.-C. Ruggirello*, *Beat Steulli*, *Franck and Olivier Turpin*, *Munich Exchange*, *Marseille Associations of Artists 1976–96*.

12 | Hôtel du Département

architect: Will ALSOP, 1990–94
boulevard Alex Fleming
metro: Saint-Just

Located on the northwest periphery of the city, at the intersection of two major highways leading into the city and out to a new technopolis.

This unorthodox building, the regional seat of government, with its bold forms and ultramarine color has received high marks from the architectural establishment, the populous and politicians. Know as "Le Grand Blue," it stands out as a vivid force in the landscape proclaiming a dynamic, forward-thinking spirit. At its core is a vast, luminous atrium that gives access to all areas. It also connects two major blocks—a fuselage-like structure and a vertical box—both suspended in space above decks resting on cruciform supports (pilotis). The sculptural character of the whole is further accentuated by a long, ovoid pod at the south end of the atrium and an aeroflot atop the roof terrace of the rectangular block. What's most appealing is that the design is adventurous and technologically ingenious without being outrageous. Take the 10-minute métro ride (the Saint-Just station occupies the basement level of the building) to see for yourself.

13 | Unité d'Habitation

architect: LE CORBUSIER, 1947–52
280 boulevard Michelet, 13008
bus: 21 or 22, exit Le Corbusier
Located between boulevards Barral and Guy de Maupassant.

Don't miss a visit to this historic, architectural monument, one of the great buildings of the 20th century. You can even stay in the small hotel that is part of the structure! (In 1997 a room with bath was 245F for one person, 285F for two.) This 18-story, "vertical housing city" containing 337 apartments and 1,600 inhabitants sparked controversy when it was built but has since become an extremely influential force within both architectural and urban-planning circles. The brutalist concrete design was termed an "inhuman beehive," and many questioned Le Corbusier's conception of a megastructure rooted to

autonomy and self-sufficiency. He had been theorizing about a *Ville Radieuse* (Radiant City) since 1935, but not until four million French families were caught in the desperate housing shortage after World War II was he provoked to turn ideals into reality.

To achieve his "apartment villas," he designed 23 different apartment types, positioned them across the full depth of the building (excellent cross ventilation), gave each a balcony (serves as a sunscreen), a double-height living room and a modern, central kitchen. In addition, he developed the roof as a recreation area and nursery school, and totally integrated shopping and service facilities into the high-rise, situating them as a "shopping street in the sky" on the 7th and 8th floors. The street includes a grocery store, café, bar, bakery, professional offices, hotel, sauna, restaurant and even a sitting area like in an outdoor plaza. As ever with Le Corbusier, all aspects of the edifice are spare and functionally efficient.

On the exterior, the raw concrete and repetitive alignment of recessed balconies and window niches avoids creating a bleak, monotonous facade because side walls and ceilings of the inset spaces are variously painted bright red, blue, yellow, green and white, and the overall grid is enriched by wide and narrow, recessed and surface, horizontal

Le Corbusier, Unité d'Habitation, rooftop

and rectangular rhythms. Perhaps to emphasize the importance of exacting human proportions, Le Corbusier has placed a relief image of his classic *Modulor* figure on the front wall, beside the entrance. Reiterating his concern with convenience, he creates a covered car entrance in the back from a free-form, cast-concrete canopy and raises the building off the ground on huge concrete support columns (pilotis) to provide parking spaces. (Cars no longer park underneath; for some reason they have been relegated to a lot behind the building.)

If you sign in with the guard, you can explore the public areas inside. Note that the elevators only stop on every third level. This results from orienting the apartments as interlocking sets of cross-over units with entrances on stag-gered-floor access corridors. The hall-ways are raw concrete, enlivened by segments painted in bright colors. Although you should visit the shopping-hotel streets, go up to the roof before you get lost.

Using the full span of rooftop footage, Le Corbusier has created an incredible communal area with spectac-ular views of the city, sea and moun-tains. The entire design and each com-ponent element is a tour de force. Preeminent are the undulating walls of the two concrete towers formed of the two ventilation shafts. One of these, sit-uated opposite a staircase-fronted stage with a backdrop wall (all concrete), appears to be part of an open-air the-ater of sorts. The parts themselves are theatrical presences with the semblance of minimal sculpture. For health-con-scious residents, there is a track running all around the circumference of the roof, and at the far south end are a swimming pool and sun terrace with sculptural forms and plants intermit-tently placed to separate the space into private areas. Nearby, next to the nurs-ery school, is a children's pool and sand-box (a curving form with star shape in the middle). A second, two-story build-ing houses a club (originally men only!) and bar. Although concrete is the dom-inant material on the roof, a wall of glass bricks and richly colored, decorat-ed floor and wall tiles provide contrast. Here as elsewhere, the wood grain imprinted in the concrete (a residue of the casting process) patterns the harsh, gray surfaces with an incongruous ref-erence to nature.

The building is presently in excellent condition. Having suffered from early deterioration, it required major recon-structive and repair work, not always done in accordance with Le Corbusier's design. Recently, however, efforts have been made to return the building to its original appearance. The surrounding landscape, a spacious, parklike setting, is clearly an enhancement to the build-ing, and this too follows the original plan. Le Corbusier's megastructure housing was conceived as a way to con-solidate the population and keep the landscape free from suburban sprawl. Ironically, unfettered suburbanization now totally envelops his building and its landscaped plot.

14 Musée d'Art Contemporain (MAC)

69 avenue d'Haïfa, 13008
04-91-25-01-07 f: 04-91-72-17-27
Tues–Sun, closed Mon June–Sept,
11–6; Oct–May, 10–5
admission: 15F
métro: rond-point du Prado, then
bus 45 to MAC

Located on the eastern periphery of the city in the Bonneveine area. It's not far to walk from Unité d'Habitation to MAC (15 min). Take the first right off boule-vard Michelet onto rue Guy de Maupassant; turn left at avenue de Marzargues; turn right at avenue d'Haifa.

MAC (also called Galeries Contemporaines des Musées de Marseille) opened in 1994 as a museum for art created since 1960 in all media. Its location in a suburban neighborhood, geographically and culturally outside the center city, is not great, and the building is pure banality. It was constructed in the 1970s by Dr. Gustav Rau, a German who planned to establish a foundation there for the display of his art collection. Rau subsequently changed his mind but donated the building to the city. When the idea for creating a contemporary art museum gained momentum in the early 1990s, the Rau building surfaced as a location. Renovation work attempted to make it appropriate, but many shortcomings couldn't be eliminated. It is an enormous, utterly bland space containing two large halls flanked by adjacent rooms and illuminated by nine bays of skylights. Unfortunately, the ceiling height is too low for much contemporary art. The building thus stunts the appearance of some work and makes it impossible to install (properly, or at all) the monumental creations of the current era.

Despite the building, MAC produces some of the most adventuresome and historically valuable exhibitions in the arena of contemporary art. Some are classic monographic or thematic shows, and others are projects conceived by artists, or commissioned by the museum. The uniqueness of MAC is perhaps most notable in its refusal to treat contemporary artworks as "objects" or artists as object makers. Moreover, the museum doesn't shy away from complex, irreverent projects that may not attract a big audience. These attitudes were particularly apparent in an amazing but difficult *Dieter Rot* exhibition (1997) in which the artist virtually transformed the entire building into a living studio. There were no barriers or display cases. Instead, you virtually had to walk

Dieter Rot installation, 1997 (MAC)

into the midst of complex installations, some of which were purposefully left in a growth or limbo state. Moreover, you were given access to the actual work space and materials the artist left behind after setting up the exhibition. Other recent exhibitions: *Richard Baquié, Ben, Chris Burden, Lygia Clark, Panamarenko, Robert Smithson, Paul Thek, Rosemarie Trockel, Tatiana Trouvé, Fluxus, Body Art, Epileptic Forest, They Collect—the Return, Installations from the Pompidou Collection.*

Special exhibitions constitute half the exhibition space of MAC. The other half, which displays the permanent collection, is organized to articulate important groupings—Nouveau Réalisme, Supports-Surfaces, Figuration Narrative, Fluxus, "individual mythologies" (Arte Povera, Pop Art . . .) and current tendencies. In addition, some artists are given a privileged presence. They include Richard Baquié, Christian Boltanski, Daniel Buren, César, Toni Grand, Simon Hantaï, Annette Messager, François Morellet, Claude Viallat. In its representation of the most recent years, the collection displays works by Absalon, Stephan Balkenhol, Barbara Bloom, John Coplans, Günther Förg, Yannick Gonzalez, Dan Graham, Suzanne Lafont, Gina Pane, Hervé Paraponaris, Jana Sterbak, Patrick Tosani, Jean-Luc Vilmouth, William Wegman. The gallery space also includes a video room. Since French art is a dominant aspect of the collection, the MAC galleries are a good place to get a judicious picture of the various directions and artists composing France's contributions to contemporary art.

Not only are poetry, music and film programs coordinated with all exhibitions but debates, conferences, artist residencies, the publication of catalogues and artist books are omnipresent activities. Within its ongoing film program (cinéMAC), the museum explores the relationship between art and film as evinced in films by artists, films about artists, documentaries on art and commercial films. Showings are held in two theaters: one at MAC and a second at La Vielle Charité. The museum has a bookstore, library and café-restaurant.

Musée César

A new museum devoted to César (Baldaccini), an artist born in Marseille and considered to be one of France's leading contemporary artists, will soon open in the city. It will probably be located in the 18th-century Château Borély, situated in Parc Borély, a green space bordering on beaches, east of the city center. Disagreements about the renovation of the original site (on place Villeneuve Bargemon near the city hall) have delayed the opening of the museum and necessitated its relocation.

Côte d'Azur

Nice

The profusion of art sites in and around Nice (not to mention the sun and beaches) makes this region a popular tourist destination. If you can avoid the summer season, you will be able to enjoy the incredible landscape and culture without the crowds. The area has a rich history as a place where modern and a smattering of postwar artists lived and worked. Not surprisingly, this history has spawned an ample quotient of clone-art showrooms and schlock galleries. There are also museums associated with one specific artist who was born, lived or died in the area. Be aware that many of these cash in on an artist's name but have only the most paltry collection of work or memorabilia by the celebrity artist. Fortunately, there are also places where you can see good quality contemporary and modern art. The region as a whole pooled its resources in the summer of 1997 for *Côte d'Azur and Modernity, 1918–1958* —a single exhibition held in 13 cities and 28 museums. It was a spectacular undertaking; hopefully there'll be successors. TGV from Paris (Gare de Lyon), 6 1/2 hr; from Marseille, 2 1/2 hr.

Villa Arson

20 avenue Stéphen Liégeard, 06105
04-92-07-73-73 f: 04-93-84-41-55
July–Sept: daily, 1–7. Oct–June: Tues–Sun, 1–6, closed Mon
admission: free
bus: 4, 7 or 18

Located just off square Baron de Berre, near the summit of boulevard de Cessole, which is a continuation of boulevard Gambetta.

Villa Arson—Centre National des Arts Plastiques is a conglomerate enterprise embracing one of the leading national art schools, an outstanding resident artist program and an impressive art center for research and exhibitions. The separate divisions are united under one director, and all teaching, art-making and exhibition activities are inextricably linked because of a shared focus on contemporary art.

Situated far from the tourist hustle and beach scene, the Villa Arson is a community onto itself. Housed in an ocher-colored late-18th-century Italianate villa encased within a five-level labyrinth of mid-20th-century buildings, terraces, courtyards, staircases and ramps cascading down a steep slope, it exists in a unique, totally nonurban setting. It's not easy to adjust to the fortresslike, brutalist style of the architecture with its cast-concrete walls (some embedded with pebbles), overhangs and recessed windows. The aura is cold and dark in places, yet the design effectively shields passageways and the interior from the blazing sun. It also takes good advantage of the setting, which abounds in Mediterranean greenery and exceptional panoramas of the city and coast. In addition, the building has been embellished by art projects and has a spacious garden area—a popular place for socializing—at the entrance (top of the hill).

Be sure to stop at the information desk to get specifics on the location of current exhibitions and outdoor installations. Be prepared to get lost but don't worry, since the meandering pathways wind everywhere you want to go and ultimately lead you back to the entry garden.

The galleries begin at the upper level, though a no-holds-barred, experimental attitude means that artists sometimes install their work outside the gallery rooms. The space specifically devoted to exhibitions is considerable, encompassing vast white-cube galleries as well as eccentrically shaped rooms. Villa Arson has an exceeding open exhibition program, highly esteemed for its support of young artists and its sanctioning of the broadest range of creativity. For example, should you have visited the Villa Arson during the summer of 1997, you would have seen a captivating group of installations by Cosima von Bonin, Richard Fauguet, Markus Geiger, Pierre Joseph, Ingrid Luche, Jason Rhoades; an exhibition of *Erotica* from the collection of Martin Kippenberger; and five large-format, outdoor projects in various media. The scope and cutting-edge character of the selections were equal to the best of any presentation at a contemporary art museum.

Each year, 15–30 artists are in residence for a 3-, 6- or 12-month period. As part of their interaction with students, visiting artists often direct workshops, pursue research or develop experimental art projects. Typically, the projects become part of the exhibition (and publication) program. Recent exhibitions: *No Man's Time*, *The Reality Principal*, *Is It about Sculpture?*, *Under the Sun*, *Bad Boys—Beach Boys*, *Sara V. Bernhard*, *Jean-Marc Bustamante*, *Dominque Gonzalez-Foerster*, *Anne Marie Jugnet*, *Michel Krebber*, *Claude Levêque*, *Olaf Metzel*, *Meuser*, *Elaine Sturtevant*, *Franz Erhard Walther*, *Heimo Zobernig*.

Jason Rhoades installation, 1997 (Villa Arson)

Among the artist projects installed within Villa Arson as permanent installations are:

Siah ARMAJANI, garden furnishings, 1995– . This American artist habitually creates outdoor environments focused on providing a place for the individual within a social space. His designs are spare, utterly functional and imbued with references to poets, philosophers or great humanists. Here the furnishings spread throughout the upper garden area are a diverse assortment of table-and-bench platforms, mobile benches with integrated wheels, flowerpotted benches, a gazebo-bench unit, mix-and-merge stage-work-meeting tables with benches, trash-can stands, lecterns and sign stands with quotations from the poet Arthur Rimbaud.

Bertrand LAVIER, *Argens sur Decaux*, 1990. In the entrance garden, on the left side, you will see one of the familiar street toilets found in French cities. Note, however, that Lavier has placed a blade structure from a large fan on top. The result—an incongruous juxtaposition of contemporary, industrial products in which one serves as a pedestal for the other—is a classic example of the artist's work. (The title refers to the two companies that manufactured the component fan and toilet.)

Jacques VIEILLE, Untitled, 1992. This sculpture, a pipelike form with bar extensions for climbing, occupies a square shaftlike cavity to the left of the lobby beside the main ramp. The work extends from the basement on up through the roof, where it is humorously topped by a cone-shaped tree (visible from outside or if you look up when in the lobby).

Michel VERJUX, *Projection*, 1990. Using the main corridor as the site for his work, Verjux has designed an architectural light-installation similar to those for which he has received great acclaim in Europe. It consists of projected squares of light that shine on the floor of the long descending path through the center of the upper buildings. The imagery echos the square skylights in the ceiling and produces a perspectival sight line that is, however, enigmatic and disorienting. The projections are only on at certain hours late in the day, so you may not be able to see this work unless your visit coincides with the schedule.

Dan GRAHAM, Untitled. In contrast to his rectangular glass-and-mirror structures that people can walk within, here Graham has created a minimalist goldfish pond with three square cube sections. The center section is covered by a pyramid with one open side, one side with mirrored glass and two sides with transparent glass. The work—one of the artist's most compelling, appealing designs—is located in a small planted courtyard at the intersection of walkways on a lower level.

Jean-Luc VILMOUTH, Untitled. On a midlevel terrace, off to the left side, Vilmouth has created an aluminum spiral staircase curving around a palm tree. The sculpture addresses the artist's conundrum about producing art without adding a supplementary element to a world already overflowing with artifacts.

Felice VARINI, *La cible* (*The Target*), 1994. Varini not only distorts space by painting a continuous image on several terrace walls but also wittily transforms the universal warning sign—the red-framed white circle crossed by a diagonal red line—into a pseudo-Mondrianesque image—a red-framed white circle with horizontal and vertical red lines. Set on walls facing out toward the city, the image is visible by the public looking up at the hilltop landscape.

Musée d'Art Moderne et d'Art Contemporain (MAMAC)

architects: Yves Bayard and Henri Vidal, 1990
promenade des Arts, 06300
04-93-62-61-62 f: 04-93-13-09-01
Mon, Wed–Thurs, Sat–Sun, 11–6;
Fri, 11–10; closed Tues
admission: 25/15F, first Sun of each month free
bus: 3, 5, 6, 16, 17, 25, exit Promenade des Arts; 7, 9, 10, exit Musée d'Art Moderne; 1, 2, exit Garibaldi.

The museum and city theater, designed as an architectural ensemble, are situated on the Paillon river promenade, which runs through the heart of the city. The cultural complex is raised above street level with stairs and escalators bringing patrons up to a grand plaza. From here one enters the museum—a building composed of four square marble-faced towers connected by glass-enclosed walkways with an open-air octagonal space in the center. The galleries, located in the towers, are large and well suited to 20th-century art. Special exhibitions are installed on the ground floor and first level; the collection occupies the upper two floors. A roof terrace has some art on it as well, though the miniature-golf-like design of the space makes it a disastrous setting for most sculpture.

The collection presents European and American art from the 1960s to the present. Apart from a particular concentration on Nouveau Réalisme—a movement strongly associated with the Niçois artists Arman, Yves Klein and Martial Raysse—there are representative works of American Pop art and color field painting, Supports-Surfaces and other reductivist tendencies in French art from the mid-1960s forward, American Minimalism, Figuration Libre, and various French artists who don't fit within specific categories. Unfortunately, the collection, admittedly fledgling, is uneven and oddly formed. Although announced as having a strong European component, work by other than French artists or French movements is virtually nonexistent. And though the Franco-American focus may have some virtue, the selection of American art is dominated by second-rate, late or atypical works. Moreover, it offers a very limited canon of artists and an ill-conceived overview of the 1960s–70s, and very little involvement with the 1990s and young artists. The same can be said of the special exhibition program. Recent exhibitions: *Giovanni Anselmo, Enrico Baj, Véronique Bigo, Jean-Marc Bustamante, Jim Dine, Mark Di Suvero, Robert Indiana, Robert Malaval, Paul Mansouroff, John Murphy, Ernest Pignon-Ernest, Man Ray, Georges Rousse, Tom Wesselmann, Bernar Venet, Paris—Nice—New York: 1960, Nice—an Abstract Look, The Exile of Russian Painting in France, From Klein to Warhol*. Hopefully, the museum's orientation will expand and loosen up as it grows.

Despite its limitations, you shouldn't be dissuaded from a visit here. You will see many fine works by French artists from the past several decades and will get a good sense of this era's history in France. Among the superb objects on display are Jacques de la Villeglé, *Boulevard Saint-Martin* (1959), César, *Dauphine* (1959/70), Niki de Saint-Phalle, *Tir* (*Shooting*, 1961), Christo, *Package on Luggage Rack* (1962), Raymond Hains, *La grande palissade* (1964), Martial Raysse, *Nissa-Belle* (*Beautiful Woman from Nice*, 1964), Daniel Spoerri, *Hommage au jardin d'hiver de la baronne Salomon de Rothschild* (*Homage to the Winter*

Garden of Baron Salomon de Rothschild, 1972), Annette Messager, *Effigie #6*. Although the museum devotes an entire room to its favorite son, Yves Klein, it's a shame that the display is so weak, composed of mainly minor works or postmortem multiples.

Musée Matisse

 164 avenue des Arènes de Cimiez, 06000
04-93-81-08-08 f: 04-93-53-00-22
Mon, Wed–Sun, closed Tues
Apr–Sept, 11–7; Oct–Mar, 10–5
admission: 25/15F
bus: 15, 17, 22

Located about 1 1/2 mi (2.5 km) northeast of Nice's center city in a hilly area amid archaeological ruins. Cimiez is an upscale suburban community.

Matisse lived in this elegant 17th-century Genoese-styled villa from 1938 until his death in 1954. The museum contains personal belongings, a selection of work from all periods of his life, including all the bronzes he made, and a series of photographs (by Robert Capa) showing him at work. Small temporary exhibitions usually focus on the theme of Matisse and his contemporaries, though occasionally the subject is Matisse's influence, and this may even include artists of the late 20th century.

Musée National Message Biblique Marc Chagall

avenue du Docteur Ménard, Cimiez, 06000
04-93-53-87-20 f: 04-93-53-87-39
Mon, Wed–Sun, closed Tues
July–Sept, 10–6; Oct–June, 10–5
admission: 30/20F

Located at the foot of the Cimiez hill, west of boulevard de Cimiez.

A main attraction here is the *Biblical Message* series (1960–66), composed of 17 paintings relating to Genesis, Exodus and the Song of Songs. In addition, there are over 500 gouaches, engravings, lithographs, stained-glass windows, sculptures and mosaics by Chagall. The museum, which was founded in 1973, acquired its collection through a bequest from the artist. The café, bookstore, gift shop and especially the gardens are usually as crowded as the galleries of the museum. It's hard to find a time when tour-bus groups aren't present, since this populars site is included in almost all the tour itineraries.

Saint-Paul-de-Vence

Fondation Maeght

 architect: Josep Lluis SERT, 1962–64
 route de Pass-Prest, 06570
04-93-32-81-63 f: 04-93-32-53-22
July–Sept, daily, 10–7; Oct–June, 10–12:30 and 2:30–6
admission: 40/30F; special exhibitions and summer months 45/40F

Unlike most art museums in France, which are government supported, the Fondation Maeght is a private entity. Created by Aimé and Marguerite Maeght (founders of the Galerie Maeght in Paris), the center features an outstanding collection of 20th-century modernism and an equally exceptional architecture and rapturous setting. The Catalan architect Josep Lluis Sert designed the ensemble of structures and garden pavilions specifically for modern art, for certain works in the Maeght collection and for the views afforded by the setting. The white concrete buildings, half-hidden on a pine-covered hillside, are human scale with striking roofs shaped like nun's coifs. Like his predecessors Walter Gropius,

Ludwig Mies van der Rohe and Le Corbusier, Sert emphasizes clear, open spaces and the social role of architecture.

Art is not only exhibited inside the structures, but it is integrated, as a result of Sert's direct collaboration with artists, with the buildings and landscape. Be sure to seek out the extraordinary art-architect projects: the GIACOMETTI courtyard; the MIRÓ labyrinth peopled with sculpture and ceramics; mosaic murals by CHAGALL and Pierre TAL-COAT; stained glass by MIRÓ, BRAQUE and Raoul UBAC; and the Pol BURY fountain. The collection on display in the galleries includes additional works by these artists, plus work by Pierre Alechinsky, Bonnard, Sam Francis, Julio Gonzalez, Hans Hartung, Barbara Hepworth, Kandinsky, Ellsworth Kelly, Wifredo Lam, Léger, Matisse, Matta, Joan Mitchell, Pierre Soulages, Antoni Tàpies and others. There is also a film program, bookstore and café-restaurant to keep you busy.

During most of the year, the collection is on display. But during the summer season, the center presents temporary exhibitions. These are characteristically mega-enterprises. Usually they are encyclopedic presentations with exemplary objects. Sometimes they even include contemporary art to establish borrowings, comparisons and cross currents with earlier work. Don't miss these exhibitions if you're in the area, and be sure to allocate several hours for a visit. Recent exhibitions: *Sculpture by Painters—Daumier to Baselitz*, *Art in Movement—Bacon to Freud*, *The Ultimate Work*, *Otto Dix—Metropolis*, *Henri Laurens*.

Vence

This quiet, little, inland town with a medieval center is about 15 1/2 mi (21 km) west of Nice. Intercity (SAP) bus, 50 min; or train to Cagnes-sur-Mer, then bus.

Château de Villeneuve—Fondation Emile Hugues

🚍 2 place du Frêne, 06140
04-93-58-15-78 f: 04-93-24-68-52
Tues–Sun, closed Mon. July–Oct, 10–6; Nov–June, 10–12:30 and 2–6
admission: 25/15F

Located in the center of the city, just off the main street.

This Mediterranean-style château became an exhibition site after it was restored in 1992. Named to honor an esteemed public figure who was the mayor of Vence, the center presents contemporary art exhibitions, usually featuring French artists. Historic shows devoted to the modern artists who lived in the region are also included in the program. Recent exhibitions: *Jean Le Gac*, *Mimmo Palladino*, *Jean-Pierre Raynaud*, *Claude Viallat*, *Supports-Surfaces*, *Definitions of Art*, *Art Brut*, *Arp and His Friends*.

Henri Matisse

Chapelle du Rosaire, 1951
route de Saint Jeannet (N210)
04-93-58-03-26
Tues, Thurs, 10–11:30 and 2:30–5:30; Wed, Fri–Sat, 2:30–5:30; closed Sun–Mon and Nov
admission: 10F

Located about 1/2 mi (800 m) north of the center of town.

With the most minimal design, Matisse created an absolutely elegant, serene yet buoyant environment for this small Dominican nuns' chapel. He had only planned to do a set of stained-glass windows but ended up virtually designing the whole chapel and its liturgical accouterments. The ensemble includes

15 narrow windows with a Tree of Life imagery (six are in the nave and nine are in the choir); a pair of apse windows with philodendron-like leaves laid against oval cactus shapes topped by the curve of the sun; a small window (beside the vestibule door) decorated with a fish caught in a net with a star above; three glazed-tile murals for the nave and sanctuary depicting the Stations of the Cross, Saint Dominic, Virgin and Child (flanked by huge cloudlike rosettes); a crucifix, six candlesticks, altar and other furniture; the door to the confessional, carved with disk and lozenge designs and painted white; the square and diamond patterning on the white floor; two chasubles richly embellished with brightly-colored cutouts of palm leaves, quatrefoils, halos, fish, stars and crosses; two exterior tile compositions (over the twin windows and doors into a sacristy)—a tondo of the Virgin and Child and heads of Saint Dominic and the Virgin and Child with a radiant cross in the middle; and a slender metal spire with cross and bell for the roof.

Chapel of the Rosary is one of the most masterful environments of the 20th century. It should be seen by anyone with an interest in art, architecture or design. Because Matisse used the windows as a source for both light and color, keeping the rest of the space white, the interior is dazzling. This is especially true on sunny days when light streams in and casts reflections of sumptuous sapphire blue, grass green and golden yellow on the spare murals with their linear black figurations and glowing white surface planes.

Galerie Beaubourg

Château Notre-Dame des Fleurs,
2618 route de Grasse, 06145
04-93-24-52-00 f: 04-93-24-52-19
Tues–Sat, 11–7; closed Mon and Feb
admission: 30/15F
bus: local service between Vence and Grasse

Located 1 1/4 mi (2 km) northwest of Vence on the winding mountain road toward Grasse.

This gallery occupies two floors of a restored 19th-century château (previously the site of a Benedictine abbey) and has a sizeable sculpture garden, chock-full of objects, on front terraces. Each year the gallery organizes three exhibitions for the grand spaces on the main floor. These often include some superb vintage works by leading postwar French artists. Though they have the gloss of a museum show, the works are for sale. Recent exhibitions: *Picabia, Accumulations from the Collections of Arman*, *Artists' Objects*, *Modernity after 1958—the Nouveaux Réalistes*.

Galerie Beaubourg specializes in French and American artists who emerged during the 1950s–60s, and some younger artists. On the ground floor there is a gift shop and many small rooms overflowing with prints and all sorts of multiples made by, or allied with the work of, gallery artists. Don't miss the chapel (main floor, near the entrance desk) with a stained-glass window by Jean-Pierre RAYNAUD (1993) and a marvelous conglomerate of mechanical assemblages, *L'odalisque* (1989), and a candelabra, *Oecuménisme* (1982), by Jean TINGUELY.

In the garden you will find sculptures by some of the gallery artists in addition to works by Sandro Chia, Claes Oldenburg, Bernard Pagès, Jean-Pierre Raynaud, Julian Schnabel. A festive atmosphere prevails since visitors can freely climb up and down the terrace levels, and many works are permeated with irony and humor. But this atmosphere, plus the excessive number of objects and crowded installation—not to mention the mediocre quality of most of the sculptures—turns the garden into a virtual amusement park.

Gallery artists: Arman, Ben, François Boisrond, Louis Cane, César, Robert Combas, Meurice Dado, Jim Dine, Bernard Dufour, Jean-Claude Farhi, Alexandre Fassianos, Jean-Olivier Hucleux, Alain Jacquet, Yves Klein, Pierre Klossowski, Nam June Paik, Philippe Perrin, Larry Rivers, Niki de Saint-Phalle, George Segal, Daniel Spoerri, Frank Stella, Jean Tinguely, Jacques de la Villeglé, Andy Warhol.

Antibes

Train from Nice, 25 min; or intercity bus, 1 1/4 hr.

Musée Picasso

Château Grimaldi, 06600
04-92-90-54-20 f: 04-92-90-54-21
Tues–Sun, closed Mon. June–Sept,
10–6; Oct–May, 10–12 and 2–6
admission: 20/10F

Picasso used a part of this superbly sited château as his studio in 1946 when he was living nearby with Françoise Gilot. When he subsequently gave a collection of his art to the city, the building was transformed into a museum. In addition to the Picassos, the collection now includes art by de Staël, Ernst, Hartung, Léger, Modigliani, Picabia, and a sculpture terrace displaying objects by Miró, Bernard Pagès, Anne and Patrick Poirier and Germaine Richier. In 1997 the museum inaugurated a series of exhibitions focused on young artists. These have featured Hubert Duprat, Pierrick Sorin, Jessica Stockholder.

Biot

A medieval hilltop village favored by tourists for its boutiques and studios specializing in glass. Although the train from Nice stops in Biôt, the station is 2 1/2 mi (4 km) from the village. It's therefore preferable to take the bus from Antibes (5 mi/6 km) which leaves you in the center of Biot.

Musée National Fernand Léger

chemin du Val de Pôme, 06140
04-92-91-50-30 f: 04-92-91-50-31
Mon, Wed–Sun, closed Tues
Apr–June, 10–12:30 and 2–6;
July–Oct, 11–6; Nov–Mar,
10–12:30 and 2–5:30
admission: 30/20F

You can't miss the museum building. It has a huge mosaic mural with a colorful array of sports-related images on its facade. Originally designed for the Olympic Stadium in Hannover, this work and over 450 paintings, ceramics, mosaics, drawings, prints and tapestries by Léger now form the museum's permanent collection. As is evident in his style and subject matter, the artist—who was associated with the cubist and purist movements—was inspired by the geometric aesthetic of the machine and themes from working-class life and popular culture. Selections from the collection are installed in the galleries and gardens that surround the building. A new wing was added in 1989 to expand the display space. Special exhibitions, focused on Léger as well as other modern and contemporary artists, are a regular aspect of the museum's program.

Vallauris

This small hillside village between Antibes and Cannes has become a major tourist attraction. It is a center of artisanal ceramics, renowned as the site where Picasso created his ceramic sculptures. Accessible by local buses from Cannes and Antibes.

Musée National Picasso *La Guerre et la Paix*

place de la Libération, 06222
04-93-64-16-05
Mon, Wed–Sun, 10–12 and 2–6;
closed Tues
admission: 13F

In response to world violence, most directly to the execution of the Beloyannis in Greece (Mar 1952), Picasso transformed this 12th-century chapel (deconsecrated during the French Revolution) into a temple of peace. The chapel is a very small vaulted space—a space so low, narrow and claustrophobic that it feels almost like a cave. By painting a panorama filled with allegoric images of War along one side and a panorama symbolizing Peace on the other, Picasso virtually filled the entire space, since images curve up the arching walls and meet at the top. On the semicircular end wall, Picasso furthered the imagery and meaning of the panoramas by creating one simple depiction: four figures of different colors stretching their arms upward in unity toward a rising sun.

Pablo Picasso

Homme au mouton, 1944
avenue Georges Clemenceau

Situated at the top of the main street of the village, opposite from the chapel of War and Peace, this bronze sculpture, *Man with a Sheep*, commemorates

Picasso's role in reviving the economy of Vallauris by making its ceramic studios world famous. After accepting this gift from the artist, the community of Vallauris made Picasso an honorary citizen.

Madoura

rue 19 mars 1962, 06220
04-93-64-66-39

These are the ceramic studios where Picasso worked. In its gallery, Madoura displays and sells examples of the artist's ceramic output as well as lots more.

Mouans-Sartoux

Northwest of Antibes and north of Cannes. Accessible by local bus between Cannes and Grasse.

Espace de l'Art Concret

Château de Mouans, place
Suzanne de Villeneuve, 06370
04-93-75-71-50 f: 04-93-75-88-88
Mon, Wed–Sun, closed Tues
June–Sept, 11–7; Oct–May, 11–6

This exhibition space, located in a 16th-century château in a charming little village, concentrates exclusively on "concrete art"—a term encompassing art with a constructivist, conceptual, geometric-abstract or minimalist orientation. Many exhibitions are culled from the private collection of Sybil Albers-Barrier, which is on long-term loan to the art center. At times artists are invited to create works in response to a specific query. Whether thematic or monographic, exhibitions aim to make visitors think about the social context of art and to question art's existential necessity. Despite the high-minded sound of all this and the cerebral base of concrete art, the exhibitions are engaging and at times even lighthearted. Indeed, this unknown little art space is a real treasure amid the plethora of tourist-oriented sites on the Côte d'Azur. Recent exhibitions: *To Compare —to Create*, *A Museum Imagined by Artists*, *Fear of the Void*, *Before and behind the Light*, *Art and Clothes*, *French Springtime*, *In Order to Irritate Us—the Mind, the Body*. Some artists represented in the collection include Carl Andre, Ernst Caramelle, Anne Marie Jugnet, Imi Knoebel, Mario Merz, David Rabinowitch, Jean-Pierre Raynaud, Fred Sandback, Niele Toroni, James Turrell.

Digne

If you want a break from the chic ambience of the Côte d'Azur, visit this charming village (also called Digne-les-Bains), high in the mountains between Nice and Provence. It's a hang-loose, thermal springs center, where you can partake of outdoor sports, pamper your body and breathe air enriched by lavender (one of the herbs grown in the region). The scenic train from Nice, 3 1/4 hr; train from Marseille, 2 1/2 hr; bus from Nice, 2 1/4 hr.

David Rabinowitch

Notre-Dame-du-Bourg, 1998

When you enter this old, modest church you won't immediately be aware of Rabinowitch's extensive design of the interior. Rather than the brilliant colors of Gothic stained glass and the figurative imagery of medieval sculpture, he has created a subdued, spare setting. His minimalist aesthetic, with its plays between angular and circular motifs, pale and deep color tones, is a perfect complement to the simple geometry of the 12th-century architecture. As you walk around, you will realize how carefully and completely Rabinowitch has refined the space and virtually all the liturgical furnishings. The stained-glass windows, massive stone altar and bishop's throne, candle holders, tabernacles, chalices, transept tapestry, processional pattern embedded in the floor of the center aisle, and even the seating are shaped by an abstract, architectonic mode that imbues the space with serenity.

The idea of having a modern artist totally design a church interior and its artifacts became a reality with Matisse's creations for the chapel in Vence. Recently France has commissioned artists to produce contemporary designs for various churches around the country. See, for example, Pierre Buraglio's Chapelle Saint-Symphorien in Paris, Jan Dibbets's windows in Bourges, and the stained glass in the cathedral in Nevers.

Lyon Region

Lyon

This lively, art-impassioned city is one of France's best-kept secrets. If you're looking for a delightful escape from Paris for a long weekend or a leisurely week, put this high on your list. Lyon is easy to reach and has a sophisticated provincial character all its own. The cultural milieu, both in- and outside the realm of the visual arts, is rich and varied. TGV from Paris (Gare de Lyon), 2 1/4 hr; from Grenoble, 1 1/4 hr; train from Saint-Etienne, 1 hr.

A clear sign that Lyon and its entrepreneurs are exploring new ways to enhance the city comes from the extraordinary parking garages—Lyon Parc Auto—recently designed by artist-architect collaborations. Not only is the very idea of aestheticizing a parking garage amazing, but the results are phenomenal! It is also notable that many of these new underground garages have resulted from the city's move to pedestrianize

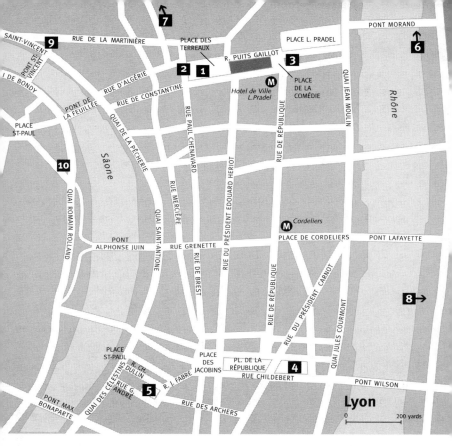

Lyon

streets and to put parking garages underground, thus freeing up space for gardens, parks, playgrounds and plazas within the congested urban landscape. A veritable killing of three birds with one stone!

In 1992 Lyon Parc Auto commissioned Jean-Michel WILMOTTE to develop a basic plan for the interior of all the garages and Yan D. PENNOR to design the graphics and signals. The company then hired artist-architect teams for specific center-city projects. This is public art at its best—well integrated into and coordinated with its setting. If you want to see how a mundane environment can be radically transformed, be sure to visit at least one of the parking garage projects noted below (Mullican, Morellet, Buren, Kosuth, Verjux).

Note: the word *parc* refers both to a parking garage and a park. (Recreation or green areas are often called gardens rather than parks in France.)

Daniel Buren with Christian Drevet

Untitled, 1994
place des Terreaux
métro: Hôtel de Ville

Although prominently placed in one of the city's grand plazas, Buren's sculpture is discreetly integrated into the setting. On three sides, the plaza is bordered by majestic buildings, including the city hall and Fine Arts Museum (Palais Saint-Pierre). A monumental fountain, *The Chariot of Liberty* (1892) by A. Bartholdi (the sculptor who created the Statue of

Liberty), dominates the fourth side. As in his creation for the Palais-Royal in Paris, Daniel Buren has again divided the space into a grid. But here, a more subtle design, mainly ground markings and water spurts, takes precedence over a framework of columns. The grid, articulated by lines patterned alternately with horizontal or vertical stripes, derives from narrow bands of black and white stone embedded in the concrete of the plaza. The lines actually extend beyond the plaza, stretching into abutting streets and spilling into adjacent areas. Art and life totally merge when the black-and-white stripes of crosswalks and the grid stripes overlap.

Buren, working collaboratively with the architect Drevet, also constructed an ersatz border of striped stone cubes on the long sides of the plaza. They then further emphasized the alignment on the side with the Bartholdi fountain by placing a second row of tall columns behind the row of cubes. The tall columns not only make reference to the cubes because they are composed of striped cubic blocks, but they also relate to the relief columns on the facade of the building opposite. This subtle interplay with the setting is a trait common to Buren's work.

In the center of the plaza, 69 mini water jets aligned within the squares of the grid spring up from the ground. The spurts rise (about 18 in, roughly the height of the stone cubes) and then peter out, and then suddenly rise again. They quite literally animate the plaza, to the delight of toddlers and the dismay of inattentive tourists. In the evenings, when the water jets glow with light, the plaza has a bejeweled appearance.

As in the case of many public artworks, this project has suffered its share of controversy. In its favor, the design must be recognized for its innovative, radical transformation of the conventional idea of a public "fountain." Like the reconceptualization of "public sculpture," here a "fountain" is no longer defined as an isolated object to be looked at. It, too, has become an experiential, environmental artwork. Despite its vanguard creativity and catalytic revivification of a downtrodden public place, the work has produced problems because its design was incompatible with a well-established use of the plaza. Almost sacred is the French convention of moving brasserie tables outdoors into public spaces when weather permits. Place des Terreaux is no exception, and water jets were a most unwelcome interference. (Another problem, though not the fault of the design, was the algae that began growing in the plaza.) As a solution, the city has turned off the jets in the area of the tables during business hours. Although this in itself doesn't critically alter the design, the presence of the umbrella-shaded tables around the Bartholdi fountain does dramatically reduce the visibility of the cube and column feature of the project. As is often the case when contemporary sculpture is set in the public arena, the difficult balance between art and life is not attained.

2 | Matt Mullican

Untitled, 1992–94
Parc Terreaux, place des Terreaux
métro: Hôtel de Ville

In this parking garage, designed by the architect Pierre FAVRE, Mullican situated his art in the main passageways, access areas and elevator lobbies. Using signs, images and objects from daily life of centuries past, he sought to arouse thinking about the history of Lyon, most particularly about its main plaza, place des Terreaux. Typically, he has merged references to bygone eras with his own vocabulary of forms and contemporary life.

In the lobby of the garage and in

front of the elevator on each of the six parking levels, Mullican has imbedded a plane of black granite in the floor. At the street entrance, an old map of Lyon is engraved on the stone surface. The other floor designs have historic motifs arranged within modified grids. As you descend the levels of the garage, the images refer to increasingly distant time frames. Complementing these images are objects encased in a large vitrine embedded in the ground of the pedestrian access area of the first level of parking. The objects are copies of artifacts (dishes, tools, toys, etc.) found in archaeological excavations. Mullican includes two of each item and arranges them in a geometric composition. Their identity vacillates from mundane object to historic treasure to abstract image. As an added means of evoking the past, Mullican reconstructs old fortification walls found on the site. These are located on the car ramp and pedestrian passage of the first level.

3 | Opéra de Lyon

 renovation: Jean NOUVEL with
Emmanuel BLAMONT, 1986–93
place de la Comédie
métro: Hôtel de Ville

Rather than compete with the old, Italianate architecture, Nouvel added high-tech elements within and restructured the building to increase its size and capabilities as a 21st-century theater. His design overflows with camouflage and accommodation even as it wreaks havoc with the former layout, boldly asserting the architect's own brand of contemporaneity. For example, the exterior suggests a two-level edifice surmounted by a majestic arched "dome." In fact, there are now 18 floors in the Opera House, five below ground, seven beneath the row of statues (the former rooftop), five in the new glass-and-steel barreled roof on top and

the ground floor lobby. Without producing a glaring appendage, Nouvel has almost doubled the size of the building.

Similarly, the historic white stone facade with its arcades and decorative carvings still dominates the outer appearance. But now there is also an inner, black-glazed facade with black entrance doorways and shiny, black granite on the ground and steps all around. This dark glass schema only mildly transforms the old edifice compared to the dramatic modernization of the lobby. Curved diagonal and perpendicular streams of escalators crisscross the space and move above and below the entrance level. Reflections also abound from mirror, glass and polished metal accouterments and sheathings. Again, a glossy black tonality and reductive, geometric aesthetic prevail. Despite the elimination of decorative details and rich colors, the space is riveting. You stop, stare and gasp when you enter but soon start reeling in the dizzying environment. The plethora of ricocheting images and disparate rhythms in a tightly compressed space crowded with circulation structures is overwhelming.

Perhaps the best impression of Lyon's Opera House occurs on the exterior at night, when black glass surfaces provide a lustrous contrast to the traditional white facade aglow with soft lighting. Enhancing the image of elegance are the touches of red from the ruby-toned globes of the old lanterns hanging within each arch.

4 | François Morellet

 Les hasards de la République,
1995
Parc République, place de la
République
métro: Bellecour or Cordeliers

Morellet has marked each of the seven levels in this garage, designed by Pierre

VURPAS, with differently colored neon tubes. In one wing the lines of colored neon, almost 33 ft long (10 m), are on the ground; in the other they are on the ground and walls; and in the access tower (containing stairs and two glass-walled elevators) they create a floating cascade spanning all levels—like a toss of multicolored pickup sticks frozen in space.

The colors punctuate an otherwise gray environment, brutally breaking up the space. They also providing markers to help patrons find their cars. Morellet has called them "stupid accidents with a beneficial tendency." Their placement is totally arbitrary according to the logic of chance—"chance, programmed with a system using the naval battles occurring during my childhood and the telephone numbers of Lyon Parc Auto." The

artist reiterates absurdity in his title by playing with the meaning of *hasards*—chance, luck, accidents—and the dual reference of "la République"—the plaza in Lyon and the French Republic.

5 | Daniel Buren

Sens dessus dessous, Sculpture in situ en mouvement, 1994
Parc Célestins, place des Célestins
métro: Bellecour

Buren reveals his finely tuned sensitivity to space and repetitive patterns in this project. *Direction Above Below, Sculpture in Place and in Movement* is by far the most spectacular of the parking garage creations in Lyon. By working on the original construction plans with the architect Michel TARGE, Buren had the openings in the core cylinder shaped as wide arches and lit indirectly from below. The visual effect of the arch openings spiraling down the concrete walls of the six-story core is phenomenal, all the more so because reflections emanating from a large, inclined, circular mirror set at the base of the cylinder accent the depth on an oblique angle and give a mind-boggling view of the whole, illuminated, arch-aligned cylinder. As if this weren't enough, a mechanical system makes the mirror pivot continuously, its velocity changing according to the speed of the cars going up and down the garage's ramps. Thus, there are times when you can no longer discern individual arches and levels, but instead experience the sensation of an endless, twisting, sparkling screw.

When you leave the garage, don't walk away until you locate the periscope Buren has placed on the plaza above, directly atop the cylinder of the parking garage underneath. Looking through its lens, you will see in a single glance the whole core cylinder from its very center. The periscope itself is a remarkable minimalist object of polished steel, its central column wrapped

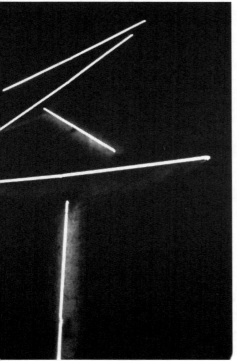

Morellet, *Les Hasards de la République*

Buren, *Sens dessus dessous*

in stripes—the artist's trademark. (This object was conceived by Buren and designed by Jean-Michel WILMOTTE.)

6 Cité Internationale

project head: Renzo PIANO, 1985–

This new neighborhood is located on the periphery of the city between the spacious, idyllic Parc de la Tête d'Or and the Rhône river. It is a choice stretch of land and will contain an interesting mix of culture, business, commercial and residential buildings. Already in place are the Palais des Congrès (Convention Center) and offices, 1995; Musée d'Art Contemporain de Lyon, 1995–96; and multiplex UGC movie theater with 14 screens, 1997. Yet to be completed are a hotel, private homes and apartment units.

6 Musée d'Art Contemporain de Lyon

architect: Renzo PIANO, 1995
81 quai Charles de Gaulle, 69463
04-72-69-17-17 f: 04-72-69-17-00
Wed–Thurs, Sat–Sun, 12–7; Fri, 12–10; closed Mon–Tues
admission: 25/13F
bus: 4, 47, 71, exit Musée d'Art Contemporain. métro: Foch or Saxe-Gambetta, then bus 4

If you're looking for a new building by Renzo Piano—the architect celebrated for the Centre Pompidou and The Menil Museum in Houston—you may think you're in the wrong place when you arrive at the museum's address. The facade is vintage 1930s and doesn't look like a contemporary museum. Clearly, it's been renovated, and when you check further, you'll see an architecture with all the finesse that has made Piano great. Beyond the facade, which was retained from the Palais de la Foire de Lyon, the side walls are delineated with a grid and constructed from orange brick—the same color found throughout the city in its tile roofs, a signature of Lyon. The back, with its glass facade opening onto a covered pedestrian street, offers yet another design. The exterior is therefore eccentrically hybrid though not at all brash.

In the interior, the ground floor is largely a reception area with a café (opening onto an outdoor terrace), auditorium, bookshop and documentation room off to the sides. In the back, embedded in the wall facing outward, is an ensemble of video screens. This *mur d'images* (wall of images) continuously displays artists' videos as well as current information about activities in the museum, Cité Internationale or the city itself. The astute positioning of the wall makes it visible not only to people inside the museum but also to pedestrians walking on the street outside and patrons inside the lobby of the glass-encased movie theater across the way. The videos are also relayed to the métro station, Gare de Vaise, where they appear on a column of video monitors.

The three upper floors of the building are open spaces in which to present art. Since the museum wanted to structure the interior for the on-site creation of artist installation projects, it requested a modifiable space, amenable to a broad diversity of requirements. In response, Piano designed the floors like empty boxes equipped with modular, movable walls and windows or skylights that can either remain open to the outside or easily be walled off. With this non-layout, it is possible to totally reorder the space and radically change the museum's appearance with each exhibition. Moreover, the flexibility (how it all works as well as the available furnishings) is perfectly invisible.

Although the 1995 opening of the new building marked the inauguration of Lyon's Museum of Contemporary Art on its own turf, its history dates back to 1983 when the city decided to create a contemporary art department in the Musée des Beaux-Arts. The department gained official designation as an independent museum in 1988. Prior to moving to its own building, it continued to present exhibitions in the Fine Arts Museum and elsewhere in the city. These included two international biennials and an outstanding show on monochrome painting, Only One Color (1988). A propensity for conceptual, minimal and non-object-oriented approaches evolved during this initial period and is still a mainstay of the museum's program.

In general, the museum favors one-person exhibitions, which are often new, ambitious installations. Indeed, Lyon has taken an admirable position in

both its exhibition and collection policy: it gives a major preference to art produced exclusively in and for the museum. That is to say, it gives artists the chance to experiment with materials, forms, ideas and big dimensions, and then acquires the installations produced under its aegis for its permanent collection. Focus is on the creative process, or, as it is termed here, the "production" of a work and an exhibition "conceived as a living spectacle." Rather than reconstitute a chronology or stylistic development through a retrospective type of exhibition, the museum seeks to give visitors a more direct experience with a single, grand artwork that is its own universe impacted with its own history. The installations are considered to be veritable scenarios, presumably requiring no prior knowledge. To be sure, they are amazing examples of vanguard creativity, but whether they function as expected—especially for visitors not versed in contemporary art—is questionable. In any event, Lyon has put itself at the forefront of encouraging and realizing unconventional projects that push the limits of artistic production.

Since new installations and other temporary exhibitions fill the galleries most of the time, the collection is rarely visible. Every so often, however, a slot in the schedule is devoted exclusively to the collection. If your timing is right (or wrong, depending on your perspective), a collection exhibition gives you the chance to see the entire museum filled with a unique body of art—international and French, from the late 1960s (beginning with Fluxus) on to the present. These shows are worth a special trip to Lyon!

Aside from its questionable all-or-nothing strategy for displaying the collection, the museum's concentration on new installations may sound great, but in reality it's not very visitor-friendly. On-site installations take a long time to set up, particularly when they entail a dramatic restructuring of the exhibition space. In Lyon's case, the downtime—a period when the museum is closed to the public—has been as long as two months. Thus, you may arrive and find there's nothing to see. Scheduling practices will undoubtedly change as the museum grows, but in the meantime be sure to check in advance so you won't be disappointed.

As the list of past exhibitions reveals, the museum has shown many blue chip artists, some for the first time in France. Recent exhibitions: *Abramovic and Ulay*, *Giovanni Anselmo*, *John Baldesarri*, *Guillaume Bijl*, *Louise Bourgeois*, *Marcel Broodthaers*, *James Coleman*, *Robert Filliou*, *Toni Grand*, *Ann Hamilton*, *Gary Hill*, *Douglas Huebler*, *Robert Irwin*, *Ilya Kabakov*, *Per Kirkeby*, *Sol LeWitt*, *Mario Merz*, *Robert Morris*, *Philippe Perrin*, *Alain Pouillet*, *Alain Séchas*, *James Turrell*, *Pierrick Sorin*, *Pat Steir*, *Krzysztof Wodiczko*, *Rémy Zaugg*, *Music on Stage*, a 1998 exhibition, also suggests that Lyon is again creating meritorious thematic projects. This one featured music-based sculptures, drawings, installations and videos by Terry Allen, Laurie Anderson, Michael Aubry, Sylvie Bossu, Angela Bulloch, Rebecca Horn, Pierre Huyghe, Marylène Negro, Peter Vogel. The museum also organized an Internet exhibition, *Version originale* (1997), in which 27 invited artists created cyberspace presentations.

The catalogues produced by the museum in association with their exhibitions range from short descriptive texts to comprehensive, scholarly publications. Many of these are bi- or trilingual. In addition, the museum organizes a successful program of artist roundtables, conferences and lectures.

Lyon Biennale

This mega-exhibition, organized by the city's Museum of Contemporary Art, has become a major event in France, rivaling other big international survey exhibitions like the Venice Biennale and Documenta. The 1997 Biennale was held in the cavernous Halle Tony Garnier (20 place Antonin-Perrin, 69007). In Lyon, biennials usually have an ostensible theme and aim to present the latest, most vanguard and significant work in all media by some 80 artists. In 1991 the inaugural show was called *The Love of Art*, and in 1997 it was *The Other*. The summer 1999 biennale holds great promise since the guest director will be Jean-Hubert Martin—the admired exhibition curator who organized *Magiciens de la Terre* when he was director of the Pompidou. At their best, biennials are a terrific way to see what's going on internationally in contemporary art. More typically, they are political footballs, peppered with a lot of bombast, showing an odd hodgepodge of very uneven work by superstars and emerging artists. Recognizing these givens, Lyon's exhibitions have received high marks and are a welcome addition to the art scene in France.

Michel Verjux

 De plain-pied et en sous-sol, 1994
Parc Croix-Rousse,
73 rue de Belfort
métro: Croix-Rousse, Hénon

This parking garage is at the north periphery of the city near Hôpital de la Croix-Rousse. It's a pleasant 5–10 min walk from the métro stations. Note: the light projections that are the essential element in this work only operate 9–12 and 2–6.

Verjux is a young French artist, acclaimed for his architecturally based light installations that literally and conceptually shed light on a space or environment. For *On the First Floor and in the Basement*, he has placed 13 light projections along the route where people walk or pass in their cars within the garage. The projections illuminate the connection between the access tower (stairs and elevators) and the parking area on each of the 10 floors. They also spotlight some other places where pedestrian and automobile circulation intersect. You can't help noticing these out-of-the-ordinary, precise, large, circular spotlights, which create dominant, nonpainted, nonsculpted, ephemeral shapes in the environment.

The architecture in this garage, by Jérôme THOMAS, is itself quite creative. By alternating full and half-circle painted images and actual openings on the outer and ramp walls, a syncopated dark-light, open-shut pattern results. This nicely complements Verjux's work, further reducing the dark, claustrophobic ambience of the underground environment.

8 | Joseph Kosuth

Les aventures d'Ulysse sous terre, 1995
Parc Gare Part-Dieu, boulevard Marius Vivier-Merle
métro: Part-Dieu

There are many parking garages in the Part-Dieu area, so be sure you go to the one at the Vivier-Merle exit of the train and métro stations. It's easy to get lost in the Part-Dieu shopping center, so be prepared!

Working in his inimitable mode of using a text to focus on the relationship between language and reality, Kosuth here cites passages from James Joyce's *Ulysses*, merging them with extracts from the underground adventures of *Alice in Wonderland* by Lewis Carroll. The new texts, titled *The Adventures of Ulysses Underground*, are an homage to the subterranean character of the garage. For example, one sign reads: "Fall into the Rabbit's Hole. Bloom. Stitch in my side. Why have I run away? I must catch my breath and move slowly toward the lights of the garage's car lanes. The glimmers flash again."

A luminous text panel greets you as you enter the lobby leading into the garage. It stretches over 42 1/2 feet along the wall opposite the elevators and stairs. Smaller panels appear on pillars behind the parked cars on all four floors. Although text signage is perhaps unwelcome for people rushing to find their cars, get to work or catch trains, the humor of the double references to literature and the garage environment in Kosuth's texts is a welcome palliative to the hustle and the bleak anonymity of urban life and parking garages. (Part-Dieu, one of Lyon's two main train stations, is located in an area recently developed with office towers and a mega-commercial center–shopping mall.) It is questionable, however, if many people take the time to stop, read and appreciate such cerebral art in a midcity parking garage.

The architectural design of this garage, created by Jean-Charles DEMICHEL and Claude DORDILLY, has some delightful elements that add class and refinement to the basic garage structure. See especially the circular windows, defined by black rims and a cross bar, inserted into white walls at the exit of each level.

Institut Lumière

 rue du Premier-Film, 69008
04-78-78-18-95 f: 04-78-01-36-62
métro: Monplaisir-Lumière
exhibitions: Tues–Sun, 2–7;
closed Mon
admission: 25/20F
films: Tues–Sun, variable hours;
closed Mon
admission: 29/25F

In a country of cinephiles and a city connected to the birth of film through its famous sons, Louis and Auguste Lumière, the Institut Lumière (created in

1982) pays tribute to the history and ongoing appreciation of motion pictures. It sees itself as a "living film museum." The cinematic experience actually begins when you emerge from the métro station and find yourself on the site of an outdoor theater, where films are presented free every Tuesday during the summer. Even when a screening is not occurring, the film-related imagery on the tiered pavilion sets the stage.

The institute is located to the right of the plaza in the unusual, Art Nouveau–styled building named Le Château by its neighbors. It was the fantasy house built by Antoine (1899–1901), founder of Lumière Establishments, a lucrative business involved with the production of photographs. The building now contains an exhibition gallery, library, film-video library, archive, offices, meeting rooms and a 100-seat theater. In 1998 a new 280-seat theater, called the *usine* (factory), opened out back in an old hangar formerly used for photo production. It was, moreover, the site where Louis Lumière screened the first film in 1895. Even if you don't stay for a film, be sure to mosey around the extraordinary factory-to-theater renovation and the extensive park area contained within the Lumière property.

The institute organizes its public showings as homages to and retrospectives of filmmakers, film stars, historic styles, thematic genres, etc. But it is not just involved with past classics. It also screens current films, including previews of new films and first showings of work by young filmmakers. In addition, it presents a monthly series of lectures by prestigious individuals from the film world and publishes a valuable magazine two or three times a year.

Dror Endeweld

Innommable-innombrable, 1995
Parc Berthelot, 99 rue de Marseille
métro: Jean Mace

In this parking garage project, *Unnameable-Innumerable*, the artist works with units—numbers and letters—and combinations of units. Each unit is depicted in a hexagonal shape, inlaid on the floor. At the entrance level, the entire lobby area is covered with a number and letter composition, precisely organized in four rows but without any apparent logic in terms of the sequential ordering of the units.

For Endeweld, the negative words "unnameable" and "innumerable" make reference to Klaus Barbie, the infamous head of Lyon's Gestapo, who had his headquarters nearby on the site now housing the Museum of Resistance and Deportation (14 avenue Berthelot). The words also capture the tone of the artist's installation, which is a commentary on the sequence of 1–12 units from -2 to 10, from part to whole. You may not grasp the nature of the sequence, since you probably didn't begin by perceiving its internal, formal logic (1 form, 2 forms; 3 forms . . .) instead of the usual conceptual logic (1, 2, 3 . . .). Fortunately, Endeweld did not apply this obtuse pattern in marking the various floors in the garage. He instead used the more common, graspable progression 0–12. Here, the number inlaid on the floor near the elevator and stairwell doors serves as a reference—as long as you remember the level where you've parked your car.

9/10 | City Murals

Throughout Lyon you will see trompe-l'oeil frescoes on the sides of buildings. Many of these are produced by La Cité de la Création, a commercial business. A tourist favorite is the fictitious house imagery wrapping around three sides of the residence at 49 quai Saint-Vincent, corner of rue de la Martinière. Another, even more clever composition, is just across the river in the old city at the

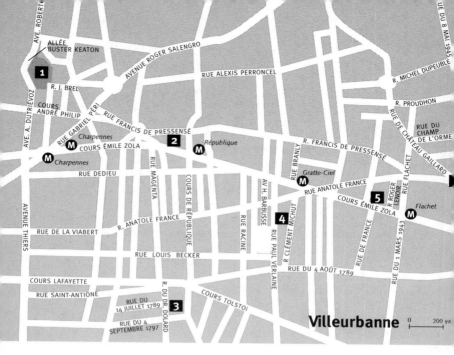

juncture of quai de Bondy and rue François Verny.

Villeurbanne

Although a suburb bordering Lyon on the east, Villeurbanne is connected to Lyon by its métro and buses and is nearer to the city center than many areas within the city limits. But it is hardly a bedroom community feeding off Lyon. Instead, it is a vigorous urban entity with a life all its own and an energetic art scene. Most of the sites noted below are within walking distance of one another. If you went at a fast pace, you might be able to see them all in a single day, except that then you wouldn't have time to enjoy the wonderful cafés, restaurants, markets and shops in the delightful center of town around the city hall.

Anne and Patrick Poirier

La fontaine des géants, 1985
espace de l'Europe Jean Monnet
métro: Charpennes

From the métro, walk a few blocks down rue Henri Rolland; cross rue Jacques Brel; enter the park; walk forward veering to the left. (This is referred to as the Tonkin neighborhood.) If you don't immediately see the fountain, follow the voices of kids who seem to be a constant presence in and around it, weather permitting.

The Poiriers typically present fragmented classical images in their art, suggesting the collapse of order or Western civilization. In *The Fountain of Giants* they have outdone themselves by creating a marvelous, witty, surreal fountain that is a perfect artwork for a neighborhood park. A heap of rocks piled high into a mountainous mass sits in a bed of

Poirier, *La Fontaine des géants*

water, with jets of water spraying inward from the corners of a surrounding shallow pool. Interspersed with the rocks are marble fragments of classical sculpture—four gargantuan eyes and one colossal mouth—and architecture. Mixed among this conglomerate are two large bronze arrows, one of which sits atop the mass pointing downward. On the one hand, the fountain fascinates children who clearly respond to its form and imagery. On the other hand, it is visually and conceptually provocative as a "serious" work of art, raising all sorts of questions about survival, heritage, contemporary culture . . . .

Galerie Georges
2 Verney-Carron

99 cours Emile Zola, 69100
04-72-69-08-20 f: 04-72-44-97-70
Mon–Fri, 9–12 and 2–6:30;
closed Sat
métro: République

This gallery, through its subsidiary Art Enterprise, has been actively involved with putting art in the urban environment in Lyon and elsewhere. It's a good place to see work by midcareer and young European artists involved with

spatial and cultural issues. Recent exhibitions: *Cécile Bart, Michel Blazy, Etienne Bossut, Daniel Buren, Patrice Carré, Marie-Noëlle Décoret, Krijn De Koning, Gloria Friedmann, Sylvie Garraud, Gottfried Honneger, François Morellet, Leonel Moura, François Perrodin, Rober Racine, Michel Verjux, Bernar Venet.*

Institut d'Art
3 Contemporain (IAC)

11 rue du Doctor Dolard, 69605
04-78-03-47-00 f: 04-78-03-47-09
June–Sept: Mon, Thurs–Sun, 1–7;
Wed, 1–8; closed Tues. Oct–May:
Mon, Thurs–Sun, 1–6; Wed, 1–8;
closed Tues
admission: 20/15F
métro: République.
bus: 1, Cité/ Nouveau Musée

From the métro, walk down cours de la République to the traffic circle at place Albert Thomas; turn right onto cours Tolstoi and take an immediate left onto rue Docteur du Dolard.

IAC (often referred to by its former name, Le Nouveau Musée) was founded in 1978 and opened its doors in an old school building on the Doctor Dolard site in 1982. A decade later, the building was finally renovated and enlarged to its present state. It now has an attractive pitched roof, glass facade, nine

Joep van Lieshout, *Baisodrome*, 1995 (IAC)

diversely scaled galleries, a library, café and auditorium. The original little schoolhouse is still present and visible, sitting in the midst of spacious new surroundings. When the museum merged with FRAC Rhône-Alps in 1998, it expanded in a different way, acquiring a large collection of contemporary art and taking on the operations of a FRAC (purchasing art for the collection, organizing small exhibitions and education programs for regional locations). The merger also produced a new, cumbersome name: Institut d'Art Contemporain: FRAC Rhône-Alps, Le Nouveau Musée.

Since its inception, IAC has presented many rigorous and enlightening exhibitions. Again and again, it has played an important role in supporting challenging, unconventional work by young and unrecognized artists or mid-career artists with little previous exposure in France. The list of artists who have had one-person exhibitions and retrospectives reads like a Who's Who of the late-20th-century avant-garde, especially in terms of art with a minimal, conceptual or cultural-commentary orientation. It includes: Carl André, Basserode, Christian Boltanski, Daniel Buren, Geneviève Cadieux, Tony Cragg, Hamish Fulton, Jenny Holzer, Anish Kapoor, On Kawara, Daniel Libeskind, Gordon Matta-Clark, Mario Merz, Leonel Moura, Guilio Paolini, Richard Prince, Martha Rosler, Niek van de Steeg, Jacques Vieille, Jeff Wall, Lawrence Weiner. Group exhibitions and the specific project series—Art et Essai—are also mainstays of the program. Recent group and project exhibitions: *Identity*, *Always Modern*, *Aperto*, *Artists/Architects*, *Towards Decoration*, *Guillaume Bijl*, *Chen Zhen*, *Braca Lichtenberg-Ettinger*, *Yan Pei-Ming*, *Thomas Ruff*, *Sam Samore*, *Joep van Lieshout*, *Gillian Wearing*, *Sam Taylor-Wood*.

Group exhibitions based on a prevailing issue show real curatorial depth and should not be missed. For example, *South Side: Apology* (1998) presented artists from countries outside the main art centers—Spain, Portugal, Italy, France—to initiate a debate on European "reality," globalization and the idea of North and South as distinctive zones. The exhibition drew attention to a range of new work not currently receiving due notice even as it provoked thinking about the categorization of art and the functioning of the art-media world. The catalogue and a lecture series in turn debated these issues in depth.

Rather than a sterile white box, the atmosphere within IAC is somewhat hang-loose and very visitor-friendly. But this is not at the expense of the art. Indeed, the museum takes care to give each work its due space and proper lighting, and to make even the most difficult art accessible to the public. Receptivity is greatly enhanced by the free brochures accompanying each exhibition. Unlike many museum handouts and publications, these neither succumb to abstruse intellectualizing nor do they substitute simplistic biographical data and generic comments for serious commentaries. Instead, they contain helpful, relevant, comprehensible information on an artist's ideas and approach to a particular theme, medium, subject, etc.

The museum also coordinates its exhibitions with lively symposia, lectures, debates, artist talks and catalogues. Within this realm is the series of colloquia organized in collaboration with the University of Lyon 2. These are multidisciplinary investigations of issues related to contemporary art, life and culture. The museum's publication enterprise—Art Edition—has, moreover, released some first-rate monographs, books of art criticism, artist books and

artist writings. If you think this all sounds too good to be true, a visit will provide evidence.

4 | Lawrence Weiner

Marelles, 1990
place Mendès-France
métro: Gratte-Ciel

Located in the town center. From rue Anatole France turn onto rue Paul Verlaine; just ahead, before you get to the Hôtel des Postes (post office), turn left into allée André Dupuis, a pedestrian passageway; walk until the passageway opens onto a courtyard; look down. Because this work is on the ground, within an interior courtyard surrounded by buildings, you won't see it until you are literally on top of it.

For this work (*Hopscotch*), Weiner has drawn hopscotch configurations on the pavement of a courtyard in the midst of a housing complex. But he has set the words CIEL and TERRE (sky and earth) above and below the number blocks. In addition, the following phrases are written on the pavement: LA TERRE (ICI BAS), LES PIERRES (GRANDES), LE CIEL (BLEU), DE GROSSES PIERRES DEPLACEES ICI ET LA ENTRE LES CIEUX ET LA TERRE [the earth (low here), the (big) stones, the (blue) sky, of enormous stones moved here and there between the skies and the earth]. Weiner—who is one of the leading conceptual artists working with language—thus merges the stone-throwing feature of hopscotch with environmental references and the formation of word groups and poetic sentences.

5 | François Mitterand Maison du Livre de l'Image et du Son

architect: Mario BOTTA, 1984–88
240 cours Emile Zola, 69601
04-78-68-04-04 f: 04-78-68-30-39
métro: Flachet
Sept–June: Mon, 2–7; Tues–Fri, 11–7; Sat, 10–8. July–Aug: Tues–Fri, 2–7; closed Mon

President Mitterrand was a major force behind the creation of this innovative book and multimedia library with a curious name—Book, Image and Sound Center. He included it in his program of *grands projets* and viewed the selection of an internationally renowned architect as an essential ingredient—a manifestation of culture on the municipal level. Conceptualized as a new kind of resource center for the general public (children and adults alike), this lending library contains collections exemplifying a broad diversity of cultural expression: books, microfilms, magazines, videos (including fiction and documentary films), CDs (music of all styles), audiotapes, records and artwork.

From the exterior, seen from cours Emile Zola, the building is quite striking. An inset geometric cutout forms a black design along the center axis (the recessed walls are black-toned glass), splitting a flat-planed, cream-and-gray horizontally striped stone facade into symmetrical halves. The dramatic cutout not only exaggerates the entrance door but also reduces the monumentality of the building. You probably haven't even registered that the glass brick structures set slightly back on the sides are also part of Botta's library. Here again the double facade cuts the scale of the building's total mass, making it an integral part of the surroundings. And though side and middle sections each have a very different appearance, on closer examination you can see how they too complement one another. Most particularly, the black steel beams and narrow, horizontal windows that demarcate a geometric pattern on the planar surfaces of the sides echo the prominent features of the stone facade. In contrast to the planarity of the

front, the back facade has a mammoth semicylindrical form projecting far beyond the glass brick walls, which again appear on the sides. As on the street facade, the center section is sheathed with the two-toned stone layered in stripes, but here the surface is punctuated by rows of loophole windows (small, recessed openings reminiscent of those in the fortification walls of castles). A parking area extends behind the building.

From the exterior, it is impossible to tell that the interior centers on a spectacular atrium with concentric circles rising up to a spare glass dome. The circles are "floating" concrete walls painted white with cutout openings behind which are windows and library stacks. All seven levels are bathed with an amazing amount of soft luminescence. In addition to the atrium light, the rear cylinder, which houses visitor consultation and reading areas, is lit from above by a skylight and from the sides by the small loophole windows. On the basement level, the cylinder shaft becomes the core of a display section for the *artothèque* (artwork library). Quite creatively, Botta has made this zone totally open, enticing and directly accessible from the main floor. The library's art collection includes original works of contemporary art, mainly prints and photographs, available for study and loan to patrons. Often they are the source of exhibitions in the library's two galleries, located on either side of the front door.

6 | Étienne Bossut

Deux fois un abri jaune
intersection of rue Greuze and rue Francis de Pressensé
métro: Flachet

From the library continue down cours Emile Zola and turn left at the third street, rue Greuze.

Bossut, Deux fois un abri jaune

A *Yellow Shelter Twice* is a surreal, humorous and socially poignant public sculpture. Set in the middle of a traffic circle, it undoubtedly brings cars to a halt (at least on the first go-round). The object consists of two pitched-roof, metal sheds set atop one another, the top one upside down, balancing its weight on its pointed edge. The sheds are, or have the semblance of, massproduced box dwellings, not unlike the housing type in the surrounding neighborhood. With their fresh coat of light yellow paint and stacked arrangement, Bossut's shelters are also suggestive of the surface cleanup and crowded conditions within urban areas designated as redevelopment districts.

7 | Patrick Raynaud

Sculpture giratoire, 1985
intersection of rue Louise Michel, rue Prudon, rue 8 mai 1945 and rue Greuze
métro: Flachet

Located three blocks from the Bossut sculpture on rue Greuze.

Like the Bossut project, Raynaud's *Traffic Circle Sculpture* is a wonderfully witty and ironic image to encounter at a traffic circle. It is its own circle of traffic signs—a composite of rows of arrows in various colors and designs, names of cities and reflector markers. Aside from being a clever commentary on the absurd concatenation of traffic signs that often exists at intersections, it calls to mind the seemingly ubiquitous habit, practiced by street engineers in all countries, of repeating the same sign ad infinitum and creating numerous variants of the same directive.

Vaulx-en-Velin

A suburb bordering Lyon and Villeurbanne on the northeast.

Ecole d'Architecture

architects: Françoise JOURDA and
Gilles PERRAUDIN, 1982–88
3 rue Maurice Audan
métro: Bonnevay, then bus 56,
direction Vaulx-en-Velin, exit
Hôtel de Ville

From the bus stop, walk across the plaza, then along the path between the Planetarium and Palais des Sports to rue Maurice Audan (5 min).

Jourda and Perraudin, an esteemed husband-and-wife team based in Lyon, designed this refreshing, distinctive building as the School of Architecture. Visually appealing and technologically inventive, it is also amazingly in tune with the needs and activities of those who use and work in its spaces. There are two separate but connected buildings: one, a long structure containing teaching facilities; the other, a half-cylinder structure for administration and faculty offices. A wide "street" with a glass-and-cable roof runs down the center of the teaching realm and extends across into the office area, where it spreads out, becoming an atrium surrounded by balconies and covered by a windowed half-dome. The street clearly has a dual role as a place for communication and a passageway for circulation.

The long wing of the school has two floors each with a different design and function. The ground floor, constructed of concrete and defined by heavy arches and vaulted ceilings, contains classrooms, seminar rooms and a library. In contrast, the upper floor, which exudes lightness from its glass, steel and wood frame, houses the studios. A similar spatial-functional division shapes the four levels of the round building. The ground floor is for information and records, the next floor has support staff offices, above this are the offices of faculty and administrators, and on top are meeting rooms and terraces. The design is simple, refined and classical with a repetition of forms and modifications allied to the hierarchy of spaces.

In both buildings, the architects' sensitivity to natural light is apparent. Though the front facade of the administrative structure is a flat plane with thin slit windows, the interior is illuminated from above and all around the curving back wall. For the classroom building, where it was especially important to control light shining into the design studios through the window walls, a sun awning was added. Made of raw fabric, it extends from the roof and attaches like a tent to poles and cables.

Grenoble

This city not only looks like a travel poster with its alpine surroundings and the charm of its old village center (winding, narrow streets, parks, plazas, medieval and 17th-century architecture), but it is also a lively university town with a significant arts scene. Train from Lyon, 1 1/4 hr; TGV from Paris (Gare de Lyon), 3 hr.

Alexander Calder

Untitled
place de la Gare

Calder's stabiles and stabile-mobile sculptures have become the classic public artwork of the 20th century. In Grenoble, the placement of a black steel stabile in front of the train station provides an upbeat welcome to the city.

Le Magasin, Centre National d'Art Contemporain

Site Bouchayer-Viallet, 155 cours
Berriat, 38028
04-76-21-95-84 f: 04-76-21-24-22
Tues–Sun, 12–7; closed Mon
admission: 15/10F
tram: direction Fontaine-La Poya,
exit Berriat

Located at the western edge of the city, in an industrial area that's an easy 15-min walk from the train station. Follow the tram along cours Berriat; just before it ends, turn left into the gated, factory-warehouse complex at 155.

Le Magasin is one of the premier exhibition spaces focused on international contemporary art in France, Europe or, for that matter, anywhere. You will probably be dumbfounded when you first enter the building and confront the incredible, open, vast, luminous interior. The structure was actually built by Gustave Eiffel for the Universal Exhibition of 1900 and then moved to Grenoble for use as a warehouse. (The odd name "Magasin" belonged to the warehouse, but the art center's founding director kept it because it also refers to Magazin—The Store, a very avant-garde exhibition organized by Vladimir Tatlin in Moscow, 1916.) Still conspicuous today is the original unencumbered,

undivided design of the space and the glass-paned roof high overhead. Even the metal and glass cubes that house offices, a bookstore and a café near the entrance barely intrude on the grand space. And without altering the structure, Le Magasin created a grand "street" (the well-known rue) down the center of the building and added an auditorium in the rear, galleries to the left and a project room to the right.

The street aims to be a passageway and social space, symbolic of the city. An artist or architect is given creative rights to the zone every four months, thus having the opportunity to produce an on-site installation, construction or exhibition there. Sometimes these develop into collaborative team efforts. The galleries are generally used for monographic, retrospective or thematic exhibitions. The project room showcases the work of a young artist or an artist who has had little or no exposure in Europe or France. And the café is an installation site where artistic transformation coincides with functional activities.

Renowned for its innovative, unconventional exhibitions, Le Magasin gives both curators and artists the freedom to take risks. Regardless of when you visit, you will see a broad spectrum of venturesome projects and compelling, provocative art. The range typically encompasses a variety of media, differing conceptual and image orientations, new styles and diverse approaches to subject matter. Recent exhibitions: Strategies of Collaboration, The City in Projects, Tell Me a Story, Really—Feminism and Art, Dramatically Different, Auto Reverse 2, Stories in Forms, Moment Ginza (Dominique Gonzalez-Foerster), Alighiero e Boetti, Maurizio Cattelan, Diller & Scofidio, Willie Doherty, Kcho, Anne Lacaton & Jean-Philippe Vassal, Mariko Mori, Allen Ruppersberg, Sarkis, Soo-Ja Kim, Joep van Lieshout, Nari Ward.

Images, Objets, Scène exhibition (Le Magasin)

Of special note are exhibitions integrating vanguard ideas and practices of art and architecture. Significantly, Le Magasin does not treat art and architecture as separate entities, nor is architecture merely allotted a token presence in the total program. Indeed, a perspective that views art in the context of culture and society, especially as it addresses the problematics of art and the city has become a priority. This is clearly evinced in projects situated in the city proper. Created in or on buildings and within the streets and neighborhoods of the urban landscape, these artworks aim to interface closely with the daily life of the city and its citizens.

Most exhibitions are accompanied by catalogues as well as helpful free brochures giving basic information on particular projects and artists. (These usually have dual French and English texts.) In-house publications as well as an excellent selection of books on contemporary art and architecture, theory, criticism, cultural studies and other related topics are available in the bookstore. Be sure to look at the inventory of artists' books.

The center runs a very popular public series every Tuesday evening. The format varies (lecture, discussion, debate, performance, video) as do the guests (artists, architects, poets, filmmakers, historians, critics, curators), but the aim remains constant: to promote and increase receptivity to contemporary art. Equally ambitious and esteemed are the international colloquia concerning issues related to contemporary creation. Since 1987 Le Magasin has also been operating its own school—Ecole du Magasin. This, too, is dedicated to contemporary art. It provides six to ten young Europeans with the unique opportunity of studying, working directly with artists and receiving professional training and hands-on experience in the development of exhibitions.

Parc Albert Michallon and Esplanade François Mitterrand

This quiet, unpretentious landscape extending back from the city museum is implanted with a reputable (albeit uninspired) array of modern sculpture. Objects from the postwar era and beyond exemplify a basically abstract orientation with a reductivist or essentialist sensibility. They represent a span of established artists from Europe and America: Alexander Calder, Anthony Caro, Eduardo Chillida, Mark Di Suvero, Eugène Dodeigne, Gottfried Honneger, Richard Nonas, Marta Pan, George Rickey, Bernar Venet, Ossip Zadkine. A walk along the pathways is a delightful, relaxing way to enjoy some of Grenoble's natural beauty if you don't have the inkling, clothing or physical stamina to hike in the mountainous terrain.

Musée de Grenoble

architects: Olivier and Antoine FELIX-FAURE, Philippe MACARY
5 place de Lavalette, 38010
04-76-63-44-44 f: 04-76-63-44-10
Mon, Thurs–Sun, 11–7; Wed, 11–10; closed Tues
admission: 25/15F

With the opening of its new building in 1994, the Grenoble Museum greatly expanded its exhibition space. (The encyclopedic collection spans many cultures from antiquity to the present.) It now has an extensive display area for 20th-century art, though contemporary work unfortunately doesn't have permanent gallery space. (The collection galleries pretty much end with a very limited selection of exemplary objects from the 1970s–80s.) This is particularly

regrettable since the collection includes many exceptional and unusual examples of recent (1990s) international trends. Every so often, the museum installs collection objects from recent years in the special exhibition space, and from time to time there are special exhibitions of contemporary art.

For the architecturally minded, the building is worth a visit. A grand hall, which runs the length of one main section of the museum, is flanked by collection and temporary exhibition galleries. Unadorned, well-proportioned and illuminated by natural light from above, they give no competition to the art. A second section, abutting the first and extending back to a curved outer wall, contains 29 galleries of 20th-century art. On the left end of this section, a bridge leads to a medieval tower—Tour de l'Isle (Island Tower)—housing the museum's drawing collection. On the right end, a ramp goes down to two lower levels that fan out providing views of the park and ultimately opening onto a garden. The architecture judiciously accommodates the lay of the land, especially where it integrates the ancient city wall and a basin of the Isère river into its structure.

Although there is a large 20th-century collection, the pre–World War II material is quite uneven and lackluster. Some superb paintings by Matisse and the fauvists, and a few important surrealist compositions are highlights, but most modern movements are represented by undistinguished works by secondary followers. Similar to many European museums, Grenoble puts great emphasis (overemphasis) on geometric abstraction—art inspired by Mondrian, van Doesburg, Malevich and the Russian constructivists but missing their skillful balance and inventive excellence.

The 1950s–70s focus is almost exclusively on abstraction—a rather conservative, formalist approach to the era. But the quality and character of the art from this era onward is outstanding. The installation of French postwar paintings, coordinated with some contemporaneous European and American art, presents strong work by Olivier Debré, Nicolas de Staël, Sam Francis, Hans Hartung, Morris Louis, Joan Mitchell, Louise Nevelson, Maria-Elena Vieira da Silva, Pierre Soulages, Antoni Tàpies. Following this are galleries displaying American art with a minimalist propensity by Carl Andre, Donald Judd, Ellsworth Kelly, Sol Lewitt, Robert Mangold, Brice Marden, Kenneth Noland, David Rabinowitch and Frank Stella. Only in the last galleries does the selection expand to include some non-abstract work. Represented are first-rate creations by Pierrette Bloch, Christian Boltanski, Christian Eckart, Jochen Gerz and Annette Messager.

If you want to buy some basic books on contemporary art and artists, check out the museum bookstore. A café-restaurant is also located off the entrance lobby.

Saint-Etienne

Train from Lyon, 45 min.

Musée d'Art Moderne de Saint-Etienne

🏛 | La Terrasse, 42000
04-77-79-52-52 f: 04-77-79-52-50
daily, 10–6
admission: 28/23F
tram 4, direction Hôpital Nord, exit place Dorian; then bus 10, exit Tardy/La Cotonne.

Located on the outskirts of the city within a park area.

Outside of Paris, this museum has one of the most comprehensive collections of modern art in France. The building, inaugurated in 1987, is a big but unim-posing, horizontal structure faced with a grid of black square tiles. It contains galleries for both temporary exhibitions and the permanent collection, a bookshop, restaurant and excellent art library (open to the public). The interior design is extremely well suited to the collection and displays of contemporary art. Although ventilation and lighting systems are exposed (following the industrialist proclivity of much late-20th-century architecture), the ambience is refined, not harsh or brutalist. Technologically controlled lighting (natural and artificial), varying ceiling heights and diverse gallery dimensions soften the space and greatly enhance the art-viewing experience. Often the museum also makes use of the broad plaza in front of the building and the expansive field of lawns beyond to display outdoor sculpture.

Some temporary exhibitions highlight contemporary art, but the strength of Saint-Etienne is not its attentiveness to the latest, most vanguard art. In terms of the post-1945 period, the museum's reputation lies with its collection. Indeed, this is one of the few museums in France where you can see a reasonable selection of work by artists not in the Franco-American axis. Considering all the critically important developments that have taken place during the past decades in Germany, Italy and Britain, to name just a few countries, and given France's close location to these hubs of activity, the typical representation of contemporary art in French museums is curiously skewed. To its credit, Saint-Etienne offers a broader view.

Even before you enter the galleries, the lobby acclimates you with the white tile wall construction, *Espace zéro* (1987), by France's esteemed minimal-conceptual artist, Jean-Pierre Raynaud. Within the galleries, the arrangement is roughly chronological with the 1950s represented by gestural and improvisational abstractions by Jean-Michel Atlan, Roger Bissière, Jean Fautrier, Simon Hantaï, Hans Hartung, Alfred Manessier, Pierre Soulages, Bram van Velde and sculptures by Alexander Calder, Robert Jacobsen and Germaine Richier. There is also a Dubuffet room with a range of objects spanning several decades of his career.

From this rather tepid, insular beginning, you move into galleries chock-full of superb art exemplifying major modes of vanguard creativity from the 1960s and 1970s. Included are pop, minimalist and conceptual works by Americans— Carl Andre, John Baldessari, Jim Dine, Dan Flavin, Donald Judd, Ellsworth Kelly, Joseph Kosuth, Sol LeWitt, Roy Lichtenstein, Morris Louis, Kenneth Noland, Claes Oldenburg and Coosje van Bruggen, Frank Stella, Andy Warhol, Tom Wesselmann. Paralleling this are French works by artists associated with Nouveau Réalisme—Arman, César, Raymond Hains, Yves Klein, Martial Raysse, Daniel Spoerri, Jacques de la Villeglé; figurative paintings by Valerio Adami, Bernard Rancillac, Jacques Monory; and artists embracing a conceptual or antiformalist orientation—Vincent Bioulès, Daniel Buren, Louis Cane, Marc Devade, Noël Dolla, Toni Grand, Olivier Mosset, Bernard Pagès, Patrick Saytour, Niele Toroni, Claude Viallat.

Also in the collection are Fluxus objects by Ben, George Brecht, Erik Dietman, Robert Filliou, Wolf Vostell; sculptures from the Italian Arte Povera movement by Luciano Fabro, Mario Merz, Giuseppe Penone, Gilberto Zorio; and German art from the 1980s by Bernd and Hilla Becher, Georg Baselitz, Lüdger Gerdes, Jochen Gerz, Harold Klingelhöller, Markus Lüpertz, A. R. Penck, Sigmar Polke, Gerhard Richter, Thomas Schütte. The 1980s are also represented by Art and Language, Christian Boltanski, Victor Burgin, Tony Cragg, Helmut Federle, On Kawara, Bertrand Lavier, Julian Schnabel and Bernar Venet. With regard to the 1990s and very recent art, the museum rotates the selection every six months.

Not only does the Saint-Etienne contemporary collection have considerable breadth, but individual works are, on the whole, distinctive examples of artists and artistic directions. For example, Hygiène de la vision (portrait-double), by Raysse, takes a witty, satirical view of 1960s values, pop culture and women. A monumental, multipartite work by the Oldenburgs, From the Entropic Library (1989), also expresses clever humor by depicting the titular image in terms of a jumble of oversized architectural fragments and building materials stacked on the floor between bookends. And the construction, Cabane (Cabana), by Buren (1991), is an installation sculpture playing with positive and negative space, geometric and repetitive design in a mind-boggling way.

Saint-Etienne has an extensive photography collection with its own gallery, so be sure to save time for this. It also has a unique design collection, which is given display space for a two-month period each year. Given that the museum only began enriching its collection in 1947, its early-20th-century holdings are uneven and hardly comprehensive. Do go through the galleries, however, for you'll see some stellar works (by Léger, Kupka, Severini, etc.) and a fine ensemble of dada and surrealist objects.

Unfortunately, there is no signage or text information about objects or artists in the collection, so you're totally on your own. The museum does publish excellent, scholarly catalogues (in French only), especially for the renowned, historical exhibitions they organize. Recent exhibitions: Robert Adams, Erik Dietman, Jochen Gerz, Bernar Venet, The Statue in the 20th Century—Rodin to Baselitz.

Thiers

This medieval mining city, known as the capital of French cutlery and knifemaking for the past five centuries, lies between Lyon and Clermont-Ferrand. Thiers is located within a national park and the landscape in and around the town is breathtaking. A train or car ride here will take you through a mountainous landscape with deep gorges, rocky peaks and rich forests. The ride itself is worth the trip. Train from Lyon, 2 1/2 hr; from Clermont-Ferrand, 1/2 hr; from Paris (Gare de Lyon) via Vichy, 3 1/2 hr.

Creux de l'Enfer, Centre d'Art Contemporain

vallée des Usines, 63300
04-73-80-26-56 f: 04-73-80-28-08
Mon, Wed–Fri, 10–12 and 2–6;
Sat–Sun, 2–7; closed Tues
admission: free

A bus goes from the train station to the art center, but it doesn't run on Sundays. Be advised that the walk is up and across very steep terrain, but it's quite do-able.

Creux de l'Enfer takes the prize for having the most extraordinary site and exhibition space. The center clings to the side of a high cliff with river rapids and a waterfall literally running through and alongside the building. The structure, now in the midst of an industrial wasteland, was formerly a cutler's forge named Creux de l'Enfer (Pits of Hell), though originally the setting was known as Passage des Fées (Fairies' Passage).

Rather than erase the old workshop environment, the renovation kept much of it intact. And rather than ignore legends relating to its history and location, the center has embraced them. Indeed, the city of Thiers itself is passionate about its identity with knifemaking and the metal industry. In its ongoing desire to convey the potential of metal, it helped organize an International Metal Sculpture Symposium in 1985. The aim was to bring art and industry, artist and artisan together. The conference was a very hands-on gathering, ultimately producing sculptures designed expressly for the immediate environment in collaboration with local metalworkers (see below). These activities in Thiers also resulted in the creation of the Creux de l'Enfer art center.

As you will discover, the drama of the surroundings permeates the interior of the center. Its space, an eccentric conglomerate of galleries, descends four levels, and the sound of water is constant. One of the exhibition areas is actually a cave. Its dripping rock surfaces are still manifest, but now it has luminous white walls. (Have no fear, you'll be given a slicker and hat at the reception desk if needed.) Since its inauguration, the center has invited artists to reside in its studio-apartment

Alain Séchas, *Professor Suicide* exhibition, 1995 (Creux de l'Enfer)

and create a work on-site with the technical assistance of industries and factories in Thiers. Most of the productions—sculptures, installations and new technology projects—have been imaginative, even risky responses to the challenge of the site. Complementing the works realized by resident artists are exhibitions. The list of artists featured—a truly international mix of young, mid-career and well-established talents—is impressive. It includes Miroslaw Balka, Elisabeth Ballet, Per Barclay, Cécile Bart, Marie-José Burki, Ernst Caramelle, Mélanie Counsell, Fischli-Weiss, Gary Hill, Fabrice Hybert, Cildo Meireles, Thom Merrick, Florence Paradeis, Laurent Pariente, Michelangelo Pistoletto, Eric Portevin, Doris Salcedo, Eric Samakh, Alain Séchas, Roman Signer, Pierrick Sorin, Sam Taylor-Wood, Diana Thater, Luc Tuymans, Patrick van Caeckenbergh.

George Trakas

Pont de l'épée, 1988
vallée des Usines

Below the mundane footbridge crossing the gorge to Creux d'Enfer, the Canadian sculptor George Trakas constructed a second footbridge, this one of shiny stainless steel and an unusual curved shape. Positioned right in front of the waterfall, and reached by stairs and walkways built along the side walls of the gorge and building, *Bridge of the Sword*, offers a phenomenal experience of the natural setting. This project and those Skoda, Raynaud and Oppenheim resulted from the metal symposium of 1985.

Vladimir Skoda

Untitled, 1985
rue de la Coutellerie

The artist placed these five faceted steel spheres, inscribed with stars, at the top of one of Thiers's steepest streets to further the image of a meeting between heaven and earth.

Patrick Raynaud

Rivière sans retour, 1985
Pont du Moutiers

River of No Return has as its focus a geometrically shaped, generic boat of Cor-ten steel. It appears marooned on the riverbank. Three identical figures—simple cutout images with their arms raised—stand on a nearby bridge facing the boat. They, like the boat, epitomize anonymity and are frozen in time.

Dennis Oppenheim

Untitled, 1985
carrefour Chambon

Traffic circle about 1 mi (2km) outside Thiers on route N89.

This tall steel tower surrounded by large hoops swirling up from the ground, has a decidedly surreal appearance. The circles are like orbits energizing the surrounding space and the structure recalls prison watchtowers, except that it is brightly colored. Typically, Oppenheim has created an imaginary structure, seemingly functional but actually pure futuristic fantasy.

Dijon–Strasbourg

Dijon

This prosperous city with an illustrious past and rich artistic legacy is a favorite site for connoisseurs of medieval and Renaissance architecture, wine and food. Despite the tourist crowds (especially strong in summer), it's an upbeat, friendly city, quite easy and enjoyable to visit. TGV from Paris (Gare de Lyon), 1 3/4 hr; train from Lyon, 1 3/4 hr.

Le Consortium, Centre d'Art Contemporain

16 rue Quentin, 21000
03-80-30-75-23 f: 03-80-30-59-74
Tues–Sat, 2–6; closed Mon
admission: free

Located on a street bordering the main market plaza (Les Halles). Enter at #16 and walk to the back of the small courtyard. The mundane shop facade without any grand signage is the place.

This is one of the most adventurous, energetic, productive contemporary art centers worldwide. Le Consortium doesn't just talk a good line about supporting young artists, innovative ventures and contemporary art; it continuously takes action and follows through on ideas. Its activities, in number, scope and character, are extraordinary. For a modestly sized institution with a bare-bones staff, it does far more (and far better) than mega-institutions with enormous budgets. The ambience of risk-taking and being really involved with art and artists—not politics, patrons, publicity or ego trips—somehow permeates throughout.

The exhibition site at rue Quentin has six fairly sizeable, skylit galleries amenable to most all types of contemporary art. It's not at all a chic environment, just empty space, looking like it's been repainted and reconstructed many times, and a no-frills operation. Le Consortium also runs a second space, L'Usine (see below). Its program is internationally oriented and embraces both young and midcareer artists. The center has, moreover, repeatedly organized exhibitions that raise significant questions about the nature and direction of contemporary currents. Recent exhibitions: *Photo-Collages*, *Moral Maze*, *The Moral Labyrinth*, *Pieces on the Ground*, *Angela Bulloch*, *Daniel Buren*, *Baltasar Burkhard*, *Maurizio Cattelan*, *Marc*

Camille Chaimowicz, *Plamen Dejanov*, *Dan Flavin*, *Sylvie Fleury*, *Liam Gillick*, *Peter Halley*, *Hans Hartung*, *Svetlana Heger*, *Pierre Huyghe*, *Sarah Jones*, *Robert Mangold*, *Sarah Morris*, *Philippe Parreno*, *Permanent Food*, *Sophie Ristelhueber*, *Rikrit Tiravanija*, *Daan van Golden*, *Rémy Zaugg*.

A unique aspect of the center is the creative relationship it has established between exhibitions and collection building within the community and for the art center. According to the setup, works in exhibitions are for sale and profits are used exclusively to buy art. Thus, the center serves as an incredible resource and source for patrons interested in developing collections of museum-quality art. In addition, the center is in a prime position to make its own purchases. Over the years, it has acquired some 90 major works of art. The recent exhibition of the Consortium collection in Paris at the Centre Pompidou (1998) was a fitting recognition of its high caliber.

The center also has an ambitious publishing operation, Les Presses du Réel. Thus far, it has released comprehensive books of writings by Vito Acconci, Paul-Armand Gette, Dan Graham, On Kawara, Richard Nonas, Gerhard Richter and Rémy Zaugg, as well as short texts on or by other artists. In addition, it publishes the magazines *Documents sur l'art* and *Prime Time* (a video magazine) and produces television shows.

It takes so little time to get to Dijon from Paris, there's no excuse not to hop on the train, if only for a day trip, to see what passion for art looks like without all the splash and flash accouterments.

L'Usine

37 rue de Longvic, 21000
03-80-68-45-55 f: 03-80-68-45-57
Tues–Sat, 2–6; closed Mon
admission: free

Rue de Longvic runs alongside cours

Général de Gaulle, a wide, tree-lined boulevard off the monumental place du Président Wilson. It's a pleasant 15-min walk from the center city. Alternatively, take bus 9 or 2, direction Campus-Cimitière, exit Prison; walk down rue d'Auxonne to rue Docteur Lavalle; turn right and then right again onto rue de Longvic. After you enter the courtyard–parking lot behind the street-side fence, head to the right toward the concrete stairs leading to a "sunroom." This is the humble, unmarked entrance into L'Usine.

In 1991 the Consortium added this supplementary exhibition space—The Factory—which occupies the ground floor of an old industrial building, still in a very worn, unrenovated state. The main gallery is a large, spare room—ideal for sculpture, installation or on-site projects—and there are several side galleries, which provide more intimate environments. Artists who have shown here include Vito Acconci, Cécile Bart, Angela Bullock, Chris Burden, Daniel Buren, Michael Corris, Didier Dessus, Jessica Diamond, Peter Downsbrough, Bruno Girard, Duane Hansen, Donald Judd, On Kawara, Bertrand Lavier, Bernd Lohaus, Miltos Manetas, Ming, François Morellet, Olivier Mosset, Steven Parrino, Udo Rondinone, Frank Stella, Beat Streuli, Elise Tak, Lily van der Stokker, Gillian Wearing.

On the upper floor of L'Usine, students from the Ecole Nationale des Beaux-Arts have studios, and a vast space on the lower level is regularly the site of performance, film, video, dance, music and theater events.

FRAC Bourgogne

49 rue de Longvic, 21000
03-80-67-18-18 f: 03-80-66-33-29
Mon–Sat, 2–6:30
admission: free

Located down the street from L'Usine, with its entrance inside the courtyard at #49.

In its two sizeable galleries in a renovated factory, this FRAC presents three or four exhibitions each year. These are solo shows or group presentations featuring art from the collection. Exhibitions have several realms of concentrations: geometric abstraction and constructivist art; minimalist and conceptual art; and work by young artists concerned with the nature and function of art. There are some excellent objects in the collection so don't dismiss a visit to a collection exhibition for something sounding more jazzy. Recent exhibitions: *Sylvia Bossu*, *Marc Camille Chaimowicz*, *Simone Decker*, *Philippe de Gobert*, *Jean Dupuy*, *Daniel Firman*, *Marcia Christiane Geoffroy*, *Philippe Ramette*, *Adrian Schiess*, *Günter Umberg*.

Université de Bourgogne

boulevard Petitjean and boulevard Gabriel, 21004
bus 9, exit Université, esplanade Erasmus

The university opened at this campus site on the outskirts of the city in 1957. At the same time, it changed from the University of Dijon to the University of Bourgogne—from a city to a regional institution—and expanded its programs to meet the needs of the 21st century. Naturally, new buildings were necessary and this meant that the 1%-for-art provision could also be activated. For the most part, the selection is nonoffensive, formalist object-type sculpture. It's not groundbreaking art but the works are engaging and add an upbeat tone to the environment. Objects are placed around the campus grounds and a few are located inside buildings. They include:

Didier VERMEIREN, *Sculpture*, 1982. Set in the main lobby of Maison de l'Université, the administration building located on the right side of the front end of the esplanade. With its columnar form isolated in the middle of the atrium, the elegant marble pedestal becomes a sculpture in its own right. It is no longer a subsidiary thing serving to elevate a work of art. It is now, itself, an autonomous object defined by its own surface, form, material and proportions. Vermeiren exaggerates its new role and significance as "sculpture" by placing one pedestal upon another. Borrowing an image-concept from Brancusi (the *Endless Column* especially comes to mind), he completely merges the categories of sculpture and pedestal, deflating distinctions between them.

Gottfried HONNEGER, *Hommage à Jacques Monod*, 1974. This work greets

Vermeiren, *Sculpture*

you as you walk down the main lawn (esplanade Erasmus) of the campus. The form of this monumental, geometric steel sculpture is similar to the minimalist work of Tony Smith. But Honneger, a leading Swiss artist, derived the image using ideas developed by the biochemist Monod in his treatise, *Chance and Necessity*. A first impression yields an image of stability and simplicity. But as you move around the structure, and as light conditions change, your perception of its volumes, planes and composition continually shifts.

Karel APPEL, *Anti-Robot*, 1976. Located toward the back of the esplanade Eramus. Appel is best known for his dynamic paintings with aggressive, destructive brushstrokes and bright colors. Here he adapts his approach from painting to sculpture, similarly rebelling against refined, aestheticized imagery. His big, clownish, pathetic figure, composed of red, yellow, blue and black planes, is the antithesis of a well-engineered, controlled automaton. Its animated presence is buoyant, a nice complement to the Honneger and well suited for this prominent location.

Julije KNIFER, *Méandre*, 1990. From the Appel, walk back to the center of the esplanade. At the corner of the main cross street, avenue Alain Savary, is the Bibliothèque Universitaire Droit-Lettres (University Library for Law and Humanities). Just inside the entrance to the right is the catalogue room (also called the grand hall). Knifer's multipartite painting of flat, white rectangular planes is located here. He radically reduced the work so it contains only the most basic pictorial elements, exactingly sized to conform with the room's architecture. His intention was to invent nothing. Instead, he sought to produce a pure presence that was simultaneously formal and existential.

Jean GORIN, *Construction plastique verticale, no. 101*, 1968/83. From the library, turn right onto avenue Alain Savary. This aluminum-and-steel sculpture is just ahead on the left side in front of the Centre Régional de Documentation Pédagogique (CRDP). Inspired by Mondrian and neo-plasticist principles, Gorin created "constructions in space" using primary colors, white and black in planes of different dimensions set in horizontal or vertical orientations. He gave the structure an architectonic and space-time character by incorporating voids into the mass and planar rhythms, and by developing different compositions on all sides.

Yaacov AGAM, *Tente*, 1974. From the Gorin sculpture, continue down avenue Alain Savary until you come to the U-shaped courtyard of the large Faculté de Sciences Mirande building on the left. Situated here is a kinetic sculpture by Agam, composed of a series of upside-down V shapes. The upright, acute-angled forms, made from polished tubular steel, sway back and forth in the wind. When pushed, their animate character reverberates all the more strongly. This work exemplifies the artist's aim to enliven the most basic elements of geometric abstraction.

ARMAN, *Divionis mechanica fossila Arman*, 1976. From the Agam, cross avenue Alain Savary and wind your way ahead through the university to boulevard Petitjean, a wide street on the lower edge of the campus. You will have arrived when you see a square concrete block, over 16 ft high. Adhering to his technique of accumulation, Arman has gathered a collection of rusted scrap-metal disk and wheel elements used in construction and embedded them into the surface of the block. The mundane waste material has a fossilized appearance. Seeing it displayed in multiple variants and excessive quantity is humorous, though laughter becomes tinged with a discomforting realization about the production and behavioral nature of modern civilization.

Antipodes, 1991–92

 architects: Jacques HERZOG and Pierre de MEURON with Rémy ZAUGG
avenue du XXIème siècle, University of Bourgogne

From the Arman sculpture, walk back toward avenue Alain Savary; turn right, look for signs on the right side for Antipodes.

Herzog and de Meuron are the hot team of Swiss architects who are developing the new Tate Gallery of Contemporary Art in London. (They were also one of the three finalists in the competition for the Museum of Modern Art's expansion project in New York.) The buildings in this complex of student dorms are all four stories high with their long, planar facades articulated by two-toned concrete and single-pane horizontal windows. Five of the units are aligned, not in a straight row, but in a staggered layout. The end units are double width with a central corridor extending on each level to an open walkway connected to the adjacent unit. The walkways become covered corridors running along the exterior of the three center units—alternatively set in front, in back and in front of the respective buildings. Thus, the corridor-walkway is a continuous street joining all five units. Inside interpenetrates with outside.

Horizontal stripes formed by the darker tone of concrete on the exterior of the units further emphasize continuity; they form an unbroken line with the concrete bands between each level of the corridor-walkway. Though the design breaks loose from some of the relentless repetition and sameness so pronounced in modern architecture, the use of harsh concrete and dark wood paneling along the corridor-walkways retains the bleak coldness and anonymity of minimalism.

Chagny

This charming small village with inter-lacing streets, little shops and a popula-tion of 6,000 is located in the midst of Burgundy wine country just south of Dijon. It enjoys a strong reputation among gourmets who come specifically to dine at the highly rated restaurant, Jacques Lameloise. The town now has the added renown (if only among the cognoscenti) of having two public art works by internationally celebrated artists. Train from Dijon, 35 min.

Richard Serra

Octagon for Saint-Eloi, 1991
place de l'Eglise Saint-Martin

This relatively small (6 1/2 ft high and nearly 8 ft wide), solid mass (57 tons) of forged steel sits in the midst of a mod-est paved plaza (used as a parking lot) in front of an old village church. The church, situated directly on the plaza, is a patchwork structure begun in the 11th century. It has a perfectly axial facade of spare Romanesque design: a flat stone wall, porch overhang with a pitched roof, centered arch window on the upper level, slanted side roofs and a gabled center section ending in a trian-gle. The facade is thus a geometric form dominated by clearly defined oblique angles and an exacting symmetry. In addition to the church, the plaza is bor-dered by two-story houses, a blind facade and a wall covered by vegeta-tion. It is essentially a closed space, accessible by two narrow streets enter-ing on angles.

Made from industrial material left in a raw, unrefined state, Serra's *Octagon* has a decidedly urban appearance. Defying traditional norms of beauty and fine art, it is here also disjunctive with the small-town rural ambience. As with most minimalist sculpture, it is a literal object—an utterly reduced, essential form bearing no referential or symbolic meaning. A connection can be made, however, to Saint-Eloi, patron of metal forgers to whom the work is dedicated. Indeed, Serra was greatly assisted in the difficult and potentially dangerous pro-duction of the sculpture by a team of skilled forgers at Creusot-Loire Industrie in nearby Le Creusot. A second connec-tion exists between the shape Serra chose and the octagonal form often found in the bases of Romanesque church columns, baptistries and lanterns.

A dominant characteristic of Serra's art is the relationship between the sculpture and the space in which it is situated. In this case, *Octagon* is not in the center of the plaza but exactingly aligned with the front door of the church at a distance equal to that from the door to the altar within the church's interior. Though you may not realize the measured positioning of the object, its noncentralized placement within the plaza is apparent. The form-space equi-librium experienced in Serra's precari-ously balanced steel plates underlies this work as well. Here, however, ten-sion results from the disproportionately small scale and angled shape of the closed, solid sculpture in the open space of the Chagny plaza with its geometri-cally defined boundary elements. *Octagon* is not huge in size, yet it is monumental because of its mass and location. Moreover, it is a forceful, provocative, even discordant presence in the plaza.

Chagny is a very traditional, close-knit community with little interest in art—especially not contemporary art. Not surprisingly, most of the townspeo-ple vehemently opposed the Serra and are still angry about the whole deal. It didn't help matters any that an old stone calvary was moved from its hal-lowed place in the middle of the plaza to a peripheral wall to clear the site for the new sculpture. Why then is this sculpture here? Mainly, it was thanks to the energetic efforts of Galerie Pietro Sparta—a local gallery, amazingly well connected to the international art scene and top echelon in the Ministry of Culture. (The state commissioned the sculpture and is its official owner.) On the one hand, the gallery established the link to Paris and Serra, and on the other hand, it was seminal in getting the town council to back the project. The council viewed the presence of a Serra as a boon to its image, hence good for tourism and the local economy.

Lawrence Weiner

Untitled, 1994
Port du Canal

This public artwork is situated on the edge of a small port serving a canal that runs through the center of France. Chagny's residents go fishing here, and it is an appealing docking place for boats—be they fancy yachts, old row-boats or small barges. At first, Weiner's sculpture appears like a wall used for the posting of official signage. It is a tall concrete block, one side facing the port and the other turned toward the canal and an overpass road. On second glance, the strange design of the stain-less-steel inlays on the facades of the block suggests this is not at all like com-monplace signage. This view is con-firmed when you get up close and read what is written on the metal surfaces.

One plate has a long arrow extend-ing from its bottom corner to the top of the concrete block. Within the plate is a blank cutout strip below which are the phrases: EXTRAITS DE L'EAU, TRANS-PORTE VERS LES ETOILES (extracts of water, transported toward the stars). The plate on the opposite side has its long arrow pointing down with a blank cutout strip above the phrases: MIS SUR L'EAU, EN DESSOUS DES ETOILES

(placed on the water, beneath the stars). One narrow side of the concrete block also bears a stainless steel plate. It covers most of the surface and its mes-sage is written in a vertical line down the center. The phrases here read: (1 CHOSE) (2 CHOSES) (3 CHOSES) (PLUS) ([1 thing] [2 things] [3 things] [more]). Weiner thus uses concise phrases to evoke meaning and a bare minimum of imagery to relate the phrases to a context.

Weiner, Untitled

Ronchamp

This tiny village is about 12 1/2 mi (20 km) from Belfort. A limited number of trains and buses make the 30-min trip daily. Beware that the weekend sched-ule is exceedingly sparse and unaccom-modating of same-day travel to and from the site. Train to Belfort from Dijon, 2 1/2 hr; from Strasbourg, 1 1/2 hr. By car: route N19.

Chapelle de Notre-Dame-du-Haut

architect: LE CORBUSIER, 1950–55
Ronchamp, 70250
daily, 9–7; winter, 9–4 or 5
admission: 10F

From the village, go under the viaduct and up the hill. It's only a 1/2 mi climb, but it can be quite an arduous walk in the summer heat.

Like the awe-inspiring grandeur and soaring space of medieval cathedrals, the hilltop pilgrimage chapel at Ronchamp arouses a sense of the sublime even in those resistant to spiritual feelings. Built at the request of Monsignor Dubourg, archbishop of Besançon, and dedicated to the Virgin Mary Our Lady on High, the chapel is an utterly theatrical, sculptural oddity—and one of the great buildings of the 20th century. You will comprehend its power when you ascend the winding, wooded road and suddenly see the majestic, upswept roof—shaped like a nun's coif or seashell—silhouetted against the sky. The impact of this sight intensifies as the stark, white base of the building, punctuated by deeply inset windows, comes into view. Walking around and inside the structure prolongs the wondrous sensation, especially since you experience the full force of the rapport between the building and site at every turn. Not only do the curves respond to the undulating landscape and the half-cylindrical side chapels to the sun's trajectory, but the sounds of choir voices reverberate within the interior and down into the valley.

Le Corbusier's reductive, unembellished aesthetic is notable in his designs for the cast-concrete altar, confessionals and outdoor podium (used for open-air masses). But his embrace of color and light effects is also evident in the intense hues of the door paintings and window glass, and in the exaggerated sunbeams shining through slit and cubic hollows scattered across a dominant wall in the darkened interior. Far more than in his other buildings, Ronchamp diverges from the repetitive, grid structure and skeletal frame that had almost become synonymous with modern architecture. It instead is a form distinguished by curves, irregularity and massive walls, which "takes possession of ineffable space" and is "an answer to a psychophysiology of [religious] feelings"—primarily "joy and meditation."

Strasbourg

This lively, prosperous metropolis is the capital of the Alsace region. Although it has a rich cultural heritage and is a very cosmopolitan city, Strasbourg has only recently become an active player in the contemporary art world. Hopefully the festive, congenial ambience of the city will not be undone by the ongoing expansion and redevelopment of various neighborhoods, or the presence of the new parliament and courts for the European Union in its midst. It's easy to walk all around the streets and neighborhoods in the center city, and the tram and bus routes provide good, fast transportation to outlying areas. If you've never been to Strasbourg, put it on your list of must see places. Train from Paris (Gare de l'Est), 4 hr; from Dijon, 4 hr.

Tramway

The redevelopment plan for Strasbourg included the pedestrianization of a major segment of the center city and the creation of a tramway system (inaugurated 1994). Not only was due attention paid to technological factors, but significant concern was given to the visual appearance of many aspects of the new transportation system. The French designer Jean-Michel WILMOTTE developed the model for the information and service columns (containing the ticket machines, schedules, etc.) at each station; the respected British architect Norman FOSTER produced the image for the tram shelters—see especially the stunning glass roof ring at Station Homme de Fer; and four artists—Jonathan Borofsky, Gérard Collin-Thiébaut, Barbara Kruger, Mario Merz—were commissioned to create public art projects. (The Collin-Thiébaut project involved designing tram tickets. These were used when the system opened but have been replaced by mundane, generic tickets.)

Barbara Kruger

Installation, 1994
place de la Gare

After entering the station—the only underground station in the tram system—you soon come upon a segment of Kruger's design. Overhead as you descend the wide bank of stairs and escalators to the platform is the question: *Ou allez-vous?* (Where are you going?). It is etched in large letters on a concrete girder spanning the entire space. The next segment—the centerpiece of the installation—is a monumental photo-text panel (serigraphed on aluminum) placed high on a concrete wall over the tracks at the end of the platforms. Its size alone gives it a domineering presence. But added to this is the brash style imbued with overblown theatricality. The panel shows a cropped, blown-up, black-and-white reproduction of a man's profile with a securely locked safe implanted in his skull. The imagery is overlaid with a diagonal, boldly printed, red-and-white sign stating *L'empathie peut changer le monde* (Empathy can change the

world). In contrast to the flamboyance of the presentational mode, the images are utterly objectified and inexpressive, and the text sets forth a philosophic idea for quiet contemplation.

Another element of the installation appears in the large light boxes with a rolling screen of advertisements, located at the front ends of the platforms. A string of commercial spots directs messages at you and then you see the pensive face of a young girl looking in a mirror and an over-text stating *Voir, c'est croire* (Seeing is believing). The message is not promoting a product, and its cerebral tone is out of sync with the bombast of the ads. Yet, this Kruger design (there are two of her compositions interspersed in the string of ads) is not so different since it purposefully apes the rhetoric and imagery of publicity communication.

Kruger, tram installation (detail)

Complementing these pictorial wall components are 12 steel triptychs embedded in the floor of the platforms at the places where the tram doors open. The center sections reproduce monograms of Strasbourgeois residents made by Hélène Schaeffer (professor in the city's School of Decorative Arts at the beginning of the 20th century) using an ornate alphabet she created. On one platform, the middle plates of two triptychs contain the words *Depart* and *Retour*, written with this alphabet and set against medieval depictions of the Strasbourgeois landscape. All of the triptychs have sloganlike phrases on their side panels.

Brief textual elements in the form of questions are also etched onto the concrete girders in the platform and entrance areas. Usually the expressions are situated as pairs formulated in terms of opposites, reversals, clashes or contingencies. For example—*Qui pensez-vous être? Qui a peur des idées?* (Who is afraid of ideas? Who do you think you are?); *Qui voit? Qui est vu?* (Who sees? Who is seen?); *Qui gagne? Qui perd?* (Who wins? Who loses?). Unlike the visually aggressive image-text panels, these phrases are barely perceptible and difficult to read unless you're positioned so light rakes across the etched letters. Similarly, the words Kruger has inscribed on the steps are somewhat hidden from view and written in simple block letters devoid of the confrontational stylistics that have become her signature. Although the visual character of the work is subdued, the individual words, word juxtapositions and sequences are evocative, particularly since they unexpectedly appear in odd locations as isolated noncontextualized blips. As a commuter, you might well climb the steps every day and never notice the inscriptions until one day, by chance, you look down and see the words *Travail, Jeu, Rire, Cri, Espoir, Peur,*

Amour, Haine, Good, Bad, Desire (Work, Play, Laugh, Cry, Hope, Fear, Love, Hate).

Using two very different modes of communication aesthetics in her installation, Kruger presents a critique of stereotypes and repeatedly questions the human condition and value judgments. Identity, power, sexuality, nationalism, sensitivity and difference are underlying issues that permeate throughout. In addition to an obvious concern with content and style, Kruger integrates her images and texts with the architecture, sensitively adjusting scale and style of each component to enhance the overall effect. For people interested in or critical of public art, this should be considered as an archetype. As a design it works well with its setting, and as imagery its potency lasts no matter how often you see it since the messages are so perplexing and nonspecific.

Musée d'Art Moderne et Contemporain

 architect: Adrian FAINSILBER, 1998
1 place Hans-Jean Arp, 67000
Mon, Wed–Sat, 10–12, 1:30–6;
Sun, 10–5; closed Tues.

Located across the Barrage Vauban (Vauban Dam) on the shores of the Ill river in a part of the city undergoing redevelopment. The back of the building parallels rue de Molsheim near place Sainte-Marguerite.

Looking at this compelling building with its panoramic terraces and gardens, it is hard to imagine that the site was until very recently an ugly wasteland where slaughterhouses once stood. The building specifically faces away from the street toward the river, thereby offering two different perspectives of the setting. The immediate surroundings yield an almost pastoral landscape, but just beyond, snatches of the historic old city and modern urbanism come into view.

The building itself has a monumental presence composed of block shapes (concrete or sheathed in white tile and rose granite) and a striking glass arcade rising in its midst. The arcade is a veritable interior street off which are exhibition galleries, a library, auditorium, bookshop and other services. A restaurant is situated on a terrace. As in his design for the Géode and City of Science and Industry in Paris, Fainsilber has created a structure of simple geometric volumes, devoid of decoration but imbued with character and astutely configured to provide amenable spaces for art and people.

In the autumn of 1998, when this museum moved into its spacious new quarters, it deliberately evinced a new emphasis on contemporary art. This is visible in the permanent collection galleries, which are largely devoted to art from the 1950s to the present. Moreover, the collection is installed along the lines of recent, revisionist attitudes toward history and art. That is to say, works are hung in a chronological order beginning with paintings by the impressionists and the visionary artist Gustave Doré from the mid-19th century. But instead of trying to reveal a formalist evolution—leading toward pure abstraction—the presentation indicates the coexistence or polymorphic progression of figurative, expressionist, symbolic and abstract art. By the end of the 20th century, this nonhierarchical mixture of diverse styles is shown to be a dominant characteristic of postmodernism. Among the works in the final section are creations by Georg Baselitz, Christian Boltanski, Robert Filliou, Jochen Gerz, Thomas Huber, Jorg Immendorf, Jannis Kounellis, Mario Merz, Nam June Paik, A. R. Penck, Sarkis. Contrary to most French museums, here the display embraces German contemporary art. Of course, Strasbourg's

proximity to Germany is largely responsible for this. The museum also has a sizeable collection of photography and dedicates a room to its famous son, Jean Arp.

In its inaugural temporary exhibition —a large, site-specific installation by Ettore Spalletti—the museum gave further evidence of its focus on contemporary art. Subsequent special exhibitions will continue this orientation.

Mario Merz

Tram installation

Located in the middle of the tram tracks extending the distance of over 3/4 mi (1.3 km). A good place to see a section of this work is just off the main city plaza—place Kléber—where the tracks run along rue Francs Bourgeois.

When you see the red light boxes in the ground between the two rails of the tramway, you've found this public art project by Mario Merz. Inside each box are numbers following the mathematical progression known as the Fibonacci series. It is named for an Italian mathematician from the 13th century who was responsible for the spread of Arab principles of arithmetic in the Christian world. In the series, each number is the sum of the two preceding terms: 1, 2, 3, 5, 8, 13, 21, 34, 55 . . .).

Merz, who has used the Fibonacci series since 1971, making it his trademark, here sees it as "a sign of the dynamic state of the whole world, all inscribed in the horizontality of the urban landscape." By placing the numbers in the ground, Merz returns to the growth that begins with the emergence of plants, animals and humans from the earth's surface. The suite contains 46 light boxes; one series of 16 and two series of 15. The boxes vary in size depending on whether they contain 1, 2 or 3 numbers. All the numbers are written in the artist's handwriting. Since the red lights are connected to the same system as the traffic signals for the tram, they go on when the first car enters a station and go out when the last car leaves. Thus they also serve as signals announcing the arrival of a tram to passengers waiting at the station.

Unfortunately, the lighting of Merz's installation had to be turned off in the mid-1990s because water and humidity were seeping into the boxes. The tramway administration is presumably working on a new system. Needless to say, without the lighting, the installation is virtually nonexistent.

Jonathan Borofsky

Woman Walking to the Sky, 1994
place des Halles

Borofsky, *Woman Walking to the Sky*

In his tramway project, Borofsky presents the comic-tragic image of a woman walking toward the sky. Although she is a rather normal figure of human scale and wearing universal blue jeans (fiberglass), her placement near the top of an 82-ft (25-m) steel pole implanted in the ground at an oblique angle makes this a monumental, startling sculpture. Like other Borofsky figures, she evokes a personage from the commedia dell'arte. But her commonplace, modern dress, carefree manner and the familiarity of her exercising gait belie a staged performance. Her space walking seems like mundane, normal behavior. Situated in an open plaza at the tram stop facing the renovated city market (now a market-shopping-office center), the sculpture functions successfully as public art. It marks a spot, arouses attention and endures as a gripping image. The pendant of this sculpture, *Man Walking to the Sky*, originally made for Documenta, is in Kassel, Germany.

Oulipo

Texts posted on the upper part of the service and information columns at each tram station.

Oulipo (Ouvroir de Littérature Potentielle—Workshop of Potential Literature), founded by Raymond Queneau in 1960, is "dedicated to the joys, games and deviations from constraint in literature." In their innovative project for Strasbourg, the group developed ironic, ludicrous texts. "During the few moments a tram rider spends in a station, it is a matter of giving him—a traveler transformed by circumstance into a reader—an ensemble of texts that awaken his curiosity and/or interest by their instructive and/or entertaining character." Oulipo's texts use word-plays, plays with the sounds or meanings of words, and relational interplays between segments. They divide into four invented structures and new literary constraints: toponymic notices— fantasy definitions related to a station's name and written in dictionary form; homophonic variations—dislocations of the sounds in the phrase "le tramway de Strasbourg"; a serial story with each episode written only with the letters contained in a station's name; and "cooked language"—known sayings (proverbs, refrains, etc.) transformed by introducing the words "tram" and "tramway" at key places. If you had any doubt that Strasbourg was a cultural haven, just imagine a review board in some other city or country selecting this project to adorn its public transportation system!

La Chaufferie

5 rue de la Manufacture des Tabacs, 67000
03-88-35-38-58
Wed–Sun, 2–7; closed Mon–Tues
admission: free

This gallery, associated with the Ecole des Arts Décoratifs de Strasbourg, is a good place to see current work by artists who are not big names but who are pushing the edge conceptually. Recent exhibitions: *Dennis Adams*, *Kate Blaker*, *François Bouillon*, *Emmanuel Saulnier*, *Alain Sonneville*, *David Tremblett*.

Palais des Droits de l'Homme, 1989–95

architect: Richard ROGERS
avenue de l'Europe
Bus 30 or 23 from place Broglie or rue du Vieux Marché aux Vins, exit Orangerie
Located 1 1/4 mi (2 km) northeast of the city center, across from the lush Parc de l'Orangerie.

Richard Rogers, the architect who designed Centre Pompidou with Renzo Piano, has once again created an creatively eccentric, high-tech building. But here the industrial aesthetic is not as brash; color articulation is limited to red accents; and priority is given to a geometry of cylinders and curves. This is late-20th-century design, steeped in advanced technology and architectural prowess though tempered by a quotient of dazzling grace and refinement.

The building (housing the Human Rights Center of the European Community), a monumental structure wrapping around a corner plot of land, is composed of various distinct units. Most dominant are two huge cylinders sheathed in stainless steel except for a horizontal band of windows near the bottom. Raised off the ground (supported by concrete columns), they terminate in a sloped roof at the top. A third, glass-sheathed cylinder, nestled between the other two and much smaller in size, serves as the entrance hall for the whole building. Behind is another window-walled structure with one side—the side fronting the river—slanted out and configured as wide steps so that offices on all levels overlook and open onto plant-laden terraces. Though each side and part of the building is distinctly different, common threads and harmonious repetitions hold it together. Its compelling design is innovative and unusual but very appealing

Parlement Européene

architects: ARCHITECTURE STUDIO, 1994–1999
Located across the river from the Rogers building.

Sheathed in glass, this monumental building virtually lines a bend in the river, extending in opposite directions from a sweeping curve at its midsection. The curve is emphasized and made

Rogers, Palais de Droits de l'Homme

more graceful by the graduated roofline which reaches its highest level at the corner curvature. A circular structure rises in the center and a pedestrian bridge gives access to office buildings across the river.

subject index

public art

parks and gardens

arts bookstores

index

we appreciate your help

If you found errors regarding information about a site we discussed or
know about sites we missed, please tell us.
art·SITES, 894 Waller Street, San Francisco, CA 94117 USA
fax: 415-701-0633, website: www.artsitespress.com

coming soon

art·SITES™

great britain + ireland

art·SITES™

france

ORDER FORM

Check your local bookstore or order directly from us.

NAME

STREET

CITY   STATE   ZIP

COUNTRY   TEL(   )

PLEASE SEND

quantity _____ @ $19.95 each $ _____

sales tax ($1.70 per book) for CA residents $ _____

shipping in US ($4 for the first book, $2.50 for each additional book) $ _____

international airmail ($7 per book) $ _____

                                          TOTAL $ _____

PAYMENT

○ Check or money order (payable to **art•SITES** in US dollars drawn on a US bank.
   Send to: **art•SITES**, 894 Waller Street, San Francisco, CA 94117 USA

○ MasterCard   ○ Visa

CARD NUMBER   EXP DATE

EXACT NAME ON CARD

SIGNATURE

ORDER BY
telephone: 415-437-2456 fax: 415-701-0633 website: www.artsitespress.com